Handcraft
ILLUSTRATED

~ 1996 ~

Published by
Boston Common Press Limited Partnership
17 Station Street
Brookline Village, Massachusetts 02147

ISBN: 0-9640179-6-2
ISSN: Pending

To get home delivery of future issues of *Handcraft Illustrated*
magazine call 1-800-526-8447 or write to the above address.

$29.95

NUMBER ELEVEN

WINTER 1996

Handcraft

ILLUSTRATED

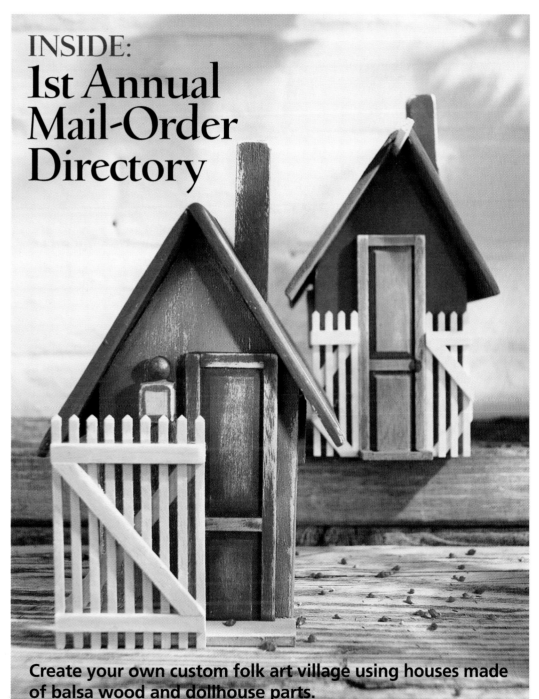

INSIDE:
1st Annual Mail-Order Directory

Create your own custom folk art village using houses made of balsa wood and dollhouse parts.

Folk Art Village
The Secret: Dollhouse Parts and Balsa Wood

How to Make Vintage Tassels
Hundreds of Versions from One Easy-Wind Technique

The Fastest Homemade Paper
Distinct Texture from Recycled Paper

Block-Print Your Own Faux Wallpaper
Use a Printing Pad You Cut Yourself

Easy-Sew Lap Quilts
Elegant but Practical Designs in an Afternoon's Time

ALSO
Silk Flower Chair Sash
Quick Chocolate Leaves
Shabby Chic Slipcover
Easy Custom Lampshades
Fabric-Covered Desk Screen

$4.00 U.S./$4.95 CANADA

0 74470 83731 2   63 >

Contents

You can use this silk flower chair sash to complement your decorating scheme, or to add color to a festive table setting. See article, page 9.

Three antique finishes, page 12

Chocolate leaves, page 17

Make your own paper, page 18

COVER PHOTOGRAPH:
Carl Tremblay

Handcraft
ILLUSTRATED

EDITOR
Carol Endler Sterbenz

EXECUTIVE EDITOR
Barbara Bourassa

ART DIRECTOR
Amy Klee

SENIOR EDITOR
Michio Ryan

EDITORIAL PRODUCTION DIRECTOR
Maura Lyons

EDITORIAL PROD. COORDINATOR
Karin L. Kaneps

DIRECTIONS EDITOR
Candie Frankel

COPY EDITOR
Gary Pfitzer

EDITORIAL ASSISTANT
Elizabeth Cameron

❧

PUBLISHER AND FOUNDER
Christopher Kimball

EDITORIAL CONSULTANT
John Kelsey

MARKETING DIRECTOR
Adrienne Kimball

CIRCULATION DIRECTOR
Elaine Repucci

ASS'T CIRCULATION MANAGER
Jennifer L. Keene

CIRCULATION COORDINATOR
Jonathan Venier

CIRCULATION ASSISTANT
C. Maria Pannozzo

PRODUCTION DIRECTOR
James McCormack

PROJECT COORDINATOR
Sheila Datz

PRODUCTION COORDINATOR
Pamela Slattery

SYSTEMS ADMINISTRATOR
Matt Frigo

PRODUCTION ARTIST
Kevin Moeller

❧

VICE PRESIDENT
Jeffrey Feingold

CONTROLLER
Lisa A. Carullo

ACCOUNTING ASSISTANT
Mandy Shito

OFFICE MANAGER
Tonya Estey

Handcraft Illustrated (ISSN 1072-0529) is published quarterly by Boston Common Press Limited Partners, 17 Station Street, P.O. Box 509, Brookline, MA 02147-0509. Copyright 1995 Boston Common Press Limited Partners. Second-class postage paid at Boston, MA, and additional mailing offices, USPS #011-895. For list rental information, please contact Direct Media, 200 Pemberwick Road, Greenwich, CT 06830; (203) 532-1000. Editorial office: 17 Station Street, P.O. Box 509, Brookline, MA 02147-0509; (617) 232-1000, FAX (617) 232-1572, e-mail: hndcftill-@aol.com. Editorial contributions should be sent or e-mailed to: Editor, *Handcraft Illustrated*. We cannot assume responsibility for manuscripts submitted to us. Submissions will be returned only if accompanied by a large, self-addressed stamped envelope. Subscription rates: $24.95 for one year; $45 for two years; $65 for three years. (Canada: add $3 per year; all other countries add $12 per year.) Postmaster: Send all new orders, subscription inquiries, and change of address notices to *Handcraft Illustrated*, P.O. Box 7448, Red Oak, IA 51591-0448. Single copies: $4 in U.S.; $4.95 in Canada and other countries. Back issues available for $5 each. PRINTED IN THE U.S.A.

Rather than put ™ in every occurrence of trademarked names, we state that we are using the names only and in an editorial fashion to the benefit of the trademark owner, with no intention of infringement of the trademark.

Note to Readers: Every effort has been made to present the information in this publication in a clear, complete, and accurate manner. It is important that all instructions are followed carefully, as failure to do so could result in injury. Boston Common Press Limited Partners, the editors, and the authors disclaim any and all liability resulting therefrom.

From the Editor

IT IS TWILIGHT, AND I HAVE BEEN SITTING IN an eighteenth-century farmhouse looking out a narrow window. A small pond, silver and level like a shard of broken mirror, lies at the bottom of a sloping lawn, which finally ends where a cornfield begins. Mist rises ghost-like, stealthily moving toward the stand of pine that rims the field.

In a few weeks, that same expanse of cornfield, which is lined with shorn rows that resemble the bristles of a scrub brush, will be blanketed with snow and firmly frozen underfoot. I know that. For many weeks, the sun has allotted smaller and smaller portions of daylight to the afternoon, bringing an early dusk that discolors the pale light to ashen yellow.

Soon it will be fittingly winter, a time when the change of weather will also cause me to change the kinds of crafts I do. I will be drawn to projects with more heft, especially quilting, and I will try again to finish the quilt with the Dresden plate pattern started years and years ago when the window through which I looked, a six-over-six as it was called, was in our just-built house in East Setauket, New York. The window overlooked a newly seeded lawn, and I remember sitting nearby holding my newborn son, Rodney, just two days old, who stretched in length only from my open palms, which cradled his head, to the folds at my elbows. How I marveled at the shape of his head, the sketch lines of hair that felt like satin on my lips, his puckered mouth murmuring in some ancient unknown language. Was he talking to all the universe in sounds that mimicked words he had heard through amniotic seas? What was he saying? I didn't know. I only wished I could hold that precious moment from the tides of change so that I did not have to lose the miracle of his infancy to time and its ability to dissolve magical experiences into dreamlike memories. But, for one brief cosmic moment, he and I seemed to remain as unchanging and as still as the snow on the land while, in reality, we were being moved swiftly through time as the Earth spun on its axis, and the sun moved soundlessly past the window.

I sometimes wonder how many windows I will look through before I am finished with the whole quilt, but I also have a suspicion that I am not in any rush to know.

Since that time, there have been many planetary revolutions, as there have been countless changes in the boy and his windowscape. The infant in my arms is now a man, reed thin, earnest, smart, and funny. Today, he looks out of a new window, one that reveals a fire escape and a discordant city smudged with soot, and filled with the sound of sirens that wail into the night. Rodney is studying special effects at film school in New York, and I often think his environment is one of his most influential teachers.

I now look out of a steel-framed window fitted into a brick wall of a factory building that has been transformed into a modern office by architects who have made honorable use of the old space. An above-ground subway stop is situated across the street, and a bell announces the arrival of two cars hitched together like a kid's ride at Disneyland. I ride the train back and forth to work, and sometimes I carry a small square with a Dresden plate pattern on it hoping to add a few stitches to its already puckered surface. I sometimes wonder how many windows I will look through before I am finished with the whole quilt, but I also have a suspicion that I am not in any rush to know.

For now, the view from my desk is at once settling and challenging as I work on developing ideas for *Handcraft Illustrated,* a magazine that I have come to know very well.

As our editors move into the new year, we are busy at work building the upcoming issues, packing page after page with such projects as floral arrangements, handmade boxes, decoupage, gilded frames, painted trunks, elegant candles, herbal soaps and waters, painted cookies, clocks, and more in four quarterly issues. We hope these issues will provide the creative inspiration for a full year of satisfying handcrafts. Have a joyous New Year.

Carol Endler Sterbenz

Notes from Readers

Readers find answers to problems such as how to restore paintbrushes with dried-on paint, and where to find oversized roses and instructions on how to make ribbbon flowers.

Unsealing Envelopes

I recently purchased some envelopes that I had intended to use to send out invitations for a special occasion, but when I went to address them, many of them had sealed themselves and couldn't be used. Is there any way to unseal them without ruining them?

CAROLYNE NAVESINK
ANN ARBOR, MI

Here's our favorite way to unseal envelopes: Place the envelopes in a plastic bag and put them in the freezer for about twenty minutes, or until the seals reopen.

Preventing Fabric Paint from Bleeding

Is there a product available that keeps fabric paint from bleeding? I tried drawing a pattern on a silk scarf with felt markers recently, and the images weren't as sharp as I'd hoped for.

SUSAN TERCETTI
LOS ANGELES, CA

Your local art or crafts supply store should carry products (antifusants) that inhibit the spreading of dye. Every brand has its own specific instructions, but most of them are used the same way: Brush or sponge on the antifusant, then wait until the fabric is dry to apply any paint.

Two brand names we've tried and recommend are Jacquard Dye-Na-Flow ($2.63 per two ounces), which can be used on any fabric, including silk, canvas, or cotton, and Deka ($2.20 per two ounces), which was created especially for use on silk.

Restoring a Paintbrush with Dried-on Paint

Is there any way to restore paintbrushes with dried-on oil paint?

NICHOLAS RODGERS
DAYTONA BEACH, FL

We recommend "The Masters" Brush Cleaner and Preservative, manufactured by General Pencil Company. The nontoxic, nonflammable product removes oil and acrylic paint, varnishes, stains, and watercolors. It also prevents buildup in the ferrule of the brush and conditions the bristles. "The Masters" is available at most art supply stores in four sizes starting at $1.25 for one-quarter ounce.

We also tested Silicoil Brush Cleaning Fluid, designed especially for cleaning brushes used with oil paint. The cleaner, made by the Lion Company, can be used with the Silicoil Brush Cleaning Tank or by pouring it in a jar and swirling the brush around in it. A one-pint container retails for $2.80.

Hand-Painting Furniture with Ease

I love hand-painted furniture, and I'd like to try my hand at it. The problem is, I'm afraid of doing an amateurish job or choosing the wrong colors. Are there any kits that give you templates and/or tell you what colors to use?

LAURA GIBBONS
WILMINGTON, DE

We recommend *Painted Furniture Patterns: 34 Elegant Designs to Pull Out, Paint, and Trace* by Jocasta Innes and Stewart Walton (Viking Studio Books, 1994). This $19.95 do-it-yourself painting book contains cutout patterns that enable you to create beautiful, original pieces from even the most ordinary furniture. The patterns can be replicated exactly or modified for smaller or larger surfaces. In addition, the authors guide you through choosing paints and brushes and provide a step-by-step guide to usage.

Drying Multiple Flowers in Silica Gel

Is it okay to dry flower heads of different species together in silica gel?

LISA BLACKETT
ALAMO, NV

It is best to dry only like flowers together, as drying times vary from species to species. The shape of a flower also dictates how it should be placed in the silica gel: Flat flowers (such as black-eyed Susans) should be placed upside down, cup-shaped flowers such as roses should be placed right side up, and spiral-shaped blooms (e.g., delphiniums) should be placed on their sides.

Delivery Service for Oversized Roses

Around Valentine's Day last year I read about a floral service that specializes in sending oversized roses nationwide, but I can't remember the company's name. Can you help?

SUSAN UMATHON
BROOKLYN, NY

You're probably thinking of Jungle Roses, a Los Angeles–based company that is owned by Joan Dangerfield (wife of comedian Rodney). Ms. Dangerfield, who has been a florist for more than fifteen years, sought out what she believed to be the largest, most beautiful species of roses for her delivery service. Although pricey (one dozen roses cost $98, not including shipping and handling), the roses we ordered were unbelievably beautiful. Jungle Roses offers a variety of packages, including long-stem roses and rose petals for use in baths. To order roses or for more information, phone 800-SEND-ROSE.

Multipurpose Stain Remover

Can you recommend a stain remover that works on a variety of stains?

SAMANTHA JONES
SANTA BARBARA, CA

We recommend The Original Kiss-Off Stain Remover. This stain remover claims to remove almost any stain, including blood, wine, wet and dry oil paint, and grass stain, and we found that it really does. Apply the Kiss-Off stick to the offending stain and wash the item, either by hand or in the machine. A 0.7-ounce Kiss-Off stick retails for about $3.98.

Hot-Glue Gun with a Variety of Nozzles

Do you know of any hot-glue guns that come with a variety of nozzles?

LEANNE DOOLEY
PORTLAND, ME

The Floral Pro Professional Glue Gun and Accessories Kit includes five interchangeable nozzles that let you apply the hot glue in a straight thin line, in wider lines, into tight crevices, and on awkward corners and edges. The gun, which retails for $59.99, works with almost any material, including paper, glass, metal, and wood. To order this product, call 800-GLUE-GUN.

Mail-Order Vintage Wallpaper

Do you have any sources for wallpaper that is similar to that made in the fifties? I'm having trouble finding anything I like. I'm looking for floral prints or large checks in particular.

ELIZA MADDEN
SANTA MONICA, CA

Dream House: A Retrospective of 40s and 50s Vintage Wallcoverings Designed for Modern Living should meet your needs. This charming line, designed by Andrea Mantel and Susan Brown of Smart Company of America, features several floral patterns with coordinating stripes and damask fabric, as well as motifs that were popular during those years, including angelfish, bubbles, oversized gingham checks, and buckaroos, and faux cowhide. Double rolls of the wall coverings start at $45; borders start at $24.95 for a five-yard roll. To locate retail stores that carry Dream House in your area, call or write the distributor: Quality Wallcoverings, 8 Sutton Place, Edison, NJ 08817; 800-570-7655. This company will also sell directly to consumers in certain states.

Storing Thread Spools

Can you offer any tips on storing thread spools other than in a sewing box? I'd like something that lets me see everything at once and keeps the spools separate from each other.

KIMBERLY MARCO
ALBANY, NY

To keep thread spools accessible and neat, try hanging each on its own peg on a pegboard or hanging hooks on a plastic-coated wire grid. Both pegboards and wire grids are widely available and can be readily mounted on a wall or on the inside of a closet door. This same concept also works well in a drawer. Cut to size, a pegboard with short pegs or a board into which short nails have been hammered is effective. Plastic drawer dividers and the slanted drawer inserts used for spice jars, both of which are available in many housewares stores and mail-order catalogs, are possibilities, too.

Using Perfume in Scented Candles

I'd like to try making some scented candles and was wondering if you could tell me how to use my perfume in place of the squares of scented wax they sell.

LINDA SABARSKY
RENO, NV

Unfortunately, perfume and cologne should not be used as a candle scent, as they are alcohol based and will not blend with wax, which is oil based. You should use either the solid type of wax you describe, which is simply a square of concentrated scented wax, or an oil-compatible liquid scent.

Transferring and Cutting Out a Stencil

Can you recommend a method of transferring and cutting out a simple stencil? I'd like to do this with a few animal-shaped patterns for a child's bureau.

JANNA BURR
FAIRBANKS, AK

Try this technique: Start by transferring the patterns to Mylar polyester film that is cloudy on one side. Lay the pattern on a flat work surface, then lay the film, cloudy side up, on the pattern. Keep several inches of margin all around the pattern to create a stable stencil. To make the tracing as accurate as possible, use a mechanical pencil to ensure that you always have a sharp pencil point.

To cut out the stencil, lay the film, cloudy side up, on a piece of plate glass (taped around the sides to prevent cuts). Use an X-Acto knife for cutting. Since you will be cutting out animals, try to cut distinct curves in one pass, as lifting the knife from a curved pattern in midcut will disrupt the fluidity of the curve. You may find it easier to cut curved shapes if you hold the knife steady and turn the film away from you as you cut. For sharp points and corners, extend your cut just beyond the pattern; running the knife blade along a ruler is the best way to cut straight lines.

Making Flowers Out of Wire Ribbon

Can you tell me where I can find instructions for making flowers out of wire ribbon?

EDITH BURGESS
CLEAR LAKE, WI

Offray Ribbon Company offers more than twenty-four "how-to" sheets detailing various ideas for using ribbon in crafts and home decor. Two specific sheets demonstrate how to use wire ribbon in order to make flowers: "All About Roses" and "All About Ribbon Flowers." In order to obtain copies of these two how-to sheets or a listing of other Offray sheets, send a letter stating your request along with a self-addressed stamped envelope to Offray How-Tos, Route 24, Chester, NJ 07930.

Slowing the Drying Time of Watercolor Paint

Is there a way to slow the drying time of watercolor paint? I've been trying to work wet into wet to get a softer effect, but the paint seems to dry too quickly—or at least before I can get the two colors to create the effect I want.

CHRIS GRAHAM
DENVER, CO

As glycerin is a retardant that is often mixed with tube watercolors to keep them from drying out, it can be added to your jar of mixing water to slow the evaporation rate of watercolor paint. Exactly how much you'll need is a matter of personal preference and experimentation, but an approximate ratio is twelve drops to a pint jar of water. Glycerin can be bought at most pharmacies.

Refinishing an Old Bureau

I recently purchased a great old bureau at a flea market with the intent of scraping off the chipping paint and putting on a new coat. The problem is that once I began, I realized that the piece has much more thick, old paint on it than I had originally thought. Scraping off the bad areas and sanding them down is not only proving to be laborious but inadequate as well. Any suggestions?

JERRY SHEPARD
WATERVILLE, ME

You could try using a hot-air gun, which will cause the paint to soften, enabling you to scrape it off more readily. Another option is to use a peel-off chemical paint stripper, which is very effective on furniture coated with multiple layers of old paint. Working in a well-ventilated area and wearing protective gloves, apply a thick layer of the peel-off stripper to the bureau, then let it sit for several hours. The stripper will gradually eat through the paint, making it simpler for you to scrape it off. Any remaining paint can be scraped off with steel wool and mineral spirits.

Before applying primer or paint to a stripped surface, be sure that the wood is dry and that it is free of dust and dirt.

Using Contact Paper as Wallpaper

Is it okay to use contact paper as a substitute for wallpaper? I have a pattern that I'd really like to use.

CASS HERRICK
PROVIDENCE, RI

We took your question to Rubbermaid, Inc. Contact paper is designed for lining drawers and shelves, and Rubbermaid recommends that you use it for this purpose only, for several reasons.

Unlike wallpaper, contact paper neither comes in dye lots nor is it cut so that edges of a pattern will line up from roll to roll—both of which are essential to doing a professional wallpapering job. Also, contact paper should never be stretched to cover a surface, as it will shrink back to its original size. Finally, the adhesion of contact paper depends on the condition of the surface to which it is applied; it will peel off raw wood and other porous surfaces and paint that has not cured.

If you're interested in learning more about installing contact paper properly, write to Rubbermaid,

Inc., 1147 Akron Road, Wooster, OH 44691-2596.

Chalk Versus Pastels

What's the difference between chalk and pastels?

ELIZABETH CAMPBELL
FREMONT, OH

Chalk is a natural product, whereas pastels are manufactured. There are three main types of chalk (black, red, and white), and they are derived from various soft stones or earths, such as carbonaceous shale (black chalk), red ocher (red chalk, also known as sanguine), and limestone (white chalk). Pastels are essentially sticks of color made from powdered pigments that have been mixed with enough gum or resin to bind them.

Reference Book on Collectibles and Antiques

Is there a book club that specializes in books on collectibles, antiques, and antique furniture? Whenever I go to bookstores, all I seem able to find are price guides or encyclopedias. I'd like to find some visual material and some background information that can help me identify what I see out there.

BILL NORTON
OLD GREENWICH, CT

Collector Books publishes books on antiques and collectibles. Their book list is extensive and covers a wide range of topics, many of which we have never seen offered elsewhere. For a free catalog, write or call the company at P.O. Box 3009, Paducah, KY 42002-3009; 800-626-5420. ◆

ATTENTION READERS

Looking for an Unusual Craft Supply?

Need advice on a home-decorating project? Drop us a line, and we'll try to find the answer. Although we can't respond to every letter, we will try and publish those answers with the widest appeal. Write to:

Notes from Readers

Handcraft Illustrated
17 Station Street
P.O. Box 509
Brookline Village, MA
02147-0509
e-mail: hndcftill@aol.com

WINTER 1996 • HANDCRAFT ILLUSTRATED   3

Quick Tips

PAINT WITHOUT BUBBLES

Rene Sommer of Carlisle, Massachusetts, stores squeeze bottles of fabric paint upside down in an egg carton. This position funnels the paint toward the nozzle and discourages air bubbles.

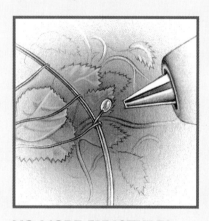

NO MORE PUNCTURES

To keep any protruding wire tips on a project from jabbing or puncturing her hands, Dorothy Hefner of Troup, Texas, seals each one with a bead of hot glue.

SUPER PAINT STIRRERS

Susannah Vogel of Winthrop, Maine, recycles foam trays from the supermarket into paint stirrers.

1. **Cut the tray into strips ½" to 1" wide. The strips are sturdy enough to mix paint.**

2. **When the paint dries, write the mix recipe or other details on the end with a permanent pen.**

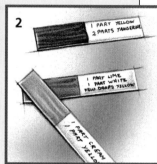

PHONE BOOK WORK SURFACE

When gluing cutouts for decoupage, Rose Maxwell of Seattle, Washington, uses an old telephone book as a work surface.

1. **Brush the glue beyond the cutout and onto the page.**

2. **As a page becomes too messy, tear it out and continue on a fresh page.**

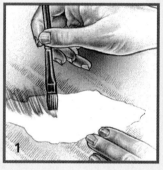

ATTENTION READERS

See Your Tip in Print

Do you have a technique you'd like to share with other readers? We'll give you a one-year complimentary subscription for each Quick Tip that we publish. Send your tip to:

Quick Tips
Handcraft Illustrated
17 Station Street
P.O. Box 509
Brookline Village, MA
02147-0509
e-mail: hndcftill@aol.com

Please include your name, address, and daytime phone number.

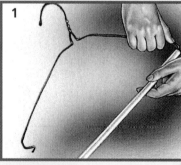

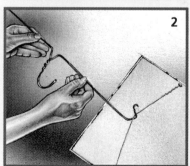

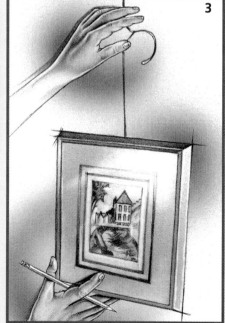

PICTURE PERFECT

Joe Citarella of Tarrytown, New York, offers this tip for hanging pictures without measuring.

1. **Remove the paper core from a dry cleaner hanger.**

2. **Unbend the hanger and slip one of the hooked ends around the picture-hanging wire.**

3. **Hold the picture against the wall by its hanger handle, moving it around until you find the best position. Carefully lift off the picture, then mark the hook position on the wall. Hammer a picture-hanging hook at this location to mount the picture permanently.**

ILLUSTRATION:
Harry Davis

QUICK BEAD PICKUP

To retrieve beads, pins, or other small items that have spilled accidentally, Jessica Miller, of Alamogordo, New Mexico, uses a vacuum cleaner covered with an old nylon stocking.

1. Cut the foot off the nylon stocking and slip its open end over the opening of the vacuum hose.

2. Wrap your hand around the stocking where it attaches to the hose, and turn on the power. The stocking foot will invert into the hose opening, and you can vacuum the beads into it.

3. Hold hose upwards so the beads don't spill out, turn off the power, and carefully remove the stocking "pouch." You can now empty the beads into a container.

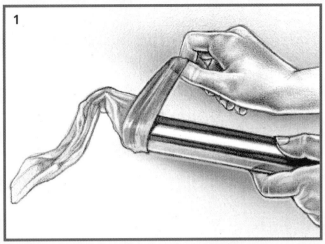

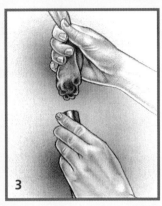

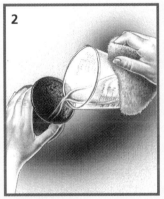

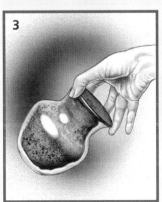

VASE REPAIR

A vase with a hairline crack that weeps water is no longer functional. Susan Rains of Joliet, Illinois, offers this remedy for the situation.

1. Cut several small chunks from a block of paraffin. Microwave them on high in a Pyrex measuring cup for 2 to 4 minutes until melted.

2. While protecting your hands from the heat, pour the hot liquid into the vase at the site of the crack.

3. Working quickly, maneuver the vase to distribute the liquid evenly over the crack.

4. Wait a few moments until the wax has cooled to a solid state, then fill the vase with water to test the seal.

COFFEE DEODORIZER

To eliminate a musty odor from old wood furniture, place a bowl of freshly ground coffee inside, then close the drawer, door, or lid. In a few days, the odor should be gone. This tip comes from Lita Watson of Iowa Park, Texas.

NO MISSING BUTTONS

To prevent machine-sewn buttons from working loose, apply a drop of washable fabric glue to the stitches when they are first made. Thanks to Susan Murray of Bristol, Virginia, for this useful tip.

INSTANT FLOWERPOT PATINA

To give new clay flowerpots a mossy patina, rub the surface of the pot with fresh parsley sprigs.

How to Block-Print a Faux Wallpaper

Love the look of wallpaper but want to avoid the expense? This simple block-printing technique creates the same look using a homemade printing pad and latex paint.

🐦 BY VI AND STU CUTBILL

MATERIALS

- **Fleur-de-lis motif or other motif for block print design**
- **Latex paint in ground coat color***
- **1 quart latex paint in print color**
- **Acrylic matte varnish***
- ***To determine amount needed, see Getting Started, step 1.**

You'll also need:
access to photocopier with enlarger; solid color computer mousepad; 2-ply chipboard; rubber cement; X-Acto knife with new blade; self-healing cutting mat; yardstick; steel ruler; masking tape; calculator; pencil and paper; colored antidust chalk; 1 sheet 12" x 18" construction paper; scissors; manicure scissors; string; retractable tape measure; plumb bob with line; two stepstools or ladders; carpenter's level; 1" and 2" paintbrushes; painter's tape or low-tack masking tape; paint roller and tray; disposable gloves; and cotton swabs.

Other items , if necessary:
hammer, spackling compound, spackling trowel, and 120-grit sandpaper (to repair nail pops and dents in wall surface); TSP (trisodium phosphate, a detergent sold in hardware stores), sponge, and plastic bucket (to clean dirty or greasy walls before painting); and broad felt-tip permanent markers in two colors (for marking tape guidelines for walls taller than 8 feet high).

To block-print this wall, we base-coated the walls using Benjamin Moore #733, then block-printed a fleur-de-lis motif using Benjamin Moore #296.

DESIGNER'S TIP

If you're an experienced faux finisher, you can take this project to the next level: Imagine using two different colors to print the motif, or printing the pattern on top of your favorite faux finish, such as a ragged effect.

ILLUSTRATION:
Wendy Wray

DIAGRAMS:
Mary Newell DePalma

COLOR PHOTOGRAPHY:
Carl Tremblay

IF YOU'VE EVER HUNG WALLPAPER, you know the down sides. First, order the wallpaper, which can take a few weeks to arrive—and cost $100 or more. Then, prep the walls, apply adhesive to the wallpaper, line up and match the pattern, and, finally, clean up the mess.

But wallpaper has many pros as well. It lets you transform a plain painted wall and allows you to choose from a wide array of multiple colors, patterns, and even textures. Our block-print wallpaper technique captures those advantages, but without the complexity and expense of wallpaper. The concept is fairly simple: We mounted a computer mousepad on chipboard for stability, cut a fleur-de-lis motif from the pad, and used it to print a repeating design on a painted wall.

Unlike stenciling, this technique re-creates the look of complex wallpaper because the mousepad lets you cut solid shapes with interior cutouts.

The part of this project that requires the most attention to detail is marking the walls for placement of the motif. To position the motifs on the wall, we measured and lightly marked guidelines using colored chalk, which can be brushed off later. Once the guidelines are in place, the actual printing goes fairly quickly.

Testing Materials for the Pad

In cutting our printing pad, we tested several different materials, including both sides (fabric and rubber) of a computer mousepad, foam core, and a Speedball cutting block. The computer mousepad used on the fabric side was the clear winner. We found we could easily make straight and curved cuts, as well as detailed cuts, using an X-Acto knife. The resulting print was softly textured, although you won't get the sharp edges that are possible with stenciling. Even though we found we could print up to twelve images before repainting the pad, we recommend repainting every time you print the motif in order to maintain the printing quality.

However, we don't recommend cutting the motif from the rubber side of the computer mousepad, as it is much more difficult to cut the detailed areas. We also rejected the foam core because it was difficult to cut curves. The Speedball cutting block was set aside because the paint didn't lay evenly on its surface.

To make a printing pad, we glued the mousepad onto a backing made from two pieces of two-ply chipboard and two pieces of one-ply chipboard. The backing provides a stable surface for the cutting process, resulting in more even and predictable cuts.

To clean the printing pad, use a soft wet rag and wipe it gently until all the paint is removed. For a more durable printing block that can be rinsed under running water and reused numerous times, mount the mousepad on a plywood block instead of chipboard.

Stu and Vi Cutbill are one of Canada's leading teams of faux-finishers.

MAKING THE PRINTING PAD

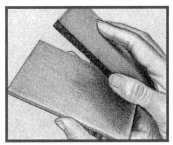

A. Make a printing pad by cementing a mousepad and several layers of chipboard together.

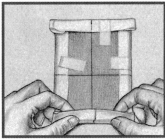

B. Wrap a photocopy of the motif around the pad. Match the guidelines on the reverse side before taping in place.

C. Use an X-Acto knife to pierce through the paper and fabric layer.

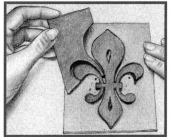

D. Make all the cuts before the cement is fully set (it takes about an hour), then peel up the waste material.

INSTRUCTIONS

Getting Started

1. Before purchasing base coat paint and varnish, determine square footage of wall surface to be covered, then refer to manufacturer's coverage estimates to calculate amounts needed.

2. Prepare wall surface. If wall is dirty or greasy, clean with TSP following manufacturer's directions. Use spackle to fill nail pops, dents, or holes. Let dry and sand smooth. Repeat, if necessary. Cover paint on baseboard and ceiling edges with painter's tape or low-tack masking tape.

3. Apply ground coat. Use 2" brush to cover spackled areas, interior corners, and areas around window and door trim. Then use roller to paint remaining wall. Let dry following manufacturer's recommendations. If necessary, paint second coat for even coverage.

Making the Printing Pad

1. Photocopy and enlarge fleur-de-lis (*see* illustration, right) or other motif to measure between 4" and 6" high. (Fleur-de-lis used to print wall measures 3⅜" x 4⅝".) If using your own motif, draft two lines to divide motif into quarters (*see* dashed lines on fleur-de-lis). Measure motif and jot down results.

2. On two-ply chipboard, draft two rectangles, each ⅜" larger all around than motif. Score and cut out rectangles using X-Acto knife, steel ruler, and self-healing cutting mat. Cut same-size rectangle from mousepad using scissors.

3. Assemble printing pad. Start by brushing rubber cement on facing sides of two chipboard rectangles. Let cement set several minutes until tacky but no longer wet, then press tacky surfaces together, edges matching, to adhere. Cement mousepad rectangle to chipboard in same way so fabric side of mousepad faces out (*see* illustration A). Turn pad chipboard side up and draft two lines on chipboard to divide surface into quarters.

4. Position motif on pad. Start by trimming photocopy paper 1½" beyond edge of motif, then extend dash lines or lines drawn in step 1 to cut edge. Lay paper on mousepad and fold edges to back of pad, matching dashed lines to those on chipboard to center image (illustration B). Tape down edges.

5. Cut out motif using X-Acto knife with new blade. Work from center of motif outwards. Cut each line in two passes: First, slice through paper and fabric surface of mousepad, concentrating on making smooth, clean cuts. Second, cut clear through rubbery part of mousepad until knife blade scratches chipboard surface (illustration C). To cut short sections, such as crossbar on fleur-de-lis, push tip of blade straight down into pad. When all cuts are made, remove paper and peel up mousepad waste (illustration D). Trim stray fibers with manicure scissors.

Marking the Wall

The directions that follow describe how to mark a wall for a 4" to 6" motif with 18" horizontal spacing, 24" vertical spacing, and alternate rows staggered in a half drop (diagram 10, page 8). On a standard 8-foot-high interior wall, a full vertical row contains four motifs, with the top motif starting 10" below the ceiling line and the bottom motif ending about 10"

above the floor (*see* step 2). To determine spacing for walls larger or smaller than 8 feet, *see* step 3. You will need a partner's help for steps 2 through 4.

1. Measure height of wall. For standard 8-foot-high walls, proceed to step 2. For walls larger or smaller than 8 feet, proceed to step 3.

2. For 8-foot walls, have partner and yourself stand on stepstools at opposite ends of wall. Stretch string horizontally across wall 10" below ceiling and tape one end. Have one partner hold untaped end of string while other uses level to check horizontal position of string. Adjust, then tape other end (diagram 1, page 8). If string sags, tape in place every 12" to 18" to secure. Hold yardstick even with string and draw soft chalk line against it. Repeat to mark remaining walls around room. Proceed to step 4.

3. For walls lesser or greater than 8 feet, use white painter's tape to gauge motif placement. First, cut tape 24" longer than wall height. Beginning a few inches from end of tape, draft lines perpendicular to tape edge every 12" (diagram 2). Then, starting at each line, draw perpendicular line equal to motif

Photocopy and enlarge fleur-de-lis to measure between 4" and 6" high.

PRINTING THE WALL

E. Load printing block with paint using 1" brush, then blot drips with cotton swab.

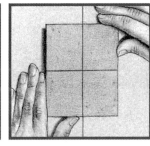

F. Position block so top center aligns with mark on wall.

G. To print, press block firmly, then lift up.

Marking the Walls

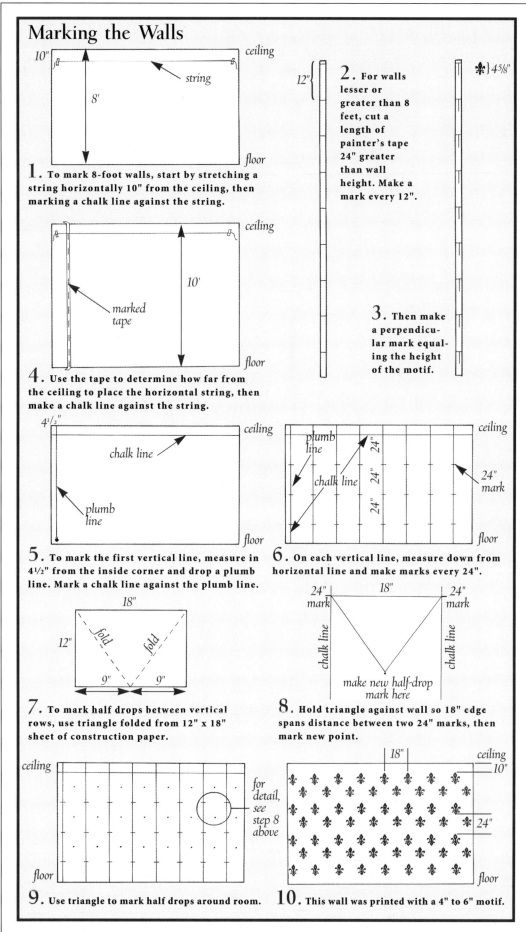

1. To mark 8-foot walls, start by stretching a string horizontally 10" from the ceiling, then marking a chalk line against the string.

4. Use the tape to determine how far from the ceiling to place the horizontal string, then make a chalk line against the string.

5. To mark the first vertical line, measure in 4½" from the inside corner and drop a plumb line. Mark a chalk line against the plumb line.

7. To mark half drops between vertical rows, use triangle folded from 12" x 18" sheet of construction paper.

9. Use triangle to mark half drops around room.

2. For walls lesser or greater than 8 feet, cut a length of painter's tape 24" greater than wall height. Make a mark every 12".

3. Then make a perpendicular mark equaling the height of the motif.

6. On each vertical line, measure down from horizontal line and make marks every 24".

8. Hold triangle against wall so 18" edge spans distance between two 24" marks, then mark new point.

10. This wall was printed with a 4" to 6" motif.

height; draw all lines in same direction (diagram 3). Darken every other line with broad-tipped marker, then darken remaining lines with a second color marker. To use tape, press it vertically against wall, adjusting its position until spacing between ceiling and top line and floor and bottom line is even. Each line represents a motif, and the two colors illustrate how motifs in two adjacent, staggered columns will fall. Depending on wall height, lines at top and bottom may be the same or different colors. If you want top and bottom printed rows to match, readjust tape position so lines at top and bottom are same color. Following step 2, stretch string even with top of first line on tape to mark guide-lines (diagram 4). Remove tape when through.

4. Mark vertical guidelines on walls. Start in corner most visible upon enter-ing room. Make chalk mark on horizon-tal line 4½" (one-fourth of 18" spread) from interior corner, then have partner drop plumb line from this mark (dia-gram 5). Hold yardstick even with plumb line and draw soft chalk line ver-tically down wall against plumb line. Make second mark on horizontal line 18" from first mark, drop plumb line, and draw vertical line as before. Repeat to mark vertical lines 18" apart all around room. On each vertical line, measure down from horizontal line and mark every 24" (diagram 6).

5. To mark half drops between vertical rows, use triangle folded from 12" x 18" sheet of construction paper. Draft lines from midpoint of one long edge to oppo-site corners, then fold on lines (diagram 7). Hold triangle against wall so 18" edge spans distance between two 24" marks, then mark new point at triangle's lower point (diagram 8). Repeat to mark entire wall (diagram 9).

Printing the Wall

1. Load printing block with paint. Use 1" brush to brush paint onto exposed fabric surface (illustration E, page 7). Blot drips with cotton swab. Make several consecu-tive test prints on scrap paper to determine if you applied enough paint and to gauge how many prints you can make on one loading. To make a clear print, press firmly on all areas of block.

2. Block-print wall. Work from top down and from left to right all around room. Load block with paint, position block so top center aligns with mark on wall (illustration F, page 7), then press firmly and lift up to make print (illustra-tion G). Continue until entire wall is printed (diagram 10). Let dry at least 4 hours, but preferably overnight. Whisk off chalk marks with soft brush or damp sponge. ◆

Silk Flower Chair Sash

Dress up your entertainment setting in a new way with this quick and easy chair back arrangement.

❧ BY CAROL ENDLER STERBENZ

MATERIALS

- 7 to 8 silk flowers, each 3" to 4" across (choose three different colors)
- 6 to 8 artificial leafy stems with 1" blossoms (e.g., freesia)
- 4 to 6 stems with 5" cascades of flowers or blossoms
- Two 27"-long foliage stems (approximately twenty-five 2" to 3" leaves per stem)
- 4 to 5 berry clusters, assorted sizes
- 2 to 3 grape clusters
- 1 to 2 miniature fruits
- 16-gauge stainless steel wire
- Green florist tape
- 2 to 3 fabric-covered 18" florist stems

You'll also need: wire cutters; ruler or yardstick; and pencil.

Other items, if necessary: ribbon or additional fabric-covered florist stems (for attaching sash to chair).

I F YOU LOVE SILK FLOWERS AND WANT another place to display them, consider this chair sash, which is designed to accent the back of a kitchen or dining room chair.

You can make this sash in about fifteen minutes using silk flowers, artificial foliage, and clusters of berries and grapes. Start by creating a U-shaped base with 16-gauge stainless steel wire, then wrap the base with green florist tape. You can attach the flowers, foliage, and fruit by coiling their own stems around the base or else by taping them in place using florist tape.

For the sashes shown at the right, I used a soft palette—a mix of soft green, purple, yellow, and white colors—but you can construct a chair sash to match a decorating scheme or to reflect the season at hand. Celebrate winter with a sash made from white flowers and gold or silver fruit, or make a springlike mixture of pastels, a fall design with autumnal colors, or a holiday arrangement using rich reds and dark greens.

If your budget is limited, consider skipping the traditional centerpiece arrangement and making matching chair sashes for your end chairs.

INSTRUCTIONS

1. Make core of sash by cutting two 23" lengths of wire, holding them together, and wrapping their entire length with florist tape. On flat work surface, bend core into upside-down U about 15" across at widest part.

2. In order to decorate core, work from ends toward center of U. Tape two or three cascading stems to each end so that blossoms dangle freely (*see* illustration A). Coil both 27" foliage stems around entire length of core, working each one from opposite direction in order to vary leaf sizes (illustration B).

3. Arrange 3"- to 4"-diameter silk flowers around core so that no two adjacent colors match each other. Once arrangement along U has been finalized, wind flower stems around core in order to attach each bloom (illustration C). Then fill in sides of sash with leafy stems containing 1" blossoms (illustration D).

4. In order to fill in remaining gaps, wind on grape and berry clusters and fruits. In order to make tendrils, wind florist stems around pencil in tight spiral. Remove pencil and unwind stem slightly to relax spiral. Trim spiral to desired length and wind onto core.

5. In order to attach finished sash to chair, use ribbon or additional fabric-covered florist stems. ◆

ILLUSTRATION:
Nenad Jakesevic

COLOR PHOTOGRAPHY:
Carl Tremblay

STYLING:
Gabrielle Derrick de Papp/Team

MAKING THE CHAIR SASH

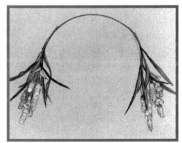

A. Tape two or three cascading stems to each end of the core.

B. Wind two long foliage stems around the core.

C. Wind the stems of the 3" to 4" flowers onto the core.

D. Use the stems with the 1" blooms to fill in the empty areas.

Folk Art Village

The secret to these fast and fabulous houses: Cut the parts from balsa wood, then decorate the exteriors with dollhouse parts.

❧ BY CAROL ENDLER STERBENZ

ILLUSTRATION:
Mary Newell DePalma

COLOR PHOTOGRAPHY:
Carl Tremblay

MATERIALS

- **4" x 36" x 1/8" balsa wood sheet**
- **1/2" x 1/2" x 36" balsa stick**
- **1/4" x 1/4" x 36" balsa stick**
- **1 package Handley dollhouse picket fence gates #7504**
- **1 package Handley dollhouse shutters #5017**
- **Yellow carpenter's glue**

You'll also need:
fine-grit sandpaper; X-Acto knife with extra blades; small pull-stroke saw (such as keyhole saw); steel ruler; pencil; self-healing cutting mat; masking tape; damp cloth; tack cloth; and 1/2" and 1/8" flat brushes.

Other items, if necessary:
2-ounce containers acrylic paint, one each in sage green, dull red, and gold (if making green house) and one each in sage green, dull red, light navy, and cream (if making red house), and one package Handley newel posts #7205 (if making green house).

Dollhouse parts can be used in a variety of ways. On the green house (right), a picket fence is positioned to the side of the door; on the red house (left), the picket fence is cut into two parts and placed on either side of the door.

YOU CAN CREATE A NEIGHBORhood of individually decorated houses for a windowsill or shelf in an afternoon's time. The trick: cutting the house walls and roof from balsa wood, then using dollhouse shutters, picket fences, and posts to add architectural details.

Start by making a basic house: a simple four-sided construction with a peaked roof. You can make it from a one-yard length of balsa wood measuring four inches wide and about one-eighth inch thick, with two narrow strips, also of balsa wood, for the chimney and interior supports. Balsa wood is very easy to cut; all you need is a metal straightedge and a sharp X-Acto knife. I originally tried building the houses from basswood, as I liked the weight and grain of the wood, but found I had to use a saw to cut it.

Because balsa wood is so thin, I experienced some problems with warping when I glued the joints together. To avoid this, use your glue conservatively and use masking tape to secure the glued sections after the glue has set and turned rubbery. Once the glue dries, the joints will be straight.

I tested Aleene's original tacky glue and Elmer's yellow carpenter's glue for assembling the houses. With both glues, the glued surfaces gripped readily, but the Aleene's glue took up to one minute for the pieces to hold on their own without sliding apart. With the carpenter's glue, I could let go after ten or fifteen seconds.

I also experienced some warping after painting the houses, but I attribute this to the fact that on my first set of houses, I used a wet and runny paint. On the second set, I used a thicker, slightly drier paint, with superior results. If your paint appears too wet, let it air-dry for a few minutes to thicken it.

After you've constructed the basic house, you can decorate it in any number of different ways using dollhouse shutters, picket fences, posts, or other architectural items. Because these components are usually made of wood, you can adapt their functions, or change their shapes entirely, using an X-Acto knife and paint. A wooden shutter, for instance, becomes a door; newel posts make great pillars for a front porch; and the top ball and block from a newel post make an interesting lantern.

INSTRUCTIONS

Cutting the Wood Pieces

1. Draft six house pieces on balsa sheet (use illustration A as cutting diagram). Using pencil and ruler, draft one 3¾" x 4" roof, one 3⅝" x 4" roof, two 3½" x 2¾" sides, one 5¾" x 2¾" front, and one 5¾" x 2¾" back (*see* illustrations B through D). To draft peaks on front and back, mark midpoint of one short edge, then mark point 2¼" from each short edge on two perpendicular edges. Draft lines connecting three points. To cut out pieces, lean on cutting mat, lay steel ruler along marked lines, and score and cut wood with X-Acto knife. Save one peak triangle to mark chimney.

2. Use balsa sticks for cutting chimney and inner supports. To draft chimney, align right-angle edges of peak triangle against edge of ½" x ½" balsa stick. Run pencil against diagonal edge of triangle to mark chimney base angle on balsa stick (illustration E). For inner supports, mark four 3¾" sections on ¼" x ¼" balsa stick. Cut all pieces using X-Acto knife and ruler.

3. Use shutters to make door and windows. For door, draft line on shutter ¾" from short edge and saw off excess; save scrap for stoop on red house. For windows, draft lines 1½" from each short edge and saw off excess; discard middle piece. To mark and cut remaining trims, proceed to step 4 for green house or step 5 for red house.

4. If making green house: For stoop, draft 2⅞" x ½"-wide strip on leftover balsa strip and cut with X-Acto knife (illustration F). For lantern, saw off top section of newel post.

5. If making red house: For pulley hoist, draft 1¼" x ¼"-wide strip on leftover balsa sheet and cut with X-Acto knife. For fence, saw off ½" from bottom of picket fence gate, even with bottom rail; then saw fencing vertically, four pickets in from each side edge, to make two sections about ⅞" across. Discard middle piece.

Assembling the House

1. Glue inner supports to house sides. Run thin bead of glue along two longer edges of each house side, lay supports on glue, even with outer edges, and press to adhere (illustration G). Wipe oozing glue with damp cloth. Let dry 5 minutes.

2. Join back and front to sides. Run thin bead of glue along two longest edges of back. Stand back and one side upright and press edges together at right angle so support touches fresh glue (illustration H). Glue second side to back in same way (illustration I). Glue front to sides to complete house base (illustration J). Hold in position about 1 minute, then tape outside edges.

3. Join roof to house. Angle larger roof over smaller roof to form peak, and test-fit on house base, creating overhang all around (illustration K). To improve fit, wear down roof edges that form peak by sanding lightly on an angle. Remove dust with tack cloth. Run thin bead of glue around top edge of house and roof edges that form peak, then reposition roof pieces on house. Adjust fit, hold 1 minute, and tape across peak. Run thin bead of glue along peak seam and smooth with finger. Let house dry at least 1 hour, but preferably overnight. Remove tape, sand edges and joins lightly, and wipe with tack cloth.

Painting and Finishing

Paint house and trims separately in sequence below, washing out brush with cold water between colors. Prop wet trims and let dry 30 minutes. When paint is dry, glue trims to house, using glue conservatively. Follow step 1 for red house and step 2 for green house, then proceed to step 3.

1. If making red house: Using ½"-wide brush, paint eaves, door, and stoop sage green. Then paint windows, fences, and pulley hoist cream; front, back, sides, and chimney dull red; and roof light navy. Add light navy dot to door for doorknob. Let paint dry 30 minutes. Glue windows to sides so eaves conceal cut edges. Glue door flanked by fences to front. Glue stoop at right angle to door. Glue chimney to roof. Glue pulley hoist to eaves at front peak. Let dry 1 hour, but preferably overnight.

2. If making green house: Using ½"-wide brush, paint fence and lamp gold. Then paint front, back, sides, and stoop sage green, and roof (including eaves), door, windows, and chimney dull red. Using ⅛"-wide brush, paint edges and top of lantern dull red. Let paint dry 30 minutes. Glue windows to sides so eaves conceal cut edges. Glue stoop at right angle to front. Glue door to front ¼" from right edge with cut edge resting on stoop. Glue lantern to left of door. Glue fence to left of door, applying glue to where it touches stoop and roof. Glue chimney to roof. Let dry at least 1 hour, but preferably overnight.

3. To wear away paint and create worn finish, lightly sand edges and other selected areas. ◆

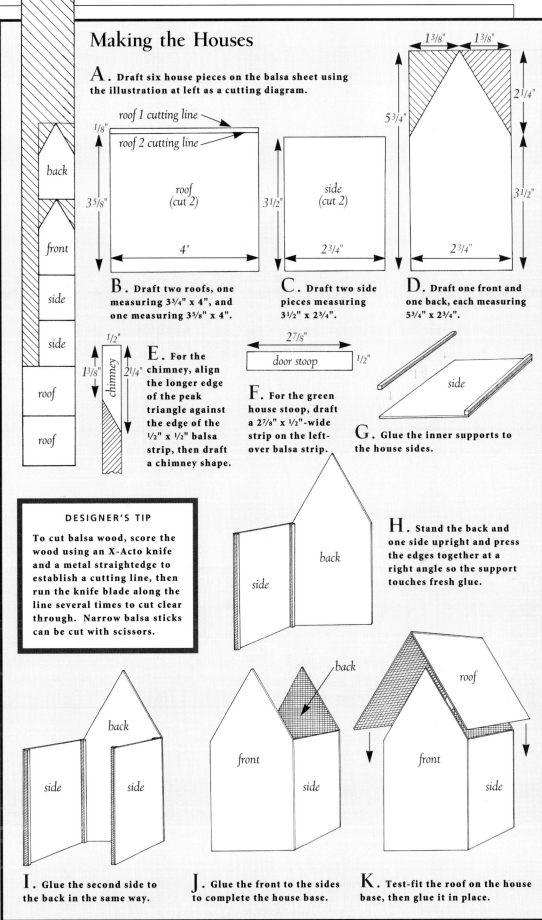

Making the Houses

A. Draft six house pieces on the balsa sheet using the illustration at left as a cutting diagram.

B. Draft two roofs, one measuring 3¾" x 4", and one measuring 3⅝" x 4".

C. Draft two side pieces measuring 3½" x 2¾".

D. Draft one front and one back, each measuring 5¾" x 2¾".

E. For the chimney, align the longer edge of the peak triangle against the edge of the ½" x ½" balsa strip, then draft a chimney shape.

F. For the green house stoop, draft a 2⅞" x ½"-wide strip on the leftover balsa strip.

G. Glue the inner supports to the house sides.

> **DESIGNER'S TIP**
>
> To cut balsa wood, score the wood using an X-Acto knife and a metal straightedge to establish a cutting line, then run the knife blade along the line several times to cut clear through. Narrow balsa sticks can be cut with scissors.

H. Stand the back and one side upright and press the edges together at a right angle so the support touches fresh glue.

I. Glue the second side to the back in the same way.

J. Glue the front to the sides to complete the house base.

K. Test-fit the roof on the house base, then glue it in place.

Three Easy Antique Finishes

Learn the secrets of giving a new piece of unfinished furniture an aged look in just a few hours.

❧ BY DEBORAH MILLER GABLER

MATERIALS
Prepping the Object

- **New, unfinished wood object or furniture**
- **Latex sealer or primer**

You'll also need: paintbrush; 220- and 400-grit sandpaper; tack cloth; and screwdriver.

Other items, if necessary: hammer (for tapping nails) and wood filler (for filling holes).

DESIGNER'S TIP

For a truly authentic piece of aged furniture, antique the furniture's hardware. Spray polished metals with a matte fixative such as Krylon 1311 to dull the surface. Then paint the hardware with a metallic paint or with the paint used on the furniture. Knobs, drawer pulls, handles, or latches will show signs of wear. For a worn wood look, rub the surface with steel wool. For metal, polish to expose a high sheen.

COLOR PHOTOGRAPHY:
Carl Tremblay

SILHOUETTE PHOTOGRAPHY:
Furnald/Gray

STYLING:
Gabrielle Derrick de Papp/Team

Two or more finishes can be combined on a single piece of furniture, as illustrated on the cabinet above.

WANT TO GIVE A NEW, unfinished cabinet, small wooden object, or piece of furniture an antique finish? In just a few hours, using water-based paints and glazes, even beginning faux finishers can replicate any one of these three aged finishes.

The techniques that are featured here (*see* samples, next page) are well suited to many types of unpainted furniture, such as shelves, boxes, cupboards, chairs, or small tables. Each finish can be applied individually, or two or more finishes can be combined on a single piece of furniture, such as the cabinet shown above.

On the cabinet, I base-coated the entire exterior surface with Pratt & Lambert's Olivette (1679) latex paint. (I used the Olivette color alone on the interior of the cabinet.) Once the base coat was dry, I covered the surface with a coat of Deco Art Weathered Wood, a special medium that produces a crackle finish when dry. I let the medium set for twenty to thirty minutes until it was tacky, then I patted on a coat of Pratt & Lambert's Victoria Blue (1276) latex paint. When dry, I sanded the piece slightly to show signs of wear at the corners, edges, and around the wooden knob, and rubbed a small amount of paste shoe polish into the corners and the grooves of the molding to replicate soiled areas. Then I polished the exterior surface with Goodard's Cabinet Maker's Wax (beeswax).

If you're interested in a crackled finish, I recommend one of two products. A two-ounce bottle of Deco Art Weathered Wood, mentioned above, is priced at around $1.99; it's better suited for smaller projects, such as the cabinet. If you decide to "crackle" a larger piece of furniture, such as a table or dresser, I recommend Tight Bond's Franklin Hide Glue, which retails for about $4.99 for a four-ounce container. The Hide Glue produces wider cracks and a bigger crackling pattern, which is better suited for a larger piece of furniture.

Getting Started

Before you can antique any piece, careful preparation of the surface is essential. Start by removing all the hardware, such as knobs and drawer pulls, then tap in any protruding nails and fill any holes, nicks, chips, or deep scratches with wood filler. Prep the wood by sanding lightly with 220-grit sandpaper, wiping it with a tack cloth, and sealing it with a latex sealer or primer. Then sand the piece again with 400-grit paper in case the primer raises the grain of the wood.

Once the primer is dry, you can apply the base coat. You can use the same color base coat for the entire piece, or paint selected areas, such as doors or moldings, in different colors. Choose your color palette to complement the style of furniture: Delicate furnishings can be painted in softer, pastel colors while heavier furnishings with bolder lines and a more hand-crafted character may look better painted in darker, country colors.

I recommend water-based (latex) paint and glazes for easy cleanup; a flat or satin finish gives the most realistic antiqued effect. The amount of sealer, paint, or glaze mixture needed will depend on the surface area to be covered. Generally, one quart will cover 100 to 125 square feet—more than enough for a large armoire. The antiquing mixture used in finish III, a 1:1 mix of linseed oil and odorless turpentine, goes much further: One cup will cover the same surface area (or one teaspoon for every two to three square feet).

Finishes I and III should be topped with a clear satin sealer, such as Flecto Varathane Diamond Finish IPN Coating. Be sure to let the finishes dry several days before sealing. Finish II should not be sealed, as it may destroy the whitewash effect created in the last step.

Deborah Miller Gabler, owner of Shady Lane Designs in Hamburg, New York, is a freelance designer and teacher specializing in custom lampshades and stenciling.

INSTRUCTIONS
Prepping the Object

1. Prep furniture by unscrewing and removing any metal hardware, such as knobs and hinges. If necessary, tap in any protruding nails and fill any holes, nicks, chips, or deep scratches with wood filler. Using 220-grit sandpaper, sand entire surface lightly. Remove dust with tack cloth.

2. To protect wood, brush on one coat sealer or primer and let dry following manufacturer's recommendations. Sand with 400-grit sandpaper and remove dust. ◆

I. Crackled Finish

1. Paint wood yellow oxide and let dry 1 hour.

2. Brush Hide Glue or Weathered Wood onto surface, covering selected areas. Let set 20 to 40 minutes or until formula begins to coagulate.

3. Using rag, pat barn red paint unevenly onto covered areas, allowing streaks and patches of base coat to peek through. To achieve crackle finish, let dry overnight.

4. To protect dried surface from chipping, apply sealer spray following manufacturer's instructions. Let dry overnight.

5. To suggest accumulated dirt, squeeze small amount burnt umber paint onto plastic lid. Dip rag in paint, sweep over surface, then blot off paint in selected areas. When nearly dry, rub paint further into surface using fingertip. Let dry several days, then apply at least one coat satin sealer.

MATERIALS
Crackled Finish

- Yellow oxide satin latex paint (for base coat)
- Barn red satin latex paint (for top coat)
- 4-ounce container Tight Bond's Franklin Hide Glue or 2-ounce bottle Deco Art Weathered Wood
- Folk Art Clearcote Acrylic Sealer Spray
- Small tube burnt umber acrylic paint
- Flecto Varathane Diamond Finish IPN Coating (clear satin)

You'll also need: paintbrushes; clean, soft rags; plastic lid; and paint-stirring sticks.

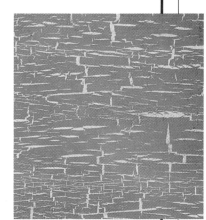

Crackled finish

II. Flaked Finish

1. Paint wood pea green and let dry 1 hour.

2. To mark spots that will be flaked, rub fingertip in furniture polish, then dab or streak it across painted surface. Let wax penetrate 15 to 20 minutes.

3. In plastic container, tint 2 parts glazing liquid with 1 part yellowish/ivory paint. Brush glaze onto surface. Let dry 4 to 6 hours, then repeat up to two more times to cover pea green base coat.

4. Run scraper across surface to lift paint from areas with furniture polish. Let dry several days.

5. To create whitewash, use water to thin white latex paint to half-and-half consistency. Dab or streak on using rag, then blot off exposed green areas.

MATERIALS
Flaked Finish

- Pea green satin latex paint (for base coat)
- Yellowish/ivory satin latex paint (for top coat)
- Latex glazing liquid
- White latex paint

You'll also need: paintbrushes; beeswax furniture polish; plastic containers; soft, clean rags; measuring cup; paint-stirring sticks; and stiff, sharp-edged plastic scraper.

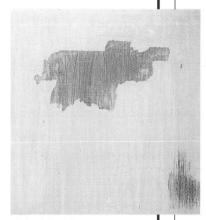

Flaked finish

III. Ragged and Spattered Finish

1. Paint wood yellow oxide and let dry 1 hour.

2. Tint glaze by mixing 2 parts glazing liquid with 1 part raw sienna paint in plastic container. To apply tinted glaze, crumple newspaper into ball, dip in glaze, dab off excess, then dab and roll across wood surface. Wipe wet glaze from raised areas of painted surface and let additional glaze accumulate in crevices and corners. Let dry overnight.

3. To spatter surface, squeeze burnt umber paint onto plastic lid. Coat toothbrush with paint. Hold toothbrush 4" to 6" from surface and run thumb across bristles. Let dry overnight.

4. In plastic container, mix 1 part linseed oil with 1 part turpentine. To add touches of patina, rub mixture into painted surface with rag.

5. To suggest accumulated dirt, squeeze small amount asphaltum oil paint onto plastic lid. Dip rag into paint, dab off excess, then rub paint sparingly into recessed areas and corners while mixture from step 4 is still wet. Let dry several days, then apply at least one coat satin sealer.

MATERIALS
Ragged and Spattered Finish

- Yellow oxide flat latex paint
- Raw sienna flat latex paint
- Latex glazing liquid
- Linseed oil
- Odorless turpentine
- Small tube burnt umber acrylic paint
- Tube of artist's asphaltum oil paint
- Flecto Varathane Diamond Finish IPN Coating (clear satin)

You'll also need: paintbrushes; newspaper; clean, soft rags; old toothbrush; plastic containers; plastic lids; measuring cup; and paint-stirring sticks.

Ragged and spattered finish

Easy-Sew Lap Quilts

Two soft furnishing fabrics make these simply designed lap quilts elegant as well as practical.

🐾 BY CANDIE FRANKEL

MATERIALS

- **2 yards each two complementary (weave, color, and pattern) 45"- to 60"-wide fabrics (both must be same width); for large pattern repeats, add yardage equal to one pattern repeat**

VERSION 1
Striped/Floral Quilt
- **5⁷⁄₈ yards (for 45"-wide fabric), 6³⁄₈ yards (for 54"-wide fabric), or 6³⁄₄ yards (for 60"-wide fabric) complementary tassel fringe**

VERSION 2
Burgundy Damask Quilt
- **10¹⁄₃ yards (for 45"-wide fabric), 11¹⁄₃ yards (for 54"-wide fabric), or 12 yards (for 60"-wide fabric) ½"- to ⅝"-wide complementary flat braid trim**
- **Four 5"-long complementary tassels**

You'll also need:
Matching thread; sewing machine; rotary cutter; scissors; tape measure; pins; fabric marking pencil; and iron.

Other items if needed:
Beacon FabriTac glue (to baste Version 2 trim).

This reversible lap quilt, sewn from just four yards of fabric, will warm up any decorating scheme. The finished quilt measures sixty inches long and approximately fifty-three inches wide.

DESIGNER'S TIP

To keep braid trims from shifting during sewing, glue them in position before you sew. Be sure to use fabric glue so that the finished lap quilt is washable.

ILLUSTRATION:
Mary Newell DePalma

COLOR PHOTOGRAPHY:
Carl Tremblay

SILHOUETTE PHOTOGRAPHY:
Furnald/Gray

MY GOAL IN CREATING THIS pair of lap quilts was to devise a simple, easy-to-sew design that looked elegant. The solution, as it turned out, hinged on my choice of soft furnishing fabrics: a pair of loose floral and striped weaves made up of thicker threads, and a pair of contrasting damask weaves.

The construction for this quilt resembles that of any traditional patchwork or whole cloth quilt that places two fabrics back-to-back—but without the batting in between. To keep the piecing to a minimum, I surrounded a center panel with four border strips.

To ensure a loose, easy drape, I needed soft, lightweight fabrics. I ruled out heavyweight upholstery fabrics in favor of lighter-weight, soft furnishing fabrics that are suited to both upholstery and window treatments. The ideal fabric would be pliable and drapable rather than stiff; its texture could vary, as long as it wasn't itchy against the skin; and its body would have resilience to resist wrinkling. These characteristics—qualities that are best determined by touch, not by sight—are collectively referred to as the fabric's *hand*.

Of the different types of fabric I examined, two top choices emerged: loose and damask weaves. Loose weaves suggest an informal mood and come in a range of prints, stripes, and other patterns. Damask carries loose threads across the weave on both the right and wrong sides to create a reversible pattern. These threads enhance the fabric's pliability, and the patterns formed are typically traditional and symmetrical, thus suited to formal interiors.

Weave, Color, and Pattern

To select two compatible fabrics for each quilt, I considered three aspects: weave, color, and pattern. Both of the quilt's fabrics needed to be one of the two weaves discussed above. A mismatch of weaves—damask paired with a less formal, looser weave, for instance—would look unprofessional.

Color is more subjective. The two fabrics can be similar in color, share a background color, or use the same colors in different proportions so that the predominant color in one fabric appears as an accent color in the second fabric. Precise color matches are not necessary, and subtle differences can actually be more visually compelling. Even though color match is not critical, the fabrics should match one another in overall tone so that the same level of lightness or darkness runs through both. In the striped/floral quilt, for example, both fabrics use colors that are slightly muted.

As far as pattern is concerned, the quilts shown here illustrate two pattern combinations that are always safe: a floral with a stripe, and two damask fabrics limited to a two-tone palette. A more adventurous choice would bring together two very different patterns, such as a floral and a paisley, or two florals. Some prints are open, showing more of the

Above, left: Version 1, striped/floral quilt. Above, right: version 2, burgundy damask quilt.

background color, while others are closed, showing a more packed pattern with less background. To ensure compatibility between two prints and to keep the eye moving over the entire surface in your final design, choose one of each. Another way to combine two patterned fabrics is to look for decorator fabrics that are designed in groups.

Purchasing Your Fabric

Rather than make a plain reversible quilt, I decided to feature both fabrics on each side, piecing them in a rectangular panel surrounded by a wide strip border. Each side is the mirror image of the other, so no fabric is wasted. I used fifty-four-inch fabric; two yards of each fabric gave me a finished quilt sixty inches long and roughly fifty-three inches wide. The design is suited to any fabric forty-five to sixty inches wide as long as the two fabric widths match.

I planned the cutting layout so that the fabric's surface pattern would be centered within the rectangular panel. Most patterned fabrics have even patterns that are suited to this layout. In other words, if I were to draw a line down the lengthwise center of the fabric, the pattern to the right of the line would show in mirror image to the left. It is, however, possible to find fabrics that jog the pattern along the selvages like wallpaper; these patterns should be avoided for this project. Two yards of fabric gave me twelve inches of play to center the fabric pattern on the panel. For pattern repeats exceeding eighteen inches, purchase additional yardage equal to the repeat depth so that you can achieve a pleasing placement. To make certain all of my rectangular panel and border pieces were cut on the straight grain, I pulled a crosswise thread across the fabric from selvage to selvage to mark the grain before I began. Without this step, I risked cutting some pieces slightly askew, with the result that they wouldn't lie properly when sewn together.

One additional note: If you use striped or plaid fabric, be prepared for an uneven pattern match when you join the end borders at the corners. On the striped/floral quilt, I machine-stitched a pleat, or tuck, near one end of each end border so that the stripes would line up with those on the adjacent side border. (To see the site of the pleat in the photo above, look for the aqua stripe in the end border that is narrower than the rest.)

For the finishing touches, I used fringe on the striped/floral quilt and braid and tassels on the burgundy damask quilt. I chose upholstery-weight trims, as dressmaker trims looked too skimpy against the upholstery fabrics.

Lap quilts designed by Nancy K. Johnson and sewn by Jeanne Beutel.

INSTRUCTIONS
Cutting the Fabric

1. To determine crosswise grain of fabric, lay fabrics on flat surface. Using scissors, snip selvage. Grasp thread at one selvage and pull gently, alternately sliding thread and pushing fabric until you reach other selvage (*see* illustration A). Cut along channel left by pulled thread.

2. To cut quilt pieces, fold each fabric in half lengthwise, right side out and with selvages and cut straight grain matching. Using rotary cutter, trim off selvages. Referring to cutting layout (illustration B) and using tape measure, insert pins into fabric to mark approximate position of panel A, so fabric design falls within A area and at least 7" of fabric extends at each end for C sections. Make cuts 1–5 as shown on each fabric. Before lifting pieces, draw small arrow on wrong side of each piece with marking pencil to indicate nap or print direction.

3. To mark midpoint of each fabric, fold each B and C piece in half crosswise and, using scissors, clip into long edge at fold no deeper than ¼" (illustration C). Use same method to mark midpoint of all four edges on A section.

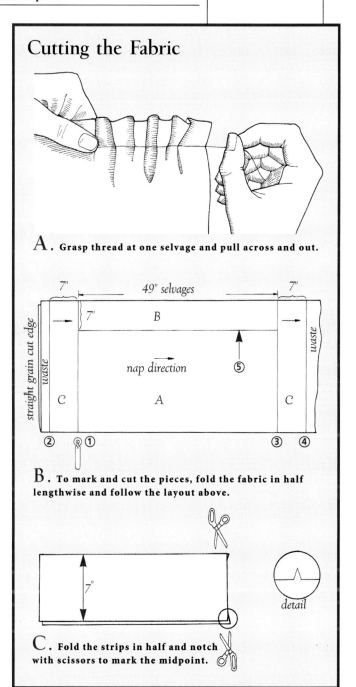

Cutting the Fabric

A. Grasp thread at one selvage and pull across and out.

B. To mark and cut the pieces, fold the fabric in half lengthwise and follow the layout above.

C. Fold the strips in half and notch with scissors to mark the midpoint.

detail

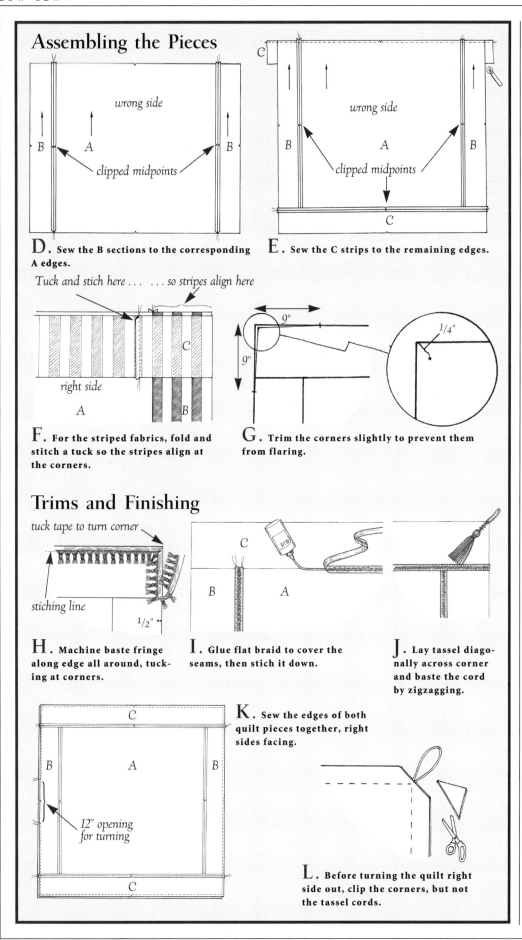

Assembling the Pieces

wrong side

B | A | B

clipped midpoints

D. Sew the B sections to the corresponding A edges.

wrong side

B | A | B

clipped midpoints

C

E. Sew the C strips to the remaining edges.

Tuck and stich here . . . . . . so stripes align here

C

right side

A | B

F. For the striped fabrics, fold and stitch a tuck so the stripes align at the corners.

9"

9"

1/4"

G. Trim the corners slightly to prevent them from flaring.

Trims and Finishing

tuck tape to turn corner

stiching line

1/2"

H. Machine baste fringe along edge all around, tucking at corners.

C

B | A

I. Glue flat braid to cover the seams, then stich it down.

J. Lay tassel diagonally across corner and baste the cord by zigzagging.

K. Sew the edges of both quilt pieces together, right sides facing.

C

B | A | B

12" opening for turning

C

L. Before turning the quilt right side out, clip the corners, but not the tassel cords.

Assembling the Pieces

Complete the appropriate steps, then repeat with second side of quilt.

1. To stitch border in place, pin B sections to 49" edges of contrasting A panel, right sides together, clipped midpoints matching, and arrows marked in step 2 pointing in same direction (illustration D). Stitch ½" from edges. Press seams open.

2. *If using unstriped fabric:* Pin C strips to remaining raw edges of contrasting A section, right sides together, clipped midpoints matching, and arrows marked in step 2 pointing in same direction; ends will extend beyond B strips. Stitch, then, using rotary cutter, trim extensions even with B edges (illustration E). Press seams open.

3. *If using striped fabric:* Lay sewn A/B section right side up. Lay striped C strip face down on A/B edge, aligning stripes at one corner. As you near opposite corner, fold and press C strip so stripes align there (illustration F). Machine-stitch fold from wrong side, trim seam to ½", and press open. Pin and stitch adjusted C strip to A/B section as in step 2.

4. *If border seams cause corners to flare:* Mark dot ¼" in from each corner. Starting 9" from corner, trim off fabric from edge to dot on each side (illustration G).

Trims and Finishing

Select appropriate options from steps 1–3, then complete steps 4–6.

1. *To add fringe (Version 1):* Lay one quilt piece flat, right side up. Place fringe along edge all around; adjust position so fringe tape falls within ½" seam allowance (illustration H). Machine-baste ⅜" from edge all around, tucking tape at corners.

2. *To add flat braid (Version 2):* Lay each quilt piece flat, right side up. Center braid on seam, so end extends about ¼" beyond area to be glued. Lift braid, then run thin bead of glue along each A/B seam. Press braid to adhere, concealing entire seam. When you reach end, trim braid ¼" beyond glued area. Machine-stitch down both edges of braid. Repeat to glue and stitch braid to each A/B/C seam, concealing cut ends of first braid applied (illustration I). Repeat on other side.

3. *To add tassels (Version 2):* Lay one quilt piece flat, right side up. Lay tassel on fabric diagonally so cord extends into corner. Zigzag over cord (illustration J).

4. To complete, lay quilt pieces on flat surface, right sides together and edges matching. Stitch ½" from edges all around, pivoting at corners; leave 12" opening along one edge for turning (illustration K). *Version 2 only:* From wrong side, press seams open, then to each side.

5. Clip corners, but in Version 2 avoid cutting the tassel cord (*see* illustration L).

6. Turn right side out and slip-stitch 12" opening closed. Press all edges, pulling fringe away from seam (Version 1). ◆

The Best-Tasting Chocolate Leaves

The winners: dark brown leaves made from Tobler bittersweet chocolate and cream-colored leaves made from Lindt white chocolate.

❧ BY FRANCOISE HARDY

CHOCOLATE LEAVES MAKE A beautiful accent for a wide range of desserts. I've always admired chocolate leaves, so I decided to make them at home, a simple process that involves melting chocolate, brushing it on a fresh leaf, and chilling. My goal, however, was not just to make the leaves, but to find the best-tasting chocolate for the task.

After evaluating four imported dark chocolates, I decided on Tobler Tradition Swiss bittersweet chocolate (3.5 ounces for $1.89). The Tobler chocolate was creamy and very chocolaty, and the slightly bitter flavor was pleasant yet not overpowering. I could find only two imported white chocolates, of which I preferred the Lindt Swiss white confectionery bar (3.4 ounces for $2.79).

With the taste preference settled, I moved on to the choice of leaf. I ended up with rose leaves because they are supple (good for support and for peeling), they have clearly dimensional veins (good for textural imprinting), and they can be found year-round in any florist shop.

Francoise Hardy is a professional craftsperson and artisan living in Boston.

INSTRUCTIONS

1. Wash leaves in soapy water, rinse well, and pat dry with kitchen towel.

2. Melt chocolate by breaking bars into individual blocks. Place 8 bittersweet chocolate blocks in one container and 6 white chocolate blocks in second. Microwave bittersweet chocolate at medium for 60 seconds, white chocolate at medium for 30 seconds. To remove lumps, stir with individual chopsticks until smooth. To keep chocolates liquefied, set each container in soup bowl half-filled with hot tap water.

Coating the Leaves

1. Line cookie sheets with waxed paper and set aside. Lay rose leaf in open palm with underside facing up; hold stem with fingertip.

2. To cover leaf with chocolate, brush chocolate from stem out to edges, layering it ¹⁄₁₆" to ⅛" thick (illustration B). Set leaf on cookie sheet, chocolate side up. Repeat, using different brush for each chocolate, to coat additional leaves (illustration C).

3. To set chocolate, place cookie sheets

For a mottled look on your leaves, as shown above, remove the leaf from the refrigerator, let it reach room temperature, and then refrigerate again for one to two days.

in refrigerator 15 minutes or until surface of chocolate is hard to the touch.

4. To remove rose leaf, hold chilled leaf chocolate side down. Working quickly so chocolate doesn't melt, gently pry up rose leaf at stem until leaf and chocolate layers begin to separate, then peel it back and off chocolate (illustration D). Discard rose leaves or press between layers of waxed paper in heavy book for future use. Lay chocolate leaves on waxed paper and refrigerate until needed.

5. To attach leaves to cake, brush small dab melted chocolate (cool to touch) on back and gently press it against side or top of cake. ◆

MATERIALS
Yields approximately 2 dozen leaves

- **3.5-ounce bar Tobler Tradition Swiss bittersweet chocolate**
- **3.4-ounce bar Lindt Swiss white confectionery chocolate**

You'll also need: microwave oven; 2 dozen 1"- to 3½"-long fresh rose leaves with stems; 2 cookie sheets; 2 custard cup–size, microwave-safe containers; 2 soup bowls; 2 chopsticks; 2 pastry brushes; waxed paper; table knife; dish-washing soap; and kitchen towel.

Other items, if necessary: heavy book (for flattening limp leaves).

DESIGNER'S TIP

To make curved or dimensional leaves, cradle the rose leaf in the bowl of a soupspoon and chill until the chocolate coating hardens.

ILLUSTRATION:
Nenad Jakesevic

COLOR PHOTOGRAPHY:
Carl Tremblay

STYLING:
Gabrielle Derrick de Papp/Team

MAKING THE CHOCOLATE LEAVES

A. Microwave the chocolate until it's almost melted.

B. Brush the melted chocolate onto the underside of the leaf.

C. Set each leaf on a cookie sheet lined with waxed paper.

D. After chilling 15 minutes, peel off the rose leaf.

The Fastest Way to Make Your Own Paper

Creating beautiful, custom paper is a breeze using our time-saving techniques and additives such as rose petals or glitter.

❧ BY MARIE BROWNING AND SUSAN WILSON

MATERIALS

Yields approximately 12 sheets 8½" x 11" paper

- **2 to 3 dozen 8 ½" x 11" sheets (or equivalent) uncoated paper**
- **5 envelopes unflavored gelatin**

You'll also need:
blender; 8½" x 11" mold and deckle; 23" x 16¾" x 6" plastic storage box with cover ("vat"); 3 to 6 terry-cloth bath towels; wire mesh strainer; twenty-four 13" x 15" pieces 100 percent cotton fabric; six to eight 13" x 15" pieces wool fabric; two 13" x 15" pieces plywood, primed or sealed; newspaper; cellulose kitchen sponges; 8-quart bowl; pitcher; spray mister; stove; teakettle; Pyrex measuring cup; 2-quart pot or Pyrex bowl; and large spoon.

Other items, if necessary:
One or two sheets cotton linter (to increase rag content); iron (to iron paper); folding drying rack with twelve or more rods and three to four dozen clothespins (for air-drying); and herbs, flowers, etc. (for color and texture; *see* "Adding Color and Texture to Paper," page 19).

ILLUSTRATION:
Nenad Jakesevic

COLOR PHOTOGRAPHY:
Carl Tremblay

These handmade papers contain a variety of additives: (from top to bottom) fresh grass clippings; dried eucalyptus leaves; white cotton thread and dried carnation petals; and chile peppers and fresh grass clippings.

TRADITIONAL PAPERMAKING IS A messy, space-consuming process that's best done outdoors or in a studio setting. Since we don't have a studio, we wanted a method we could do in our kitchen.

To make paper, you suspend pulverized pieces of plant fiber in a vat of water, resulting in a mixture called a slurry. For color and textural interest, you can introduce ingredients such as flower petals, spices, herbs, or glitter (*see* "Adding Color and Texture to Paper," page 19). A two-piece framed screen, known as a mold and deckle, is inserted into the slurry. As it is lifted out, the water drains away, leaving a thin layer of fibers on top of the screen. These wet fibers are then transferred, or couched, onto a separate flat surface and allowed to dry, which yields a sheet of paper. At some point during the process, the paper may be treated with size to prevent written ink from bleeding.

Our fast papermaking technique involves three shortcuts: using cotton fabric for couching, air-drying or ironing the paper dry, and sizing the paper by adding gelatin to the slurry.

All papermaking techniques start with a fiber source. The simplest means of creating paper employs used paper as the fiber source. We tested used copier paper (tree fiber) and business stationery (tree and cotton rag fiber), but you can also use junk mail letters and envelopes, computer paper, newsprint, construction paper, thin paper bags, tissues, napkins, or paper towels. Be sure to remove any staples in the paper or glassine windows in the envelopes. Avoid glossy-coated papers and photographs since water cannot easily break down their coatings.

To make slurry, tear the paper into postage stamp–sized pieces, presoak them, pulverize them with water in an ordinary blender, then mix them with more water in a vat. Cotton linter, a sheet of processed cotton fibers, can be used to increase the paper's rag content, which improves durability and longevity.

Testing the Couching and Drying Techniques

Couching is fairly easy, no matter which material you choose. We tested four options: cotton fabric, wool fabric, nonwoven interfacing (Pellon), and three-ply cardboard. Once the pulp was couched onto the support material, we laid a second piece of the same material on top, in effect, making a sandwich. Then we made a stack of four or more sandwiches for each material.

Each couching material had its merits, but cotton was the most versatile. It readily grabbed and held the wet pulp during couching, created a pleasing linenlike texture, and produced smooth sheets, with just a hint of curl to the deckled edges.

We then tested three drying methods: pressing the paper sandwiches with a dry iron, placing them in a 175-degree oven, and air-drying them. The ironing method worked extremely well for cotton, turning out a bone-dry sheet of paper in a matter of minutes. If you don't have time for ironing, use clothespins to attach the sheets to a drying rack, and let them dry overnight.

Putting a fountain pen to our test papers exposed their one major flaw: The ink spread. To prevent this from happening, the untreated paper needed to be sized. We tested two ways to add a liquid size: mixing it into the slurry or brushing it onto the surface of the dry waterleaf.

We tried the mix-in method with three sizes: liquid starch, Mod Podge, and gelatin. When the papers were dry, we ran a felt-tip pen, a watercolor brush loaded with paint, a dip pen loaded with India ink, and a calligraphic fountain pen across the surface. The gelatin paper worked quite well for the pens, but a drop of watercolor paint bled. Brushed-on gelatin size created the best surface for all the media, especially the watercolor paint, but it was too time-consuming, so we recommend adding gelatin to your slurry, unless you're using watercolors.

Marie Browning is a fine arts specialist and craft instructor. Susan Wilson is a freelance craftsperson and contributor to HANDCRAFT ILLUSTRATED.

MAKING THE PAPER

A. To make the slurry, put pre-soaked postage stamp-sized pieces of paper in a blender.

B. Flower petals, glitter, or other accents can also be added at this stage.

C. To pull a sheet, insert the mold and deckle into the vat at an angle . . .

D. . . . then level off and shake to settle the pulp on the screen.

E. Lower the mold as if it were hinged on one edge . . .

F. . . . then lift up that edge to release the wet pulp.

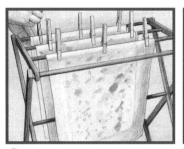

G. To air-dry, clip each sandwich and let it dry overnight.

H. Peel the dry paper off the couching cloth.

INSTRUCTIONS

1. Rip paper and cotton linter into postage stamp–sized pieces. Place in 8-quart bowl. Fill bowl with warm water, submerge pieces, and let soak at least 20 minutes, but preferably overnight.

2. Line counter next to sink with triple layer of bath towels. Set vat on towels next to sink, then lay one piece plywood next to vat, with longer sides parallel to counter edge. Layer ten to twenty sheets uncreased newspaper on plywood, followed by one piece wool fabric and one piece cotton fabric. Pour warm water into vat until half full (approximately 14 quarts).

Making the Slurry

1. Make pulp by measuring 1 cup soaked paper. Using spoon, place in blender (see illustration A), then add fresh water until three-quarters full. Blend on high in short 5- to 10-second spurts three or four times. Pour pulp into vat. Repeat, then add more water to vat until about two-thirds full (approximately 18½ quarts). Pulverize remaining paper in same way, then set aside in bowl placed in sink.

2. To make size, measure 5 cups boiling water into 2-quart pot or Pyrex bowl. Add gelatin and stir until dissolved. Pour into slurry and blend thoroughly with fingers. Add any other ingredients (illustration B; see also "Adding Color and Texture to Paper," right).

Pulling and Couching the Sheets

1. To suspend pulp fibers in vat, agitate water with hand. To prepare cotton cloth for couching, spray-mist lightly.

2. To pull paper, hold mold mesh side up and fit deckle on top. Grasp both pieces firmly together. In one slow, continuous motion, lower unit into vat at an angle (illustration C), then straighten so fully submerged and horizontal.

3. Slowly lift unit straight up until deckle breaks surface of water and pulp resting on screen is just barely submerged. Shake lightly in all directions to even out pulp (illustration D). Lift unit out of water and hold steady as water drains. Tip slightly to continue draining.

4. Rest bottom of mold on edge of vat, then lift off deckle and set it aside, taking care that no dripping water hits pulp surface. If pulp is marred or uneven and you want to start over, proceed to step 5. To couch pulp layer, proceed to step 6.

5. To shed pulp from screen without couching, hold mold horizontally, screen side down, and lower it until pulp just touches surface of water. Bob to release pulp back into slurry. Start again.

6. Using slow, continuous motion, stand mold upright on short edge, parallel to and about 2" in from left edge of cotton cloth (wet pulp will stick to screen), then lower mold onto fabric (illustration E); there should be a 2" margin of fabric all around. As water surges up through screen, blot with damp sponge. Lift left edge of mold, checking to make sure pulp is clinging to fabric. Slowly lift mold up and off fabric (illustration F).

7. Lay fresh cotton cloth on top of pulp to complete sandwich. To begin next sandwich, lay another new cotton cloth on top. Repeat steps 1 through 6 to pull and couch additional sheets. To draw off wetness, lay down wool cloth as you complete every second or third sandwich. As sheets of pulp on screen begin to look thin, uneven, or broken, add new pulp to vat from reserve pulp. Repeat until pulp is gone. Lay down cotton cloth to complete final sandwich. Lay wool cloth on top, followed by 10 to 20 sheets crease-free newspaper. Top pile with second piece of plywood. *Note:* To prevent a clogged drain, strain remaining slurry and discard wet pulp in trash.

Drying the Sheets

1. Set plywood/paper pile in shower stall or bathtub. Stand on plywood a few minutes, shifting weight around, so water trickles out sides of pile. Repeat to remove as much water as possible.

2. If you wish to iron sheets dry, use dry iron on cotton setting to press individual sandwich on both sides until dry. Repeat as necessary.

3. If you wish to hang sheets to dry, set up drying rack, then fold edge of sandwich over rod and clip with clothespins (illustration G). Set rack aside to dry overnight.

4. To remove dry sheets from cotton couching cloth, lay sandwich on flat, clean surface and peel off top layer. Lift corner of dry paper and peel sheet off bottom cotton fabric (illustration H). ◆

ADDING COLOR AND TEXTURE TO PAPER

Adding color and texture to your paper is simple. To create a natural look, consider celery, leeks, corn husks, irises, bulrushes, bamboo leaves, grass clippings, or wheat straw. Start by cutting the ingredients into one-inch pieces. Boil them in water for approximately two hours, strain them in a colander lined with cheesecloth, and add them to the slurry.

You can also create a variety of textures by using thread, wool, jute string, or cotton fabric. Simply cut them into small pieces and add them to the slurry.

Onion skins and dried flower petals, which add color and texture, can be added to the blender along with your chunks of paper. For flecks of metallic color, consider mixing gold, silver, or copper leaf, or glitter directly into the slurry.

Three Projects to Make from Handmade Paper

These three designs are well suited for paper you've made yourself or for specialty paper purchased by the sheet.

❧ BY FRANCOISE HARDY

ILLUSTRATION:
Micheal Gellatly

COLOR PHOTOGRAPHY:
Carl Tremblay

To make any of these three projects, you'll need handmade paper. You can make your own following the directions on page 18, or purchase handmade paper by the sheet.

WHEN I FIRST DISCOVERED handmade paper, both by purchasing it and later by making my own (*see* "The Fastest Way to Make Your Own Paper," page 18), I also began searching for easy, elegant project ideas. Successful projects, I found, had ample flat surfaces that displayed the papers' most distinct characteristic—rich, beautiful, and varied texture. Three of my favorites are featured here: an insert folio, a customized jacket for a purchased book, and a picture frame.

The simplest project is the insert folio. Here, a single sheet of handmade paper becomes a folder for a printed insert, such as a wedding invitation or a birth announcement. The handmade paper must be a bit larger than the unfolded invitation—about one-quarter inch larger all around—to surround and set off the insert when the folio is opened. If you plan to make your own paper for the folios, you'll need to purchase a mold and deckle (the basic tool used in papermaking) that is the proper size. Your invitation or announcement can be a single- or double-fold style, but the printing should appear on the inside.

The second choice—using handmade paper to customize a purchased book—is suitable for address books, guest registers, datebooks, diaries, and blank books. Since the binding becomes part of the finished design, it should coordinate with the color and texture of your handmade paper. You'll need two sheets of eight-and-one-half-by-eleven-inch handmade paper to cover one book. If this size paper is positioned on the book vertically, the book cannot be any larger than nine and one-half inches across by nine inches high. If the paper is positioned horizontally, as in my sample project (*see* photo, left), the maximum book size is twelve and one-half inches across by six and one-half inches high. You will also need two sheets of endpaper; possibilities include pastel or charcoal drawing paper, finely textured paper, construction paper, or kraft paper.

To make one picture frame, you will need two to three sheets of eight-and-one-half-by-eleven-inch handmade

Making the Insert Folio

A. Measure a sample insert in its open position. Select a mold and deckle to make the correct size of paper, or purchase paper and trim it down to size.

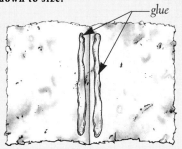

glue

B. To join the folios and inserts, fold the sheets of paper in half, then apply glue along each side of the fold.

C. Slip the insert inside so the folds touch, close the folio, and weight with a book.

paper. The largest frame size possible from this size paper measures seven by nine and one-half inches, or three-quarters of an inch smaller all around than the paper dimensions.

The best papers for these projects will be of a light to medium weight. Extra-thin papers will be translucent and compromise the coverage, while very thick sheets tend to break or crumble when folded. You can discourage breakage by creasing all folds lightly with your fingers, instead of using a ruler or bone folder, but the issue is best avoided at the outset if possible.

Francoise Hardy is a crafter and artisan living in Boston.

I. Insert Folio
INSTRUCTIONS

1. Unfold one invitation and measure vertically and horizontally. Use mold and deckle ¼" larger all around to make one sheet of paper per invitation, or purchase handmade paper this size (illustration A, previous page). If you cannot obtain paper the correct size (with deckle edge all around), trim down larger sheets.

2. Determine cord or ribbon yardage by making prototype folio. Fold one sheet handmade paper in half, slip invitation inside so folded edges align, then wrap sample cord or ribbon once around both pieces at fold (illustration C). Tie ends in bow or knot, as desired, and trim excess. Untie bow or knot, measure cord or ribbon length, multiply by number of folios planned, and divide total by 36".

3. Fold all handmade paper in half, then unfold and stack. Pour white glue onto plate and dilute with tiny amount of water. Stack invitations to one side.

4. To assemble folios, lay one handmade sheet on flat surface, and brush ½"-wide band of glue on each side of fold (illustration B). Avoid spreading glue all the way to the top and bottom edges of paper. Set invitation into position so folds align and deckle extends evenly at top and bottom edges, then close folio and press to adhere. Repeat to assemble remaining folios. Stack finished folios in several piles, weight with heavy books, and let dry overnight. Cut lengths of cord or ribbon as determined in step 2 and tie as for prototype.

Covering a Purchased Book

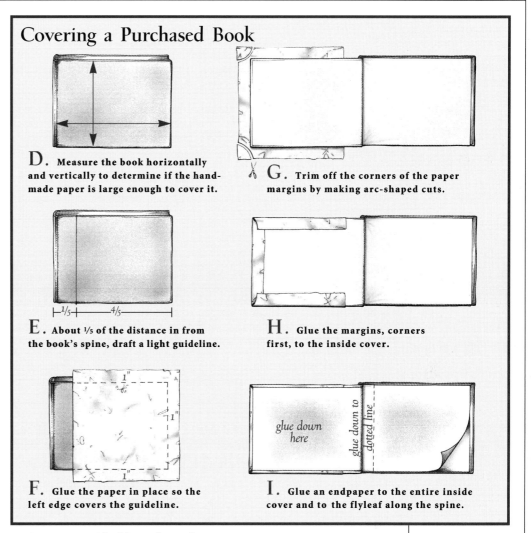

D. Measure the book horizontally and vertically to determine if the handmade paper is large enough to cover it.

E. About ⅕ of the distance in from the book's spine, draft a light guideline.

F. Glue the paper in place so the left edge covers the guideline.

G. Trim off the corners of the paper margins by making arc-shaped cuts.

H. Glue the margins, corners first, to the inside cover.

glue down here

glue down to dotted line

I. Glue an endpaper to the entire inside cover and to the flyleaf along the spine.

II. Covering a Clothbound Book
INSTRUCTIONS

1. Start by measuring book horizontally and vertically (illustration D). To cover book with 8½" x 11" sheet of handmade paper, book can measure up to 9½" across by 9" high (for vertical placement of paper) or up to 12½" across by 6½" high (for horizontal placement of paper). Determine which placement book requires.

2. Mark guideline for paper placement. Divide horizontal measurement of book by 5, measure this distance from spine, and mark light pencil line parallel to spine (illustration E). Position paper on cover with left edge touching guideline. If desired, trim off deckle from left edge using X-Acto knife, steel ruler, and self-healing cutting mat.

3. Prepare for gluing by covering work surface with kraft paper. Pour about one tablespoon glue onto plate; stir in few drops of water for spreadable, but not watery, consistency. Brush glue evenly onto cover, from guideline out to edges. Position paper on cover so left edge conceals guideline; smooth with palm. Wipe off oozing glue with damp washcloth.

Trim excess paper 1" beyond top, side, and bottom edges of book (illustration F).

4. Glue inside front cover. Start by opening book flat. Make arc-shaped cuts across corners (illustration E). Fold up and glue arced edges onto book corners first, then fold and glue allowances onto inside cover (illustration H). Press to adhere. Repeat steps 3 and 4 to glue back cover in place.

5. Glue endpapers to inside covers. Start by opening one cover so book lies flat. Position endpaper on top so book is concealed. Slide top edge of paper even with top of book pages, then mark paper even with bottom of book pages. Remove paper from book and draft line through mark parallel to top edge; cut precisely using X-Acto knife against steel ruler. Reposition paper on book so ⅛" of handmade paper shows beyond left edge, then mark paper even with book pages at far right. Remove paper, draft line at mark, and cut. Brush glue on inside cover and onto about 1" of flyleaf. Press endpaper in place and press to adhere against inner spine (illustration I). Repeat process to cover back inside cover. Weight with heavy book and let dry overnight.

Making the Picture Frame

J. Use graph paper to draft the frame template.

K. To make a prop template, use a rectangle the same size as the frame.

L. To complete prop template, draft lines 1 through 4.

M. Use the templates to cut a frame, back, and prop.

score here on reverse side

frame

back

prop

N. Glue the frame to the handmade paper. Trim the paper within ¾" all around.

3/4"

O. Fold back and glue down the flaps, then cut away the corners in an arc shape.

P. Glue the lower margin, then glue thin slivers of chipboard to the remaining three edges.

Q. Set the back in position, then glue and fold the side and top margins.

R. Glue the prop to the paper. Trim the paper, then trim off the corners.

S. Glue the prop to the back of the frame.

MATERIALS
Picture Frame

- Two to three 8½" x 11" sheets handmade paper
- Photo, 4" x 6" or smaller
- 2-ply chipboard
- White glue

You'll also need:
Graph paper; pencil; tape; steel ruler; utility knife; self-healing cutting mat; scissors; ceramic or glass plate; stiff-bristled brush; kraft paper; craft stick; and heavy book.

III. Picture Frame
INSTRUCTIONS

1. Make frame template by measuring photo, or decide on standard photo size 4" x 6" or smaller. Draft rectangle on graph paper ⅛" smaller all around than photo, then draft concentric rectangle 1" to 3" beyond it, but not exceeding 7" x 9 ½", to indicate frame width (illustration J).

2. Make template for frame prop by drafting same size rectangle as larger rectangle in step 1. Mark lines to divide rectangle into quadrants, then mark bottom and left edges into ⅓ and ⅔ segments (illustration K). Draft lines 1 through 4 as follows: Draft line 1 from left edge point to upper right corner; line 2 from upper left corner through intersection of line 1 and vertical quadrant line, ending at horizontal quadrant line; line 3 from lower edge point to end of line 2, then continuing for another ½" to 1"; and line 4 parallel to line 2 and connecting lines 1 and 3 (illustration L).

3. Cut frame parts from chipboard. Tape templates to chipboard and set on self-healing cutting mat. Using steel ruler and utility knife, score and then cut marked lines straight through to mat to make one frame and one prop. Score (cut halfway through) reverse side of prop along line 2 (illustration M). Reuse frame template to cut one back.

4. Lay down kraft paper to protect work surface during gluing. Pour about one tablespoon glue onto plate, dilute with a few drops water, and stir with craft stick for spreadable, but not watery, consistency. Brush glue evenly onto one side of frame and out to edges. Set frame glue side down on handmade paper and press to adhere. Mark and cut paper ¾" beyond frame edge. Draft diagonal lines connecting inside corners and cut triangular flaps, using utility knife to start cuts at center and scissors to finish (illustration N). Brush on glue and fold back flaps onto edges of frame; press to adhere. To reduce bulk, cut arcs ⅜" beyond at four outside corners (illustration O).

5. Snip off flap points even with frame edge. Glue and fold up lower allowance (illustration P), then press to adhere. To prevent a tight picture opening, glue thin slivers of chipboard along remaining three edges (illustration P). To attach back of frame, start by brushing glue on top and side paper allowances (bottom remains open for inserting photo). Set back chipboard piece in position, fold arced sections onto corners, then fold each allowance onto back (illustration Q). Press all surfaces to adhere.

6. Cover prop with handmade paper. Start by brushing glue on unscored surface, then press glue side down on paper. Trim paper ½" beyond prop edges and cut arcs ⅜" beyond three corners (illustration R). Fold and glue arced sections onto corners, then fold up and glue paper allowances onto prop. Press all surfaces to adhere.

7. To cover back of frame and prop with handmade paper, use each as template to draft same shape on paper. Using scissors, cut out each shape ⅛" inside marked lines. Test-fit pieces, retrim if necessary, and glue in place. Press to adhere. Gently bend prop at score line. Apply undiluted glue to back of prop flap and glue to back of frame so bottom and left edges of frame and prop align (illustration S). Weight with heavy book and let dry overnight. ◆

How to Make a Decorative Tassel

These tassels may look complicated, but their construction is simple: Wrap multicolored threads around cardboard, tie off, and then finish as desired.

❧ BY BARBARA KELSEY

MATERIALS
Basic Tassel

- Six 70-yard spools/skeins (or equivalent) of cotton, rayon, or silk embroidery thread in 4 to 6 colors adjacent on the color wheel and with similar tone, thickness, and sheen
- Strong thread, any color (for binding hanging loop and tassel neck; may be one of above threads)
- 14 inches ¼"-diameter upholstery cord (for hanging loop)
- Button, upholstery, or other strong thread (to bind tassel head)

You'll also need:
5" x 7" corrugated cardboard; tape; ruler; scissors; shallow box; comb with widely spaced teeth; and line or drying rack.

ALTHOUGH THE TASSELS PICtured here differ in their finishing touches, they were made using the same technique: wrapping thread around a rectangle of cardboard, tying off the thread, and then trimming the ends. By varying the length of the cardboard and the number of winds, you can create tassels of any dimension.

I make these ornate tassels in several sizes. Larger versions, such as the seven-and-a-half-inch-long ones shown, can be used in pairs to trim neckroll pillows, table runners, or drapery ties. Singly, they work well as Christmas tree ornaments, or they can be attached to lamp pulls, desk keys, or drawer handles. Smaller versions, about two to three inches long, can be glued to pin backs or stickpin findings and displayed on a beret or lapel.

Whatever the size, the construction technique is the same. Each tassel was made by winding silk and rayon thread from six individual spools around a five-by-seven-inch piece of cardboard. On the thinner jewel collar tassel (the first tassel pictured at right), the thread was wound 120 times, and on the others, 155 times.

Color is one of the most important factors when designing a successful tassel. For a sophisticated scheme, use colors that are adjacent on the color wheel (rather than complementary) and similar in tone, or shade. Adjacent colors are closely related, yet different enough to introduce visual interest. Each of the tas-

These tassels were made using the same technique but with different finishing touches. From left to right: jewel collar, beaded, ombré, gimp collar.

sels shown uses six threads: one each of ivory, copper, and peach, and three of mustard gold.

One inspiration for selecting colors that work well together is decorator fab-

ric. If the dominant colors in a multicolored design aren't immediately obvious, try squinting at the fabric, and three or four colors should appear more distinct.

You can add or delete individual threads at any time during the tassel-winding process. For example, if a spool runs out, you can introduce a new strand of the same color. You can also modulate the color balance. In the three plumper tassels shown, the copper thread was omitted during winds 100 to 140, and then reintroduced from winds 141 to 155. This prevented the copper, which was darker than the other threads, from becoming too prominent.

Another important design factor is the choice of thread. My tassels are made from a mixture of rayon and silk threads of a similar thickness and sheen. Mixing various weights and finishes can produce a frizzy tassel. The surface of the thread should be smooth and silky,

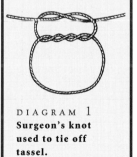

DIAGRAM 1
Surgeon's knot used to tie off tassel.

ILLUSTRATIONS
A, B, & C:
Nenad Jakesevic

DIAGRAM 1 &
ILLUSTRATIONS D–H:
Mary Newell DePalma

COLOR PHOTOGRAPHY:
Carl Tremblay

MAKING THE BASIC TASSEL

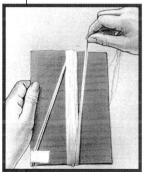

A. Wind the threads around a cardboard form.

B. Reach desired thickness, then tie tassel using surgeon's knot (diagram 1).

C. Turn the cardboard form over and cut the threads.

not fuzzy, because part of a tassel's appeal is the way the threads move when handled. Threads with a soft and fuzzy finish, such as wool, may have wonderfully intense colors, but they will stick to each other, especially as the tassel ages. In testing different types of thread, I found that embroidery thread (i.e., silk twist, pearl cotton, and cotton floss) hung straighter and made a neater, more orderly tassel than did fine threads intended for crochet and knitting (i.e., rayon chainette and crochet cotton).

After the tassel is made, you can accent its throat with upholstery trim, beads or "jewels." Or you can dye the tassels to create another variation.

Barbara Kelsey is a fiber artisan who lives in Newtown, Connecticut.

INSTRUCTIONS
Basic Tassel

1. To contain spools during winding, place them in shallow box. If using skeins, wind into balls and place in box. Tie 6 free thread ends together in overhand knot. Tape knot to lower left corner of cardboard (reverse if left-handed), then wind threads around center, maintaining even tension (*see* illustration A). To add new strand during winding, tape strand end to knot, hold strand together with existing threads, and resume winding. To remove a strand, cut it 2" below lower edge of cardboard and resume winding other threads. Stop winding when bundle is about 1" thick around (about 155 wraps), or desired thickness. Cut threads 2" beyond lower edge of cardboard, tie ends, and tape down knot on back side of cardboard.

2. Secure thread bundle. Start by cutting 18" length of button, upholstery, or other strong thread. Slip thread between cardboard and thread bundle, wrap twice around center of bundle, pull ends tight, and tie surgeon's knot (illustration B and diagram 1). Turn cardboard over and cut thread bundle at center (illustration C).

3. Add hanging loop. Fold 14" upholstery cord in half. Tie granny knot 2" from fold (knot will be loose). Wrap free cord ends around center of bundle, and tie ends in square knot (illustration D). Adjust cord so square knot conceals surgeon's knot.

4. To bind hanging loop, start by cutting 14" length of tassel thread from any spool. Tighten granny knot, then hold loop sections together just above knot (illustration E1). Using illustration E2 as reference, fold thread end, lay it against cord with folded end at top, and begin wrapping free thread end around cord. Wind tightly for ¼" to ⅜". To draw loop

inside, slip thread end through loop (illustration E3) and pull both ends firmly. Trim off ends (illustration E4).

5. Hold hanging loop and use large-toothed comb to gently smooth and separate threads. Use illustration F1, thread #1, as reference for binding tassel. Winding directly from spool, fold end of thread, lay it against body of tassel, folded end down, and begin winding thread around tassel about 1" below granny knot. Wind tightly for ½" to 1", concealing loop as you go. To draw loop inside, slip thread end through loop (illustration F4, thread #1) and pull both ends tightly in opposite directions. Carefully snip off free ends.

6. Trim tassel. Start by shaking it, then suspend it from a line or drying rack and comb through threads. Trim ends at bottom of tassel until even (illustration G). Since threads will relax over time, let tassel hang for several days, then retrim as necessary.

TASSEL VARIATIONS
I. Gimp Collar Tassel

Make basic tassel, binding neck for 1" with contrasting thread (step 5). To size upholstery trim for collar, cut trim straight across at one end, fold cut end ⅜" to wrong side, and glue. Fit trim around neck of tassel, cutting off excess ⅜" beyond fold. Fold and glue this end ⅜" to wrong side. Wrap collar around tassel neck so folded edges butt, then hand-tack together. To prevent collar from slipping, tack edges to neck binding.

II. Beaded Tassel

Make basic tassel through step 4. Thread upholstery needle with 1¼ yards chainette and set aside. Begin binding neck of tassel (step 5), stopping as soon as starter wraps are snug; hold thread end secure. Insert threaded upholstery needle into tassel head directly above wrapping thread and draw it out at opposite side, leaving a 7" tail (illustration H1). Repeat two more times at equal intervals around neck, leaving 14" loops at each pass (illustration H2). Slip off upholstery needle. To secure tails and loops, let them fall alongside tassel threads and finish binding neck, as in step 5, for ½".

To apply beads, cut chainette loops at midpoint. Thread one strand onto upholstery needle, pull taut, and pick up three beads. Apply dot of glue to strand 1½" below collar; slip bead onto needle, slide onto glue, and hold steady 10 to 15 seconds until glue sets. Apply new dot of glue 1½" from first bead and attach sec-

ond bead at this spot. Glue third bead 1½" from second bead. Glue three beads on each of five remaining strands. Trim each strand even with third bead. Wrap neck with upholstery trim as in tassel variation I.

III. Jewel Collar Tassel

Wind basic tassel 120 times and bind through step 2. For hanging loop, fold black cord in half and tie overhand knot 3" from fold. Slip carnelian disk onto cord, slide up to knot, and make second closely spaced knot to secure. Add silver bead and secure with third knot. Tie free cord ends around bundle in square knot, as in step 3; omit step 4. For step 5, bind tassel neck with rattail for 1½". Glue velvet ribbon around neck, folding and overlapping end; trim excess. Trim bullion openwork braid to fit around collar and glue down. Glue velvet buttons to braid, evenly spaced all around.

IV. Ombré Dyed Tassel

Make basic tassel through step 4. To bind tassel using two colors, lay ends of both colors against neck, and make loop in thread #1 (illustration F1). Wrap thread #1 for ⅛", anchoring thread #2 as you go. When finished, hold end of thread #1 aside, and make loop in thread #2 (illustration F2). Wrap thread #2 for ⅜", and hold end aside (illustration F3). Resume wrapping with free end of thread #1 for ⅛". Slip both free ends through their respective loops (illustration F4), and draw threads tight. Finish off following steps 5 and 6.

Pull on rubber gloves. To mix dye, pour 1 cup cold water in one wide-mouthed jar, add ½ teaspoon dye, and stir to dissolve. Fill other jar three-quarters full with cold water. To promote capillary action, dip bottom half of tassel into water for a few seconds, lift, and squeeze out excess. Take care to keep upper half of tassel dry. Dip bottom third of damp tassel into dye for a few seconds, lift out, and wring immediately. To create ombré effect, redip bottom fourth of tassel into dye, lift out, and hang one minute to drain. Gently squeeze out excess moisture, and shake to separate strands. Hang overnight or until dry. When dry, retrim any raveled ends. ◆

Tying the Tassels

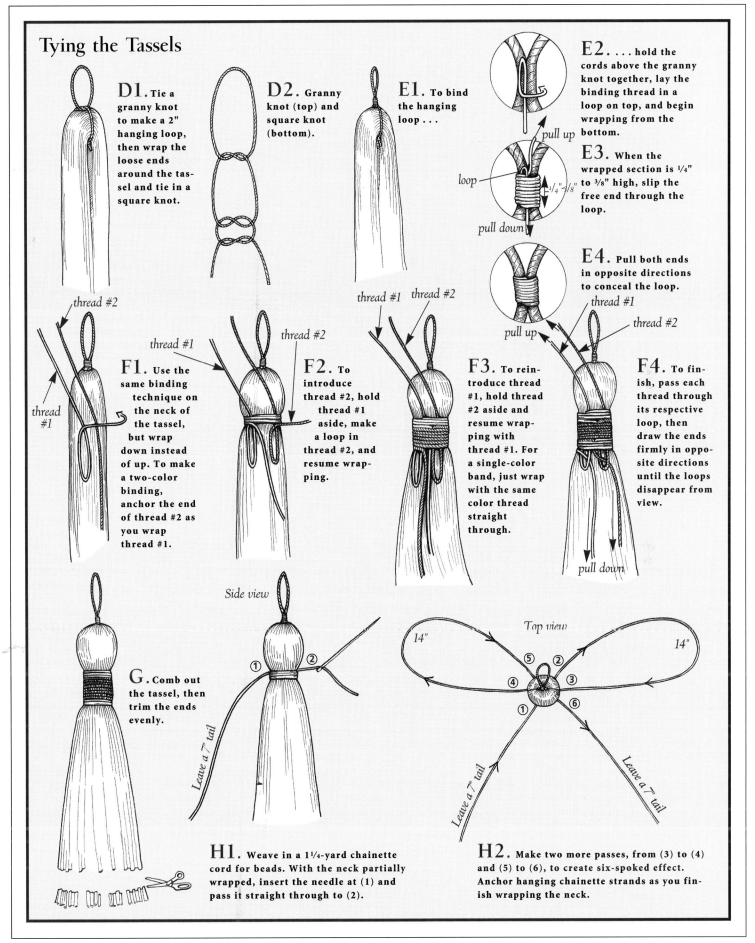

D1. Tie a granny knot to make a 2" hanging loop, then wrap the loose ends around the tassel and tie in a square knot.

D2. Granny knot (top) and square knot (bottom).

E1. To bind the hanging loop . . .

E2. . . . hold the cords above the granny knot together, lay the binding thread in a loop on top, and begin wrapping from the bottom.

pull up

loop

pull down

E3. When the wrapped section is 1/4" to 3/8" high, slip the free end through the loop.

1/4"-3/8"

E4. Pull both ends in opposite directions to conceal the loop.

pull up

thread #1

thread #2

thread #2

thread #1

thread #2

thread #1

thread #2

thread #1

thread #2

F1. Use the same binding technique on the neck of the tassel, but wrap down instead of up. To make a two-color binding, anchor the end of thread #2 as you wrap thread #1.

F2. To introduce thread #2, hold thread #1 aside, make a loop in thread #2, and resume wrapping.

F3. To reintroduce thread #1, hold thread #2 aside and resume wrapping with thread #1. For a single-color band, just wrap with the same color thread straight through.

F4. To finish, pass each thread through its respective loop, then draw the ends firmly in opposite directions until the loops disappear from view.

pull down

G. Comb out the tassel, then trim the ends evenly.

Side view

①

②

Leave a 7" tail

H1. Weave in a 1 1/4-yard chainette cord for beads. With the neck partially wrapped, insert the needle at (1) and pass it straight through to (2).

Top view

14"

14"

⑤ ②

④ ③

①

⑥

①

Leave a 7" tail

Leave a 7" tail

H2. Make two more passes, from (3) to (4) and (5) to (6), to create six-spoked effect. Anchor hanging chainette strands as you finish wrapping the neck.

How to Make a Fabric-Covered Desk Screen

This handy decorative accessory hides a mess and adds a touch of class to any desktop.

BY FRANCOISE HARDY

This small desk screen offers an attractive alternative to cleaning up your desk when guests are expected.

WHEN I'M EXPECTING guests, I've often wondered what to do with the messy stack of paperwork spread out over my desk, especially when I'm in the middle of something important and don't want to put everything away. This small desk screen solves the problem.

Although I designed my screen using a traditional color scheme (burgundy and gold), you can create a less formal screen by substituting a country print fabric, and painting the railing white. Whatever fabric you select for the screen covering, you'll need to coordinate it with three types of trim: braided trim for the side and bottom edges of the outside panel; narrow cord to surround the railing; and two colors of grosgrain ribbon to serve as hinges. In the materials list at left, color A refers to burgundy, the dominant color in the fabric I chose. I matched my braided trim to the burgundy color, and then used burgundy grosgrain ribbon for one set of hinges. To coordinate with the second fabric color, gold (color B), I selected gold narrow cord and gold grosgrain ribbon for the second set of hinges. You can follow this plan, or create your own color scheme.

In designing the screen, I made two decisions that prevent the screen from folding flat. I chose the appeal of wooden dollhouse railing, which is wider than the screen panel thickness, and ball feet made from wooden beads. You can make a screen that folds, however, with a few modifications. Start by making the spacing between the panels equal to two panel thicknesses, instead of one. Omit the dollhouse railing and the ball feet, and instead glue a flat braid around the outer edges.

Several different types of adhesive are required for this project: spray adhesive, white tacky glue, and hot glue. Although they all serve the same purpose in the end, they're not interchangeable. I used spray adhesive to glue the fabric panels to the artist's canvas because the adhesive won't bleed through the fabric the way a wet glue might. I could have used hot glue for attaching the grosgrain ribbon hinges and the trim to the edges of the panels, but hot glue hardens quite fast. Using white tacky glue allowed me to spread glue along the entire length of the trim, and then go back and position it carefully. Hot glue is ideal, however, for the railing and the ball feet because it adheres those small elements quickly.

Francoise Hardy is a Boston-based artisan and craftsperson.

INSTRUCTIONS

Covering the Artist's Canvas

1. If using 8" x 16" artist's canvas, proceed to step 2. If using 12" x 16" artist's canvas, cut panel to 8" x 16" size by drafting line 4" in and parallel to one 16" edge. Work on self-healing cutting mat, and use utility knife and steel ruler to score and cut through marked lines. Discard excess.

2. Cover panels with fabric. To start, use rotary cutter to cut six 10" x 18" rectangles from fabric, with 18" edge running lengthwise along fabric. Working outdoors, or in well-ventilated space, lay fabric rectangles face down on top of several layers of newsprint. Apply spray adhesive, following manufacturer's recommendations. Center each artist's panel canvas-side down on fabric, and press lightly to adhere. Trim away fabric corners in gentle arc about ⅜" beyond panel corner (*see* illustration A).

3. Turn each panel over and smooth fabric with palm, then turn panels over and position fabric-side down. Fold each arc-shaped edge onto panel corner, then fold remaining allowances onto back of panel, and press to adhere (illustration B).

Assembling the Screen

1. Attach horizontal grosgrain ribbon hinges. Start by laying three fabric-covered panels face down, with long edges about one panel-thickness apart (illustration C). Cut color B ribbon into four 4½" lengths. Lay each ribbon across two panels, 2" from, and parallel to, shorter edges as in illustration C. Adhere with tacky glue.

2. Attach vertical hinges. Start by cutting

color A ribbon into two 12½"lengths. Brush glue onto panel edges between horizontal hinges. Press new ribbon into place so it joins two panels; fold raw ends under, exposing ¼" of horizontal hinge, then glue in place (illustration D).

3. To join front and back panels, squeeze glue evenly across wrong side of remaining panels, leaving indicated areas free of glue to wire on feet (illustration D). Position panels glue-side down on top of hinged panels, and press to adhere. Weight with heavy books, and let dry at least 1 hour, but preferably overnight.

4. Measure and mark dollhouse railing into three 7½"- to 8"-long identical sections, with marks falling between balustrades. Saw along marked lines, then sand lightly. Gild railings and balls using gold paste and following manufacturer's directions.

5. Attach railing. Start by standing screen upright. Run bead of hot glue along top edge of one double panel (illustration E). Set railing, upside down, into glue, let set 5 to 10 seconds, then stabilize with packing tape. Repeat to attach two remaining rail sections. Stand screen upside down so railings rest on work surface. Glue ⁷⁄₁₆" braided trim to side and bottom edges of each outer panel, as well as bottom edge of center panel. Trim ends to fit. If desired, seal ends with fray preventer.

6. Attach ball feet to outside panels. Cut four 2" lengths of steel wire. Insert wires into two outside panels ¾" from corner, pushing each wire down through braided trim, in between panel boards, to depth of about 1" Apply hot glue to bead holes, set each bead on wire, and let set. Stand screen upright and remove packing tape from around railing. Glue narrow cord to each panel around base of railing, then trim to fit. Let screen dry 1 hour. ◆

Constructing the Desk Screen

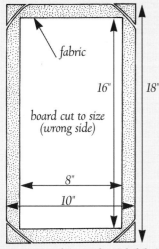

A. To cover the panels with fabric, apply spray adhesive to the fabric, then center each artist's panel, canvas-side down, on the fabric. Trim away the fabric corners.

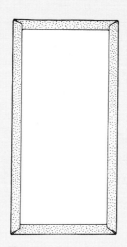

B. Fold each arc-shaped edge onto the corner, then fold remaining edges onto the back of the panel.

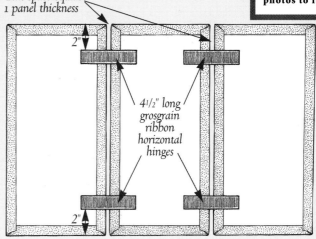

C. To assemble the screen, position the panels face down, then glue 4½" lengths of the ribbon across two panels, 2" from, and parallel to, the shorter edges.

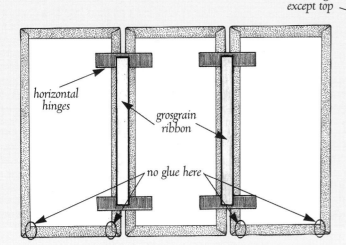

D. Join the two panels along the vertical edges, using 12½" lengths of ribbon. Join the front and back panels by gluing the two surfaces together, but leave the indicated areas free of glue in order to wire on the feet.

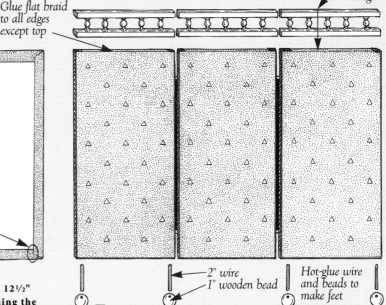

E. Attach the railing to the top of the screen using hot glue, then attach the ball feet to the outside panels.

The Best Household Tools for Graining

Don't buy specialized tools. You can create a variety of beautiful grained effects using your fingers, a corncob, or cellophane.

🐚 BY DEBORAH MILLER GABLER

To decorate the lid of the square box at left, the author rolled her index finger around the outermost edge. On the oval box at right, the center of the lid was decorated with continuous fingerprint impressions.

This frame was decorated using the edge of a fingernail.

To decorate this box, we wiggled a feather in a fanning motion.

CREATING A FAUX GRAINED FIN-ish only requires three items: a graining tool, a paint recipe, and the object to be grained. Although some formulas recommend using specialized tools such as combs or rollers, I've discovered some of the best effects can be created with common household items.

Six of my favorite tools are shown in the photographs on page 29: fingers, fingertips, a feather, a corncob, a candy mold filled with glazing putty, and a crumpled ball of cellophane. One of the most creative tools I've found is my hand. Not only do fingerprints dabbed randomly or in a repeated progression add interest, but the side of one's cupped hand tapped in concentric arcs across a large surface makes an unusual softly mottled pattern.

I've also used crumpled waxed paper, plastic wrap, tissue paper, or cheesecloth with good results. Over the years, I've experimented successfully with corks, steel wool, pieces of glazing putty, household and sea sponges, and polyfoam brushes as well. You're also free to use more specialized graining tools, such as combs, brushes, or rollers, but these are usually more expensive and difficult to find than everyday objects.

Paint recipes for graining also vary widely, but I've found that a mixture of vinegar and paint works the best. The sugar content in the vinegar helps the paint adhere. When the mixture is brushed over a surface and allowed to set a few minutes, it becomes thick enough to retain a soft impression from the tool at hand.

You can mix your recipe using powdered artist's pigments or watercolors. Of the two, I prefer the effects created by mixing watercolors with vinegar. For starters, watercolors are more readily available and offer a greater variety of ready-mixed colors. Since they are water soluble, they dissolve almost instantly in vinegar.

Artist's powdered pigments are not as readily available, and come in fewer shades, meaning you must mix them to achieve special colors. They do, however, produce brighter, more saturated color. This is due in part to the powder formulation, which, unlike watercolor, is intended to bind to oil- as well as water-based mediums. I found during my testing, however, that some of the powdered particles did not dissolve in the vinegar—bursting and dispersing instead as I brushed the paint on the surface. Thus, I had less control over the end result. If you're graining a large surface area, such as a piece of furniture, powdered pigments may be more economical to use, but I prefer the paler and more delicate effects achieved with watercolors.

Deborah Miller Gabler, owner of Shady Lane Designs in Hamburg, New York, is a freelance designer and teacher specializing in custom lampshades and stenciling.

CHOOSING A BASE COAT COLOR

You can apply vinegar paint over either a flat latex or an eggshell oil-based paint. I prefer using a latex, or bottled acrylic paint for small projects, because of the fast drying time and easy cleanup. Allow the base coat to dry thoroughly before graining. The most frequently used color combinations on early grained pieces were variations of earth tones. Simulating such woods as rosewood, maple, and cherry relied upon a warm palette—often a yellow ochre base coat covered with burnt sienna paint. Green and burnt umber paint were also applied over yellow ochre to create a multicolored graining effect.

A cool palette, used to simulate woods including walnut, butternut, and apple, had a buttermilk-colored base coat with burnt umber vinegar paint; a second variation used indigo vinegar paint accented with burnt umber and black. For the darker woods, a red-orange base coat was decorated with a burnt umber/burnt sienna mixture or vinegar paint tinted with black. Nonwood colors also played a part, including pale blues, greens, pinks, and reds. If you are embellishing a previously painted object with a complementary base coat, make sure that the surface is clean by washing it with soap and water, wiping it with vinegar, and then allowing it to dry. —DMG

INSTRUCTIONS

Mixing the Vinegar Paint

For each 4 square feet of surface area to be covered, mix approximately ¼ cup of vinegar paint as follows: In glass jar, dissolve ½ teaspoon sugar in 1 cup vinegar. Squeeze 1" of watercolor paint into shallow bowl. Add ½ teaspoon vinegar/sugar mixture to paint and mix well to liquefy. Dilute further by adding up to ¼ cup vinegar/sugar mixture, stirring to achieve consistency of thin cream. Use remaining mixture to mix other colors or thin paint as needed. Let paint stand 15 to 20 minutes to thicken slightly.

Working with Vinegar Paint

1. In preparation, cover work surface with newspaper and waxed paper. *Note*: If pinstriping is desired, begin process by pressing pinstriping tape onto the object at this time.

2. To apply vinegar paint, use foam brush on one plane surface of object. If tiny bubbles appear, use extra foam brush to sweep drop of detergent across affected area to break up surface tension. Let paint rest on surface until no longer runny, 3 to 10 minutes depending on humidity and temperature.

3. To create graining, make random or repetitive impressions on wet surface with one or more tools (*see* photographs below

MATERIALS

- **Wooden item, sealed and painted with base coat color** (see "Choosing a Base Coat Color", page 28)
- **Winsor & Newton 8 ml tube(s) watercolor paint, in one or more of the following colors: alizarin crimson, burnt umber, burnt sienna, Hooker's green, Prussian blue, or lampblack**
- **Cider vinegar**
- **Granulated sugar**
- **Satin spray varnish**
- **Nonyellowing, clear shellac**

You'll also need: low, wide-mouthed glass jar with cover; shallow bowls (one per paint color); assorted tools for graining; 1" or 2" natural bristle paintbrush (choose size appropriate to object); 1" or 2" foam brush (choose size appropriate to object); measuring cup; measuring spoons; newspaper; waxed paper; and ammonia.

Other items, if needed: liner brush (for adding accent color); painter's tape (for masking off border areas); sponge (for keeping paint in border areas from running); automotive pinstriping tape (for creating narrow pinstriping); and liquid dish detergent and extra foam brush (if paint solution forms bubbles when applied).

for ideas). To erase undesirable designs, sweep foam brush over surface and start over. If paint becomes too thick to work with or color is too intense, dilute by sweeping foam brush loaded with vinegar over surface.

4. *To add accent color:* Squeeze small amount of second watercolor paint into shallow bowl. Moisten liner brush with vinegar only, dip into paint, then streak, dab, or dot wet surface. Run second tool, such as feather or corncob, across surface

to subtly blend new color and develop new texture.

5. *To create borders or crisply defined edges between textures:* Allow painted surface created in step 3 to dry completely. Mask off border or area to be defined with painter's tape. Using natural bristle brush, apply shellac to exposed area to set and protect pattern. When dry to touch (about 15 minutes), remove tape. Using liner brush, apply vinegar only to unshellacked area to reactivate paint, and grain with contrasting texture. Wipe away paint that creeps into shellacked area with damp sponge.

6. *To complete pinstriping:* Allow painted surface created in step 3 to dry completely. Using natural bristle brush, apply thin coat shellac to exposed area. Let dry about 15 minutes, then remove pinstriping tape laid down in step 1. Touch up base coat color if needed (*see* "Choosing a Base Coat Color," page 28).

7. Spray varnish onto completed surface as soon as it is dry to prevent humid air or moisture from fingers from reactivating vinegar paint. Continue to grain remaining surfaces of object one by one as desired. When finished, use natural bristle brush to apply clear shellac on all surfaces, let dry 2 hours, then brush on second coat. Let dry overnight. Clean brush with ammonia. ◆

TIPS AND TECHNIQUES

- Try rolling a piece of glazing putty across the painted surface, or dab at the surface with a crumpled piece of cellophane or tissue paper. If desired, add a few randomly placed fingertip impressions.

- Sweep the convex edge of a feather through the fresh paint or textured pattern using a sawing or scalloped motion. Or wiggle the feather in a fanning motion across the corner of a box or wide picture frame.

- Roll a corncob through the vinegar paint, or pivot it around to create a textured circular flower.

- Walk the chiseled edge of a foam brush or the edge of a feather along the inside and outside edges of a frame to create a striated pattern.

- Hold the chiseled edge of a foam brush upright and, pivoting from one corner, slowly swing it in a circular motion to replicate the end cut of a log.

- Cup your hand and gently walk the fleshy side of it across a large vinegar-painted surface in overlapping waves and arcs.

- Use the end of a cork or a small sponge to stamp random imprints onto a combed or mottled surface.

SIX HANDY GRAINING TOOLS

FINGERS Lay the palm side of your fingers flat against the surface, then lift up and repeat.

FINGERTIPS For this effect, make random dots using your fingertips.

FEATHER Sweep the edge of a feather using a slight back-and-forth motion.

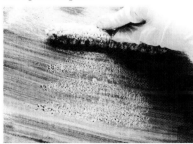

CORNCOB Make side-by-side impressions by pressing a corncob to the surface.

CANDY MOLD FILLED WITH GLAZING PUTTY Use this tool like a printing block.

CRUMPLED BALL OF CELLOPHANE This tool is effective for creating an allover background texture.

How to Make a Fabric-Covered Lampshade

Master two key steps: Use the existing shade as a template for cutting a new shade, and cover the new shade with fabric.

❧ BY DEBORAH MILLER GABLER

MATERIALS

- Lampshade to re-cover
- 45"-wide densely woven, lightweight or medium weight fabric *
- Braid trim, or substitute (for top ring) *
- Fringe, or substitute (for bottom ring) *
- ⅝"-wide cotton/rayon grosgrain ribbon *
- ½ yard 40"-wide lampshade laminate paper
- White tacky glue
- Fray preventive

*To determine yardage, see Getting Started, steps 1 and 3.

You'll also need: self-healing cutting mat; 18" steel ruler; X-Acto knife; single-edged razor blade; 2- to 3-dozen wooden spring-clip clothespins; iron; compass; scissors; pencil; scrap paper; and calculator.

Other items, if necessary: spray lacquer (to prevent rust on older rings); and paperweights (for weighing down lampshade arc).

ILLUSTRATION:
Nenad Jakesevic

DIAGRAMS:
Judy Love

COLOR PHOTOGRAPHY:
Carl Tremblay

Covering a lampshade with fabric, wallpaper, or sturdy gift wrap is simple. The trick: Instead of glue, use laminate paper, which reduces the mess and speeds up adhesion.

YOU HAVE A BEAUTIFUL LAMP with a less-than-beautiful shade, and you want to cover the shade with fabric that matches something in your decorating scheme such as a couch or a pillow. The solution is easier than you think: Use the existing shade as a template for creating a new shade, then cover the new one with fabric.

The original shade must be smooth, not pleated, and have a straight, rather than a curved or bell-shaped, silhouette. First, cut the old shade away from the wire rings at the top and bottom. Next, use the old shade as a template to cut a new shade. Then attach the fabric to the new shade using laminate paper (which makes gluing unnecessary). And finally, assemble the new shade using wire rings and grosgrain ribbon to cover the shade's edges. You can also add finishing touches by gluing lace, rickrack, fringe, or beading to the shade.

Laminate paper features a stiff paper backing for the shade on one side, and peel-off adhesive on the reverse.

The shade shown above measures four inches by ten inches by seven and one-fourth inches. The measurements denote, in order, the shade's top diameter (four inches), the shade's bottom diameter (ten inches), and the distance down the side of the lampshade (seven and one-fourth inches). These directions, however, apply to any size lampshade.

Deborah Miller Gabler, owner of Shady Lane Designs in Hamburg, New York, is a freelance designer and teacher specializing in custom lampshades and stenciling.

INSTRUCTIONS
Getting Started

1. To determine ribbon and trim yardage, measure and jot down (a) diameter of lampshade top ring, (b) diameter of bottom ring, and (c) length of side seam (*see* diagram 1, next page). For grosgrain ribbon (which goes on both the top and bottom rings) add (a) + (b) and multiply by 3.14. For top ring trim, multiply (a) by 3.14. For bottom ring trim, multiply (b) by 3.14. Round all figures to nearest quarter yard.

2. Remove existing shade by setting shade on level surface, then running razor blade around top ring to cut through shade material (*see* illustration A). Turn shade upside down and repeat along bottom ring. Make straight cut along vertical seam and release shade from rings. Gently bend shade in half and make small crease on each curved edge to mark midpoint.

3. To determine fabric yardage, lay lampshade arc pattern flat, weighting with paperweights, if necessary. Measure from point X to point Y as shown on diagram 2, next page, then round to nearest quarter yard.

4. If necessary, apply spray lacquer or rust preventive, following manufacturer's recommendations, to prevent older lampshade wires from rusting. Let dry.

Covering the Shade

1. Create matching lampshade arc from laminate paper. Lay laminate paper shiny side down, place lampshade arc pattern on top, and trace around it. Mark midpoint on each curved edge of laminate paper. Use X-Acto knife and work on cutting mat to cut out laminate paper arc. To make overlap for gluing, cut one straight edge ½" beyond marked edge. Cut curved edges first, then run blade against edge of steel ruler to cut straight edges. Transfer midpoint marks to shiny side of laminate paper.

2. Laminate fabric to paper. Start by ironing fabric smooth, then laying it right-side down on flat work surface. Lay laminate paper arc, shiny side up, on top of fabric. Align ruler on midpoints, then position arc so ruler runs along bias of fabric (illustration B). Remove ruler and hold arc down firmly with one hand. Use free hand to slowly peel away paper backing, drawing it under and away from arc as you press exposed laminate onto fabric surface (illustration C). When backing is completely removed, run palm back and forth across surface to make sure paper is fully adhered.

3. Trim fabric ¼" beyond one straight edge, then even with all remaining arc edges. Apply bead of glue to wrong side of ¼" extension. Brush glue smooth, then fold glued edge onto shiny surface of laminate paper and press firmly.

Assembling the Shade

1. Test-fit top ring. Start by standing lampshade arc upright, with fabric facing you. Hold top ring against paper side of shade, and clip together at top center with clothespin so clothespin spring touches ring (illustration D). Working each side alternately from center toward back, and keeping top of arc even with top of ring, clip clothespins every 2" to 3" to hold arc snugly against ring. As you approach back of lampshade, clip edge without fabric foldover first.

2. Repeat step 1 to test-fit bottom ring, but stand shade upside down on clothespins (illustration E). When entire ring is clipped, stand shade right-side up. If back seam buckles, open clothespin at top of seam, gently ease excess toward top edge with palm, and re-clip.

3. Glue rings to shade. Stand shade upside down. Remove clothespins from bottom edge and lift out bottom ring. (Bottom opening should retain its shape without ring.) Stand shade upright and remove clothespins at top. Repeat step 1, this time applying bead of glue to small sections of top ring before clipping in place. While glue is wet, examine lampshade from inside for gaps. Adjust clothespins as necessary to shift ring into better position, or ease excess paper toward back seam. Turn lampshade upside down and repeat all of step 2 before gluing bottom ring. Lift out bottom ring, apply glue, and drop back into position, securing with clothespins.

4. Secure back seam by removing clothespins at each end of seam, running bead of glue along inside edge of overlap, brushing glue smooth, and gently pressing seam closed. To ensure strong bond, set

seam face down on clean work surface, remove clothespins as needed so seam lies flat, and run fingers along seam inside shade. Replace clothespins at ends of seam, and let dry at least 1 hour. Remove all clothespins.

5. Run razor blade around top and bottom rings to even shade. To mark guideline for grosgrain ribbon, adjust compass

so that, in closed position, steel point extends 3/8" beyond lead point. Rest steel point on top ring, adjust so lead touches shade 1/4" below top ring, and drag lead around top rim (illustration F). Repeat to mark lower rim.

6. Attach grosgrain ribbon along top edge. Zigzag glue onto end of ribbon for 3", then spread evenly using tip of glue bottle. Starting at back seam, align lower edge of ribbon with lead line, then fold excess over wire to inside and crease it below wire with fingernail (illustration G). Continue gluing ribbon in 3" sections. When you reach a ring support, clip ribbon on inside of shade so it lies flat. At back seam, overlap ribbon 1/4", trim off excess straight with grain, and glue down. Repeat to trim bottom rim of lampshade with grosgrain ribbon.

7. If attaching additional trim to top or bottom of shade, run bead of glue along grosgrain ribbon. Starting at back seam, press trim into place parallel to edge all around. Cut off loose ends, and seal with fray preventive. ◆

A. To remove the existing shade, run a razor blade along the top and bottom edges.

B. Align the ruler on the midpoints of the lampshade arc, then position the arc so the ruler runs along the fabric's bias.

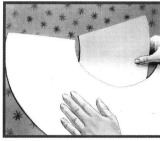

C. Position the laminate paper arc face down on the fabric. To seal, peel off the backing by drawing it from underneath the paper arc.

D. Clip the clothespin on the wire ring and shade as deep as possible to avoid crimping the shade.

E. Clip the top of the shade using the clothespins first, then turn the shade upside down and clip along the bottom edge.

F. Use a compass to draft a guideline that runs parallel to the rim . . .

G. . . . then use the guideline to position the grosgrain ribbon correctly.

Lampshade Geometry

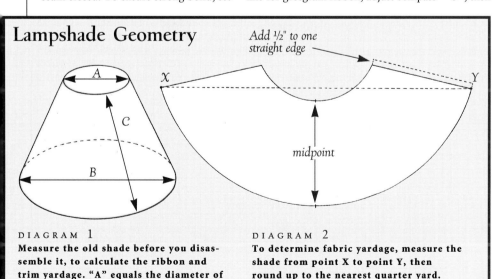

Add 1/2" to one straight edge

midpoint

DIAGRAM 1
Measure the old shade before you disassemble it, to calculate the ribbon and trim yardage. "A" equals the diameter of the lampshade top ring; "B" equals the diameter of the bottom ring; and "C" equals the length of the side seam.

DIAGRAM 2
To determine fabric yardage, measure the shade from point X to point Y, then round up to the nearest quarter yard. Mark the midpoint along each curved edge, and extend one straight edge to provide an overlap for gluing.

DESIGNER'S TIP

Laminate paper also works well with wallpaper or sturdy gift wrap. This means you can make a lampshade to match an existing room, or use that gorgeous gift wrap you've been saving.

The Best Way to Make Ribbon Roses

A simple rolling technique transforms wire-edged ribbon into realistic and shapeable roses.

❧ BY NANCY OVERTON

You can arrange a small bouquet of roses and leaves, as shown on this blanket, or use the roses singly, with or without the leaves, and attach each one to a corner of the blanket.

MATERIALS

- **Wire-edged ribbon** (to determine amount, *see* chart, next page)
- **Sewing thread to match ribbon**
- **30-gauge wire**

You'll also need: hand-sewing needle; scissors; and needle-nose pliers.

ILLUSTRATION:
Mary Newell DePalma

COLOR PHOTOGRAPHY:
Carl Tremblay

STYLING:
Gabrielle Derrick de Papp/Team

NO MATTER WHAT NEW METHods I encounter for making ribbon roses, I always return to the classic rolling technique. This method, long favored by milliners and apparel designers, creates roses from ordinary flat satin ribbons. To make the roses even more realistic and lifelike, I applied the same technique to wire-edged ribbon, with superb results.

The rolling method is easy enough to learn with any ribbon, but I found the wire-edged ribbon exceptionally easy to manipulate because it holds its shape. To form the rose, roll a core bud along the ribbon edge, then hand-tack it with needle and thread. The wire-edged ribbon is less prone to spring apart during rolling and tacking, making it easier to handle.

Once I started rolling roses from wire-edged ribbon, I kept discovering new ways to use them. Large cabbage-style blooms make a striking accent on hats or large gift packages while medium and small sizes can be combined to decorate pillows, lapel pins, or picture frames. A single, small bud can lend a sophisticated accent to a place card, while a tiny spray of roses can decorate a blanket.

If you combine a series of roses in a cluster configuration, vary the ribbon widths and the bud fullness, and use related rather than identical colors. Generally, solid colors show off the flower form, and ribbons from one color family make the best-looking arrangements. Variegated ribbons can produce quite realistic roses as long as the color

changes are subtle. One variegated ribbon I tested changed from violet to pink to white across its one-inch width. Using the roll technique, the white edge sometimes appeared at the bottom of the bloom, and other times along the petal edges, resulting in a rose that looked garish and artificial. A second test using a ribbon that ranged from violet to red to red-orange was more successful.

Leaves are also critical for achieving a convincing natural look. For making clusters of roses, I recommend combining ribbon leaves and inexpensive flocked leaves in several sizes in order to ensure variety.

Tack clusters of roses and leaves or individual roses to fabric, such as blankets, hats, or pillows, with needle and thread. If you're attaching the roses to other surfaces, such as frames or boxes, you can use a hot-glue gun. You can also make a small bouquet of roses by inserting a wire stem into each rose base, then wrapping it with green florist tape.

Nancy Overton, a resident of Oakland, California, has designed products for the craft industry and how-to books for more than twenty years.

INSTRUCTIONS
Making the Rolled Rose

1. Unfurl ribbon as needed directly from roll without cutting. Fold down end diagonally so tail equals ribbon width (*see* illustration A, next page). Fold tail section in half vertically (illustration B). Fold in half again and hand-tack at base through all layers (illustration C). Do not break off thread.

2. To create rose petals, fold excess ribbon back diagonally, then roll base tightly down around corner as indicated in illustration D and onto ribbon edge. Once folded edge is wrapped completely around bud, forming small cone, hand-tack base as in step 1 (illustration E). Repeat folding, rolling, and tacking process to add more petals (illustration F). As rose increases in size, make diagonal folds longer to create larger, more open petals (illustration G).

3. Once rose reaches desired size, cut ribbon, leaving 2" tail. Hand-sew running stitch along cut edge, pull to gather, and tack to base of rose (illustration H).Trim excess fabric from base of rose if desired.

Making the Folded Leaf

1. Cut appropriate length of ribbon (*see* chart, next page) for each leaf. Fold down ribbon ends diagonally from top center so tails are equal (illustration J). Fold each tail section in half vertically (illustration K), then in half again (illustration L).

2. Secure folds by binding wire around tails near base of leaf. Twist wire in tight spiral; clip off ends (illustration M).◆

Making the Rose

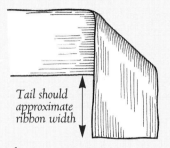

A. Fold down the ribbon end diagonally so the tail extends one ribbon width.

Tail should approximate ribbon width

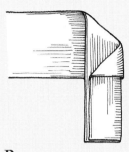

B. Fold the tail section in half vertically . . .

C. . . . and in half again to make a bud. Tack the bud at the base.

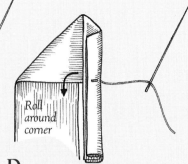

D. Fold the excess ribbon back diagonally, then roll the base tightly down around the corner and onto the ribbon edge.

Roll around corner

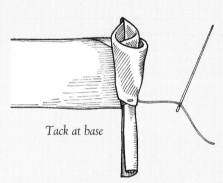

E. Stop rolling when the folded edge surrounds the bud. Tack the base again.

Tack at base

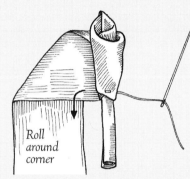

F. Fold the ribbon back and repeat the rolling and tacking process to add new petals.

Roll around corner

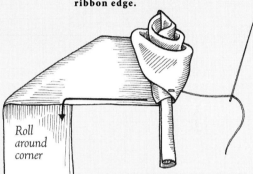

G. To make the larger, outermost petals, increase the length of the diagonal fold.

Roll around corner

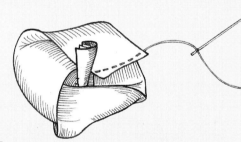

H. To finish the rose, cut the ribbon, leaving a 2" tail. Turn the rose upside down, then hand-gather the tail and tack it to the base.

I. Finished rose.

Making the Leaf

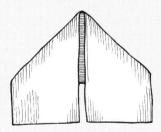

J. Cut a piece of ribbon, then fold down the ends diagonally so the edges are even.

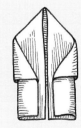

K. Fold each tail section in half towards the center . . .

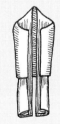

L. . . . and in half again.

M. Wind thin wire around the leaf base and twist it until secure.

HOW MUCH RIBBON DO YOU NEED?

Use this chart to determine how much ribbon is needed to make roses and leaves using standard ribbon widths.

RIBBON WIDTH	RIBBON LENGTH NEEDED	
	PER ROSE	PER LEAF
7⁄8"	10"	3"
1½"	18"	4"
2¼"	24"	6"

Fast Faux Marbling Techniques for Tabletops

You don't need the tools, materials, or experience of a professional marbler to create these fast and easy faux marble finishes.

❧ BY VI AND STU CUTBILL

MATERIALS

- **Wood surface**
- **1 quart latex wood sealer**
- **1 quart semigloss black latex paint**
- **1 quart dark green latex paint**
- **1 quart teal green latex paint**
- **1 quart latex glaze**
- **Acrylic varnish**

You'll also need:
Several lint-free cotton cloths about 16" square; cheesecloth (machine wash and dry before use); sandpaper grades 100 to 220; wet-dry sandpaper grades 400 and 600; tack cloth; short-nap roller; foam brushes; plastic containers or buckets; old measuring cup or ladle; paint sticks; disposable gloves; tape measure; and calculator.

Other items, if necessary:
Wood putty (to fill nicks in wood surface); cotton cloth about 6" square (for negative veining technique); plastic wrap (for plastic wrap drifting technique); and bowl of water, clean cotton cloth, and 1" round stencil brush (for spritz fossil technique).

ILLUSTRATION:
Nenad Jakesevic

DIAGRAMS:
Mary Newell DePalma

COLOR PHOTOGRAPHY:
Carl Tremblay

SILHOUETTE PHOTOGRAPHY:
Furnald/Gray

STYLING:
Gabrielle Derrick de Papp/Team

The finish on this tabletop was created using the negative veining technique. Start with a black latex base coat, then apply two glaze mixtures: one using dark green glaze and one using teal glaze.

MOST FAUX MARBLING PRO-fessionals rely on expensive tools, traditional materials, or special training to create their effects. To create this trio of fast and easy marbling techniques, we substituted everyday tools, commonly found materials, and simplified methods.

The three effects that we present here—negative veining, plastic wrap drifting, and fossil spritzing—are designed for relatively small surfaces, such as wooden tabletops, rather than walls. This makes the work easier to control because the surface can be laid horizontally.

Real marble is multicolored and directional. Endless pattern and color varieties exist, which give even beginners a certain amount of freedom in creating a convincing marble look. Creating a faux marble surface requires a base coat with one or more layers of glaze applied over it. By manipulating the glaze with the necessary tool, you can create depth, movement, and visual texture. To give you an idea of how different color combinations play out, we worked up each sample in two different color schemes: cream base coat with peach and gray glazes, and black base coat with dark green and teal green glazes (*see* samples, pages 35 and 36).

I. Negative Veining Technique

Veined marble is one of the simplest and easiest marbles to reproduce. This stone is characterized by subtle color gradations, which give a sense of movement, accented by distinct veins.

The most common tool used to create a veined effect is a goose feather dipped in paint. The feather is dragged across the surface, leaving veins of paint behind. This method is called positive veining because it entails the laying down of paint.

Our method, which we call negative veining, works in the opposite way, by picking up glaze. To create this effect, wrap a section of cotton cloth around your thumb, then put your thumb (or thumbnail) into the wet glaze and pull it diagonally across the surface to uncover veinlike ripples of the base color. While adding paint for positive veining takes control and experience, removing paint is easier for beginners, and allows more artistic leeway.

II. Plastic Wrap Drifting Technique

The plastic wrap drifting technique, which results in a diagonal drift of mottled color, is more subtle than the negative veined effect. To create this diagonal background movement, professional marblers use a special cotton cloth, which allows them to remove small amounts of color while keeping some color in place. Because the cotton can absorb too much paint, this technique requires experience. Our method, however, uses plastic wrap, which does not absorb paint as readily as cotton cloth. This gives the glaze longer stay-wet time. The longer the stay-wet time, the more time the faux finisher has to manipulate the glaze in order to create a realistic effect.

To create subtle diagonal drifts of color, hold a length of plastic wrap at both ends, crinkle the ends slightly to encourage folds, then lay it diagonally across the surface. Move the glaze around by rubbing your hand across the surface of the plastic, then lift off the plastic to reveal the drifts of color.

III. Spritz Fossil Technique

The spritz fossil technique is used to create the look of "floating" or "fossil marble," which features small holes and pebble-like variations of color. A professional marbler creates this effect by using an oil-based base coat and a second layer of oil-based glaze. The marbler then sprinkles droplets of paint thinner onto the surface, which eat into the glaze, leaving a pebblelike spot of the base color showing through the glaze overcoat. The excess liquid is then blotted off.

Our technique is similar, except we use latex base coat paint and glazes, and water for the droplets. Overall, we've

NEGATIVE VEINING

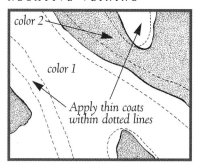

A. Apply the two glazes with a cloth in a downward diagonal drift; make one color dominant, and include thick and thin areas.

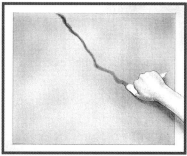

B. Make a diagonal vein through a thinly glazed area by lifting off the glaze.

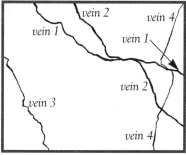

C. For a convincing look, make two veins intersect and travel together for a few inches before they break off.

Color samples below, top to bottom, using cream base coat and peach and gray glazes: negative veining technique, plastic wrap drifting technique, and spritz fossil technique.

found that latex paints and glazes are easier to clean up, environmentally safe, and create faux finishing effects comparable to oil-based paints.

We do not recommend this technique for use on walls, as the water will drip down and leave streaks.

Preparing and Painting Your Project Surface

Faux marble techniques can be created on just about any surface. However, to achieve the most realistic look, we recommend using surfaces that are smooth, grain-free, and easy to paint. Medium-density fiberboard (also known as MDF board) is ideal for tabletops because the thickness makes the finished product strong enough to use, and the board's smooth surface is easy to work on. If you can't find MDF board, you can substitute finer grades of plywood, fiberboard, or particle wood, or solid wood with little grain and no knots. For any of the above alternatives, make sure the surface is smooth and the wood is hard.

All woods need one or two coats of primer/sealer to prevent the base coat from being absorbed into the surface, while still providing the "tooth" that is needed to make paint adhere. Ask your lumber dealer for the appropriate sealer for the wood you are using. If your wood is not smooth, sand it lightly after the first coat of sealer has dried, wipe it clean, and apply a second coat.

After the sealer is completely dry (follow the manufacturer's recommendations for specific times), apply the base color. We recommend using a semigloss latex paint. Because the surfaces shown here are relatively small, you do not need as much glaze "open" time as you would if working on a large surface, or on walls. Therefore, working with oil-based glazes is unnecessary. Apply the paint using a short-nap roller or a foam brush to avoid leaving brush marks. If necessary, apply a second base coat, sanding

lightly between coats. Allow the base coat to dry completely before you begin applying the glaze.

Stu and Vi Cutbill are one of Canada's leading teams of faux-finishers and the inventors of the Cutbill system of block printing.

INSTRUCTIONS
Getting Started

1. Smooth wood surface by filling nicks with wood putty. Let dry, then sand with 100-grit sandpaper and remove dust with tack cloth. Repeat sanding and tack cloth process with increasingly finer grades of sandpaper to make surface as smooth as possible.

2. Apply latex sealer with foam brush and let dry, following manufacturer's recommendations. Sand lightly with 400- or 600-grit wet-dry sandpaper, and wipe clean with tack cloth. If wood still feels scratchy, apply second coat of sealer coat and let dry.

3. Base-coat wood surface using roller or foam brush and let dry. If first coat is uneven, sand lightly with 600-grit wet-dry sandpaper and apply second base coat. Let dry thoroughly, following manufacturer's recommendations.

4. When preparing paint-glaze mixtures, use separate container or bucket for each color. Allow 1 cup of glaze mixture for every 30 square feet. Mix 3 parts glaze and 1 part dark green or peach paint, then repeat to mix 3 parts glaze and 1 part teal or gray paint.

Three Marbling Techniques

Choose Method I, II, or III below. To allow glazes enough stay-wet time, work on no more than 9 square feet at a time. To prevent noticeable joins when glaze must be applied in sections, rub the wet glaze along the edges until smooth and thin. Once you have completed the marbling steps, proceed to the "Finishing" section.

I. Negative Veining Technique

1. Using crumpled cotton cloth, apply glaze mixtures across surface in diagonal drift; apply one color to about 70 percent of surface, and other color to about 30 percent of surface (*see* illustration A, solid lines). Vary your touch so glaze is thick in some areas and thin in others (illustration A, dotted lines) with a hint of base coat showing through. To tone down and blend glaze colors, press fluffed-up cheesecloth against wet surface.

2. To make first vein, wrap 6" square of cotton cloth around thumb, grabbing excess bulk in palm. Starting at far edge, put thumb into wet glaze and pull it diagonally across surface, passing through thinly glazed areas. To avoid making vein too straight, jiggle hand every few inches to create craggy shift in line, then continue along same diagonal path. To vary vein thickness, lessen pressure until thumbnail scratches surface, then increase pressure, using side or pad of thumb to remove wider band of glaze (illustration B).

3. To make second vein, start 4" to 5" from first vein in another lightly glazed spot. Draw vein diagonally in same manner, angling it so it intersects first vein. Draw second vein along first vein for 1" to 2", then break off from first vein and continue on in original second vein direction. Add a few more veins in lightly glazed areas; for realistic look, make between four and six veins total (illustration C). If glaze becomes too tacky to work, dampen thumb cloth with water. To make some veins appear deep and recessed, dab veins with cheesecloth.

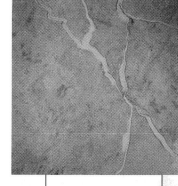

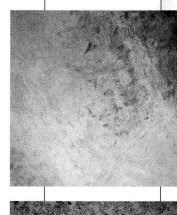

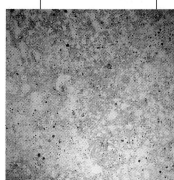

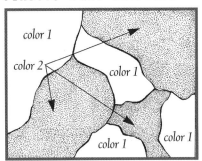

D. Using a cloth, apply the two glazes in random patches in roughly equal amounts.

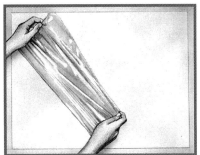

E. Hold a piece of plastic wrap so crinkles form in the middle, then lay it down on the wet glaze.

F. Gently rub the surface of the wrap, then peel off the wrap to reveal the veining.

II. Plastic Wrap Drifting Technique

1. Using separate cotton cloth for each color, apply glaze mixtures to surface in random pockets; apply colors fairly evenly, so each one occupies about

Color samples above, left to right, using black base coat and green glazes: negative veining effect, plastic wrap veining finish, and spritz fossil finish.

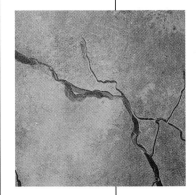

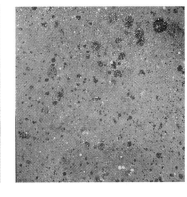

50 percent of surface (illustration D). To tone down and blend glaze colors, press fluffed-up cheesecloth against wet surface.

2. To create subtle diagonal veining, hold 2-foot length of plastic wrap at both ends. Crinkle ends slightly to encourage folds, then lay plastic diagonally across surface (illustration E). To move glaze, rub your hand across surface of plastic;

press harder to lift more glaze, or less hard to leave glaze on surface (illustration F). Lift off plastic to reveal veining. Repeat to add veins across remaining surface, changing to fresh plastic every two to three pulls. To make some veins appear deep and recessed, dab them with cheesecloth.

III. Spritz Fossil Technique

1. Using separate cotton cloth for each color, apply glaze mixtures to surface in random pockets. Apply colors fairly evenly, so each one occupies about 50 percent of surface (illustration G). To tone down and blend glaze colors, press

fluffed-up cheesecloth against wet surface.

2. To spritz surface, dip fingertips into bowl of water, bend fingers in toward palm, and press thumb against them. Hold your hand directly over glazed surface and release your fingers in a snap, so droplets hit glazed surface with force (illustration H). Let drops "eat" into glaze for a few seconds, then use folded cotton cloth to blot remaining water. Spritz and blot several more times until one-third of glaze has been lifted off. Let dry 1 hour.

3. To spatter surface, dip round stencil brush into glaze, hold brush a few inches above surface, and run thumb across bristles to release a fine spray. Repeat over entire surface with each glaze color (illustration I).

Finishing

Let glazed surface dry at least 4 hours, but preferably overnight. Using foam brush to prevent bubbles, apply acrylic varnish to entire surface. Let dry 1 hour, or as manufacturer recommends; sand lightly with 600-grit sandpaper. For a strong, durable finish, apply a total of 4 to 5 coats varnish, sanding between coats. ◆

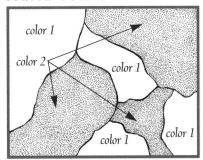

G. Using a cloth, apply the two glazes in random patches in roughly equal amounts.

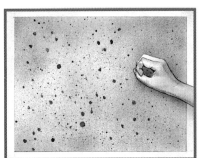

H. Wet your fingertips, then snap them against your thumb to shoot droplets onto the surface.

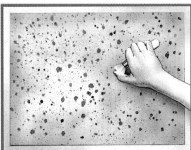

I. When the surface is dry, add a fine spray of glaze using a stencil brush.

Shabby Chic Slipcover

Forget patterns. The secret to making this loose and baggy slipcover:
Measure and cut the fabric against your chair, then stitch relaxed seam lines.

🐦 BY CANDIE FRANKEL

A CUSTOM-MADE, SHABBY CHIC slipcover like the one shown here might cost hundreds of dollars in an upholstery store, but with the right know-how, you can sew a professional-looking version in a weekend's time for less than half the cost, depending on the fabric.

This loose, baggy slipcover style is relatively new in home decorating—when I couldn't find any instructions for making my own, I used traditional methods as a springboard to determine the best overall approach. My testing led me to two easy but critical steps: First, instead of using patterns, I cut and fit the fabric directly against the chair; and second, to achieve a fit that was relaxed but professional looking, I stitched certain seams three-quarters of an inch beyond the customary fitted seam lines.

To orient myself, I canvassed half a dozen home-decorating books that described methods of sewing slipcovers. One approach measured and cut pieces of muslin fabric against the chair to derive patterns, which were then used to cut the slipcover fabric. A second technique called for measuring and cutting the actual slipcover fabric against the chair, pin-fitting the cut pieces inside out, then proceeding straight to the sewing machine. The muslin pattern approach is ideal when you want to make more than one slipcover. The same pattern can be used to create a wardrobe of slipcovers for a single chair or a set of matching slipcovers for two or more identical chairs. For a single slipcover, however, measuring and cutting the fabric directly on the chair is a real time-saver.

My second important discovery involved seam lines and the way I created the baggy fit. Instead of trying to introduce bagginess right off, I pin-fit each seam the traditional way for a snug fit, then ran a new line of pins three-quarters of an inch beyond the first line to mark the eventual seam line. This allowed better control of the fit, and prevented the final slipcover from crossing the visual border from baggy to outright sloppy. Rather than sew the pieces as pinned, I unpinned them first and proceeded section by section. This gave me the opportunity to trim symmetrical pieces and pairs, such as the front arms, so that their

The shabby chic style recalls the slightly baggy silhouette of nineteenth-century dustcovers. The durable, natural fiber fabrics used then are just as appropriate today: cotton ducks, coarse linens, and cotton/linen blends in white or neutral shades.

edges matched. In an earlier attempt, I skipped this step and produced some unattractive joins, particularly where the outside arm and inner and outer backs converged.

Welting is essential to the shabby chic look. The three-eighths-inch welting I sewed myself (you could also buy contrasting welting) helps give the baggy shape some definition and support. I was a bit skeptical when one source advised installing the welting and sewing the

seams in one step (I like to machine-baste welting along one edge first), but I found this method worked beautifully and saved time.

I sewed the slipcover shown above from Richloom Fabrics' "Signature III Collection" Harmonica pattern in sage. *Note*: The yardage requirements and directions that follow are intended for solid color fabrics or ones with small- to medium-scale prints that do not require meticulous matching.

COLOR PHOTOGRAPHY:
Carl Tremblay

ILLUSTRATION:
Mary DePalma

STYLING:
Gabrielle Derrick de Papp/Team

Measuring and Cutting the Slipcover

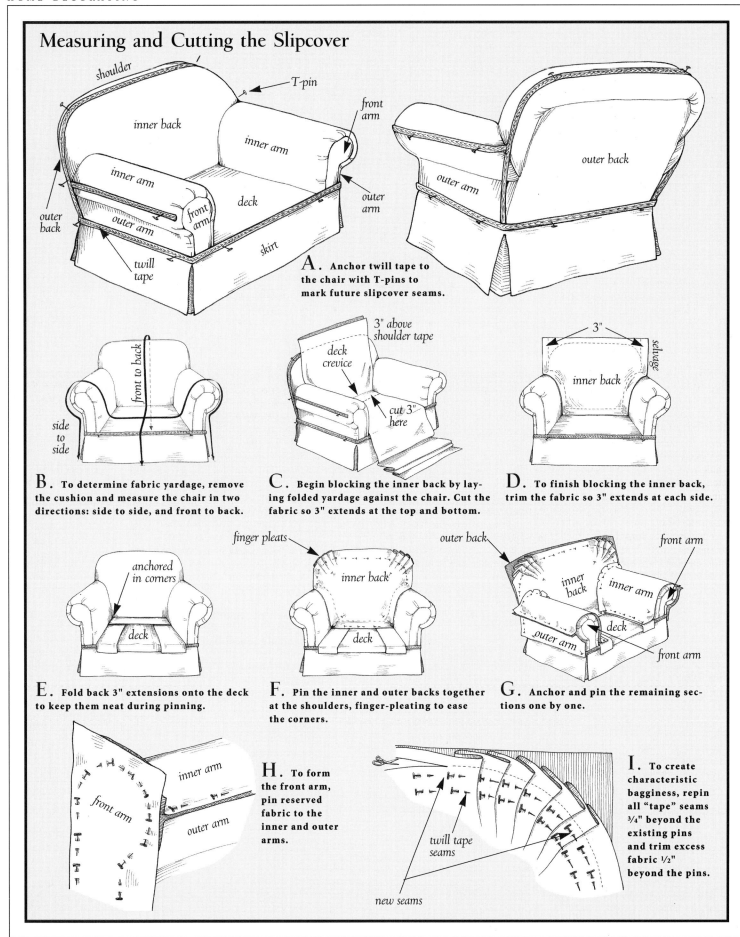

shoulder

T-pin

inner back

inner arm

front arm

inner arm

deck

outer back

front arm

outer arm

outer back

outer arm

twill tape

skirt

A. Anchor twill tape to the chair with T-pins to mark future slipcover seams.

outer back

outer arm

front to back

side to side

B. To determine fabric yardage, remove the cushion and measure the chair in two directions: side to side, and front to back.

3" above shoulder tape

deck crevice

cut 3" here

C. Begin blocking the inner back by laying folded yardage against the chair. Cut the fabric so 3" extends at the top and bottom.

3"

selvage

inner back

D. To finish blocking the inner back, trim the fabric so 3" extends at each side.

anchored in corners

deck

E. Fold back 3" extensions onto the deck to keep them neat during pinning.

finger pleats

inner back

deck

F. Pin the inner and outer backs together at the shoulders, finger-pleating to ease the corners.

outer back

inner back

inner arm

front arm

deck

outer arm

front arm

G. Anchor and pin the remaining sections one by one.

inner arm

front arm

outer arm

H. To form the front arm, pin reserved fabric to the inner and outer arms.

twill tape seams

new seams

I. To create characteristic bagginess, repin all "tape" seams ¾" beyond the existing pins and trim excess fabric ½" beyond the pins.

INSTRUCTIONS

Getting Started

1. Start by plotting slipcover seams. Wrap twill tape around shoulder, along outside arms, and around chair body even with deck (*see* illustration A). To anchor tape, use T-pins: Pierce tape and upholstery, then pivot shank 180 degrees and press down into upholstery.

2. Next, calculate welting yardage. Add (a) total twill tape measure from step 1, (b) cushion perimeter times 2, and (c) 18" shrinkage allowance. If using purchased welting, eliminate shrinkage allowance. Jot down total.

3. Last, calculate fabric yardage. Remove cushion and measure chair front to back and side to side (illustration B). Measure floor to deck-level tape and multiply by 8. Measure cushion width front to back and add cushion depth times 3. Add all measurements and divide by 36". If making welting, add ½ yard per 10 yards welting (step 2). Add 1 yard fitting allowance. Add 8 percent of total for shrinkage. Jot down all measurements for future reference.

4. To preshrink fabric, machine-wash and -dry at medium setting.

Blocking the Slipcover

Shape the slipcover by pinning together rectangles of fabric that correspond to the chair sections (inner back, outer back, etc.; *see* illustration A). To provide pinning ease, cut each rectangle 3" larger all around than its corresponding chair section. To determine the appropriate dimensions, measure the fabric directly against a chair section. This measuring and cutting process is called blocking.

1. Begin blocking by folding fabric yardage lengthwise, wrong side out. Smooth it against inner back of chair so end of fabric extends 3" above shoulder

MATERIALS

- 54"-wide slipcover fabric (to calculate yardage, see "Getting Started," steps 1 through 3)
- ³⁄₈" preshrunk cotton welting cord or purchased welting in contrasting color (to calculate yardage, see "Getting Started," step 2)
- Thread to match slipcover fabric
- 36" slipcover zipper (for cushion)

You'll also need:
chair; sewing machine; 10 yards twill tape; T-pins; quilter's pins; tape measure; calculator; dark-colored chalk; scissors; iron; washer/dryer; pencil; and scrap paper.

Other items, if necessary:
rotary cutter (to cut bias for welting); and yardstick (to draft straight cutting lines).

tape and excess runs across deck. Make small chalk mark 3" beyond deck crevice. Fold fabric straight across at mark and cut along fold (illustration C).

2. Complete blocking first rectangle by unfolding cut piece from step 1 wrong side out. Lay it against inner back of chair, so one selvage extends 3" beyond shoulder at widest part. Mark fabric 3" beyond opposite shoulder. Fold and cut fabric at mark as in step 1 (illustration D). Set aside excess. Label section "inner back" and trim off remaining selvage.

3. To block rectangles for most remaining sections (outside back, inner and outer arms, and deck), repeat steps 1 and 2. For each piece, remember to mark fabric 3" beyond chair's widest point, to cut fabric straight across, and to label all pieces. Proceed section by section, top down, to cut one outer back, two inner arms, two outer arms, and one deck (illustration A). Set aside two large scraps for front arms,

which will be added in "Anchoring and Pin-Fitting," step 5. Remaining yardage will be used to cut skirt, welting, and cushion.

4. Measure cushion from front to back, add cushion depth times 3, and cut fabric to this measure. For welting, cut fabric yardage calculated in "Getting Started," step 3. Reserve remaining fabric for skirt.

Anchoring and Pin-Fitting

In this set of steps, the rectangles and pieces are pinned together, then trimmed further to match the actual contours of the chair. Place the fabric on the chair wrong side out. Anchor the fabric to the chair's upholstery with T-pins, and pin-fit the pieces together using quilter's pins.

1. Start by anchoring deck. Lay fabric on chair deck and fold 3" extensions on three inner edges. Anchor four corners, leaving extensions free (illustration E).

2. Pin-fit shoulder seam by smoothing outer back piece across shoulder so edges extend 3" beyond chair. Anchor top and bottom. Trim lower edge 1" below deck-level tape. Anchor inner back piece so 3" extends onto deck. Pin this extension to folded deck extension. Pin inner and outer backs together at shoulder, following shoulder twill tape; finger-pleat inner back to ease corners (illustration F).

3. Shape inner back piece by pressing it against (but not into) inner back and inner arm crevices. Let excess fabric fall against chair arm. Beginning at top of each crevice and working downwards, mark excess fabric 3" beyond crevice, resmoothing fabric as needed to create ease as you move around chair arm. Trim on marked lines (illustration G).

4. Pin arms by smoothing and anchoring outside and inner arms on chair arm. Inner arm should extend 3" onto deck. Trim lower edge of outer arm 1" below

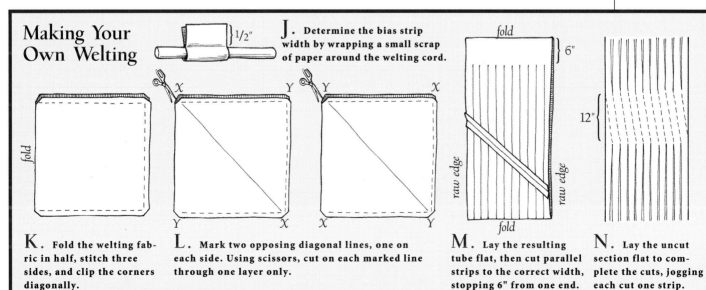

Making Your Own Welting

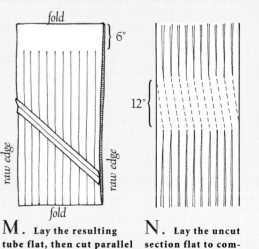

J. Determine the bias strip width by wrapping a small scrap of paper around the welting cord.

K. Fold the welting fabric in half, stitch three sides, and clip the corners diagonally.

L. Mark two opposing diagonal lines, one on each side. Using scissors, cut on each marked line through one layer only.

M. Lay the resulting tube flat, then cut parallel strips to the correct width, stopping 6" from one end.

N. Lay the uncut section flat to complete the cuts, jogging each cut one strip.

Adding the Skirt and Covering the Cushion

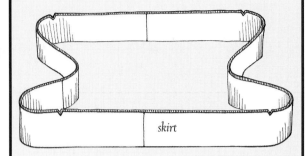

O. To make a self-lined skirt, join the skirt sections in a continuous loop.

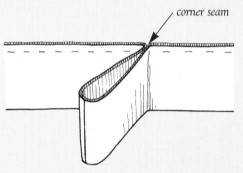

corner seam

P. Sew the skirt to the sides, back, and front of the slipcover from the center out to the corners.

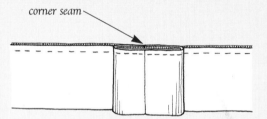

corner seam

Q. Fold the excess fabric flat and stitch it to form an inverted box pleat.

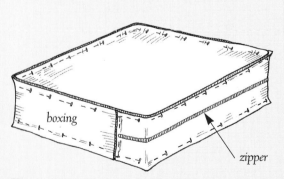

boxing

zipper

R. Cover the cushion by cutting and pin-fitting the zippered boxing strip first. Then pin-fit the fabric sections.

deck-level tape, even with outer back. Pin outer and inner arms together, following twill tape. Pin deck extensions together along straight edges, but angle pins towards outside deck corners for proper fit when skirt is joined. To ease inner arm, trim fabric 3" beyond inner arm and inner back crevices as in step 3. Starting at top of arm and continuing around curve down towards deck, pin seam allowances together 1" from inner arm and inner back crevices. Once edges straighten out, do not pin. To create ease, clip into fabric allowance, stopping just before pins. Trim ½" beyond pins. When you reach end of pins, angle cut down and out away from inner back/inner arm crevice. To complete join, pin-fit outside arms to outside back (illustration G).

5. To pin-fit front arms, anchor scrap fabric to each front arm so bottom edge falls 3" below deck-level tape. Pin-fit to outer and inner arm, following contours (illustration H).

6. Create characteristic bagginess by repinning all "twill tape" seams ¾" beyond existing pins, then removing first set of pins. Repin front arms to accommodate increased allowance. Adjust where arm and back meet. Remove anchoring T-pins. Try lifting slipcover off chair, arms first. If it is too tight, reposition pins along outer back/outer arm seams for more allowance. Trim excess fabric ½" beyond pins (illustration I).

7. With pinned slipcover on chair, notch seam allowances every 10". Remove all pins. To make sure pieces are symmetrical, fold in half or layer pairs, then trim corresponding edges to match. Repin pleats. If using purchased welting, proceed to step 1, "Sewing the Slipcover and Cushion."

Making Your Own Welting

1. Wrap small section of scrap paper around welting cord, then trim ½" away from cord (illustration J). Measure unfolded paper to determine width for bias strips.

2. Cut fabric yardage for welting, allowing ½ yard of fabric for 10 yards of welting (see "Getting Started," steps 2 through 3). Fold fabric in half, sew edges together on three sides, and clip corners diagonally (illustration K).

3. Label one corner and its diagonal opposite X. Label other two corners Y. Using chalk and yardstick, draft diagonal line from X to X. Turn piece over and draft diagonal line from Y to Y. Using scissors, cut on each marked line through one layer only (illustration L).

4. Unfold and open cut piece; shape to form a tube and press seams open. Lay tube flat and trim raw edges straight. Use rotary cutter to cut strips to width determined in step 1, or use yardstick and chalk to mark strips to width determined in step 1 and cut with scissors. Stop cutting 6" from one end (illustration M). Unfold and lay uncut section flat. To complete cuts, jog each cut by one strip width (illustration N).

5. Make welting by enclosing cord in strip, raw edges matching. Machine-baste using zipper foot.

Sewing the Slipcover and Cushion Cover

1. Join pieces by pinning and sewing right sides together, matching notches in the following order and enclosing welting in seams preceded by a W: Inner arms to deck; inner back to deck; inner arms to inner back; (W) inner arms to outer arms; (W) outer back to inner back/outer arms/inner arms; (W) front arms to inner arms/outer arms. Machine-baste welting ½" from lower edge of slipcover all around, butting ends for neat finish. Mark center of back, front, and sides of slipcover by notching; notches will be used to line up skirt.

2. To make self-lined skirt, place slipcover on chair, right side out. Measure from lower edge to floor, multiply by 2, add 1", and then cut four sections this length across fabric width. Sew short ends together in continuous loop; press seams open. Fold in half, raw edges matching, and press. On raw edge, notch center of each panel (illustration O). Remove slipcover from chair. Match notches to center notches made in step 1, and pin from notches out to corners of slipcover; machine-stitch. To make inverted corner pleats, fold excess fabric evenly on each side of corner seam, then machine-stitch (illustrations P and Q).

3. For cushion, start by making boxing strip. Cut one strip equal to cushion depth plus 1¼" across width of fabric. Anchor to cushion, leaving zipper section of cushion exposed. Cut second strip 1½" wider than first strip and 1" longer than exposed zipper section. Cut strip in half lengthwise and install zipper between halves. Sew strips together at short ends to make boxing strip. Test-fit on cushion, adjust as needed, and trim excess zipper tape. Cut remaining cushion fabric (from "Blocking the Slipcover," step 4) in half. Anchor each piece to cushion and pin-fit to boxing strip. Trim edges, then notch each edge at center. Disassemble, true up to make sure pieces are symmetrical, and sew as for slipcover, installing welting in seams (illustration R).

4. When chair and cushion slipcovers are sewn, remove twill tape from chair. Ease slipcover on chair, right side out, and tuck deck extensions and inner back/inner arm seams into crevices. Put cushion slipcover on cushion and set cushion on chair deck. ◆

Field Guide

Use these assorted shabby chic fabrics to jump-start your slipcover designs.

Name/Manufacturer
Color

1. Piccolo Washed
Bronze

2. Starfish
Putty

3. Thayer Fabrics
Pueblo Cinnamon

4. Cupid's Arrow
Putty

5. Pacific Weavers
Flat Gold #5002

6. Sconset
Taupe

7. Pacific Weavers
Mauve

8. Connelley Washed
Natural

9. Robert Allen
Celery #068003

UPHOLSTERY CHIC

These shabby chic fabric samples represent a relatively new category of upholstery fabric. The term "shabby chic" was coined to describe the washed, faded, and slightly crumpled look popular in today's slipcover designs (*see* "Shabby Chic Slipcover," page 37).

All of the fifty-four-inch-wide fabrics shown here are woven from fiber combinations (i.e., cotton/linen, cotton/rayon) that will shrink and wrinkle slightly when washed, which contributes to their shabby look. At the same time, their beautiful designs and colors keep them safely in the chic category. For specifics on where the fabrics were purchased and their price per yard, *see* the Sources and Resources section on page 46. ◆

COLOR PHOTOGRAPHY:
Carl Tremblay

Mail-Order Directory

Our First Annual Mail-Order Supplier Directory

GENERIC ART SUPPLIES

DANIEL SMITH
4150 First Avenue South
P.O. Box 84268
Seattle, WA 98124-5568
800-426-6740
Offers: Catalog of artists' materials, from paints, brushes, paper, and canvas to frames, metallic leafing supplies, and books.
Reference catalog $5 (includes $5 certificate). Free supplemental catalogs.

DICK BLICK ART MATERIALS
P.O. Box 1267
Galesburg, IL 61402-1267
800-447-8192
Offers: Large selection of artists' supplies, including paints, brushes, paper and boards, screen-printing materials, printmaking tools, craft supplies, ceramic tools, and software. **Free catalog.**

FLAX ART AND DESIGN
P.O. Box 7216
San Francisco, CA 94120-7216
800-547-7778
Offers: Tools and supplies for artists as well as gifts for art enthusiasts.
Free catalog.

GRAPHIC PRODUCTS CATALOG
5601 International Parkway
P.O. Box 155
Minneapolis, MN 55440-0155
800-326-7555
Offers: Tools and supplies for architects, engineers, contractors, designers, desktop publishers, and computer-aided designers.
Free catalog.

GRAPHIK DIMENSIONS LTD.
2103 Brentwood Street
High Point, NC 27263
800-221-0262
Offers: Supplies and materials for do-it-yourself framing.
Free catalog.

THE JERRY'S CATALOG
P.O. Box 1105
New Hyde Park, NY 11040
800-U-ARTIST
Offers: Full line of art supplies and furniture, as well as gifts and books for the art enthusiast.
Free catalog.

OTT'S
102 Hungate Drive
Greenville, NC 27858
800-356-3289
Offers: Discount art supplies from paints, brushes, calligraphy supplies, and palettes to drawing materials, canvas, markers, and varnish.
Free catalog.

PEARL PAINT CO., INC.
308 Canal Street
New York, NY 10013-2572
800-221-6845 X2297
Offers: Wide selection of art and craft supplies, including paints, mediums, canvas, framing materials, books, drawing materials, paper, gold leaf, and accessories.
Catalog $1.

PIERCE TOOLS
1610 Parkdale Drive
Grants Pass, OR 97527
503-476-1778
Offers: Tools for the ceramist, doll maker, sculptor, and potter.
Free catalog.

SAX ARTS AND CRAFTS
P.O. Box 51710

New Berlin, WI 53151
800-323-0388
Offers: A full supply of art supplies, tools, and materials, as well as books and gifts for the art enthusiast.
Catalog $5 (can be applied toward first purchase).

TORRINGTON BRUSH WORKS, INC.
63 Avenue "A", P.O. Box 56
Torrington, CT 06790
800-262-7874 (Connecticut)
800-525-1416 (Florida)
Offers: Wide selection of brushes and accessories, from China bristle and nylon paint brushes to dusters, foam brushes, artist brushes, mops, and tube brushes. **Free catalog.**

GENERIC CRAFT SUPPLIES

AMERCAN ART CLAY CO., INC.
4717 West 16th Street
Indianapolis, IN 46222
800-374-1600
Offers: Craft supplies, toys, books, and accessories relating to products such as Fimo polymer clay, Friendly Plastic modeling material, and more. **Free catalog.**

CRAFT CATALOG
6095 McNaughten Centre
Columbus, OH 43232
800-777-1442
Offers: Wide selection of craft supplies, including wood turnings, paint, jewelry findings, brushes, stencils, trims, and ribbons.
Free catalog.

CRAFT KING
P.O. Box 90637
Lakeland, FL 33804
800-769-9494
Offers: Discount craft supplies covering a wide range of topics, including beads, books, doll parts, floral supplies, paint, ribbon, and wood items. **Free catalog.**

CREATIVE CRAFT HOUSE
P.O. Box 2567
Bullhead City, AZ 86430
520-754-3300

Offers: Wide assortment of craft items and supplies, including beads, leather supplies, miniatures, baskets, jewelry findings, dried foliage, and shells. **Catalog $2.**

EARTH GUILD
33 Haywood Street
Asheville, NC 28801
800-327-8448
Offers: Tools, materials, and books for handcrafts. Specific topics include basketry, dyeing, spinning, yarns, weaving, rug making, leatherwork, candle making, beading, and modeling clays. **Catalog $3.**

HOME-SEW
P.O. Box 4099
Bethlehem, PA 18018
610-867-3833
Offers: Sewing and craft supplies, including thread, notions, glues, lace, ribbon, scissors, trims, and doilies. **Free catalog.**

KIRCHEN BROS.
Box 1016, Skokie, IL 60076
708-647-6747
Offers: Assorted craft supplies, focusing specifically on doll making, miniatures, jewelry findings, and beads. **Free catalog.**

LARK BOOKS
50 College Street
Asheville, NC 28801
800-284-3388
Offers: Catalog of books, kits, and gifts for craft enthusiasts.
Free catalog.

MAPLEWOOD CRAFTS
Humboldt Industrial Park
1 Maplewood Drive
Hazleton, PA 18201
800-899-0134
Offers: Wide range of seasonal craft kits, as well as beading and needlecraft supplies, books, tools, plastic canvas, paint, dolls, and floral craft materials. **Free catalog.**

NEWARK DRESSMAKER SUPPLY
6473 Ruch Road, P.O. Box 20730
Lehigh Valley, PA 18002-0730
610-837-7500
Offers: Sewing, craft, and needle-

work supplies, including beads, bridal basics, fabric, jewelry findings, ribbon, and silk flowers. **Free catalog.**

OPPENHEIM'S LADIES' BOOK
120 East Main Street
North Manchester, IN 46962-0052
800-461-6728
219-982-684
Offers: Assorted craft supplies, ranging from fabric and buttons to sewing and craft notions. **Free catalog.**

SUNSHINE DISCOUNT CRAFTS
P.O. Box 301
Largo, FL 34649-0301
800-729-2878
Offers: Large assortment of craft supplies, including modeling clays and accessories, beads, dolls, miniatures, brushes, and wood items. **Free catalog.**

SPECIALITY CRAFT SUPPLIES

ADVENTURES IN CRAFTS
P.O. Box 6058
Yorkville Station
New York, NY 10128
212-410-9793
Offers: Decoupage prints, tools, kits, and books, as well as unfinished wood items. **Catalog $3.50.**

BEAR CLAWSET
27 Palermo Walk
Long Beach, CA 90803
310-434-8077
Offers: Bear-making supplies and materials, from fur, growlers, and joints to patterns and books. **Catalog $2.**

EASTERN ART GLASS
P.O. Box 341
Wyckoff, NJ 07481
800-872-3458
Offers: Glass and mirror etching and decorating supplies. **Free catalog.**

EMBOSSING ARTS COMPANY
P.O. Box 626
Sweet Home, OR 97386
503-367-3279
Offers: Rubber stamps, brass stencils, card making, and embossing supplies. **Catalog $3 (specify retail catalog).**

G. SCHOEPFER, INC.
460 Cook Hill Road
Cheshire, CT 06410

800-875-6939
Offers: A complete line of eyes for dolls. **Free catalog.**

MAINE STREET STAMPS
P.O. Box 14, Kingfield, ME 04947
207-265-2500
Offers: Selection of rubber stamps, stamp pads, and embossing powder. **Catalog $2.**

POUR-ETTE CANDLE MAKING SUPPLIES
1418 NW 53rd
Ballard, WA 98107
206-525-4488
Offers: A complete selection of supplies for candle making, including wax, molds, and wicks. **Free catalog.**

STAMPENDOUS, INC.
1357 South Lewis Street
Anaheim, CA 92805
800-869-0474
714-563-9501
Offers: Rubber stamps, books, stamp sets, papers, postcards, stamp pads, markers, embossing powder, foils, and tools. **Catalog $6.**

SURMA
11 East 7th Street
New York, NY 10003
212-477-0729
Offers: Ukrainian Easter egg decorating dyes, tools, kits, and supplies. **Free catalog.**

TINKER BOB'S TINWARE
209 Summit Street
Norwich, CT 06360
203-886-7365
Offers: A complete selection of reproduction colonial tinware. **Catalog $3.**

BEADS

THE BEAD DREAMER
P.O. Box 16
Newport News, VA 23607-0016
804-245-5844
Offers: Catalog of beads, charms, leather, and findings. **Catalog $2.**

BEADS GALORE INTERNATIONAL, INC.
2123 South Priest #201
Tempe, AZ 85282
602-921-3949
Offers: Large selection of stone, glass, silver, and trade beads, as well as findings, pendants, and earrings (minimum order $30). **Free catalog.**

BUCK'S COUNTY CLASSIC
73 Coventry Lane
Langhorne, PA 19047
800-942-4367
Offers: Jewelry kits, supplies, and tools, as well as an assortment of beads. **Catalog $2.50.**

CENTRAL CASTING
1150 6th Street
Berkeley, CA 94701
800-745-1350
Offers: Wide assortment of cast lead-free pewter pieces and parts, including ethnic designs, spiritual images, metaphysical themes, coins, keys, and wildlife (minimum order $150). **Catalog $5.**

CONTEMPORARY BEADS & CASTINGS, INC.
114 Wilkins Avenue
Port Chester, NY 10573
914-939-6833
Offers: Pewter castings in a variety of finishes, as well as polymer, clay, ceramic, and glass beads (minimum order $150). **Catalog $6.**

CREATIVE BEGINNINGS
475 Morro Bay Boulevard
Morro Bay, CA 93442
800-367-1739
Offers: Wide assortment of antiquated silver- and brass-plated charms and ornaments for jewelry making or embellishing craft projects. Also offers findings, books, paints, and kits. **Free brochure.**

ENTERPRISE ART
P.O. Box 2918
Largo, FL 34649
800-366-2218
Offers: Large assortment of beads, rhinestones, and findings, as well as assorted craft supplies such as Fimo, Friendly Plastic, kits, Western wear supplies, and paint. **Free catalog.**

ORNAMENTAL RESOURCES
Box 3010, 1427 Miner Street
Idaho Springs, CO 80452
800-876-6762 (Orders and catalog)
303-567-2222 (Customer service)
Offers: Wide variety of beads, findings, books, supplies, and tools (minimum order $25). **Catalog $15.**

DECORATIVE BAKING AND COOKING

A COOK'S WARES
211 37th Street
Beaver Falls, PA 15010-2103

412-846-9490
Offers: Gourmet cooking and baking supplies, books, equipment, and ingredients. **Catalog $2.**

AMERICAN SPOON FOODS, INC.
P.O. Box 566
Petoskey, MI 49770-0566
800-222-5886
616-347-9030
Offers: Wide range of condiments and cooking supplies, including preserves, jellies, conserves, and marmalades; fruit butters; salad dazzlers; dried fruit and fruit mixes; honey; pancake mixes; and gifts. **Free catalog.**

GRAPEVINE TRADING CO.
59 Maxwell Court
Santa Rosa, CA 95401
707-576-3950
Offers: Dried berries and fruits as well as crystallized edible flowers. **Free catalog.**

KING ARTHUR FLOUR BAKER'S CATALOGUE
P.O. Box 876
Norwich, VT 05055-0876
800-827-6836
Offers: Wide assortment of baking-related supplies and gifts, including bread-making equipment and books, baker's appliances, grains and yeasts, cake and pastry supplies, and pasta equipment. **Free catalog.**

KITCHEN KRAFTS
P.O. Box 805, Mt. Laurel, NJ 08054
800-776-0575
609-778-4960
Offers: Food-crafting supplies, equipment, books, and ingredients. **Free catalog.**

LEHMAN'S NON-ELECTRIC "GOOD NEIGHBOR" HERITAGE CATALOG
One Lehman Circle
P.O. Box 41
Kidron, OH 44636-0041
216-857-5757
Offers: Large assortment of food, gifts, housewares, cutlery, cookware, crockery, canning and juicing supplies, toys, signs, camping equipment, cleaning supplies, books, lawn and gardening equipment, and farming tools. **Catalog $3.**

SUR LA TABLE
410 Perry Avenue North
Seattle, WA 98109
800-243-0852
206-682-7212
Offers: Cooking equipment,

housewares, and gifts, including cake-decorating supplies, Calphalon cookware, large selection of copper cookware, and more. **Free catalog.**

SWEET CELEBRATIONS INC.
7009 Washington Avenue South
Edina, MN 55439
800-328-6722
Offers: Wide assortment of dessert supplies and accessories, including baking equipment, bridal figures, cake decorating tools, candy-making supplies, doilies, molds, ornaments, pans, party-theme accessories, recipes, and books. **Free catalog.**

WILLIAMS-SONOMA
P.O. Box 7456
San Francisco, CA 94120-7456
800-541-2233
Offers: Large selection of housewares and cookware, including glasses, dinnerware, linens, herbs, cooking and baking equipment, flatware, appliances, and chef's clothing. Also offers recipes, books, cleaning supplies, and gifts. **Free catalog.**

FLORAL SUPPLIES

BEST BUY FLORAL SUPPLY
P.O. Box 1982
Cedar Rapids, IA 52406
800-553-8497
Offers: Floral containers, vases, and supplies, ribbon, baskets, and artificial flowers, foliage, and arrangements. **Free catalog.**

BOUNTIFUL GARDENS
18001 Shafer Ranch Road
Willits, CA 95490-9626
707-459-6410
Offers: Organic seeds, tools, tips, and books. **Free catalog.**

BURPEE GARDENS
300 Park Avenue
Warminster, PA 18974
800-888-1447
Offers: Herb seeds and plants, flower seeds and bulbs, vegetable seeds and roots, trees, shrubs, gardening supplies, seed tapes, and kits. **Free catalog.**

DUTCH GARDENS
P.O. Box 200
Adelphia, NJ 07710-0200
800-818-3861
Offers: Bulbs, tubers, corms, and perennials shipped straight from the

Netherlands, as well as gardening supplies. **Free catalog.**

GARDENER'S EDEN
P.O. Box 7307
San Francisco, CA 94120
800-822-9600
Offers: A full supply of gardening tools and supplies, as well as gifts for gardening enthusiasts. **Free catalog.**

GARDENER'S SUPPLY CO.
128 Intervale Road
Burlington, VT 05401-2804
800-444-6417
Offers: A full line of supplies, equipment, and tools for gardeners. **Free catalog.**

LIBERTY SEED COMPANY
P.O. Box 806
New Philadelphia, OH 44663
216-364-1611
Offers: A complete catalog of vegetable and flower seeds, perennials, bulbs, books, mulch, and gardening supplies and tools. **Free catalog.**

MAY SILK
16202 Distribution Way
Cerritos, CA 90703
800-282-7455
Offers: Silk flowers, plants, foliage, trees, arrangements, and accessories. **Free catalog.**

NICHE GARDENS
1111 Dawson Road
Chapel Hill, NC 27516
919-967-0078
Offers: Nursery-propagated wildflowers, Southeastern U.S. native plants, perennials, ornamental grasses, and unusual trees and shrubs. **Catalog $3.**

PACIFIC BOTANICALS
4350 Fish Hatchery
Grants Pass, OR 97527
503-479-7777
Offers: Organically grown and wild-crafted herbs. **Free catalog.**

PARK SEED FLOWERS AND VEGETABLES
Cokesbury Road
Greenwood, SC 29647-0001
800-845-3369
Offers: Large selection of herbs, flower seeds, bulbs, and plants, vegetables, fruits, berries, and garden supplies. **Free catalog.**

SHEPHERD'S GARDEN SEEDS
30 Irene Street
Torrington, CT 06790

203-482-3638
Offers: Vegetable, herb, and flower seeds, as well as seed collections, gardening supplies, and select cooking equipment. **Free catalog.**

SMITH & HAWKEN
Two Arbor Lane
Box 6900
Florence, KY 41022-6900
800-776-3336
Offers: Supplies, tools, equipment, clothing, furniture, and gifts for gardeners. **Free catalog.**

SOUTHERN EXPOSURE SEED EXCHANGE
P.O. Box 170
Earlysville, VA 22936
804-973-4703
Offers: Wide selection of vegetable/flower seeds and books.
Catalog $2 (refundable with first order).

THOMPSON & MORGAN
P.O. Box 1308
Jackson, NJ 08527-0308
800-274-7333
Offers: Wide assortment of perennials and annuals, flower and vegetable seeds, houseplants, and bulbs.
Free catalog.

WHITE FLOWER FARM
P.O. Box 50
Litchfield, CT 06759-0050
203-496-1661
Offers: Wide range of annuals, perennials, shrubs, bulbs, vines, and gardening tools and supplies.
One catalog free; $5 for year subscription.

PAINTING, FAUX FINISHING, AND STENCILS

ARTEX MANUFACTURING COMPANY
5894 Blackwelder Street
Culver City, CA 90232-7304
210-870-6000
Offers: Full line of Nova Color, an artists' acrylic paint suitable for use on canvas, paper, fabric, wood, plaster, masonry, and most non slick, nonoily surfaces.
Free catalog.

ARTIST'S CLUB
5750 NE Hassalo, Building C
Portland, OR 97213
800-845-6507
Offers: Books, kits, projects, and

supplies for tole and decorative painting. **Free catalog.**

ASW EXPRESS
5325 Departure Drive
Raleigh, NC 27604
800-995-6778
Offers: Mail-order catalog of artists' supplies, including airbrushes, boards, canvas, easels, frames, inks, paints, paper, and silk-painting supplies. **Free catalog.**

CO-OP ARTISTS' MATERIALS
P.O. Box 53097
Atlanta, GA 30355
800-877-3242
Offers: Catalog of artists' supplies and accessories, including oil and acrylic paints, easels, brushes, drawing materials, studio tools, adhesives, portfolios, modeling materials, frames, and more. **Free catalog.**

CRAFTS JUST FOR YOU!
2030 Clinton Avenue
Alameda, CA 94501
800-272-3848
Offers: The complete tole-painting catalog. Includes such items as books, kits, paint, brushes, and accessories. **Catalog $5.**

CUTBILL & COMPANY
274 Sherman Avenue North, Unit 213
Hamilton, Ontario, Canada L8L 6N6
800-960-3592
Offers: Block-printing supplies and materials, including kits, glazes, and block-printing pads. **Free catalog.**

GAIL GRISI STENCILING, INC.
P.O. Box 1263
Haddonfield, NJ 08033
609-354-1757
Offers: Wide selection of precut stencils and stencil paints.
Catalog $3 (refundable with first order).

JANOVIC/PLAZA'S INCOMPLETE CATALOGUE FOR DECORATIVE AND SCENIC PAINTERS
30–35 Thomson Avenue
Long Island City, NY 11101
800-772-4381
(outside New York)
718-786-4444
Offers: Brushes, tools, and materials for both home and commercial painting, as well as many specialty items used in restoration and preservation work. **Free catalog.**

NEW YORK CENTRAL ART SUPPLY, INC.
62 Third Avenue
New York, NY 10003
800-950-6111
(outside New York)
Offers: Fine art catalog offering paints, pastels, mediums, brushes, canvas, easels, and more. **Free catalog.**

THE OLD FASHIONED MILK PAINT COMPANY, INC.
436 Main Street
P.O. Box 222
Groton, MA 01450
508-448-6336
Offers: Collection of authentic reproduction paint supplies, including milk paint, antique crackle finish, and more. **Free catalog.**

OLD VILLAGE PAINT COLOURS
Stulb's Old Village Paint
P.O. Box 1030
Fort Washington, PA 19034
215-654-1770
Offers: A collection of authentic acrylic restoration paints, Colonial Williamsburg Simulated Buttermilk paint, paste stains, clear glaze products, and beeswax polish.
Free catalog.

POTTERY BARN
P.O. Box 7044
San Francisco, CA 94120-7044
800-922-5507
Offers: Small selection of faux finishing products, including woodwash and distressing kit, crackle glaze, stencil kits, colorwash kit, and books. Catalog devoted mostly to furniture, housewares, and gifts.
Free catalog.

STENCIL HOUSE OF NEW HAMPSHIRE INC.
P.O. Box 16109
Hooksett, NH 03106
800-622-9416
603-625-1716
Offers: Precut stencils, stencil paints, stencil brushes, and varnish.
Catalog $3.50 (refundable with first order).

STENCIL WORLD INC.
P.O. Box 1112
Newport, RI 02840
401-847-0870
Offers: Large assortment of precut stencils, as well as stenciling books, supplies, and paint.
Catalog $3.50.

STU-ART
2045 Grand Avenue
Baldwin, NY 11510
800-645-2855
Offers: Catalog of artists' supplies, including frames, mats, watercolor paper, and picture-saver panels.
Free catalog.

PAPER SUPPLIES

BAUDVILLE
5380 52nd Street, SE
Grand Rapids, MI 49512-9765
800-728-0888
Offers: Software, bordered paper, postcards, place cards, name badges, note cards, plaques, embossers, accessories, and specialty products. **Free catalog.**

THE BOOKBINDER'S WAREHOUSE
31 Division Street
Keyport, NJ 07735
908-264-0306
Offers: Full range of bookbinding supplies, including leather, vellum, parchment, paper, finishing tools, book cloth, books, and related supplies and equipment. **Free catalog.**

COLOPHON BOOK ARTS SUPPLY, INC.
3046 Hogum Bay Road NE
Olympia, WA 98516
360-459-2940
Offers: Supplies, equipment, and books related to marbling, paper-making, and bookbinding.
Free catalog.

GOLD'S ARTWORKS INCORPORATED
2100 North Pine Street
Lumberton, NC 28358
800-356-2306
Offers: Papermaking supplies, including cotton pulp, molds and deckles, kits, and pigments.
Free catalog.

HANDMADE RECYCLED PAPER BY LOTUS DESIGN
P.O. Box 1993
Union City, CA 94587
800-487-5279
Offers: Handmade recycled papers and papermaking supplies (minimum order $100). **Free catalog.**

ON PAPER
3342 Melrose Avenue NW
Roanoke, VA 24017
800-820-2299
Offers: A complete line of paper supplies, including designer paper, preprinted stationery and sets, novelty paper, colored paper, software, books, and office products.
Free catalog.

POTPOURRI

A WORLD OF PLENTY
P.O. Box 1153
Hermantown, MN 55810-9724
218-729-6761
Offers: Potpourri and sachet ingredients, oils, herbs, teas, and tools. **Catalog $1.**

THE GINGER TREE
245 Lee Road #122
Opelika, AL 36801
334-745-4864
Offers: Full line of potpourri and supplies. **Free catalog.**

SAN FRANCISCO HERB CO.
250 14th Street
San Francisco, CA 94103
800-227-4530
Offers: Complete line of spices for cooking and crafting and potpourri recipes and ingredients.
Free catalog.

TOM THUMB WORKSHOPS
P.O. Box 357
Mappsville, VA 23407
804-824-3507
Offers: Potpourri, herbs, spices, essential oils, dried flowers, and crafts. **Free catalog.**

SEWING AND FABRIC

ATLANTA THREAD & SUPPLY CO.
695 Red Oak Road
Stockbridge, GA 30281
800-847-1001
Offers: Wide assortment of thread, notions, buttons, scissors, drapery hardware, press boards, and other related supplies and equipment.
Free catalog.

CLOTILDE INC.
2 Sew Smart Way B8031
Stevens Point, WI 54481-8031
800-772-2891
Offers: Large selection of sewing supplies, notions, equipment, and tools, including sewing machine accessories, tables, books, patterns, and gifts.
Free catalog.

THE FABRIC CENTER
485 Electric Avenue, P.O. Box 8212
Fitchburg, MA 01420-8212
508-343-4402
Offers: Large selection of fabrics for home decorating use, including lightweight fabrics for draperies and bedding, multipurpose fabrics suitable for almost any interior use, and heavyweight fabrics designed for upholstery applications.
Catalog $2.

NANCY'S NOTIONS LTD.
P.O. Box 683
Beaver Dam, WI 53916-9976
800-833-0690
Offers: Wide assortment of sewing supplies and notions, including fabric, patterns, books, lace, thread, and videos. **Free catalog.**

SEW/FIT COMPANY
P.O. Box 397
Bedford Park, IL 60499
800-547-4739
708-458-5600
Offers: Sewing supplies and tools, books, cutting mats, needles, sewing machine feet, rotary cutters, and thread. **Free catalog.** ◆

Sources & Resources

The following are specific mail-order sources for particular items, arranged by article.

Most of the materials necessary for the projects in this issue are available at your local craft supply store, florist's, fabric shop, or bead and jewelry supply. Generic craft supplies, such as scissors, all-purpose glue, paint, ribbon, and thread, can be ordered from such catalogs as Craft King, Dick Blick Art Materials, Newark Dressmaker Supply, Pearl Paint Co. Inc., or Sunshine Discount Crafts. The following are specific mail-order sources for particular items, arranged by article. The suggested retail prices listed here were current at press time. Contact the suppliers directly to confirm prices and availability of products.

How to Block-Print a Faux Wallpaper, *page 6*
Fleur-de-lis motif from Dover Publications. Computer mousepad for $5.99 from Viking Office Products. Block-print material from $17.95 from Cutbill & Company.

Silk Flower Chair Sash, *page 9*
Silk flowers from $2 per stem, 24" leafy stems from $4.90, cascades of blossoms from $4.50, 27" foliage stems from $2.90, all from May Silk.

Folk Art Village, *page 10*
Balsa wood available from Pearl Paint. Dollhouse picket fence gates for $4.25, shutters for $2.95 a pair, and newel posts for $1 from Fred's Carpenter Shop.

Three Easy Antique Finishes, *page 12*
Unfinished wood objects from $4.99 from The Park Shoppe. Deco Art Weathered Wood from $1.35 from The Artist's Club.

Easy-Sew Lap Quilts, *page 14*
Fabric from $11.99, tassel fringe from $3.99, flat braid trim from $2.59, and tassels from $1.99, all from Calico Corners.

The Best-Tasting Chocolate Leaves, *page 17*
White chocolate starting from $1.59 from Dairy Fresh Chocolates. Fresh rose leaves $3.68 per pound from A World of Plenty.

The Fastest Way to Make Your Own Paper, *page 18*
8" x 10" mold and deckle for $29.95 from Kindred Spirit.

Three Projects to Make from Handmade Paper, *page 20*
Handmade marbled or painted paper from $9.50 per sheet and endpaper from $5.50 per sheet from The Bookbinder's Warehouse, Inc. Chipboard from 95¢ from Dick Blick.

How to Make a Decorative Tassel, *page 23*
Embroidery thread from 33¢ per skein from The American Needlewoman. Fabric-wrapped beads from 50¢ from Tinsel Trading. Dye from $3.79 from The Jerry's Catalog. Openwork braid from $2.59 and black silk cord for 99¢ per yard, both from Calico Corners. Velvet ribbon from $2.50, half-round buttons from $1, and rattail from 85¢, all from North End Fabrics.

How to Make a Fabric-Covered Desk Screen, *page 26*
Fabric from $5.95 from North End Fabrics. Gold Rub 'n Buff paint from $2.19 from The Jerry's Catalog. Unfinished wood dollhouse railing from $5.95 from Fred's Carpenter Shop. Four wood beads for 79¢ from Enterprise Art.

The Best Household Tools for Graining, *page 28*
Unfinished wood item from $4.99 from The Park Shoppe. Winsor & Newton watercolor paints from $1.93 from Pearl Paint.

How to Make a Fabric-Covered Lampshade, *page 30*
Fabric starting at $8 from Calico Corners. Lampshade laminate paper from $6.25 per half yard from The Park Shoppe.

The Best Way to Make Ribbon Roses, *page 32*
Wire-edged ribbon from $1.20 per yard from Newark Dressmaker Supply.

Fast Faux Marbling Techniques for Tabletops, *page 34*
Lint-free cloths from $2.95 from Cutbill & Company. Cheesecloth from $2.90 and round stencil brush for $5.50, both from Dick Blick.

Shabby Chic Slipcover *page 37*
Pictured is Richloom Fabrics Group's Signature III Collection "Harmonica" pattern in Sage ($18.99 per yard; welting from 99¢ per yard), available from Calico Corners.

Field Guide, *page 41*
Piccolo Washed, $16.99 per yard; Starfish, $26.99 per yard; Cupid's Arrow, $25.99 per yard; Connelley Washed, $17.99 per yard; and Sconset, $18.99 per yard, available from Calico Corners. Thayer Fabrics, $25.95 per yard; Pacific Weavers starting at $13.95 per yard; and Robert Allen, $23.95 per yard, available from North End Fabrics.

Gilded Candles, *back cover*
Gold composition leaf from $4.10 from Pearl Paint.

❧ ❧ ❧ ❧ ❧

The following companies are mentioned in the listings provided above. Contact each individually for a price list or catalog.

A WORLD OF PLENTY
P.O. Box 1153, Hermantown, MN 55810-9724; 218-729-6761

THE AMERICAN NEEDLEWOMAN
P.O. Box 6472, Fort Worth, TX 76115 800-433-2231

ARTIST'S CLUB
5750 NE Hassalo, Building C Portland, OR 97213 800-845-6507

THE BOOKBINDER'S WAREHOUSE, INC.
31 Division Street, Keyport, NJ 07735 908-264-0306

CALICO CORNERS
203 Gale Lane, Kennett Square, PA 19348-1764; 800-777-9933

CRAFT KING
P.O. Box 90637, Lakeland, FL 33804 800-769-9494

CUTBILL & COMPANY
274 Sherman Avenue North, Unit 213 Hamilton, Ontario, Canada L8L 6N6 800-960-3592

DAIRY FRESH CHOCOLATES
57 Salem Street, Boston, MA 02113 800-336-5536

DICK BLICK ART MATERIALS
P.O. Box 1267, Galesburg, IL 61402-1267 800-447-8192

DOVER PUBLICATIONS, INC.
31 East 2nd Street, Mineola, NY 11501 (telephone orders not accepted)

ENTERPRISE ART
P.O. Box 2918, Largo, FL 34649 800-366-2218

FRED'S CARPENTER SHOP
Route 7, Pittsford, VT 05763 802-483-6362

THE JERRY'S CATALOG
P.O. Box 1105, New Hyde Park, NY 11040; 800-U-ARTIST

KINDRED SPIRIT
1714 Government Street, Victoria, British Columbia, Canada V8W lZ5 604-385-4567

MAY SILK
16202 Distribution Way, Cerritos, CA 90703; 800-282-7455

NEWARK DRESSMAKER SUPPLY
6473 Ruch Road, P.O. Box 20730 Lehigh Valley, PA 18002-0730 610-837-7500

NORTH END FABRICS
31 Harrison Avenue, Boston, MA 02111 617-542-2763

THE PARK SHOPPE
54 Lake Street, Hamburg, NY 14075 716-648-2577

PEARL PAINT CO., INC.
308 Canal Street, New York, NY 10013-2572; 800-221-6845 X2297

SUNSHINE DISCOUNT CRAFTS
P.O. Box 301, Largo, FL 34649-0301 800-729-2878

TINSEL TRADING
47 West 38th, New York, NY 10018 212-730-1030

VIKING OFFICE PRODUCTS
24 Thompson Road, P.O. Box 1052 East Windsor, CT 06088-1052 800-421-1222 ◆

Quick Decorating Ideas

Turn everyday items into a fabulous sideboard setup.

RELAXED ELEGANCE

Instead of relying on traditional formal solutions, the new decorating philosophy emphasizes relaxed elegance. Raiding closets and drawers for common household items, then turning them into great decorative accents, is the norm.

To create a two-tier sideboard, first push a table up against the wall and stack magazines in adjacent piles. Create a centerpiece by tying string around a cardboard box. Cut foliage to the height of the box plus three inches, then slip it behind the string to create a hedge all the way around the box. Drape a curtain over the magazines and half of the table, gathering it in soft folds. Set the box on top of stacked magazines. Drape a second curtain on the table and tuck the edges under.

To finish the centerpiece, stuff newspaper inside the box, then fill the cavity with fruit. Top the pile with bunches of grapes. Cut rose stems to five inches and wrap each in a water-soaked paper towel, then enclose the paper towel in a plastic bag. Insert the roses between the fruit. Add English ivy and lemons cut in narrow slices. Make candleholders by slicing off the bottom one-eighth inch of an apple or pear. Carve a tube-shaped hollow in the core, then insert a candle into the hole. Use pieces of ivy for napkin rings. To create a pedestal cake plate, overturn a large bowl, then center and position a dinner plate on the bowl footing. Use Fun-Tack (or substitute) to further secure the plate. ◆

COLOR PHOTOGRAPHY:
Carl Tremblay

STYLING:
Gabrielle Derrick de Papp/Team

Great Marriages

Looking for new combinations of color? Use these pairs to spur your imagination.

Hunter green and yellow

Tomato red and light aqua

Light aubergine and lime green

COLOR PHOTOGRAPHY:
Carl Tremblay

SILHOUETTE
PHOTOGRAPHY:
Furnald/Gray

COLOR IDEAS

One of the single most powerful elements in decorating is color. You can use these combinations of surprising and exuberant colors the next time you set out to change simple shapes into smashing design statements, or experiment with your own color combinations to expand your visual vocabulary.

The combinations here can be applied to different portions of a single piece of furniture, like a tabletop and its legs or a dresser and its drawers. Or break up the color pair by applying them to nearby spaces, like a window frame and a door. (*Note*: To achieve the high gloss finish on these stools, we used enamel sign paint. It's a little messier to clean up, but worth the trouble.) ◆

Quick Projects

To inspire new interest in napkins you've had for awhile, it's easy to decorate the edges in unexpected ways. Here are some ideas to get you started.

DECORATIVE EDGE

A. Painted Border

Select a plain hemstitched napkin. Lay the napkin flat on a protected work surface. Use a flat, stiff brush to apply a light coat of fabric paint to one hemmed edge; to paint an angled line at each corner, lay a plastic ruler diagonally from the corner and run the brush against it. Rotate the napkin and paint each adjacent border a different color. Let it dry. Turn the napkin over and paint the underside of the hem in the same color sequence.

B. Silk Flowers

Select a plain hemstitched napkin. Use a needle and thread to tack a cluster of silk flower petals every two inches around the entire napkin hem.

C. Pom-Pom Fringe

Machine-stitch pom-pom fringe around napkin so the pom-poms extend just beyond the folded edge. When you return to the starting point, overlap the tape ends, trim off the excess, and stitch down securely. Apply fray preventative to the exposed tape end to prevent raveling.

D. Self-Fringe

Select a loosely woven yarn-dyed fabric napkin with a ¼" machine-stitched hem. Cut off ¼" hem. Then use a pencil and a straightedge to draft a light line 1" all around from the cut edge. To make fringe, ravel each edge by pulling off the outside threads one by one until the marked line is reached.

E. Appliqué Motif

Select a plain hemstitched napkin in a pastel color. Open the napkin, lay it flat, and arrange two white embroidered motifs on one corner in a mirror image. Mark the position of each motif with straight pins. Then use fabric glue to attach the motifs one at a time.

F. Ribbon and Lace

Machine-stitch 1½"-wide Cluny-style cotton lace around a napkin about ¼" from the edge. When you return to the starting point, overlap the lace ends by 1", trim off the excess, and fold the free end under by ½". Then stitch down. Use fabric glue to attach ¼" grosgrain ribbon to the lace edge to conceal the stitching. ◆

COLOR PHOTOGRAPHY:
Carl Tremblay

Gilded Candles

Transfer sheet of gold composition leaf onto piece of brown kraft paper. Remove protective cellophane wrapper from pillar candles, touching exposed wax as little as possible. Lower candles one by one horizontally onto leaf, then roll to adhere gold leaf to candle surface. (Candle has enough adhesiveness of its own so you don't need size.) Repeat to affix additional sheets of leaf until entire surface is gilded. Leave gaps ungilded for an antique look, or fill gaps by tearing leaf into small pieces and applying by hand. Use cotton ball to burnish leaf and brush off any leftovers.

COLOR PHOTOGRAPHY: **Carl Tremblay**   STYLING: **Gabrielle Derrick de Papp/Team**

NUMBER TWELVE

SPRING 1996

Handcraft
ILLUSTRATED

Victorian Spring Basket

Quick-Preserve Fresh Roses with Paraffin

Folk Art Rooster
Antique This Wood and Copper
Figure in Minutes

Perfectly Pressed Flowers
Perfect Flowers Everytime with
Our Unique Padded Press

Decorating Frames with Wallpaper Borders
Transform Any Frame Instantly

The Best Shortcuts for Faux Fresco Painting
Substitute Stucco for Plaster;
Create Texture with Glazes

Lace-Bordered Stationery
Learn the Antique Craft
of Pergamano

ALSO
Gilded Icing Monogram
Foolproof Verdigris Finish
Quick Marbled Giftwrap
Faux Spanish Tile Floorcloth
Homemade Fragrant Waters

$4.00 U.S./$4.95 CANADA

61 >

0 74470 83731 2

Contents

Make this wood-and-copper rooster in a day's time. See article, page 6.

Handpainted keep-sake box, page 12

Lace-bordered announcements, page 18

Wallpaper-covered frames, page 41

COVER PHOTOGRAPH:
Carl Tremblay

Handcraft
ILLUSTRATED

EDITOR
Carol Endler Sterbenz

EXECUTIVE EDITOR
Barbara Bourassa

ART DIRECTOR
Amy Klee

SENIOR EDITOR
Michio Ryan

MANAGING EDITOR
Keith Powers

EDITORIAL PROD. COORDINATOR
Karin L. Kaneps

DIRECTIONS EDITOR
Candie Frankel

COPY EDITOR
Gary Pfitzer

EDITORIAL ASSISTANT
Elizabeth Cameron

❧

PUBLISHER AND FOUNDER
Christopher Kimball

EDITORIAL CONSULTANT
John Kelsey

MARKETING DIRECTOR
Adrienne Kimball

CIRCULATION DIRECTOR
Elaine Repucci

ASS'T CIRCULATION MANAGER
Jennifer L. Keene

CIRCULATION COORDINATOR
Jonathan Venier

CIRCULATION ASSISTANT
C. Maria Pannozzo

PRODUCTION DIRECTOR
James McCormack

PROJECT COORDINATOR
Sheila Datz

PRODUCTION COORDINATOR
Pamela Slattery

SYSTEMS ADMINISTRATOR
Matt Frigo

PRODUCTION ARTIST
Kevin Moeller

❧

VICE PRESIDENT
Jeffrey Feingold

CONTROLLER
Lisa A. Carullo

ACCOUNTING ASSISTANT
Mandy Shito

OFFICE MANAGER
Tonya Estey

Handcraft Illustrated (ISSN 1072-0529) is published quarterly by Boston Common Press Limited Partners, 17 Station Street, P.O. Box 509, Brookline, MA 02147-0509. Copyright 1996 Boston Common Press Limited Partners. Second-class postage paid at Boston, MA, and additional mailing offices, USPS #011-895. For list rental information, please contact List Services Corporation, 6 Trowbridge Drive, P.O. Box 516, Bethel CT 06801; (203) 743 2600; fax (203) 743-0589. Editorial office: 17 Station Street, P.O. Box 509, Brookline, MA 02147-0509; (617) 232-1000, FAX (617) 232-1572. Editorial contributions should be sent to: Editor, *Handcraft Illustrated*. We cannot assume responsibility for manuscripts submitted to us. Submissions will be returned only if accompanied by a large, self-addressed stamped envelope. Subscription rates: $24.95 for one year; $45 for two years; $65 for three years. (Canada: add $3 per year; all other countries add $12 per year.) Postmaster: Send all new orders, subscription inquiries, and change of address notices to *Handcraft Illustrated*, P.O. Box 7448, Red Oak, IA 51591-0448. Single copies: $4 in U.S.; $4.95 in Canada and other countries. Back issues available for $5 each. PRINTED IN THE U.S.A.

From the Editor

L ITTLE DID I KNOW SOME THIRTY-FIVE YEARS ago that a cross-stitch border of dogwood, and the smell of boxwood after a drenching rain, would configure the shape of my future. At certain moments in my life, I've spent time looking back to see where I came from, partly so I might know a bit more about where I'm headed.

Several years ago, my husband, John, and I were camping in the Blue Ridge Mountains of Virginia. One day, we decided to visit Staunton, a town I had visited each summer as a child. My paternal grandparents had immigrated there from Europe, and although they had since passed away, I wanted to find the little house where I had spent so many happy summers.

As a child, the ride from our home in New York to Virginia seemed to take forever, and it wasn't until we had stopped at a country store and gas station within the Staunton city limits that we knew we were almost there. I remember the store's porch, which held a cooler filled with soda bottles lodged in icy slush. We would plunge our arms elbow-deep into the cooler and fish out bottles of Dr. Pepper. Nothing tasted better on a hot summer day.

When John and I stopped to ask for directions, however, there was no country store—just a sleek gas station with a Coke machine and snack dispensers. An attendant told us to drive down the road and make a right at Fredericks Street. The sun had moved from behind thick clouds as we made our turn, brightening a modern subdivision of new homes, placed in neat rows on the low mountain. We drove slowly up and down the paved street, but I grew discouraged by the unfamiliar sights. We had parked on the side of the road for a rest when I inadvertently found myself staring at the roof of my grandmother's house, now caught in the glare of the afternoon sun. The memories came rushing back.

I remembered the white curtains on the wide open windows. My grandmother had cross-stitched dogwood, the Virginia state flower, along their borders. I think this was her way of connecting to her new country. To this day, I love cross-stitch. On one wall she had hung a framed piece of schnerenschnitte, paper artfully

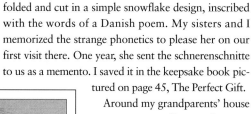

I remembered the white curtains on the wide open windows. My grandmother had cross-stitched dogwood, the Virginia state flower, along their borders.

folded and cut in a simple snowflake design, inscribed with the words of a Danish poem. My sisters and I memorized the strange phonetics to please her on our first visit there. One year, she sent the schnerenschnitte to us as a memento. I saved it in the keepsake book pictured on page 45, The Perfect Gift.

Around my grandparents' house was a cement walkway, where my grandfather used to sit and survey the garden when it was too hot to work the soil or pick the vegetables. The walkway was bordered by perfectly trimmed boxwood bushes. Often, a late afternoon thunderstorm passed through. When the rain stopped and the sun returned, the musty scent of boxwood filled the walkway. Today, I often work with boxwood in my dried flower designs, and I never fail to stop and breathe more deeply when I pass boxwood after a rain.

In this same walkway, my father and grandfather sat together smoking Cuban cigars after dinner. Sometimes they played their harmonicas, the sweet notes bouncing off the surrounding mountains. Years later, I bought a harmonica. I also found a ring designed in the shape of a cigar band, which I wear today.

As appealing as my memories were, the house in front of me presented a disappointing reality. The overgrown boxwood hedges nearly obscured the windows. A refrigerator shrouded in plastic stood by the front door and seemed to breathe in and out as wind blew around the corner of the house. The strong fragrance of boxwood was present and reassuring, but the smell of a just-lit cigar confused me momentarily. I turned around to see a construction worker holding a cigar in his hand. He explained that the house was being razed to make room for the next subdivision.

I took one last look around and went back to the car. The memories I carried back with me that day were more vivid than the ones with which I had come. And those are the ones I'll choose to build upon.

Notes from Readers

Learn how to choose fresh roses, distinguish between newspaper and newsprint, locate garden figurine molds and cameo soaps, and achieve a crackled finish without a kit.

Choosing Fresh Roses

What characteristics should I look for when buying roses to make sure I get fresh, long-lasting blooms?

ABIGAIL HINELINE
NORTH PLATTE, NE

In the January 1996 issue of *Florist's Review,* René Van Rems, AIFD, PCFI, of the California Cut Flower Commission, says fresh roses should have the following characteristics: (1) a firm neck, i.e., the part of the stem found under the calyx, (2) guard petals in place, (3) a firm head (pinch lightly to check), (4) no brown color around the edges, (5) green stems (examine the bottom too), (6) visible veins that are not wrinkled, and (7) a straight neck. Van Rems also recommends avoiding roses that begin to wilt after being taken out of the cooler, or those with small heads that look like Hershey Kisses.

Fabric Stiffener for Delicate Fabrics

Can you recommend a fabric stiffener that can be used on very fragile material such as organdy? I want to be able to shape the fabric without having it stick together.

DOLORES BERKHIMER
GRASS VALLEY, CA

A spray-on fabric stiffener called Stiffen Stuff might give you the control you're looking for. Be sure to test it first by spraying it on a scrap of the cloth, then let it dry. Clotilde Inc. (2 Sew Smart Way, B-8031, Stevens Point, WI 54481-8031; 800-772-2891) sells it by mail order in two sizes: six ounces ($2.80) and a sixteen-ounce refill ($4.16).

Searching for Parchment Flower Supplier

I have been searching for a company that carries parchment flowers, specifically roses in shades of white to dusty rose on one spray, and magnolias in peach, blue, and white. Can you help?

SANDRA STEVENS
NEPTUNE, NJ

We were able to locate one source for parchment flowers, May Silk in Cerritos, California. The company carries a parchment French rose, but no magnolias. The two-inch-diameter, open rose costs $1.90 per stem. It comes in burgundy, blue, mauve, purple, and white (subject to availability). To order flowers or to receive May Silk's catalog, call or write the company at 13262 Moore Street, Cerritos, CA 90703; 800-282-7455.

Sources for Garden Figurine Molds

Can you recommend a supplier for molds I can use to make simple figures—rabbits, groundhogs, frogs, etc.—for my garden?

MARILYN C. SIMON
BETHANY, CT

A company called Deep Flex Plastic Molds makes a variety of rubber and latex molds for figures such as rabbits, frogs, hedgehogs, foxes, and tortoises. The larger molds are about twelve inches high and cost about $46; the smaller molds are three and one-half to five and one-half inches high and cost about $11. For outdoor use you want to use concrete (not plaster, which will absorb moisture); the company's technical advisor recommends a product called Outcast, which you can finish with acrylic paint and sealer. You may need additional tools such as a trim knife and cleaning supplies. For technical help, call Deep Flex at 800-251-1402 or write: 1200 Park Avenue, P.O. Box 1257, Murfreesboro, TN 37133-1257.

Materials for Wicker Furniture Repair

Where can I find split half-reed to repair wicker and bamboo furniture?

JEAN HERING
STUDIO CITY, CA

Many caning supply stores sell this material by mail; one in your area is Frank's Cane and Rush Supply, 7252 Heil Avenue, Huntington Beach, CA 92647; 714-847-0707. The company provides a free catalog and also has a retail store.

Whistler Brushes by Mail Order

I'm looking for a mail-order company that carries brushes for decorative painting, specifically badger-hair softener, hog-hair softener, sword liner, dragger, and stippler, all from a company called Whistler.

KATE BRENNAN
LAREDO, TX

New York Central Art Supply (800-950-6111 or 212-477-0400) and Pearl Paint (800-221-6845) are two mail-order companies that carry the Whistler line of specialty faux finish brushes. (These brushes are not available directly from the manufacturer, Loew-Cornell, in Teaneck, New Jersey). Badger softeners and hog-hair softeners are made from pure badger hair or hog hair, respectively, and are generally used only with oil-based paints, although more advanced decorative painters use them with acrylic or latex paints for certain special effects. Stipplers are wide, thick brushes that distribute paint with a spattering, or wavering, stroke. Draggers are even wider and give you a subtle mixture of wide stripes. Liners are thin, long-bristled brushes that give you a precise, fine line.

Neither company carried a sword liner, but Janovic/Plaza (800-772-4381 or 718-786-4444) carries a brush called a sword striper, used for painting freehand lines.

Removing Mildew from Painted Surface

I've noticed some mildew on a painted wood bench that is located underneath an arbor in my garden. Is there a way to remove the stain without repainting the entire bench?

CAROLINE CARUTHERS
WARREN, CT

You can try wiping the mildewed areas of the bench with a solution of water and chlorine bleach in a 3:1 ratio. But test a small area first (underneath the seat) to make sure the solution doesn't harm the paint finish.

Chances are, though, that despite the cleaning, the mildew will return, as it thrives in shady areas that don't get enough sun or air circulation. A better long-term solution might be to strip off all the mildewed paint, then clean those areas with a bleach and water solution or a mildew fungicide. Let the areas dry thoroughly, then apply a mildew-resistant primer and a fresh coat of paint.

Newsprint Versus Newspaper

Some of your project material lists call for newsprint and some call for newspaper; what's the difference?

PAULA JACKSON
COUNCIL BLUFFS, IA

We're glad you asked. The two names can be misleading: *newsprint* is the technical term for the blank paper that is printed with ink to produce a *newspaper*, i.e., the daily or weekly paper you read. Given the names, you would expect it to be the reverse. You can find the plain, unprinted newsprint sheets at art supply stores.

Locating Glue-On Button Shanks

Do you know of a source for glue-on button shanks? I like to make my own buttons out of various materials, and have searched everywhere without success.

ANA TRONCOSO
PRINCETON, NJ

So did we. You might try using the back half of a flat brass, self-covering button from a kit. One company that sells flat buttons-to-cover is Atlanta Thread & Supply, 695 Red Oak Road, Stockbridge, GA 30281; 800-847-1001. The glue you use will depend on the materials being joined; silicone glue is a good choice for joining different types of materials, such as metal to plastic.

Looking for Cameo Soap

Can you help me find a source for cameo soaps? They have a relief design like those found on cameo jewelry.

VELMA R. BRUMBAUGH
BONNERS FERRY, ID

We found an easy way for you to make your own cameo soaps. Craft King Discount Craft Supply, in Lakeland, Florida (800-769-9494), sells various cameo soap molds for about $2.95 each, and one-pound blocks of soap for about $7 (five pounds for $28). To make soap, you melt the chipped soap in the microwave, add color and/or fragrance, and mold it.

Crackle Finish Without a Kit

I used a kit to create a crackle finish on an old painted table, but the overall crackle pattern appeared feathery. How can I avoid this on future projects?.

KATE CHRISTIANSEN
BELLEROSE, NY

This feathery effect seems to be inherent in commercial, water-based, acrylic crackle kits. The crackling tends to occur along the brushstroke lines, resulting in an artificial-looking finish. Instead of a crackling kit, we recommend using Bull's Eye spray-on shellac and LeFranc and Bourgeous crackle picture varnish. Spraying shellac, instead of brushing it on, gives you an even finish over a painted surface. You can then apply the crackle picture varnish and rub in a color such as burnt umber to highlight or accentuate the crackle pattern.

Removing Wax from Tablecloth

I had the dripping wax from a few candles overflow onto my tablecloth. Is there a safe way to remove the wax?

FRAN SITARSKI
BUFFALO, NY

Before you launder or professionally clean the tablecloth, try the following remedies. If the wax was not very hot when dripped, it may not have seeped into the cloth. In that case, you can try gently scraping it up with a spoon. If that approach doesn't work, chill the wax by applying something cold, such as a frozen food package, and then try to remove it.

If the wax still remains, place a brown grocery bag under the tablecloth in the area of the spilled wax, then place a second bag on top of the tablecloth over the spill. With an iron set to moderate heat (synthetic setting), run the iron over the brown bag. The wax will melt onto the paper. Move the bags both under and on top of the tablecloth until the paper has absorbed all the spilled wax. You will know the wax has been removed when the bags no longer pick up the melted wax.

How to Pry Up a Damaged Tile

What's the best way to pry up a damaged vinyl floor tile without ruining the tile surrounding it?

JAMIE MOORE
HAZELTON, ID

The first step in removing a vinyl tile is to warm it in order to make it more pliable. Place a piece of aluminum foil on the tile, then carefully warm it with an iron set at low to moderate heat. To remove the tile, cut into the center with a utility knife and pry it up from the center outward with a putty knife.

Dyeing Marble Flooring

Is there a way to dye marble flooring? My entryway and kitchen floors are white and gray marble-tiled, and I'd like to warm them up a bit.

SUSAN E. KRZYWICKI
STUDIO CITY, CA

We don't recommend dyeing marble. Although marble is porous, which allows it to stain and take color, a dye will only affect the top layer of the marble and the grout in between. This will wear off quickly, particularly in high-traffic areas, creating a patchy, scuffed look. It is possible to shellac the marble for a yellowish, warmer cast, but this finish eventually wears off too.

Sealing Wax with Wicks

I recently used a sealing wax stick to seal some envelopes but was unhappy with the results. When I held the stick over a candle to soften the wax, it frequently ignited. When the wax did soften, it often dripped and cooled before I could use it on the stationery. How can I avoid this in the future?

LINDEN MCARDLE
LANSING, MI

One of our photographers used a sealing wax stick with a built-in wick to seal her wedding invitations. The stick with a wick is superior because, when lighted, it supplies a constant source of heat, allowing you to melt the wax directly over the area being sealed. Pearl Paint's main store carries a rainbow assortment of sealing wax with a wick, starting at $1.45 for a two-inch stick. The company can be reached at 800-221-6845 or 212-431-7932.

Seaching for "Rottenstone"

I have been unable to find anyone who knows what rottenstone is, where I would buy it, or anything else about the product. I would appreciate your help.

E. G. CHADWICK
SPRINGFIELD, VT

Rottenstone is an abrasive powder made from volcanic ash and is available in the wood-finishing section of many hardware stores. We used Rainbow Rotten Stone from Empire Blended Products, Inc. in Bayville, New Jersey, to finish the pot in our "Bittersweet Topiary" article (*see* photograph on page 22, September/October 1995).

Lampshade Frames

Do you have a source for ordering lampshade frames? I'm specifically looking for tulip-shaped wire frames that I can cover myself.

MICHELLE HAMPTON
HOUSTON, TX

You can contact Munro Corporation at 800-638-0543 or 810-594-1590 for lampshade frames, parts, and accessories. The address is 3954 West Twelve Mile Road, Berkley, Michigan 48072.

Variations on Hand-Molded Soap

Charlene Brussat, of Jacksonville, Oregon, wrote to tell us how she made the soap (with a few variations) featured in our article "The Fastest Way to Make Hand-Molded Soap" (November/December 1995). To shred the soap, she substituted a salad shooter for the Mouli grater. She added color to the soap before she microwaved. And instead of hand-rolling the soap into balls, she sprayed hollow cookie cutters (both tin and plastic) with nonstick cooking oil and pressed the foamy soap mixture into them to create seasonal shapes.

Solution for Dried Jewelry Glue

What can I do to keep my tube of jewelry glue (Goop) ready to use immediately? Opening and closing the cap while I work is a nuisance. But if I leave the cap off, the glue often dries out at the tip, causing me to squeeze out more than I need.

JENNIFER LONG
SYRACUSE, NY

You can remove the cap from the tube and invert the tube in a glass of water. The water prevents the glue from drying out, and it conveniently keeps the glue at the tip of the tube where you need it for quick application. However, this method cannot be used on water-soluble white glues.

Turning Beach Glass into Ornaments

I'd like to make Christmas ornaments out of colored beach glass. Do you have any suggestions?

FELICIA HOBBS
SAN FRANCISCO, CA

You might try wrapping individual stones with short lengths of 18- or 24-gauge gold, silver, or brass wire, then linking them like chandelier crystals or wiring them into clusters or star shapes. Attach a loop of wire or a standard tree ornament hook to hang the ornament. Beading wire is less strong but can be used to wrap a delicate "belt" or "cage" around larger pieces of glass, which you could then incorporate into a wreath. Different sizes and colors of glass would also be pretty arranged around the base of a candle or in a glass bowl. ◆

Quick Tips

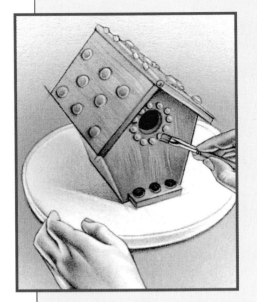

LAZY SUSAN WORK SURFACE

An old lazy Susan or a turntable designed to go inside a kitchen cabinet makes a handy crafting aid. Patricia Baralt of Tustin, California, designs flower centerpieces on her turntable, rotating it as she works so that she can easily view all sides of the arrangement. Frances Tabor of Midland, Texas, uses hers when painting small three-dimensional objects.

BLENDING COLORS

Joan Allen of Eatontown, New Jersey, submits this variation on the moist paper towel palette (see Quick Tips, September/October 1995).

1. Layer moist paper toweling in a Styrofoam tray, then lay a sheet of tracing paper, cut to fit, on top.

2. Squeeze out the acrylic paint colors. The tracing paper makes an ideal surface for blending colors.

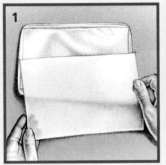

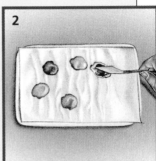

REUSABLE FLOWER STAND

To spray dried roses, Anne Welter of Sheridan, Wyoming, has devised a reusable stand.

1. Cut drinking straws in half and insert the pieces part of the way into florist foam bricks.

2. Insert the dried rose stems into the straws so the roses stay upright, and mist the roses lightly with clear acrylic spray.

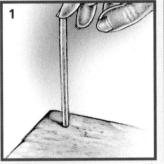

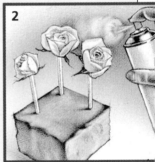

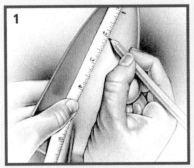

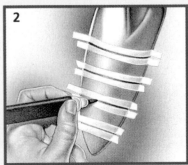

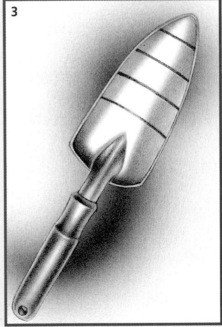

TROWEL RULER

Use a permanent marker to draw lines one inch apart on both sides of your trowel blade. The lines will help you gauge hole depth or the distance between plants when you are transplanting seedlings or perennials.

1. Measuring from the tip, mark the blade in 1" increments.

2. Lay parallel pieces of narrow tape to straddle each mark.

3. Color the narrow area between the tape guidelines with a permanent marker.

ILLUSTRATION:
Harry Davis

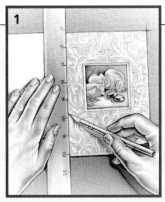

FRAMES FROM GREETING CARDS

Mary McCreery, of Boynton Beach, Florida, writes that fancy greeting cards are an excellent source for pretty borders and mats, which can be used for paper projects or to frame photos.

1. **Open the card flat. Use an X-Acto knife and a straight-edge to cut off the front just inside the fold.**

2. **Cut a window opening inside a frame, following the card's printed design. Remove the unwanted section.**

3. **Use the frame to mat a photograph or a small painting.**

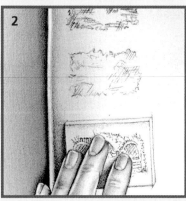

RUBBER STAMP CLEANUP

To loosen and clean water-based inks from rubber stamps without wetting the wooden base, Freda Clax of Tinton Falls, New Jersey, uses tea bags.

1. **Press the wet stamp down onto a used, moist tea bag.**

2. **Press the stamp onto a paper towel to shed the excess ink. Repeat using the same tea bag until the stamp comes clean.**

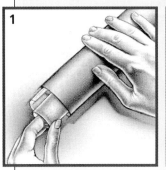
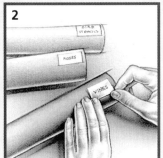

CONVENIENT PATTERN STORAGE

To keep her painting patterns clean and crease-free, Debra Mossey of Vernon, Vermont, uses cardboard tubes.

1. **Roll the pattern, stencil, or artwork slightly smaller than the tube's diameter, then place it inside.**

2. **Label each tube, and place patterns inside.**

EASY BEAD HANDLING

To prevent tiny seed beads from rolling around, Emily Giustino of Long Beach, California, finds Post-it Notes a handy aid.

1. **Tear off a set of three to four notes so that they remain attached to one another (the extra paper thickness discourages curling).**

2. **Press the adhesive portion of the bottom note onto the beads.**

3. **Turn the notes so the beads are face up. Write the bead color number or pattern symbol on the plain part of the note for easy reference as you work.**

4. **The beads can now be picked up easily with the point of your needle.**

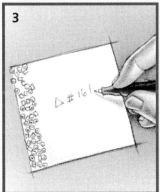
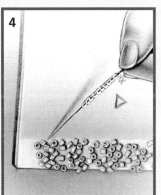

STABILIZING A WOBBLY BASKET

Any wobbly basket can be stabilized almost instantly by attaching a plain ring from a wooden embroidery hoop to the base. Choose a ring that's slightly smaller than the basket base. Set the basket on the ring, maneuvering it until the balance is right, then hot-glue the ring in place.

Folk Art Rooster

Use ready-made antiquing solutions to instantly weather a handcrafted wood-and-copper rooster.

❧ BY CANDIE FRANKEL

MATERIALS

- **Thin copper sheet, at least 6" x 11"**
- **4" x 24" x ¼" basswood**
- **4"-diameter x ½"- to 1"-thick wood or cork disk**
- **16-gauge steel wire**
- **Modern Options Patina Antiquing Kit**
- **Modern Options Instant Iron**
- **Modern Options Instant Rust**
- **Wood glue**

You'll also need:
body, tail feather, and foot patterns (*see page 47*); bandsaw or coping saw; tin snips or aviation shears; drill with ¹⁄₁₆" bit; hammer; wire cutters; three to four 1½" clamps; small pieces wood or chipboard (to use with clamps); scrap board; finishing nail; 100- and 220-grit sandpaper; masking tape; small disposable plastic cups; access to photocopier with enlarger; scissors; pencil; ballpoint pen; fine-tip permanent pen; goggles; work gloves; hot-glue gun; and newsprint.

Other items, if necessary: metal file (if using aviation shears).

ILLUSTRATION:
Nenad Jakesevic

COLOR PHOTOGRAPHY:
Carl Tremblay

STYLING:
Gabrielle Derrick dePapp/Team

This rooster body looks like antique iron, but it's made of wood that has been treated with Instant Iron and Instant Rust, for a genuine rusted metal finish.

ROOSTER WEATHER VANES WERE a common sight on top of New England barns in the early 1900s. Made by welding together two reliefs of cut and embossed copper, these weather vanes are difficult to find today and can cost thousands of dollars. I wanted to create a smaller, affordable reproduction for display indoors.

I have no special metalworking skills, so to simulate the design and antique patina of the originals, I began investigating alternate construction and finishing methods that are easy for a beginner. After experimenting, I came up with two effective shortcuts: a mixed media approach that combines copper sheeting, for the tail and legs, and basswood, for the rooster's body; and the use of a Modern Options patina kit and solutions to create authentic antique finishes on both copper and wood. These products

are the key to the convincing patinas. In a few hours' time, I saw the copper pieces age from shiny burnt apricot to an ashy green, and the wood rooster body turn into a piece of rusted iron. The rooster looks as though it is made entirely from metal that has aged and weathered after years of outdoor exposure.

The solutions I chose are Instant Iron and Instant Rust, for the rooster body, and Patina Green, sold separately or as part of the Modern Options Patina Antiquing Kit, for the tailfeathers and feet. (This kit is also used in "Foolproof Verdigris Finishing," page 35.) All three solutions are easy to use and can be purchased separately. If this is your first attempt at this type of project, I recommend buying the kit. It provides a better introduction to the overall process, includes special solutions for cleaning and sealing your project pieces, and supplies the equipment you'll need to get

started, such as latex gloves and disposable brushes. You'll be using only a small amount of each solution for your rooster, leaving plenty for other projects in the future. The kit's disposable items can be easily replenished with a visit to your local hardware or paint store.

I was intrigued to discover that, unlike typical "faux finish" products, which create a painted surface that imitates verdigris or rust, the Modern Options solutions produce the real thing. Essentially, the solutions accelerate the chemical oxidation that occurs naturally, causing copper to turn green and iron to develop rust. Being made of wood, the rooster body must be "rusted" in a two-stage process. First, you apply a couple of coats of Instant Iron. This solution contains particles of real iron that adhere to the surface in a thin layer. The surface dries overnight, and then you can brush Instant Rust across it. The oxidation process begins immediately, with the first traces of rust appearing in about twenty minutes and continuing to intensify over several days' time. Keep in mind that while the solutions brush on easily like paint, they do contain powerful chemical compounds. *Be sure to read the full instructions on the bottles and in the kit before proceeding, and wear splash goggles to protect your eyes.*

To cut out the wood and copper rooster pieces, you can use commonly found or specialized tools. My design calls for two identical wood rooster bodies to be glued together, much like the double relief construction of the originals, with the copper feet and tail feathers positioned and sandwiched in between. Although the body looks hefty once assembled, each half is only one-quarter inch thick, making for easy cutting. If you don't have access to a band saw for cutting, you can use a coping saw. Move the blade so the teeth point toward the handle. Hold the saw so the blade is vertical and the handle is at the bottom. Rest the basswood sheet on the tabletop so the area marked with the pattern hangs over the edge. To saw, move the blade up and down, always working away from your body. The saw cuts on the downward stroke. After both pieces are cut out, tape them together and sand the edges simultaneously until they match.

To cut the copper sheeting, you can use tin snips or aviation shears. I prefer tin snips for the smooth clean-cut edge they make, but they do require strength and endurance to operate. You may prefer using aviation shears instead, which have a second spring-type pivot that provides extra leverage and makes the cutting go easier. The drawback to aviation shears is the tiny ridges that appear along the cut edge. Although the ridges can be filed down with a metal file, you may end up spending just as much or more time than if you had used tin snips and taken frequent breaks. Whichever tool you choose, be sure to wear work gloves when cutting the copper, since the cut edges are sharp. You can find copper sheeting at hardware, roofing, and plumbing supply stores.

To hold my rooster upright, I devised a base from an old cork stopper (recycled from a wide-mouth cookie jar) and a piece of heavy wire. Another option for the base is two wooden plaques glued back to back and rusted to match the rooster body.

The rooster design is by Ritch Holben, an architect and designer from Nahant, Massachusetts.

INSTRUCTIONS
Cutting the Pieces

1. *Trace patterns on basswood and copper.* Photocopy patterns, enlarging so body is 7" high (*see* page 47). Cut out patterns. Tape body pattern to basswood and trace outline with pencil; press eye with ballpoint pen to mark wood. Turn pattern over and trace second body in mirror image. Tape feather and foot patterns to copper; trace with permanent pen.

2. *Cut out and sand bodies.* Using bandsaw or coping saw, cut wood on marked lines. Tape two body halves together, then sand cut edges by hand with 100-grit sandpaper until they align; reposition tape as needed; sand again with 220-grit sandpaper until smooth (illustration A). To indent eye on each side, set finishing nail head against wood and tap pointed end with hammer (illustration B). Remove tape and label both inside surfaces (these will not be treated with patina).

3. *Cut feathers and foot.* Using tin snips or shears and wearing gloves and goggles, cut feathers and foot pieces on marked lines. To straighten bent or curled edges after cutting, lay them flat on wood board and pound with hammer (illustration C). Use metal file to wear down ridges on edges cut with shears.

Creating the Patinas

Note: Apply Modern Options patina solutions to wood and copper pieces in stages. Follow product directions carefully. Provide adequate ventilation, protect work surface with newsprint, and wear rubber gloves (included in kit) and goggles. Pour small amount of solutions needed into plastic cups, rinse out brushes (also included in kit) between coats, and dispose of brushes and cups when through.

1. *Treat wood body pieces and base with Instant Iron and Instant Rust.* Shake Instant Iron vigorously before using. Brush onto edges and outer surface of body halves and base. Let dry 1 hour, then apply second coat. Let dry overnight. On second day, apply one coat Instant Rust and let dry. For more intense rusting, apply second and third coats, allowing 20 minutes' drying time between coats. Let dry overnight.

2. *Treat copper pieces with Patina Green.* Following kit directions, clean tail feathers and feet with Metal Master, rinse well, and dry. Lay pieces flat on newsprint. Brush Patina Green solution (from antiquing kit) lightly onto exposed surfaces, brushing in direction tail feathers would grow (illustration D). Let dry 30 minutes, apply second light coat, and let dry again. Turn pieces over and repeat.

3. *Apply protective sealer.* Let all wood and metal pieces cure 3 to 4 days. Following kit directions, brush on very light coat of Primo Primer and Sealer and let dry.

Assembling the Pieces

1. *Glue pieces together.* Lay bodies flat, rust finish facing down. Apply wood glue to unfinished surface of each body. Set feathers and foot in position on one body piece, as marked on patterns, then set second body piece on top (illustration E). Clamp sandwiched pieces, using scrap wood pieces to prevent dents. Let dry overnight, then unfasten clamps. Sand edges of body lightly to expose iron finish.

2. *Attach rooster to stand.* Mark center of wood or cork disk. Lay rooster flat on work surface so legs overhang edge, then bend legs down slightly. Using 1/16" bit, drill 1/2"-deep hole into body at arrow, as marked on pattern (illustration F). Drill into center of disk. Cut 5 1/2" length of wire. Apply dot of hot glue to each end, then insert ends into drilled holes in stand and rooster (illustration G). ◆

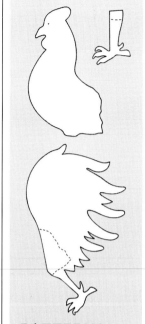

PATTERNS
See page 47 for pieces and enlargement instructions.

MAKING THE ROOSTER

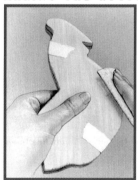

A. Tape the two cut rooster bodies together, then sand the edges simultaneously until they align.

B. To make an eye, turn a finishing nail upside down on the mark, then tap the pointed end to dent the wood.

C. Pound any bent copper edges flat with a hammer.

D. Brush copper pieces with patina solution in the direction tailfeathers would grow.

E. Sandwich the copper feathers and feet between the two body pieces and glue them together.

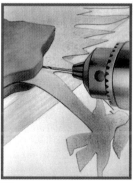

F. Drill a hole in the rooster body and another hole in the center of the base.

G. Join the rooster to the base with a short piece of 16-gauge wire.

Victorian Spring Basket with Waxed Flowers

Quick-preserve fresh roses with paraffin and a cold bath, then use them to decorate a basket.

&. BY CAROL ENDLER STERBENZ

MATERIALS

- **Basket with handle**
- **6 medium light-pink roses**
- **6 medium yellow roses**
- **4 pink rosebuds**
- **1 yard 1½"-wide white velvet ribbon**
- **3 bricks (¾ pound) household paraffin**
- **Thin craft or florist wire**
- **White thread**

You'll also need:
empty 16-ounce can; 1-quart saucepan; stove; knife; cutting board; chopstick; jar of water; deep bowl of cold water; pruning shears; waxed paper; 2 empty cereal or cracker boxes; tape; ruler; X-Acto knife; scissors; tongs; needle; paperweight; and hot-glue gun.

Other items, if necessary: green florist tape (for preventing waxed stems from cracking).

ILLUSTRATION:
Nenad Jakesevic

COLOR PHOTOGRAPHY:
Carl Tremblay

Light-pink and yellow waxed roses adorn this basket. Within a few hours of waxing, the edges will brown slightly, lending the look of antique velvet.

AFTER MANY YEARS OF MAKING pretty but predictable Easter baskets—I hot-glued dried flowers to the rim and tied the handle with ribbon—I began looking for a fresh approach that would be both beautiful and unique. This year I decided to imitate the porcelain baskets of England and France.

To achieve a porcelain effect, I turned to the Victorian practice of waxing fresh-cut roses. The process is simple: Dip each flower head in molten paraffin for two to three seconds, just long enough to coat it with a wax layer. The wax hardens to the touch within a minute; it then takes about twenty minutes for the dense flower heads to harden clear through so that they can be safely wired to the sides of a basket.

While the method works well with all types of roses and buds, I found that hot wax can alter a rose's color. I used light-pink and yellow roses in my basket design, but I also tried waxing red, medium-pink tinged with red, and white roses to see how they would fare. After a few hours, several colors turned slightly brown near the edges and on the outer petals, a natural result of the moisture loss that waxing incurs. Browning made the white roses look dingy and unappealing, but it actually enhanced the light-pink and yellow roses, giving them the antique effect found in Victorian velvet roses. Note: Wax-preserved roses will last anywhere from seven to fourteen days. By two weeks, most of my roses had turned brown.

I combined two ways of controlling moisture content so that the entire rose does not brown and wilt upon impact with the wax. I let the liquid wax cool slightly so it was warm but not hot when it touched the plant matter. I melted the wax—ordinary household paraffin—in a can set into a saucepan of simmering water. As soon as the wax was liquefied, I turned off the stove but kept the double-boiler setup intact. When the water was no longer visibly simmering, I began dipping the roses. I found that the hot water bath surrounding the can kept the wax warm and liquefied for two or three successive dippings. At the first signs of thickening, I turned the stove back on, brought the wax back to its hot liquid state, and began again. Without this reheating, the cooling wax was too dense to coat each flower smoothly. Immediately after lifting the rose from the molten wax, I plunged it into a bowl of cold water.

I also experimented with three ways of supporting the freshly dipped roses: laying them flat on waxed paper, suspending them upside down, and standing them upright. Laying the wet roses flat distorted the shape of the head, while the upside-down position allowed drips to collect and harden on the tips of the petals. The upright position clearly produced the smoothest, most blemish-free coating, because any lingering liquid wax ran back down in between the petals. To hold the roses upright, I made a stand by turning an empty cereal box on its side and making X-shaped cuts in the surface. As soon as each rose was coated, I trimmed back its stem to two inches and inserted it into one of the openings. When all my roses were waxed, I carefully lifted each one and dipped its cut stem into warm wax to seal in moisture.

Waxing rose leaves is just as easy. Use tongs to hold each single leaf or cluster by the stem, dip it into the molten wax, then lay it on waxed paper until the wax hardens, about three minutes. Apply just a light coating of wax for the leaves. While no real danger of browning leaves exists, overwaxing will give them a slightly artificial look, and the thick wax will crack easily if overhandled.

Once you've waxed your roses and leaves and let them harden, you can wire them in a pleasing arrangement to the sides of a basket. To prevent the waxed stems from cracking or breaking during the wiring, you may want to wrap them in green florist tape first. Choose a thin craft or florist wire, wind it around the rose and leaf stems, then insert the ends into the weave of the basket and twist them together on the inside. After attaching the roses to the basket, you can soften and fill out the rim of the basket with a ruffled ribbon. I hand-tacked tiny pleats

MAKING THE SPRING BASKET

A. Dip each rose into the liquid paraffin, then dip into cold water.

B. Trim the rose stem, then prop it upright in a cereal box stand so the wax can cool.

C. Seal the cut ends of each rose stem by dipping them in warm liquid paraffin.

D. Dip the leaves in the paraffin using tongs, then lay the leaves flat on waxed paper to dry.

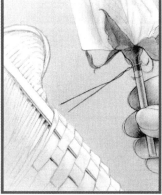

E. Attach the waxed roses to the basket with thin wire. Twist the wire ends together inside the basket.

F. Hand-tack small pleats in white velvet ribbon, then hot-glue the ribbon to the basket rim.

step 2. Holding each leaf cluster stem with tongs, quickly dip into warm liquid paraffin and remove, then lay flat on waxed paper until wax hardens, about 3 minutes (illustration D).

Assembling the Basket

1. *Attach waxed roses to basket.* Weight basket with paperweight if top-heavy. Wrap each rose, bud, and leaf stem with florist tape if desired. Wrap 3" length of wire once around a rose stem and twist, then insert wire ends into two separate openings between basket slats near base of handle (illustration E). Draw wire ends to inside of basket so rose rests snugly against outside; twist ends together to secure. Wire three pink and three yellow roses and two buds to each side of basket, then wire leaves in place around them.

2. *Make and attach ribbon decoration.* At middle of ribbon, pinch-pleat width of ribbon and hand-tack using needle and thread. Tack additional pleats every 3" along ribbon length in both directions. Starting as close to basket handle as possible, hot-glue middle pleat to basket rim. Glue adjacent pleats 2½" apart around rim in both directions to create ruched effect (illustration F). Trim off ends where they meet and glue down.

3. Remove the paperweight and fill basket with colored eggs, or as desired. ◆

Use a green basket and darker roses for a more dramatic look.

across the width of a white velvet ribbon, then hot-glued it to the basket rim to suggest ripples of porcelain.

Keep in mind that the added weight of waxed roses, particularly near the rim, can make a basket top-heavy. You can easily remedy this problem by placing some dyed hard-boiled eggs inside, or by laying the basket gently on its side and allowing the eggs to cascade out onto a display surface.

INSTRUCTIONS
Waxing the Roses

1. *Set up double boiler and work area near stove.* Using knife and cutting board, cut three paraffin bricks into ½" pieces. Drop two-thirds of pieces into can, set can in saucepan, and add water until half full. To make stands, tape boxes closed, lay flat, and make sixteen ½" X-shaped cuts, 4" apart, across each top surface. Lay sheet of waxed paper on counter. Using pruning shears, clip rose and bud stems 6" below calyx and set in jar of water. Clip and set aside 4 to 6 three-leaf clusters.

2. *Wax roses and buds.* Bring double-boiler water to boil, then reduce to simmer. Using chopstick, stir paraffin until liquefied. Drop in more paraffin with tongs and melt until can is three-quarters full. Turn off heat. When water stops simmering, hold rose upside down by stem and dip it at slight angle into warm liquid paraffin, without touching rose to can, and hold for 2 to 3 seconds (*see* illustration A). Remove immediately, dip into bowl of cold water, and lift out. Clip stem to 2" and set upright in stand (illustration B). Wax remaining roses and buds in same way, reheating to liquefy paraffin whenever it becomes dense or cloudy. Remove double boiler from stove. When roses have hardened at least 5 minutes, remove one by one from stand, dip each stem into warm liquid wax to seal cut end (illustration C), and replace in stand. Let all roses harden 20 minutes or longer.

3. *Wax leaves.* Reheat paraffin as in

Pinafore Chair Cover

Create the look of farmhouse chic with a low-sew seat cover.

🐾 BY JEANNE BEUTEL

MATERIALS

- **Country chair (cross rail back)**
- **2⅛ yards 45"-wide cotton fabric**
- **Thread to match fabric**
- **Heavy-duty thread in contrasting color**

You'll also need:
sewing machine; iron; shears; rotary cutter; rotary cutting guide marked for 45-degree angle; dust-free chalk; clear acrylic ruler; pins; pencil and paper; and dressmaker's tape measure.

DESIGNER'S TIP

If you're making several matching slipcovers for a set of chairs, make one pattern from muslin instead of fitting each seat individually. Then use the muslin pattern to mark and cut all the seats. Reconfigure the cutting layout so you cut one continuous front ruffle strip for each slipcover instead of piecing sections together to make up the needed length.

ILLUSTRATION:
Mary Newell DePalma

COLOR PHOTOGRAPHY:
Carl Tremblay

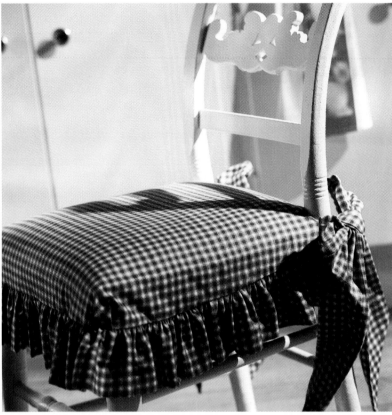

Create this country seat cover without using a pattern: Simply fit the fabric directly on your chair to create a box lid and ties.

TO CREATE A FABRIC SEAT COVER for this ordinary yard-sale chair, I took my cue from the chair's design. The contour of the back and the chair's overall silhouette reminded me of a farmhouse kitchen, so I decided to pursue a country look.

The chair was made of wood, which had been covered with several layers of paint, and it had an upholstered seat. For an overall touch-up, I added two coats of white acrylic paint over the existing paint layers. I knew the fresh coats would add to the desired affect—particularly if I chipped through them at spots to let another color peek through. After letting the paint dry, I applied paste wax to protect the finish.

I wanted to keep the upholstered seat in place because it made the chair more comfortable to sit on. The fabric was in surprisingly good shape, but the pattern was too formal for the country look. To avoid re-upholstering the seat, I decided to make a simple cover-up to conceal the existing fabric.

The cover-up had to evoke the farmhouse feeling and stay in place on the chair. My inspiration was an old pinafore-style apron with a small plaid print and ruffles. Using that style as a starting point, I added sashes to tie in bows around the post to keep the seat cover in place.

In general, the cover-up idea works best with small overall prints or solid colors. A larger or more pronounced pattern is not as suitable because the small area of the seat won't show off the pattern to its full effect. You can use striped fabrics, although the overall effect is stronger and more lively when the stripes run diagonally across the ruffle. To achieve this effect, the fabric strips that make up the ruffle must be cut on the bias instead of the straight grain.

Jeanne Beutel is a designer from Glen Cove, New York.

INSTRUCTIONS
Cutting the Fabric

1. *Measure chair seat.* Using tape measure, take the following seat measurements (*see* illustration A): (a) from front to back, beginning and ending at apron edge; (b) across widest part of seat at front, beginning and ending at apron edge; (c) around seat front, beginning and ending at back posts; and (d) between back posts. Jot down all measurements.

2. *Cut basic slipcover pieces.* Refer to Sample Cutting Layout (*see* next page) and use rotary cutter. Lay fabric flat, right side up. At one corner of fabric, cut seat rectangle measuring (a + 1") x (b + 1"). For sashes, cut four 6" x 54" strips. For ruffle, cut two strips 7" x (1.25 x c); cut one strip 7" x (2.5 x d). Set aside remaining fabric for facings.

3. *Miter-cut sash and ruffle strips.* Stack sash strips so two face up and two face down. On top piece, make mark dividing 54" edges into 30" and 24" segments; reverse mark on opposite edge. Cut diagonally between marks to yield eight miter-cut sash strips. Stack two longer ruffle strips face up. Using 45-degree mark on cutting guide, miter-cut strips at one end as in Sample Cutting Layout.

Fitting the Seat

1. *Pin-fit seat front.* Center seat rectangle right side up on chair seat; fold back corners diagonally from posts so fabric lies flat. Tuck and pin front corners (illustration B).

2. *Rough-cut seat front to fit around posts.* Using shears, cut diagonally into each folded-back corner to inner chair post (illustrations B and C, cut 1). Fold fabric flaps up against post and slit cut edge to outer edge of chair post (illustrations B and C, cut 2). Allow fabric to relax and hang down against side and back of chair. Rub chalk along fabric to mark lower edge of apron rim on sides of chair. Trim off corners below tucks (illustration C). Remove pins and finger-press tucks to mark them.

3. *Complete post cutaways.* Lift fabric from chair and lay flat. Using chalk, draw line from back edge to side edge ¼" inside cuts 1 and 2; curve gently at cut 1 (illustration D). To ensure symmetry, fold fabric in half and pin; cut on marked rim and post cutaway chalk lines through both layers, then turn piece over and cut on any remaining chalk line. Trim rounded corners, and clip into fabric edge a scant ¼" to mark tuck folds.

4. *Mark and cut two facings.* Fold reserved fabric in half right side in. Lay folded seat fabric on reserved fabric as template and draw chalk line along cutaway edge and back and side edges for 2½". Remove folded seat fabric. Measure and mark reserved fabric 2½" from marked line to complete facing outline. Cut on marked outline through both layers (illustration E).

Sewing and Assembly

1. *Sew four sashes.* Pin eight sash strips right sides together in pairs. Machine-stitch matching sewing thread ½" from edge on long and diagonal edges; leave short end open. Clip corners, turn right side out, and press.

2. *Sew front and back ruffles.* Join two front ruffle strips by sewing diagonal edges together; press seam open. Fold each ruffle strip in half lengthwise right side in, and stitch short ends. Turn strip right side out and press with raw edges matching. Using heavy-duty thread, machine-baste ⅜" and ⅝" from raw edges. Draw up bobbin threads to gather.

3. *Join sashes, ruffles, and facings to seat.* Repin seat corner tucks to match clips and machine-baste ½" from edge. Pleat open end of each sash accordion-style to measure 1½" (illustration F detail), then machine-baste to cutout edge

of right side of seat fabric ½" in from back and side edges (illustration F). Fold sashes onto center of seat, then pin front and back ruffles to seat edge, adjusting gathers to fit; allow ½" between ruffle ends and cutout edge (illustration G). Pin facings right side down on cutout edge. Machine-stitch through all layers ½" from edge all around (illustration H).

4. *Fit finished cover on chair.* Clip corners, then turn slipcover right side out. Fit onto chair seat and tie sashes around posts in bows (illustration I). ◆

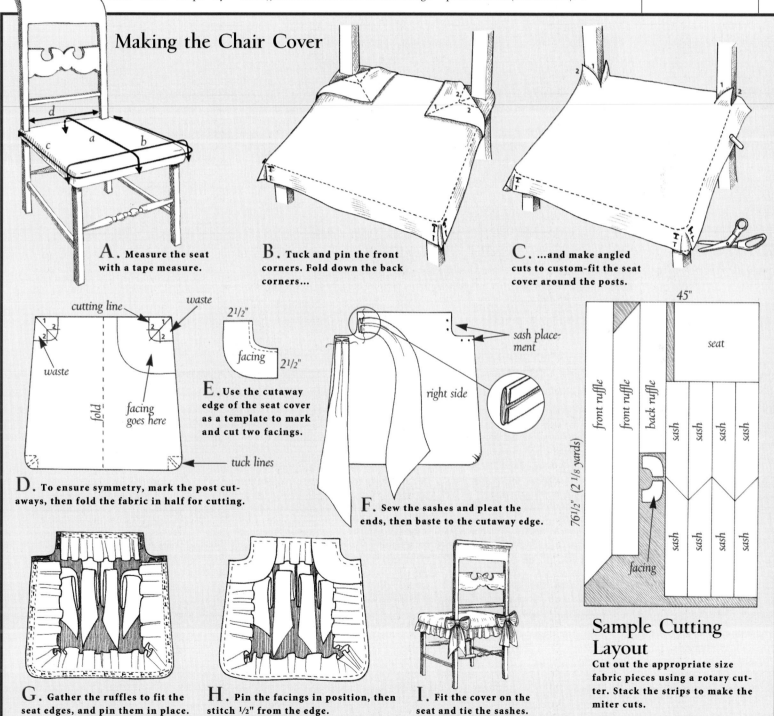

Making the Chair Cover

A. Measure the seat with a tape measure.

B. Tuck and pin the front corners. Fold down the back corners...

C. ...and make angled cuts to custom-fit the seat cover around the posts.

cutting line waste
waste
fold
facing goes here
tuck lines

D. To ensure symmetry, mark the post cutaways, then fold the fabric in half for cutting.

2½" facing 2½"

E. Use the cutaway edge of the seat cover as a template to mark and cut two facings.

sash placement
right side

F. Sew the sashes and pleat the ends, then baste to the cutaway edge.

G. Gather the ruffles to fit the seat edges, and pin them in place.

H. Pin the facings in position, then stitch ½" from the edge.

I. Fit the cover on the seat and tie the sashes.

45"
seat
front ruffle front ruffle back ruffle
sash sash sash sash
sash sash sash sash
facing
76½" (2 ⅛ yards)

Sample Cutting Layout

Cut out the appropriate size fabric pieces using a rotary cutter. Stack the strips to make the miter cuts.

Handpainted Keepsake Box

Use two easy-to-learn brush strokes to create a rose garland design.

🖎 BY LINDA STURM, CDA

MATERIALS

- 7" x 5" x 2½" oval wooden box with lid
- Four ½" mushroom plugs (for legs)
- 2-ounce DecoArt Americana acrylic paints: Shale Green DA152, Antique Teal DA158, Light Buttermilk DA164, Brandy Wine DA79, Honey Brown DA163, Yellow Ochre DA8, Lamp (Ebony) Black DA67
- 2-ounce DecoArt Dazzling Metallics Glorious Gold DA71 acrylic paint
- 2-ounce DecoArt Wood Sealer DS16
- Krylon Matte Spray Finish #1311
- Wood glue

You'll also need:
rose and bud patterns (*see* page 14); Sta-Wet palette; Bettebyrd "Aqua-Sable" brushes: 400 liner #2, 200 flat #8 and #10; Robert Simmons Tolemaster liner brush #10/0; ¾" flat brush; 1" foam brush; palette knife; small jars with water; stylus; 220-grit wet-dry sandpaper; tack cloth; tracing paper; #1 and #3 pencils; plastic eraser; and paper towels.

Other items, if necessary:
Old toothbrush and scrap paper (for spattering).

COLOR PHOTOGRAPHY:
Carl Tremblay

SILHOUETTE PHOTOGRAPHY:
Furnald/Gray

STYLING:
Gabrielle Derrick dePapp/Team

Making this wooden keepsake box requires learning two basic brush strokes: a comma and a C stroke.

THE PAINTED DESIGN ON THIS oval wooden box may look complicated, but it uses just two basic brush strokes—a comma and a C stroke—that have been the hallmark of folk artists around the world for centuries. The ability to execute these brush strokes is the key to successful decorative painting, and while professional strokework takes years of practice, you will be pleasantly surprised at your first attempts.

Before you begin painting the box, practice the basic brush strokes on a piece of stiff paper, much the way you practiced writing letters when you were learning script. For each stroke, you'll notice that a rhythm develops and the strokes begin to appear smoother and more graceful. For a comma stroke, used to develop rose and bud petals, and as an accent, press a liner brush firmly against the surface and then lift it up gently as you complete the stroke. For a C stroke, used to accent and shade leaves, roses,

and buds, pick up the paint with a flat brush, which creates a chiseled edge; begin with light pressure, add more pressure in the middle of the stroke, and end with a light liftoff. Straight lines and dots may seem straightforward, but practice will help you learn to control the pressure needed to produce thick and thin bands, or delicate circles and ovals of color. The important thing to remember is that because the brush does most of the work, make sure you select the correct size and type of brush for each stroke in the design. The motifs will seem to flow from the brush itself, and you will be amazed at how inspiring even practicing brush strokes can be.

Once you are comfortable working the basic brush strokes, you can begin painting the oval box. Proceed in three stages: (1) Sand the box

and paint the background color; (2) transfer the design to the box lid and sides; and (3) paint the leaves, roses, and buds using the same brush strokes you practiced on paper.

A closing note about paint: Don't be intimidated by having to mix paints. I prefer mixing my own colors so that the colors appear more related and natural-looking in my painting. Colors taken straight from the bottle will make the roses and leaves appear harsher and slightly less realistic. If you opt not to mix colors, try to match purchased colors to the mixed colors as closely as possible.

Linda Sturm, of Cowlesville, New York, is a Certified Decorative Artist (CDA) and a member of the Society of Decorative Painters.

INSTRUCTIONS
Preparing the Box Surface

1. *Paint box with base coat colors.* Sand wood lightly and remove dust with tack cloth. Using foam brush, apply wood sealer to box and lid. Let dry ½ hour, then resand and wipe dust. Using ¾" flat brush, paint box and lid Shale Green, thinning paint slightly with water for smooth application. Let dry ½ hour, resand, and wipe dust. Apply second coat if needed. When base coat is dry, paint base, box interior, lid rim, and lid interior Antique Teal. Paint mushroom plugs Glorious Gold and set aside.

2. *Transfer designs to box and lid.* Using #3 pencil, trace rose and bud patterns. Cut out tracings on designated cutting lines. Turn each tracing face down and retrace using #1 pencil. Lay lid tracing face up on lid and transfer design lines with stylus, pressing lightly to avoid denting wood. Position box tracing against outside of box so lower edge touches base, and transfer with stylus. Reposition tracing and repeat transfer process around box until you reach the starting point.

Painting the Leaves

1. *Begin by mixing four leaf colors on palette.* For shading color, mix 6 drops Antique Teal and 1 drop Lamp Black with palette knife. Use #2 liner brush to mix remaining colors as you need them:

PAINTING THE LEAVES

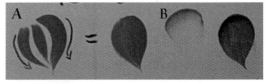

A. Start by basecoating each leaf...

B. ...then shade each leaf at the base.

For medium cool green (color 1), mix a small amount of shading color into Shale Green. For medium warm green (2), mix small amount of Honey Brown into medium cool green. For light cool green (3), mix additional Shale Green into medium cool green.

2. *Base-coat each leaf.* Use #2 liner brush and three overlapping strokes (*see* illustration A). Load brush with paint by pressing bristles flat into fan shape, then shed excess on paper towel. Press brush firmly against surface, then lift gently as you complete stroke to shape leaf tip. Follow design to paint leaves 1, 2, and 3 using color mixes described in previous step. Rinse and dry brushes on paper towel when changing colors.

3. *Use side-loaded brush to shade each leaf at base.* Dip #10 flat brush into shading color so that only half of bristles are coated. Shed excess on paper towel. With leaf tip at right, run brush in C stroke along base of leaf at left. Start stroke with very light pressure, increase pressure as you approach center, then lift brush from surface gradually to end off (illustration B).

Painting the Roses and Buds

1. *Begin by preparing palette.* For pink roses (color P), mix 5 drops Light Buttermilk and 1 drop Brandy Wine. Set out remaining colors as you need them: Brandy Wine to shade pink roses, Yellow Ochre for yellow roses (Y), Honey Brown to shade yellow roses, and Light Buttermilk for overstrokes.

2. *Base-coat roses and buds using #2 liner brush.* For smooth coverage, thin paint slightly with water, then flatten brush to load paint. Following design at right for color placement, use P and Y colors described in previous step to paint circle for each rose and oval for each bud (illustrations C and I).

3. *Use side-loaded brush to shade roses and buds.* Use #10 flat brush for roses, #8 flat brush for buds. Shade pink roses and buds with Brandy Wine, yellow roses and buds with Honey Brown. Run appropriate brush in C stroke along base and bowl of each rose and bud (illustrations D and J).

4. *Paint overstrokes to develop rose and bud petals.*

Refer to design for stroke placement. Flat-load #2 liner brush in pink paint for pink roses and buds, or Yellow Ochre paint for yellow roses and buds, then dip tip of loaded brush in Light Buttermilk. Proceed as follows:

Strokes 1, 2, and 3: Set brush down and pull comma stroke around and under bowl: Press brush firmly against surface, draw it in gentle curve, then lift up gradually to end stroke in sharp point. Pick up a bit more Light Buttermilk on tip of brush (always flattening when loading) and add one or two tiny commas alongside first stroke (illustrations E and K).

Stroke 4: Wipe brush on paper towel, but do not wash. Flat-load base color, pick up small amount of Light Buttermilk on one corner of brush, then touch brush to palette to soften line where colors change. With Light Buttermilk corner of brush at top, paint C stroke under bowl. Leave a crescent of base color visible under stroke (illustrations F and K).

Strokes 5, 6, 7, 8, and 9 (roses only): Load brush as for stroke 4. With Light Buttermilk corner of brush at bottom, apply paint in short, freeflowing strokes from outside of base in toward center; reload brush as needed (illustration G).

5. *Paint stamens inside bowl of each rose and bud.* Load 10/0 liner brush with Light Buttermilk paint. Tilt brush handle toward you, touch tip of brush to surface, then lift to produce tiny oval dot. Paint line of five dots for roses, three dots for

PATTERNS
See page 14 for patterns.

PAINTING THE ROSES AND BUDS

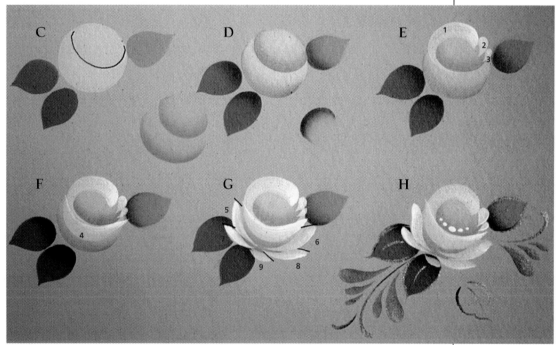

C. **Paint each rose circle pink or yellow.**

D. **Shade the base and bowl with two C strokes.**

E. **Paint the upper petals with comma strokes.**

F. **Paint a petal under the bowl with a C stroke.**

G. **Paint the other petals with short strokes.**

H. **For stamens, paint five tiny oval dots.**

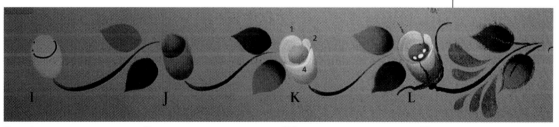

I. **Paint each bud oval pink or yellow.**

J. **Shade and define the bowl with a C stroke.**

K. **Paint small and large petals to fill out the bud.**

L. **For stamens, paint three tiny oval dots.**

buds, making center dot slightly larger (illustrations H and L).

Adding the Details

1. *Paint stems and line work.* Thin shading color with water, then load onto 10/0 liner brush and tip with Glorious Gold. Paint thin vines and stems in smooth motion. To outline leaves and paint veins, load brush with Glorious Gold and tip with shading color (illustrations H and L).

2. *Paint bud calyxes.* Load 10/0 liner brush with shading color and tip with Glorious Gold. Beginning at base of bud, paint thin stroke up and out from bud, quivering brush as you go and ending in sharp point. Add dot of shading color at base to accentuate it (illustration L).

3. *Paint filler comma strokes.* For each group of strokes, load #2 liner brush with medium warm green (2) leaf color and tip with Glorious Gold. Paint largest stroke in group first, then successively smaller ones (illustrations H and L).

4. *Spatter surface using toothbrush (optional).* To load bristles, scrub toothbrush into Antique Teal slightly thinned with water. To release fine spray, hold brush handle about 4" above sheet of scrap paper and run your thumb across bristles. If spatters are tiny, paint is too thick; if spatters are large and do not hold shape, paint is too thin. Adjust paint as needed, then spatter box; move your hand to avoid concentrating spattering in one area.

5. *Apply protective sealer.* First, glue gold mushroom plugs to base for legs. Let box dry overnight. Use plastic eraser to lift off any remaining pencil lines. Following manufacturer's directions, spray with several light coats Krylon Matte finish; let dry between coats. ◆

Rose Garland Patterns

Box lid, actual size

Box side, actual size

Quick Bouquet Party Favor

Create this arrangement in about ten minutes using a pot, floral foam, dried flowers, and sheet moss.

❧ BY FRANCOISE HARDY

MATERIALS

- **40 miniature dried yellow chrysanthemum heads with stems**
- **2½"-diameter terra-cotta pot**
- **Floral foam (water-absorbing type)**
- **Sheet moss**

You'll also need:
Table knife; spray mister; and ruler.

BEFORE YOU THROW OUT THAT dried flower wreath, swag, or arrangement from last year, consider recycling some of the beauty in a miniature party favor. This tiny arrangement takes about ten minutes to make, and requires just forty miniature dried flowers, a two-and-one-half-inch terra-cotta pot, a small block of floral foam, and a bit of sheet moss. From a single wreath or swag, you can gather enough flowers to make six to eight favors, one for each place setting around your table.

To secure the stems, I recommend standard water-absorbing floral foam rather than dried flower foam. Water-absorbing foam is softer and less likely to damage thin, fragile stems. A standard four-and-three-eighths-by-four-by-three-inch brick of such foam yielded eight tiny blocks, enough for eight arrangements. You can also recycle small sprigs left over from a fresh floral arrangement.

For the arrangement shown at right, I used miniature dried yellow chrysanthemums. I have found that small flowers, up to one-half inch across, are better proportioned for this diminutive pot size. Variations on this design are endless: You could make each favor from a different color chrysanthemum, or use a different flower for each arrangement, or mix flowers within an arrangement. For a scented favor, consider lavender; for a more elegant favor, use miniature dried rose buds. For a formal arrangement, use stems of lavender or stalky herbs like rosemary; for a Victorian arrangement, mix a few stems each of tea roses and larkspur.

You can also substitute a different container for the small terra-cotta pot. Consider pots with more surface detail, either applied relief-like in the Della Robbia tradition, or pots with hand-painted patterns or decoupage images. Or recycle chipped china tea cups to serve as delicate containers for the small bouquets. Whatever your choice, make certain that the container is stable enough to support the weight of the floral material.

Francoise Hardy, who lives in Boston, is a freelance artisan and craftsperson.

You can use any small dried flower for these favors.

INSTRUCTIONS

1. *Place foam in pot.* Cut a block measuring 1½" x 2" x 2". Push block down into terra-cotta pot until ⅜" below rim (*see illustration A*).

2. *Prepare miniature chrysanthemums.* Break off two or three forked stems 7¼" long, then add individual stems, 3" to 7¼"

long until you have about 40 flowers.

3. *Make arrangement.* Gather flowers into bouquet with bottom of single and forked stems even (illustration B). Push stems down into center of foam about 1" until secure (illustration C). Spray-mist moss lightly until pliable, then arrange over foam (illustration D). ◆

ILLUSTRATION:
Nenad Jakesevic

COLOR PHOTOGRAPHY:
Carl Tremblay

STYLING:
Gabrielle Derrick de Papp/Team

MAKING THE PARTY FAVOR

A. Fill the pot with a water-absorbing floral foam.

B. Gather about 40 flower heads, making the stem ends even.

C. Plunge the stems into the center of the foam.

D. Cover all traces of the foam with moss.

Easy-Paint Organdy Tablecloth

Use translucent fabric, a leaf pattern, and squeeze-bottle paint to create an elegant table cover.

❧ BY FRANCOISE HARDY

MATERIALS

- 1³/₈ yards 45"-wide organdy
- 1¹/₂ yards 36"- to 45"-wide silk shantung
- **Plaid Fashion Fabric Paint in color to match shantung**
- **Thread to match shantung**

You'll also need:
leaf patterns (*see* page 46); access to photocopier with 11" x 17" paper size and enlarger; sewing machine; iron; sewing shears; scissors; rotary cutter; transparent tape; fabric marking pencil; ruler; 90-degree triangle; painter's tape; brush; pins; and indoor clothesline and clothespins.

PATTERNS
See page 46 for patterns.

You can make this organdy and silk shantung tablecloth in less than a day.

DESIGNER'S TIP

To encourage fabric paint to flow smoothly, store the container upside down. When painting, stop occasionally to shake the paint down toward the nozzle.

ILLUSTRATION:
Michael Gellatly

COLOR PHOTOGRAPHY:
Carl Tremblay

SILHOUETTE PHOTOGRAPHY:
Furnald/Gray

STYLING:
Gabrielle Derrick dePapp/Team

THIS ELEGANT TABLECLOTH IS assembled from a square of sheer organdy that is painted and then bordered in silk shantung. The design maximizes the beauty and translucence of organdy and the ease and convenience of painting with a squeeze bottle applicator.

You can make and decorate the tablecloth in four simple stages: (1) tape photocopies of the leaf pattern together to make one single large pattern; (2) lay a square of organdy over the pattern; (3) trace the pattern using fabric paint in a squeeze bottle and let it dry throughly; and (4) sew a silk shantung border around the edges of the tablecloth.

I chose organdy for the center panel because it is sheer, yet firm. Designs can be traced directly onto it, and it resists pulling when tableware is placed on it. A tightly woven sheer fabric such as faille silk would be too opaque for tinting as well as tracing, and too limp to lie flat,

making it unsuitable as a table covering. Even among organdies, however, there are differences in weight. To test the fabric for this project, unfurl the bolt and lay the end over the edge of the counter, preferably over a piece of white fabric, to see the color and how crisply the material falls. I recommend a soft shade for the organdy, a strong color for the border, and a paint color similar to the border color.

Fabric paint comes in three forms: plastic vials or jars, screw-top squeeze bottles (like high-tack glues), and capped squeeze bottles with a microfine drawing tip. I tested all three types. I found that using a brush to paint from an open vial resulted in a painterly and "artistic" effect, but coverage was uneven. Screw-top bottles yielded a coarsely rendered line with a depression in the middle left by the dispenser tip. Fine-

tip applicators produced the most controlled line and were almost as easy to draw with as a pen.

Plaid's Fashion Fabric Paint gave the best all-around performance. It comes in an attractive matte finish, doesn't require heat setting to become permanent, and the fine tip worked particularly well with the leaf pattern, which is outlined rather than filled in. Tulip Colorpoint offered a similar applicator tip, but the paint required heat setting with an iron. If you select paint from another manufacturer, be sure to use a matte paint rather than glittery or high gloss; when these dry, they can look like cheap plastic.

To display your finished tablecloth to best advantage, lay a solid light-colored cloth on the table first, then place the tablecloth over it. The undercloth color will filter through, and the painted design will appear to float on the surface. Surprisingly, I found that the tablecloth looked better from the unpainted side: Instead of a raised ridge of paint resting on the surface, the color bled through evenly for a flat "printed" look. Since the shantung border is the same on both sides, the decision regarding the "good" side is up to you.

Francoise Hardy is a professional craftsperson living in Boston. The tablecloth was designed by Michio Ryan.

INSTRUCTIONS
Painting the Organdy Tablecloth

1. *Prepare organdy.* Wash fabric gently in cold water to remove sizing, then hang to dry. Press with iron at low heat to remove wrinkles. Trim off selvages if necessary to eliminate puckering. Trim off one end so length equals width; piece will be 43" to 45" square.

2. *Prepare leaf pattern.* Using photocopier, enlarge patterns 1 and 2 (page 46) so each one just fills 11" x 17" sheet, then make six photocopies of each. Using transparent tape, tape copies together in 3-row x 4-column grid so designs match at edges. Trim off 7"-wide section at lower edge to make pattern 44" square (*see* illustration A, right).

3. *Paint leaf design on organdy.* Using painter's tape, tape pattern to work surface. Lay organdy on top and tape down firmly so organdy lies smooth, taut, and square (illustration B). Following design lines visible through organdy, apply paint to surface with squeeze bottle. To prevent jagged or irregular lines, use a loose, sweeping, fluid motion; do not try to trace design lines exactly. To prevent blobs, apply less pressure at the beginning and end of each stroke. Remove tape from surface and hang-dry organdy for 24 hours.

Sewing the Organdy Tablecloth

1. *Prepare silk shantung for border.* Using rotary cutter, cut four 9" x 51"-long strips from silk shantung parallel to selvage. Press long edges ½" to wrong side. At one end of each strip, measure ½" in from midpoint and mark dot; Mark two more dots on folded edges 4½" from end. Draft two lines connecting three dots to make 90-degree "arrowhead"; use triangle to confirm that arrowhead is square (illustration C and detail).

2. *Sew strips together with mitered corners.* Pin marked end of one strip to unmarked end of second strip, right sides together. Machine-stitch on marked lines, backstitching at beginning and end and pivoting at arrow point. Trim excess fabric ½" from stitching and clip off point (illustration D). Repeat until all four strips are joined together in one continuous piece (illustration E). On wrong side, press each seam open (illustration F). Turn border right side out and pick out corners with pin. With the folded edges aligned, press border to crease outer edge.

3. *Attach border.* Lay border flat and center painted organdy on top. Sandwich edge of organdy between inner border edges and pin. Topstitch through all layers all around (illustration G). Remove all pins. ◆

Making the Tablecloth

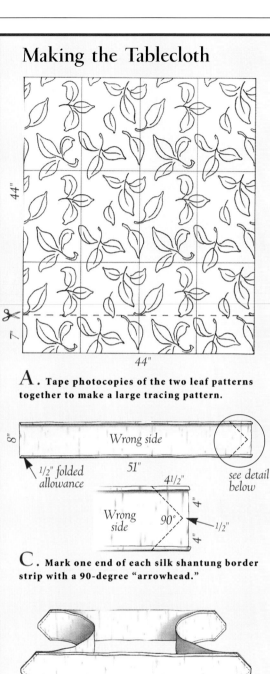

A. Tape photocopies of the two leaf patterns together to make a large tracing pattern.

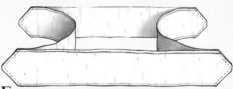

C. Mark one end of each silk shantung border strip with a 90-degree "arrowhead."

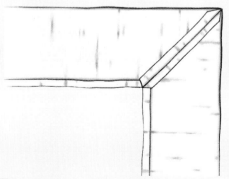

E. Join the remaining strips to make one continuous border piece.

F. Press each seam open on the wrong side.

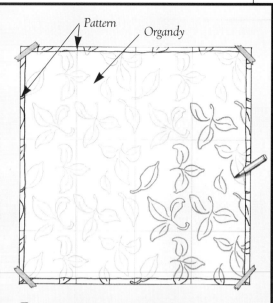

B. Lay a square of organdy over the pattern and trace the design with a fabric paint applicator. When done, hang-dry for 24 hours.

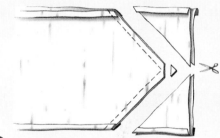

D. Join two strips together by machine-stitching on the marked lines, then trim away the excess fabric.

G. Turn the border right side out and press it flat. Slip the painted organdy inside the border fold and topstitch the inner edge all around.

Lace-Bordered Stationery

Create elegant paper lace on parchment paper using pergamano, a fifteenth-century craft.

❧ BY MARIE BROWNING

MATERIALS

- **1 sheet 8½" x 11" parchment paper (plus practice sheets)**
- **White waterproof drawing ink**

You'll also need:
access to photocopier with enlargement feature; 1 sheet 8½" x 11" vellum or acetate sheet; mapping pen; double-ended ballpoint embossing tool; 6" x 8" embossing pad; white beeswax; and masking tape.

Other items, if necessary:
single-needle perforating tool; 6" x 8" piercing pad; self-healing cutting ma;, X-Acto knife; and tweezers (for optional piercing).

ILLUSTRATION:
Wendy Wray

COLOR PHOTOGRAPHY:
Carl Tremblay

PATTERN:
Roberta Frauwirth

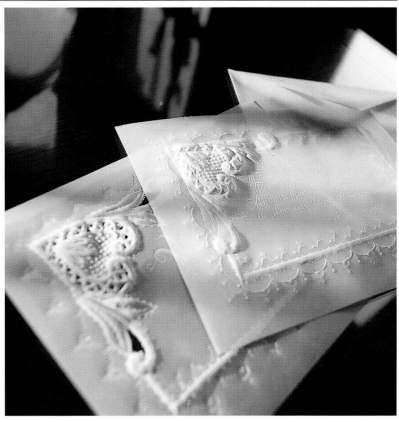

You can use pergamano to make cards commemorating special occasions such as weddings, births, or anniversaries.

HISTORICAL TIDBIT

Pergamano was first practiced in fifteenth-century Spanish convents. With Christopher Columbus's discovery of the New World, paper lace work was introduced to South America, where it has been quietly kept alive. The wide popularity of parchment craft in Europe today is due mainly to one woman, Martha Ospina. When she moved to Holland from her native Columbia in 1987, she began teaching the craft as a way to make friends and learn the Dutch language.

PERGAMANO IS THE FIFTEENTH-century art of creating lacy filigree designs from parchment paper. Traditional techniques include tracing the design, embossing a relief, and perforating and cutting the paper. Contemporary crafters have incorporated modern techniques, including painting, dorsing (coloring from the back), and three-dimensional effects. The combination of these various techniques creates an intricate, elegant look that makes pergamano appear more complicated than it actually is.

The Spanish nuns who invented pergamano worked on parchment made from the processed linings of sheep and goat intestines (*see* Historical Tidbit, right). Modern pergamano substitutes heavyweight parchment paper, which is made from cotton fibers that have been treated with glycerin and sulfuric acid. Like real parchment, parchment paper is strong yet semitransparent and has a light gray color that changes to milky white when embossed. The paper is available in a variety of thicknesses (referred to in pounds), with the thickest and heaviest paper typically 65 pounds.

In addition to parchment paper, which costs about $1 per sheet, you will need several specialized tools: a mapping pen, a ballpoint embosser, a perforating tool, and embossing and piercing pads. (All of the required tools are available by mail order, with prices starting around $3. *See* Sources and Resources, page 46).

The mapping pen, also called a dip pen or a lettering pen, has a small split nib with a cylindrical base and is used to ink in the basic design. For safety during shipping, some suppliers insert the nib point first into the pen, but it is easily removed and reinserted so the point faces up. The ballpoint embossing tool, or stylus, is used to impress the inked design on the wrong side of the parchment, creating a raised surface on the front. It is fitted with small and medium points, one at each end, to handle different line thicknesses. Rubbing the point in white beeswax (sold as a thread lubricant in the notions department of sewing stores) helps prevent the paper from tearing. The perforating tool has a sharp needlelike point for piercing holes in the parchment paper. Both embossing and piercing must be done on soft pads with give. You can purchase commercially available pads (prices start around $5), or you can substitute a computer mousepad for the embossing pad and a three-eighths-inch-thick piece of insulating foam for the piercing pad.

The pergamano design presented here (*see* patterns, page 47) includes both a beginner's version, which involves basic inking and embossing skills, and an advanced version, which adds the slightly more time-consuming and challenging piercing technique. Either approach produces an intricate, sophisticated border design suitable for any special announcement, such as weddings, anniversaries, or births.

Whichever version you choose, I recommend proceeding slowly and carefully, and taking a break between steps to maintain your focus and concentration. You may also want to practice each technique on a test piece of parchment paper. Your practice samplers can be used later as holiday tree ornaments, bookmarks, greeting card inserts, or even cutouts for decoupage.

To frame your finished design, mount it over a piece of dark colored paper, as this will best show off the embossed and pierced design.

Marie Browning is a fine arts specialist and craft instructor living in Victoria, British Columbia.

INSTRUCTIONS

Note: If you're making the beginner's pattern, you'll need to photocopy the design onto clear acetate so you can ink the pattern onto the right side and emboss the scalloped border on from the wrong side. If you're doing the advanced pattern, which doesn't require the pattern reversal, you can photocopy on ordinary copier paper.

Beginner's Design

1. *Trace pattern on parchment paper with white ink.* To make a reversible pattern, enlarge and photocopy pattern (page 47) on tracing vellum or clear acetate to measure 4⅞" x 7⅛". Center parchment paper on pattern, then tape together on wrong side. Shake white ink well. Dip mapping pen nib into ink and trace dots first (*see* illustration A), then medium and heavy lines (do not ink thin lines at inner and outer borders). Start at top left corner if right-handed, top right if left-handed, and work down and across, rotating paper as needed for easier access. Apply more pressure for heavy lines, less pressure for medium lines. When finished, wash pen nib promptly in water and dry. Let ink dry 30 minutes, then remove tape and photocopy pattern.

2. *Emboss parchment paper with ball-point tool.* Lay inked parchment paper face down on photocopy pattern, tape together, and place on embossing pad. To emboss, press smaller ballpoint into white beeswax, then gently trace thin lines omitted during inking in step 1 until paper turns milky white; remove pattern. Emboss remaining dots and lines on from wrong side, lubricating tool with beeswax as needed. Use larger point to fill in interior areas of leaves, heart, tendrils, and border with embossing until parchment paper stretches slightly and turns milky white (illustration B). On right side, embossed areas will appear slightly raised.

PERGAMANO PATTERN
See page 47 for patterns.

Advanced Design

1. *Trace pattern on parchment paper with white ink.* Follow Beginner's Design, step 1, but enlarge and photocopy pattern on ordinary copier paper (reversible pattern is not needed).

2. *Emboss parchment paper with ball-point tool.* Lay inked parchment face down on embossing pad. Following Beginner's Design, step 2, emboss all dots and lines except thin lines along inner and outer borders.

3. *Pierce parchment paper with single-needle tool.* Tape pattern and parchment paper together as in step 1. (If embossed design and pattern do not match perfectly, align and pierce designs in sections, making slight adjustments in position as needed.) Lay pattern and paper face up on piercing pad, then slip self-healing cutting mat between pad and tabletop. To pierce hole, hold tool vertically, then push it straight down into parchment paper and pull it straight up; to pierce holes in succession, allow one hole width or less between holes. Pierce all lines and dots on pattern that were not previously inked or embossed. Then pierce outline of heart, leaves, and tendrils; interior of heart; heart lattice border; interior of leaves; and outline of area between tendrils and leaves (illustration C).

4. *Perforate or tear parchment paper along pierced lines.* Using fingertip, tip of X-Acto knife blade, or tweezers, carefully punch out areas between tendrils and leaves and small sections within lattice border (illustration D). ◆

PERGAMANO IN FOUR STEPS

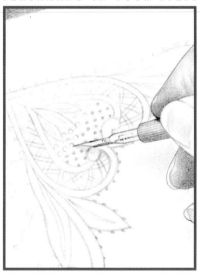

A. Use a split-nib mapping pen and white ink to trace the design lines on parchment paper.

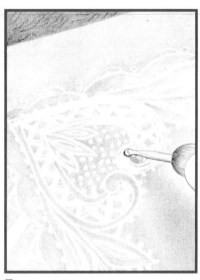

B. To emboss the design, turn the parchment paper over and trace the inked areas with an embossing tool.

C. For the advanced design, use a single-needle tool to pierce tiny holes.

D. For a lacy look, tear away sections of the parchment paper along the perforations.

The Best Shortcuts to Faux Fresco Painting

Substitute stucco for lime plaster, a paint roller for a trowel, and create texture with a wallpaper smoother.

❧ BY VI AND STU CUTBILL

MATERIALS

- Benjamin Moore latex eggshell-finish paint, 1 quart each peach 047, green 245, deep peach 077, deep green 518
- Latex glazing liquid*
- Stucco paint, dry mix, or patch compound*
- Matte acrylic varnish*

* Measure square footage of wall to determine amount needed

You'll also need:
Grapevine stencil or design of your choice; plastic wallpaper smoother; medium-nap paint roller and tray; painter's tape; two 1-gallon buckets; old measuring cup; paint stirring sticks; drop cloths; 3"-wide paintbrush; 3"-wide foam brushes; 1" and ½" stencil brushes; newsprint; damp cloth; 100-grit sandpaper; scissors; sanding block; paper towels; knife; and calculator.

Re-create a Renaissance look with modern fresco techniques. To finish, add a stencil design and distress the wall.

DESIGNER'S TIP

Other glaze color combinations:
- pale gray and gold
- pale rose and light coffee
- powder blue and lemon yellow
- light apricot and copper
- beige and lime green

Other stencil motifs:
- acanthus leaves
- architectural pediments
- fruit
- flowers

ILLUSTRATION:
Nenad Jakesavic

COLOR PHOTOGRAPHY:
Furnald/Gray

I F YOU WERE TO USE TRADITIONAL methods to create the texture and washed color of fresco painting in your own home, it would be a time-consuming, labor-intensive process. Fresco painting requires lime plaster, pure pigments, and a working partnership with someone willing to trowel on layers of wet plaster while you quickly paint on decorative motifs—all *before* the plaster dries.

We developed a shortcut method for fresco painting that substitutes the methods and hard-to-find materials used by fresco artists during the Middle Ages and Renaissance. We used stucco thinned with water instead of lime plaster; a paint roller instead of a trowel to apply the mixture; and a plastic wallpaper smoother to add texture. We also substituted common liquid acrylic paint for pure powdered paint pigments.

In traditional *fresco buono,* once the fresh, coarsely textured lime plaster was applied with a trowel, the artist then roughed out a design (called a cartoon) using charcoal or red pigment and applied a second, thinner layer of plaster made of finer sand and more lime putty. This second layer was applied in small sections so the cartoon could be colored in and completed while the plaster was still moist. In northern climates, lime plaster might remain moist for two weeks, whereas in the Mediterranean, the second layer dried within a few days, resulting in patchy sections of art instead of a sweep of smooth illustrated plaster. (For more information on traditional fresco techniques, *see* Historical Tidbit, page 21.)

In our technique, we sidestep the wet-dry problem completely by allowing the stucco surface to dry completely before adding any color. To re-create the subtle mottling of color on frescoed walls that have aged, we first applied a wash of peach and green glaze to the stucco-coated wall. The washed colors suggest the deterioration caused by uneven wearing and fading. We further enhanced the old, faded effect by laying (plain) newsprint on the surface and lifting off some of the glaze. The overall effect is a pale, chalky matte finish with no hard edges of color. You can intensify the color of the wall by adding more layers of washed color. This will produce more visual texture and give one the sense of seeing through many glowing layers of color.

To imitate the painted images of old frescoes, we used a stencil and slightly darker shades of the peach and green background hues to create a leaf pattern. Finally, we applied a few dramatic techniques: sanding the surface of the stucco with a block wrapped in sandpaper and chipping at the surface with a knife. This created chips, cracks, and worn spots, completing the distressed, aged effect we were seeking.

Stu and Vi Cutbill are one of Canada's leading teams of faux finishers and the inventors of the Cutbill system of block printing.

INSTRUCTIONS
Creating the Fresco Texture

1. *Prepare work area.* Clean wall surface so that it is dry and free of grease. Mask trim and molding with painter's tape. Lay down drop cloths under wall.

2. *Prepare stucco.* Mix dry stucco and water in bucket following manufacturer's

CREATING THE FRESCO

A. After applying the stucco mix with a roller, skim the surface with a plastic wallpaper smoother.

B. Tint the stucco surface with colored glazes for a worn, aged look.

C. Lay newsprint across the wet glazes and rub gently to lift off and "fade" the color.

HISTORICAL TIDBIT

Original fresco painting was called fresco buono. This method depended on the use of a wet plaster wall because it was by means of the plaster's curing process that a layer of crystals formed, entrapping the applied pigment and giving the illustration its enduring color and incandescence. Unfortunately, this method also required skilled artists to render their art quickly and in small sections while the plaster was moist.

A second, less-permanent method, which provided longer working time, was called fresco secco, in which pigment was applied to dry plaster and then bound to the wall with gums from plants or eggs, or glue made from sturgeon.

Fresco continued as an art into the twentieth century largely due to Diego Rivera, who learned the technique in Italy and brought it back to Mexico. Rivera also trained artists in the United States, and many of them used the technique to create murals in post offices and other government buildings as part of a public works project during the Depression.

D. Stencil the designs onto the surface using darker shades of the glaze colors.

E. Distress the wall further by breaking off chips of stucco.

instructions, or put ready-mixed stucco paint or compound into bucket. Dilute with water, if necessary, to achieve cake batter consistency. Transfer to paint tray.

3. *Apply stucco to walls in 4-foot-square sections.* Use brush to apply stucco close to taped areas, then roll 1/16" to 1/8" layer of stucco onto open areas as you would roll on paint. Texture will be ripply from roller. To flatten texture, lightly skim wallpaper smoother across surface, first vertically and then horizontally, leaving some dappled roller marks untouched to suggest layers that have been worn away (*see* illustration A). Repeat this technique across entire wall, working in sections and blending edges while stucco is still wet. When finished, wash tools promptly with water. Let dry overnight.

4. *Seal stuccoed wall.* Apply thin coat of varnish with roller. Let dry following manufacturer's recommendations.

Glazing and Stenciling

1. *Mix peach and green glazes.* Use 2 parts glazing liquid and 1 part paint for each. Make enough peach (047) glaze to cover 80 percent of wall area and enough green glaze (245) to cover 20 percent of wall area. Typically, 1½ cups of mixed glaze will cover about 175 square feet. Check product labels for coverage estimates and use calculator to determine amounts needed for your walls.

2. *Tint wall with glazes.* Working one 4-foot-square section at a time, use foam brush to apply peach glaze randomly across 80 percent of surface, then fill in remaining spaces with green glaze (illustration B). While glaze is still wet, lay newsprint on surface, rub gently with palm, and lift off (illustration C). This action will lift color from high points of surface and concentrate color in low areas, for uneven faded effect. Repeat across glazed area with same newsprint sheet. Proceed section by section across wall, first applying glazes and then pressing fresh paper against it. Let dry at least 3 hours.

3. *Stencil grapevine design on wall.* Using painter's tape, tape stencil to wall in random position. Moisten 1" stencil brush with deep green paint. Work brush in circular motion on paper towel until bristles are almost dry, then work brush in circular motion over leaf cutout of stencil. Repeat to fill in all leaves in stencil, then use ½" brush and deep peach paint to stencil vine (we omitted grapes). Reposition stencil to suggest rambling vine and repeat as desired over surface of wall (illustration D).

Finishing

1. *Sand wall to distress surface.* Run sanding block with 100-grit sandpaper over entire wall, then use circular motion over stenciled areas to make paint look worn. To break off chips of stucco, use edge of X-Acto knife tipped at an angle (illustration E). When finished, gently wipe surface with damp cloth. Finish with one or two coats acrylic varnish. ◆

Use a darker shade of the background hue for stenciling.

Fast and Easy Ottoman from Fabric and Foam

Assemble an exquisite footstool using precut plywood, slats, and curtain rod finials.

❧ BY MICHIO RYAN

The Kilim fabric covering and attenuated legs create an English manor house feel for this ottoman. Experiment with other fabrics to change the style.

DIAGRAMS:
Mary Newell DePalma

COLOR PHOTOGRAPHY:
Carl Tremblay

STYLING:
Gabrielle Derrick dePapp/Team

FOR A BEGINNER, THE IDEA OF building furniture can appear daunting, if not impossible. With that beginner in mind, I designed an easy-to-assemble ottoman using wood, foam, upholstery fabric, and curtain rod finials (decorative knobs). You can make the entire piece using basic tools: a drill, saw, staple gun, hammer, and scissors.

Essentially, the ottoman is made of two components, a seat and legs. The seat consists of a plywood rectangle reinforced on the underside with pine boards. The top of the seat is upholstered with a plump layer of fabric-covered foam. The legs are actually curtain rod finials that are attached to the seat with hanger bolts, rather than wood screws, to give them more stability. The complicated joinery, webbing, and tied springs used for tradi-

tional upholstery have been replaced with an assembly of ready-cut parts. The wood parts are so simple they can be precut to size at the lumberyard.

In planning the ottoman, I made some basic design decisions. For the legs, I selected curtain rod finials that were graceful, yet sturdy. I sanded them and applied a walnut stain. I also added domed upholstery tacks to define the lower seat edge.

I chose plywood for the seat because of its inherent strength. Plywood is made of layers of wood arranged so the grain of each layer alternates with the ones above and below it. This cross-graining makes a plywood plank resistant to splitting or bowing, whereas a plank of solid wood tends to split along the grain. I used precut, one-by-four pine boards for the rein-

forcing slats, making sure there was no oozing pitch on the wood. Solid birch and oak are also strong woods but unnecessarily expensive for this project. The slats serve three purposes: (1) they reinforce the seat's edge to prevent bowing under weight; (2) they provide a soft surface edge for inserting the decorative tacks; and (3) they elevate the seat slightly for more comfortable use.

Before you get started, here's a quick overview of the project's major steps. First you'll glue and screw the slats to the bottom of the plywood; then drill holes and install the T-nut and hanger bolt to anchor the legs to the base of the ottoman. Attach the T-nut (which looks like a metal sleeve with a flared cuff) to the base, then test-fit each leg by screwing half of the hanger bolt into the T-nut and thread the other half into the leg.

Once you've made the frame, you can tackle the upholstery. First, center the foam on the plywood, then add a layer of batting followed by muslin, pulled taut and smooth. Position the upholstery fab-

Making the Frame

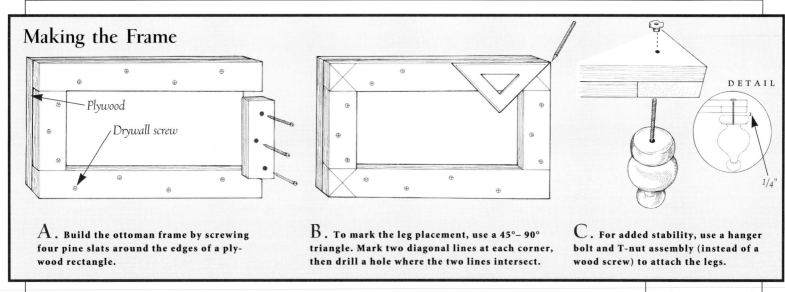

DETAIL

1/4"

A. Build the ottoman frame by screwing four pine slats around the edges of a plywood rectangle.

B. To mark the leg placement, use a 45°– 90° triangle. Mark two diagonal lines at each corner, then drill a hole where the two lines intersect.

C. For added stability, use a hanger bolt and T-nut assembly (instead of a wood screw) to attach the legs.

---

ric on top and staple it down with hospital-style corners. Then, decorate the ottoman with a neat line of brass upholstery tacks, which will easily pierce the soft pine edging. Reattach the legs and stand the ottoman upright, and it's ready to use.

INSTRUCTIONS
Building the Ottoman Frame

1. *Assemble basic frame.* Measure and mark 6' pine slat into two 24" and two 8" sections. Saw on marked lines; discard excess. Position one long slat on plywood, edges matching. Using $\frac{1}{16}$" bit, drill four to five holes along slat length at least 1" from edge. Drill through board $\frac{1}{8}$" into plywood; even spacing is not necessary. Squiggle a bead of yellow carpenter's glue between board and plywood, then screw drywall screws into holes to join pieces. Join remaining slats around edge of plywood in same way (see illustration A).

2. *Mark four corners of frame for leg placement.* Align long edge of triangle against long slat edge, matching triangle point to corner. Draft diagonal line. Repeat on opposite edge of slat so slanted lines intersect, then mark remaining corners in same fashion (illustration B).

3. *Drill holes for legs.* Lay frame down so newly attached slats face upward; set scrap wood blocks of equal thickness under corners. Using $\frac{5}{16}$" bit, drill each corner where diagonal lines intersect; drill straight down through pine slat and plywood until bit reaches scrap wood.

4. *Test-fit legs.* Using pliers, remove existing screw, if any, from finial. Screw hanger bolt into finial, stopping when $1\frac{3}{4}$" of bolt remains exposed. At each plywood corner, tap T-nut shank into drilled hole with hammer. Insert hanger bolt into frame from underside and screw into T-nut until even with plywood. The $\frac{1}{4}$" of hanger bolt that remains exposed is needed to accommodate the upholstery

fabric thickness (illustration C and detail).

5. *Stain legs.* Using $\frac{5}{16}$" bit, drill four holes 5" apart and $\frac{3}{4}$" deep in scrap 2' x 4' board. Sand legs lightly, then wipe off dust with tack cloth. Insert hanger bolts into holes so legs stand upside down. Wearing gloves, rub in stain with lint-free rag. Let dry. Brush on two coats varnish, letting dry between coats.

Upholstering the Ottoman

1. *Cut 36" x 45" rectangle from upholstery fabric.* Lay fabric flat. Determine center of printed design (to appear at center of ottoman) and mark with safety pin. Measure out from safety pin $22\frac{1}{2}$" to each selvage and 18" to each raw edge, then mark with chalk. Using yardstick and chalk, draft lines through marks to make rectangle; use triangle to confirm that corners are square. Use shears to cut fabric along marked lines (illustration D). Finally, cut a 36" x 45" rectangle from muslin and a 27" x 37" rectangle from batting.

2. *Attach foam cushion.* Set foam on plywood, then drape batting over foam so edges hang evenly down sides. To reduce bulk, cut 6" squares from corners of batting (illustration E). Center muslin on batting, smooth surface, then flip stack over. Grip middle of one long muslin edge, pull muslin onto long slat, and staple about $\frac{3}{4}$" from outer edge. Staple opposite

---

Cutting the Fabric

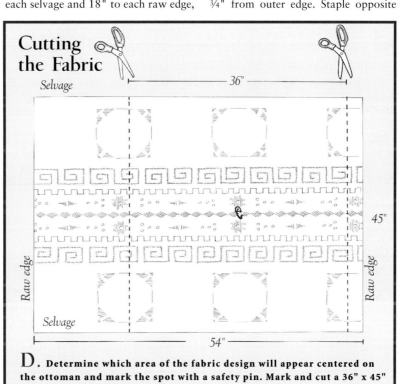

Selvage

36"

45"

Raw edge

Raw edge

Selvage

54"

D. Determine which area of the fabric design will appear centered on the ottoman and mark the spot with a safety pin. Mark and cut a 36" x 45" rectangle so the pin is at the center.

---

muslin edge in same way, then staple short edges, using consistent pressure to pull muslin taut but not tight (illustration F). Working from center of each edge out and alternating between long and short edges, continue stapling opposite sides in pairs so that staples are positioned 1" apart. Check tension frequently on top, dome, and seat sides as you go. To make adjustments, pry up staples with flat head screwdriver. Stop when staples are 4" from corners.

3. *Shape cushion corners.* Continue stapling towards corners, increasing tautness to compress foam and create rounded silhouette. At corner, pull muslin onto board at 45-degree angle and staple (illustration G). Pull and tuck the excess muslin on each side away from corner, draw firmly

over slat edge, and staple down. Check that dome is smooth on seat side and top, then trim fabric within ¾" of staples.

4. *Attach upholstery fabric.* Center fabric rectangle on dome, turn over, and apply provisional staples 3" apart, working from center out as in step 3; stop 4" from corner. Trim excess fabric ½" beyond inner board edges, then fold fabric under ½" so crease aligns with edge, and staple close to fold. Continue folding and stapling along edges, stopping 1" to 2" from inside corners; remove provisional staples (illustration H).

5. *Shape upholstery corners.* Draw fabric up onto corner at 45-degree angle, the same as for muslin, and staple on outer side of drilled hole. Pleat excess fabric on either side of hole neatly, and fold towards

hole hospital-style. Trim away excess bulk from under fold with scissors, then staple securely. Cut small lozenge-shaped openings so that holes are visible (illustration I).

Finishing the Ottoman

1. *Reattach legs.* Screw leg anchor bolts into position. Attach floor glides or castors if desired.

2. *Attach upholstery tacks.* To facilitate spacing, cut two 16" and two 26" lengths of painter's tape. Draft line ⅜" from lower tape edge, then mark line in 1" increments. Apply tape to ottoman base with lower edges matching. Push upholstery tack at each mark partway into wood (illustration J). When entire line of tacks is positioned, remove tape and tap in tacks with rubber mallet. ◆

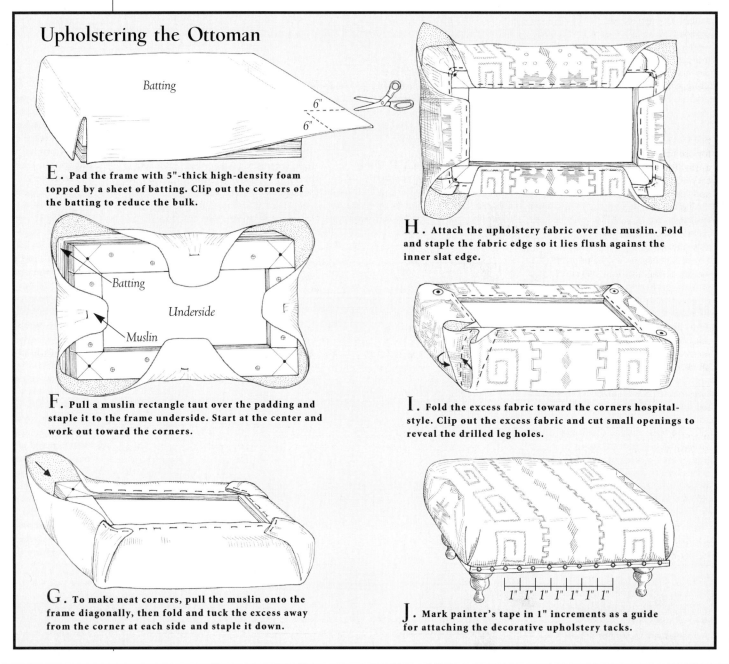

Upholstering the Ottoman

E. Pad the frame with 5"-thick high-density foam topped by a sheet of batting. Clip out the corners of the batting to reduce the bulk.

Batting

6"
6"

F. Pull a muslin rectangle taut over the padding and staple it to the frame underside. Start at the center and work out toward the corners.

Batting
Underside
Muslin

G. To make neat corners, pull the muslin onto the frame diagonally, then fold and tuck the excess away from the corner at each side and staple it down.

H. Attach the upholstery fabric over the muslin. Fold and staple the fabric edge so it lies flush against the inner slat edge.

I. Fold the excess fabric toward the corners hospital-style. Clip out the excess fabric and cut small openings to reveal the drilled leg holes.

J. Mark painter's tape in 1" increments as a guide for attaching the decorative upholstery tacks.

1" 1" 1" 1" 1" 1" 1"

Soothing Scented Waters

Fragrant and decorative waters are both convenient and inexpensive to make following these simple steps.

☙ BY FRANCOISE HARDY

MATERIALS

- **Several clean decorative glass bottles or decanters**

  Rose Water
- 2 cups distilled water
- ¼ cup vodka
- 10 drops rose essential oil
- ½ cup fresh or dried deep red rose petals

  Freesia Water
- 2 cups distilled water
- ¼ cup vodka
- 8 drops freesia essential oil
- 2 sprigs fresh or dried freesia

  Orange Water
- 3 cups distilled water
- ¼ cup vodka
- 10 drops orange essential oil
- 1 to 2 tablespoons dried orange rind slivers

You'll also need: clean 1-quart glass jars (one per recipe); glass measuring cup; and funnel.

Other items, if necessary: eyedropper (if essential oil vial does not include one); strainer to fit funnel (to strain out damaged plant matter); and chopstick (to insert fresh or cured materials into bottles).

WITH THE COST OF COMmercially prepared scented waters being relatively high, it makes sense to explore ways to make your own fragrant waters. The ingredients are inexpensive and easy to find, and you can decant them into decorative bottles.

The basic ingredients of our scented waters are distilled water, vodka, a few drops of a fragrant essential oil, and plant matter such as rose petals, freesia, or dried orange peel twists. The essential oil, which is highly concentrated, provides the scent, while the plant matter enhances the beauty of the bottle. The distilled water guards against impurities, and the alcohol acts as a preservative. You can find distilled water at pharmacies (where it's sold for use in steam vaporizers); essential oils are available at specialty bath and apothecary shops, such as Crabtree & Evelyn and Caswell-Massey.

The process for making scented water is simple: The liquid ingredients, fragrant oil, and plant matter are combined in a glass jar, swirled gently, and set aside to age (*see* recipes at right). After one week's curing, the liquid can be decanted into decorative bottles, with new petals or sprigs added for decorative appeal. Display the bottles in your bedroom, bath, or guest room, and uncork them to release the scent. Or you can quickly add scent to a room by placing the water in an atomizer and misting the area.

Francoise Hardy is a professional artisan and craftsperson living in Boston.

Scented waters make fragrant and decorative accessories for bed and bath.

INSTRUCTIONS
For each recipe, proceed as follows:
1. *Combine all ingredients.* Measure water and vodka and pour into jar. Add oil using eyedropper (*see* illustration A). Drop in fresh or dried material (illustration B). Cover jar and swirl gently.

2. *Let mixture cure, then decant it.* Store jar in cool, dark place 1 week. Using funnel, pour scented water into bottles (illustration C). As you pour, strain out any materials that are damaged. Poke petals, sprigs, or slivers into bottle using chopstick (illustration D). ◆

DESIGNER'S TIP

To remove cloudy spots from a glass bottle that has a narrow opening, fill the container with water and drop in a commercial denture-cleaner tablet. After the tablet has stopped bubbling, pour out the water and rinse thoroughly.

ILLUSTRATION:
Nenad Jakesevic

COLOR PHOTOGRAPHY:
Carl Tremblay

MAKING SCENTED WATER

A. **Add the essential oil to water and vodka.**

B. **Drop in fresh or dried material such as petals.**

C. **Age the mixture for 1 week, then decant it.**

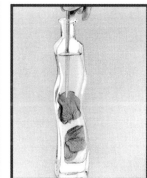

D. **Using chopstick, add petals to the bottle.**

Gilded Monogram

Use 23-carat gold leaf to create edible, yet beautiful, cake monograms.

❧ BY JO GOLDSMITH

MATERIALS
Royal Icing

- 1⅓ cups sifted confectioners' sugar
- 1 egg
- ¼ teaspoon cream of tartar

Gilding

- 1 egg
- 2 to 3 sheets edible 23-carat gold leaf

You'll also need:
Computer with word-processing software and printer *or* typeface book/source and access to photocopier with enlarger; pastry bag; #3 (round) stainless steel cake-decorating tip; handheld electric mixer; clean, dry, glass or stainless steel mixing bowls; stainless steel mixing spoon; stainless steel spatula; measuring cup; measuring spoons; sifter; cookie sheet(s); waxed paper; cup; fork; small dish; scissors; tape; butter knife; new fine-tipped artist's brush; tweezers; and clean dishtowel.

Other items, if necessary:
coupler; additional pastry tips.

ILLUSTRATION:
Nenad Jakesevic

DIAGRAM:
Judy Love

COLOR PHOTOGRAPHY:
Carl Tremblay

STYLING:
Gabrielle Derrick dePapp/Team

For added beauty, you can vary the width of the letters by moving the pastry tip slower for thicker lines and faster for thinner ones. For example, the S stroke above is broader in the center and more slender at the outer curves.

MAKING AN EDIBLE GILDED monogram is easier than it looks, thanks to three secrets I discovered during testing. For starters, use a computer to print out the style and size of monogram you like best, then use the letter printout as a template to trace the letters using piped royal icing. Finally, gild the monogram using egg whites (instead of size) and edible 23-carat gold leaf.

Several sources provide styled individual letters for your monogram, but one foolproof source is a computer with word-processing software and a printer. Simply type in the letters you want, select a font and size, and print out the results. If you don't have access to a computer, you can photocopy (and enlarge, if necessary) letters from a typography book, a magazine, or a newspaper.

To re-create the letters using royal icing, cover the printout or photocopy with waxed paper, then pipe the design. The royal icing will harden overnight, creating a delicate but solid version of the letters. I tested two methods of piping the icing: using a disposable parchment pastry bag outfitted with a round cake-decorating tip, and using a zipper-lock bag with the corner snipped off. I discovered that piping the monogram requires a great deal of control, so I recommend the cake-decorating tip and pastry bag.

Cake-decorating tips come in more than two hundred varieties, such as round, star-tip, and scroll. Tips with the number 1 through 12 have plain round holes of varying size. For this design, I used a #3 tip, which produces a stream of icing slightly broader than the thinnest strokes of the template I chose. Part of the beauty of these letters is the varying

width of the strokes. The S stroke, for instance, is slender through the outer curves but broader through the center. Used conventionally, the stainless steel pastry tip is designed to deliver a uniform stream of icing. I was able to achieve, however, thick and thin variations by varying the speed at which I moved the tip along the surface. For a thicker line, I slowed down; for a thinner line, I went faster.

If you want to be able to change tips, you'll need to fit the pastry bag with a coupler. To use the coupler, slip it into the empty pastry bag, snip off the tip of the bag so the icing can flow through, place the metal pastry tip on the coupler from the outside of the bag, and then screw on a plastic ring to hold the tip in place (*see* diagram, page 27). To change tips, simply unscrew the ring, remove the old tip, and replace it with your new choice.

When making royal icing, make sure that all utensils are scrupulously clean, for fats and oil cause the icing to break down. I recommend using glass or stainless steel bowls, utensils, and tools. Avoid plastic if possible because it retains oils (think of a plastic container that is permanently discolored because it held tomato sauce). If you must use plastic equipment, including plastic couplers, it should be dedicated to use with royal icing only, versus buttercream or other types of icing. *Note:* The royal icing recipe included with this article contains raw egg whites, which should not be eaten by pregnant women, infants and young children, the elderly, or anyone else whose health might be compromised

AN EGG-FREE RECIPE FOR ROYAL ICING

Royal Meringue Icing
Yields 3 cups

- 4 cups sifted confectioners' sugar
- 3 tablespoons meringue powder

If using electric mixer, beat ingredients together with 5½ tablespoons water 8 to 10 minutes on medium-low speed. If using handheld mixer, beat with 6 tablespoons water 10 to 12 minutes at high speed. Continue with beating very slowly to prevent sugar dust. Icing is ready when it forms stiff peaks.

Note: For stiffer icing, use ½ teaspoon less water. (Icing can be refrigerated in a tightly closed container for up to 2 weeks, but must be rebeaten at low speed before using.)

by such ingredients. For an alternative recipe that uses meringue powder instead of egg whites, see "An Egg-Free Recipe for Royal Icing," page 26.

When piping the monogram letters, make several of each one, then choose the best ones for gilding. A few notes about gilding: Be sure to use edible gold leaf (.999 percent) for this project; composition gold leaf includes trace metals that should not be ingested. Use an extremely thin layer of egg white to adhere the leaf. After you apply the leaf, brush from the top surface down to avoid dislodging it.

Jo Goldsmith is a food consultant, designer, and freelance writer from Brookline, Massachusetts.

INSTRUCTIONS
Getting Started

1. *Make monogram template.* If using a computer to make template for monogram, type desired letters on-screen, then specify font and type size so surname initial measures about 3" high and outside letters measure about 1¾" high. (In our three-letter monogram, the surname initial is larger and centered. Exact spacing is not essential on-screen, as you can arrange the letters properly on the cake.) Once letters are properly sized, print out results. If using typeface book, photocopy and enlarge selected letters from alphabet to sizes described above.

2. *Prepare egg white.* During evening before making royal icing, separate 1 egg. Let egg white stand overnight, unrefrigerated, to encourage evaporation and promote viscosity.

Making the Icing Monogram

1. *Mix icing.* Sift together sugar and cream of tartar. In mixing bowl, beat egg white until fluffy, then beat in sugar mixture in ½-cup increments. Beat about 10 minutes or until icing is smooth and forms stiff peaks.

2. *Prepare pastry bag.* Push coupler down into bag tip, then snip off tip ¼" beyond coupler. Place #3 metal tip on coupler and screw on ring (see diagram at right).

3. *Fill pastry bag.* Then transfer icing using spatula (illustration A). Press icing down toward tip of bag. Stop when bag is half full. Fold in side edges diagonally, and roll down top. To prevent remaining icing from hardening prematurely, dampen dishtowel and lay it over open icing bowl.

4. *Pipe icing monograms.* Tape printout or photocopy of letters to cookie sheet(s). Cover with waxed paper, then tape paper in place. Hold cone near tip with one hand and gently compress folded top with other hand to regulate icing flow. Pipe icing onto waxed paper, tracing over letters (illustration B). For thin lines, move steadily; for thicker lines, go slower so icing can build up. Change to larger or smaller tip, if desired. Pipe several versions of each letter, then let harden 24 hours or longer before gilding.

Gilding the Monogram

1. *Prepare work area.* Lay book of gold leaf on fresh waxed paper, then transfer single sheet of leaf to paper using blade of butter knife. Tear gold leaf into small pieces with clean, dry fingertips. Select best-formed letters and set on waxed paper with gold leaf; handle carefully since letters are fragile. Separate egg and lightly beat egg white in small dish with fork.

2. *Apply gold leaf.* Working one letter at a time, brush very, very thin coat of egg white onto small section of letter, no larger than 1" square. Using tweezers, lift piece of leaf and let touch down on egg white area; it will cling and adhere instantly (illustration C). Smooth very gently with same brush, working from top surface down toward sides (illustration D). Gild remaining surface in same way, working slowly to prevent crinkles. When surface of entire letter is gilded, use flakes and skewings to fill in gaps. Let dry overnight before placing on cake. ◆

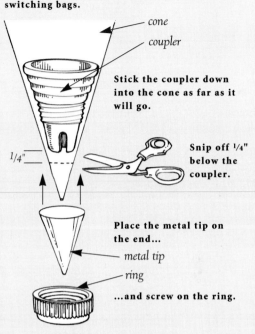

DIAGRAM 1
Attaching the Coupler and Tip
Fit the pastry bag with a coupler and a metal cake-decorating tip as shown. The coupler allows you to change to a different tip without switching bags.

cone
coupler

Stick the coupler down into the cone as far as it will go.

¼"

Snip off ¼" below the coupler.

Place the metal tip on the end...
metal tip
ring
...and screw on the ring.

DESIGNER'S TIPS

■ To pipe smooth lines of icing, avoid jerky motions and abrupt changes in speed.

■ To smooth a bubble in the icing, use a watercolor brush dipped in water.

■ Take your time when applying the gold leaf and work on small sections at a time.

MAKING THE GILDED MONOGRAM

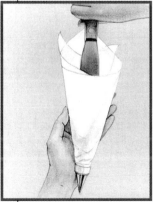

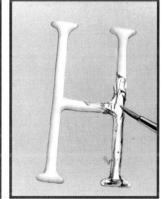

A. Using a spatula, fill the pastry bag halfway with royal icing.

B. Pipe the icing onto a sheet of wax paper that has been placed over the monogram template.

C. Let the letters harden, then apply egg white "size" and edible gold leaf.

D. Brush down gently toward the wax paper to adhere the leaf without dislodging it.

Faux Hand-Painting a French Country Dresser

Achieve the look of finely detailed hand-painting quickly and easily with reproduction art giftwrap and decoupage medium.

BY DEBORAH MILLER GABLER

MATERIALS

- **Small unfinished wooden object**
- **Source for paper cutouts (giftwrap, magazines, etc.)**
- **2-ounce acrylic craft paints (see "Getting Started," step 1, for colors)**
- **Royal Coat Decoupage Medium**
- **Water-based wood sealer**

You'll also need:
scissors; curved manicure scissors; X-Acto knife with new blade; 2" foam brush; ½" flat artist's brush; tweezers; sponge; 220- and 400-grit wet-dry sandpaper; waxed paper; tack cloth; #0000 steel wool; and ½"-wide Scotch Magic tape.

Other items, if needed:
matte acrylic spray sealer (to strengthen thin paper) and commercial antiquing medium *or* linseed oil, odorless turpentine, brown-tone oil paint, disposable plate or dish, and palette knife; and lint-free cloth (to add antique patina).

DESIGNER'S TIP

To fix any air pockets on the adhere cutouts, slice into the pocket with a utility knife and brush on more decoupage medium. Then smooth the piece down.

ILLUSTRATION:
Nenad Jakesevic

COLOR PHOTOGRAPHY:
Carl Tremblay

The floral designs on this pine jewelry chest look hand painted, but they are actually paper giftwrap cutouts applied by a decoupage technique.

PAINTING FLOWERS, LEAVES, AND tendrils on a decorative object normally requires the talents and training of a skilled artist. You can produce a similar effect using decoupage. By cutting apart printed illustrations and applying them in configurations, you can imitate the designs on expensive hand-painted furnishings.

There are three secrets to successful faux hand-painting using decoupage. The first secret is to choose illustrations that are well designed and painterly in character. The second is to prepaint the decorative object so that its base color matches the background color of the cut images. This frees you to cut fine leaves and tendrils with a bit of a border around them, minimizing the danger of their tearing apart. The third secret is to seal the entire surface (after the cutouts are pasted down) with at least a half-dozen coats of decoupage medium. This fills the minuscule drop between the edge of the cut paper and the surface. In this way, the image lies flat and smooth against its background, persuading the eye that the design is painted (not glued) on.

Modern decoupage mediums such as Royal Coat Decoupage by Plaid or Mod Podge are much quicker than traditional decoupage techniques. Traditional decoupage calls for the use of watered-down glue to adhere a motif to an object, followed by many layers of varnish. Modern decoupage mediums can be used to both glue down the cutouts and seal them. Varnish takes up to eight hours to dry, compared with thirty minutes for the modern mediums. This relieves you of the constant cleanup between applications. And when it is time to clean up, you can use soap and water instead of solvent.

The little dresser in the photograph at left was faux hand-painted in the style of an eighteenth-century French country dresser. The motifs are from Giftwrap by Artists, 18th Century English Floral Patterns published by Harry N. Abrams, one of seven volumes in a series. This giftwrap series offers a wide variety of fine reproductions by world-renowned painters, allowing you to choose images that are painterly and decorative in character.

You can also choose other sources for illustrations. Search through stores and antique shops for antique prints, greeting cards, magazines, and package labeling. Always test the quality of the paper for both durability and colorfastness.

To test for colorfastness, apply some decoupage medium to a small corner section of your sample. If the colors begin to bleed, or if the paper disintegrates, it is unsuitable. In some cases, it is possible to reinforce lightweight paper, such as the giftwrap used here, by spraying both sides with an acrylic sealer. Magazine images can be mechanically reproduced on a color copier, sprayed with the sealer, and then cut out quite easily.

To plan your design, examine the entire sheet of giftwrap, looking for suitable motifs. Using sharp manicure scissors, roughly cut out pleasing groupings of flowers, allowing a one-half-inch margin around each configuration. Place these cutouts on the object you want to decorate, moving them around until you are satisfied with the arrangement; then cut them out more precisely. You may want to do some piecing to make a symmetrical spray of flowers or to redirect the flow and direction of a trailing vine. The featured dresser required six floral sprays and their connecting leafy vines, all of which were cut from one-quarter of a full sheet of giftwrap.

To finish the design, fine-cut some additional smaller images for use as fillers as needed. Build the design as you go along, testing the placement of each image before applying the decoupage medium.

After allowing the piece to dry overnight, you can clean it by rubbing lightly with a damp cloth, and if necessary, you can gently remove any noticeable brush strokes with #0000 steel wool. However, be sure to let the piece cure for four weeks before doing a major cleaning in which pressure is applied.

Deborah Miller Gabler, owner of Shady Lane Designs in Hamburg, New York, is a freelance designer and teacher.

DECOUPAGING THE DRESSER

A. Plan a basic layout using images cut from wrapping paper.

B. Use manicure scissors to trim the cutouts close to the edges.

C. Brush the decoupage medium on the back of each cutout.

D. Lay the cutout in position and rub until it adheres.

E. Add smaller cutouts to fill out the design.

F. To "jump" across gaps, slice the paper, then slide the rest of the section down.

G. Use transparent tape to make a stencil for striping.

INSTRUCTIONS
Getting Started

1. *Establish color schemes.* Select giftwrap or other printed paper for cutouts. Choose one container of paint to match paper background color and one container in coordinating color for striping and interior surfaces. To make thin papers more durable, spray both sides lightly with acrylic sealer and let dry as manufacturer recommends.

2. *Prepare wood surface for decoupage.* Remove any hardware and loose pieces, such as drawers or lids. Sand all surfaces lightly with 220-grit sandpaper, then dust. Apply wood sealer with foam brush, let dry as manufacturer recommends, then resand and dust. Apply one coat background color to all exterior surfaces with foam brush; let dry 20 minutes, then paint interior surfaces, if any, with coordinating color. Let dry 1 hour, sand lightly with 400-grit sandpaper, and dust. Apply second coat(s) and let dry overnight.

Applying the Decoupage Cutouts

1. *Plan basic layout.* Using scissors, cut motifs or grouped images from selected paper, allowing ½" margin beyond image. Arrange cutouts on painted surface to establish general size and shape of decoupage design; fine details will be filled in later (*see* illustration A).

2. *Trim basic layout pieces with manicure scissors.* Hold scissors steady at slight angle and slowly rotate paper to create beveled edge. Trim as close to image as possible (illustration B).

3. *Using decoupage medium, glue cutouts to surface.* First, lay trimmed cutouts on painted surface to confirm design placement, retrimming if needed. Turn each cutout upside down on waxed paper. Using flat artist's brush, smooth thin layer of medium across wrong side, out beyond edges (illustration C). Pick up cutout with tweezers and position it glue-side down on object. Rub cutout from center out to edges to remove air pockets and wrinkles and promote firm bond (illustration D). Wipe excess at edges with damp sponge. Glue down additional cutouts one by one to build design as planned. Once basic cutouts are in place, cut, position, and glue on smaller images as needed to fill out and balance design (illustration E)

4. *Continue images across gaps in surface.* For surfaces with drawer fronts, doors, and lids, glue and smooth cutout to wood on one side of gap, then use X-Acto knife to slice paper even with wood edge.

Carefully slide remainder of image marginally to expose gap, and align cut edge with corresponding wood edge (illustration F).

Finishing and Antiquing

1. *Paint contrasting striped border using tape as stencil.* Affix tape to wood surface even with edge. Affix parallel tape, allowing ⅛" gap between tape strips. To paint striping, brush contrasting paint between tape strips (illustration G). Let dry 10 minutes, then lift off tape. Let dry 1 hour.

2. *Varnish entire surface using decoupage medium.* Using foam brush, apply six to eight thin coats of medium, allowing 20 to 30 minutes drying time between coats. Work in good light to confirm that coverage is smooth and even. Let dry overnight. To remove brush-strokes, rub gently with steel wool.

3. *Add antique patina.* Let piece cure several days, then apply commercial or homemade antiquing medium if desired (*see* "Antiquing Recipe" above). Test antiquing medium in inconspicuous place to ensure compatibility with cured decoupage medium. To apply, wrap cloth around index finger, dip in medium, and rub corners of each flat surface, fading toward center of surface so corners look dirtier. Also rub medium into recessed or routed areas. Let cure at least 4 weeks, then reattach any hardware. ◆

ANTIQUING RECIPE

To make your own antiquing medium, mix 1 tablespoon odorless turpentine, 1 tablespoon linseed oil, and a small dot of brown oil paint, such as burnt umber, asphaltum, or raw sienna; choose the hue that's most compatible with the base coat colorations specifically for use in this flourishing craft.

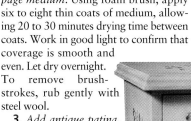

How to Make a Covered Box

Substitute laminated fabric for complicated metal hinges.

✍ BY MARY JO HINEY

This box was covered with rayon, which can be safely glued to process, crescent, or mat board. Avoid thin fabrics; the glue could bleed through.

DESIGNER'S TIP

To draft accurate lines, mark your measurements with pencil point dots. Instead of lining up the ruler against the dots, slip the pencil point into each dot and move the ruler up to the pencil tip. Give all the dots a final space check with your pencil before drawing the line.

COLOR PHOTOGRAPHY:
Carl Tremblay

DIAGRAMS:
Judy Love

MOST MAKE-IT-YOURSELF BOX instructions include some sort of external hinge to attach the lid to the body of the box. My method simplifies the process by using fabric for the box's hinge. The secret: laminating the box bottom, sides, and lid to the same piece of fabric.

Before starting the project, it's important to understand your materials. The best board for making a sturdy box is process board, which can be found at art stores or anywhere posters are laminated and framed. The second-best alternative is crescent board, also available at art supply stores; a third option, should you need it, is mat board. I recommend a thickness of approximately one-sixteenth inch, as this is easily cut with a utility knife. Thicker cardboard is more difficult to cut, and the directions and measurements that follow are not designed for it. For a sturdier box, the directions call for layering two thicknesses of board together, which should measure approximately one-eighth inch.

A few notes about your tools: Always use a new, sharp blade in your utility knife. A sharp blade is safer than a dull blade because you don't have to press as hard to make the cut. Measure and mark the board for box parts with a steel ruler (not a yardstick) and a sharp pencil; a steel ruler is more accurate.

You can glue a variety of fabrics onto this box, except for thin silks and polyesters, which do not laminate well. Cotton prints are exceptionally forgiving to work with.

My dictionary defines *laminate* as "to cover with or bond to one or more thin layers," but in reality it's just a fancy word for gluing layers together. I recommend Aleene's Thin-Bodied Tacky glue for your laminating tasks because it has the perfect consistency for box making.

Mary Jo Hiney is a craft designer and author of how-to books.

INSTRUCTIONS
Drafting and Cutting the Pieces

Note: In this project, A is the inside box bottom and sides; B is the inside lid; the three parts of C make up the outside box sides; D is the box base; and E is the box lid.

1. *Draft 12 box pieces.* Draft box pieces A, B, C, D, and E on process board, referring to illustration A for dimensions. Use steel ruler and sharp pencil. Draft all solid (cutting) lines and dash (scoring) lines, butting edges when possible. Use grid ruler or triangle to confirm right angles. For A, draft 11½" x 16½" rectangle, then draft parallel lines 3½" in from each edge. For C, draft one long piece with dash lines as shown, then draft five additional reinforcement pieces with solid lines: one C1, two C2s, and two C3s. Draft two Ds and two Es. Trim corners diagonally on E pieces. Label each piece lightly in pencil.

2. *Refine piece A.* Draft four new cutting lines to extend each 9½" box side a scant ¹⁄₁₆" at each end (*see* illustration A). This will ensure that box ends fit together snugly.

3. *Cut out box pieces.* Start by laying board on self-healing cutting mat, then align steel ruler on each marked line and draw utility knife blade along edge of ruler in multiple clean, smooth strokes. Cut straight through board on solid lines; score, or cut halfway through, board along dashed lines.

4. *Cut four fabric pieces.* To cover A/B, C, D, and E: Refer to illustration A for dimensions; use rotary cutter, cutting guide, and self-healing mat.

Laminating

Note: The following steps describe how to laminate box pieces A and B to the fabric. As you assemble the box, follow the same basic laminating procedure for other pieces when directed.

1. *Prepare work area.* Lay down brown kraft paper and place moist and dry rags nearby for cleanup. Position box piece A

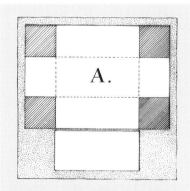

LAYOUT DIAGRAM
See page 46 for patterns.

so unscored surface faces up. Lay 18" fabric square to one side, wrong side up. Pour glue into paint tray, load roller with glue, then roll on edge of kraft paper to shed excess.

2. *Laminate A and B to fabric.* Once roller is covered with glue, run roller across box piece A out to edges. Set piece A glue-side down on one end of fabric. Apply glue to piece B and set it in position 1/16" from piece A (illustration A). Turn entire assembly over and smooth down fabric with palm, making sure edges adhere completely.

3. *Laminate fabric flaps.* Turn piece board-side up. Using scissors, trim excess fabric 3/4" from board edges all around, trim corners diagonally, and clip into inside corners (illustration B). Roll 3/4" band of glue along outer edges, fold down fabric flaps, and press to adhere (illustration C). Turn piece fabric-side up and smooth with palm. Sharpen inner and outer corners and edges with fingers as necessary. Let dry 5 minutes.

Assembling the Box

1. *Form basic box shape.* To make score lines more pliable, lay A/B piece on flat surface, fabric-side up. (Fold each extension back, one at a time, until extension lies flat on A, and roll scored fold with dowel. To form box sides, bring four extensions up at right angles; piece B, which forms lid, will flap loose. Cut four 1½"- to 2"-wide strips of fabric, then laminate each to outside corner as shown in illustration D to further reinforce box shape.

2. *Prepare piece C.* Laminate the five reinforcement pieces to scored surface (illustration E). Then laminate piece C, scored side down, to fabric; do not glue edges yet. Let dry 2 minutes, then fold each score line back and roll with dowel as in step 1. Unfold C and lay flat. Using scissors, slit fabric allowance at C2-C3 score lines along one long edge; fold over and glue allowances as shown in illustration F, keeping top edges and one side edge of C3s free (illustration F).

3. *Attach C to box.* Apply glue to wrong side of piece C, then press C1 section against box front, even with upper rim; lower edge will extend 1/8" below box, creating well for box bottom. Continue wrapping C around box, laminating C2s to sides and C3s at back; laminate C3 with side flap first, then butt second C3 with folded side edge against it. Glue top flaps of C3s to box lid B (illustration G).

4. *Attach D and E to box.* Laminate two D and two E boards together, then laminate each to remaining two fabric pieces. Laminate D to box underside and E to box lid (illustration H). Weight box with several heavy books and let dry overnight. ◆

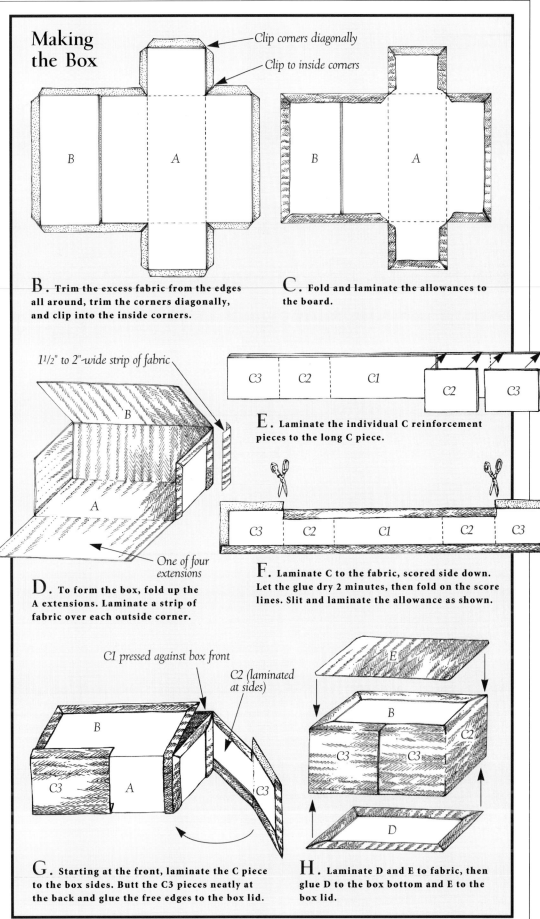

Making the Box

Clip corners diagonally

Clip to inside corners

B. Trim the excess fabric from the edges all around, trim the corners diagonally, and clip into the inside corners.

C. Fold and laminate the allowances to the board.

1½" to 2"-wide strip of fabric

D. To form the box, fold up the A extensions. Laminate a strip of fabric over each outside corner.

One of four extensions

E. Laminate the individual C reinforcement pieces to the long C piece.

F. Laminate C to the fabric, scored side down. Let the glue dry 2 minutes, then fold on the score lines. Slit and laminate the allowance as shown.

C1 pressed against box front

C2 (laminated at sides)

G. Starting at the front, laminate the C piece to the box sides. Butt the C3 pieces neatly at the back and glue the free edges to the box lid.

H. Laminate D and E to fabric, then glue D to the box bottom and E to the box lid.

Perfectly Pressed Flowers

Make a padded press that cushions and dehydrates for perfect flowers every time.

❧ BY CELLESTINE HANNEMAN

A variety of flowers and foliage are suitable for pressing. Clockwise from top: heather, rabbit's-foot fern, Johnny-jump-up (viola), geranium incanum, coreopsis, and rose leaves.

I ENJOY DESIGNING WITH PRESSED flowers but have often been disappointed by samples pressed between the pages of a book (the most common method) or in a conventional press. After harvesting my share of distorted and discolored plant material, with petals shrunken and thick parts of the flowers smashed, I decided to seek an alternative. I could see that even pressure could damage petals of varying thickness, and that poor or uneven evaporation could cause discoloration. To solve these problems, I began searching for a material or method of pressing that would preserve the contour and color of my flowers, accommodate their varying thicknesses, and allow air to circulate and evaporate at the same time.

I found the answer at a lingerie manufacturer's outlet store, when I spotted semi-sheer nylon tricot fabric. I got the idea of pairing it with polyester batting to create a pressing pad. I thought the batting would be springy enough to yield to thick flower centers, while the smooth, delicate tricot surface would support even the most paper-thin petals. The combined fiber layers would allow air to circulate, moving the moisture away from the flowers to prevent decay.

I took the material home and began experimenting. I laid fresh daisies face down on a fifteen-inch-square piece of chipboard covered with tricot-covered batting, set a second tricot-batting pad over them, and placed an even weight on top. In my early experiments, flowers in the middle of the pad became discolored because they didn't dry thoroughly or quickly enough—the longer a flower is held in a damp, airless enclosure, the greater the chance for decay to develop. The flowers near the edges, however,

dried very well in about a week's time. Since moisture seemed to be trapped at the center of the pad, I concluded that evaporation would probably occur more efficiently with a smaller pad. I reduced the pad size to five and one-half by eight inches, and this smaller pad has produced perfect pressed flowers every time.

Cellestine Hanneman, of North Hills, California, created this flower-pressing method while searching for a way to press flowers from wedding bouquets.

INSTRUCTIONS
Making the Pressboards

1. *Cut pressboard material.* Cut twelve 6" x 8½" pieces each from tricot, web, and batting. To assemble twelve pads, work through steps 2 to 5 twelve times assembly-line style.

2. *Join web to batting.* Lay batting on ironing board, then lay web on top, adhesive face down. Using wet press cloth and wool setting, touch iron to press cloth for 10 seconds; do not let weight of iron press down on batting fibers. Repeat, moving iron to new sections of press cloth, until entire surface has been covered. Let cool, then, beginning at corner, peel off paper backing from web (*see* illustration A).

3. *Join batting to chipboard.* Lay newsprint across work surface to catch spray. Following manufacturer's directions, apply spray adhesive to web side of batting and one side of chipboard. Press adhesive surfaces together firmly; batting will extend beyond chipboard (illustration B).

4. *Join tricot to batting.* Apply spray adhesive to batting surface of chipboard/batting piece. Lay the tricot on top and press gently to adhere (illustration C).

5. *Reinforce batting with additional adhesive.* Gently split batting apart so that half is attached to tricot and half to the chipboard. Lay both pieces so that batting faces up, and spray them with adhesive. Reassemble pieces, pressing adhesive surfaces firmly together (illustration D). When glue is dry, trim off all fibers even with chipboard edge (illustration E).

Pressing the Flowers

1. *To press flowers face forward,* lay them face down on plain chipboard, close together but not touching. Set padded pressboard, tricot side down, on top so flowers are sandwiched in between.

2. *To press flowers in side view,* push petals upward and lay flowers on their sides on padded pressboard. Set plain chipboard on top.

3. *Finishing pressing process:* Stack pressboard sandwiches in warm, dry area and weight with light (3-pound) weight. Leave undisturbed 5 to 7 days. To hasten drying process, warm oven to 100 degrees, turn off heat, and place pressboards inside. Leave oven light on and rewarm oven each day. This method will prevent discoloration of flowers such as geranium florets.

Making the Pressboards

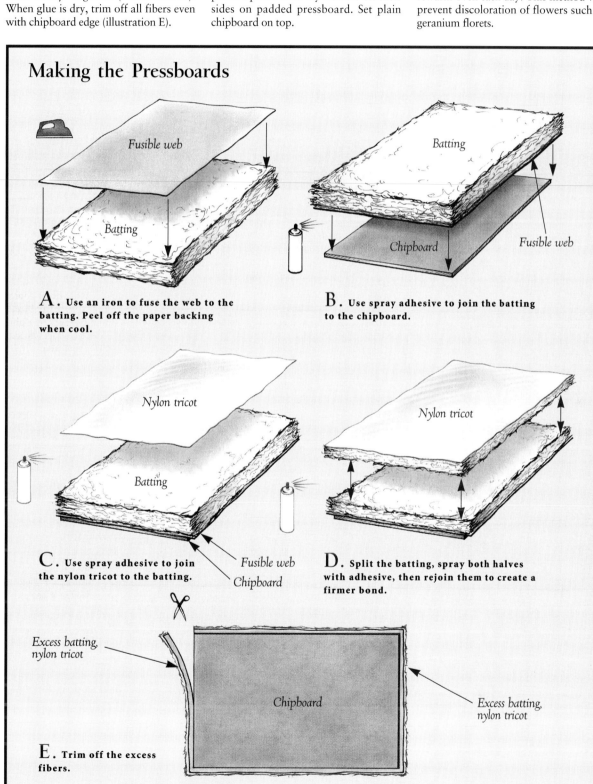

A. Use an iron to fuse the web to the batting. Peel off the paper backing when cool.

Fusible web

Batting

B. Use spray adhesive to join the batting to the chipboard.

Batting

Chipboard

Fusible web

C. Use spray adhesive to join the nylon tricot to the batting.

Nylon tricot

Batting

Fusible web

Chipboard

D. Split the batting, spray both halves with adhesive, then rejoin them to create a firmer bond.

Nylon tricot

E. Trim off the excess fibers.

Excess batting, nylon tricot

Chipboard

Excess batting, nylon tricot

Making a Pressed Flower Bookmark

MATERIALS
Pressed Flower Bookmark

■ **Pressed flowers and leaves**
■ **Heavy card-stock paper, two colors**
■ **Clear acetate laminating film**
■ **Tacky glue**

You'll also need:
8" x 10" piece of glass (edges masked with tape); scissors; pencil; steel ruler; X-Acto knife; tweezers; laundry softener; facial tissue; newsprint; teaspoon; two ½" stiff brushes; and heavy book.

Other items, if necessary:
Iron and press cloth (to enhance laminated bond).

The purple flowers in this bookmark are geranium incanum, the leaves are Cape honeysuckle, and the curved tendrils come from a vine.

To make a pressed flower bookmark, be sure to choose flowers that have a durable color. Flowers and leaves will eventually fade, especially when exposed to direct sun or fluorescent lights. (A flower bookmark, safely tucked away inside a book, will retain its colors for many more years than flowers displayed in a picture on a wall exposed to direct sunlight.) You can expect green leaves to lose all of their color after one year, turning to beige or sepia tones. Ivy is the exception; it retains its green color for two years or more. Other options are white or gray leaves such as dusty miller and acacia; they appear to retain their color indefinitely.

Most of the plants you'll need are sold in small pots with flowers in full bloom at your local nursery. The exceptions are Queen Anne's lace, which is available as a cut flower, and buttercup, which is a wildflower. You can use any leaves, ferns, or vine tendrils that will work with your design, or weeds and grass that have gone to seed.

The paper for your bookmark should be a heavier card or cover stock for added durability. For the border around the bookmark, choose a second paper in a contrasting color.

INSTRUCTIONS

1. *Cut card-stock paper to size.* Measure and mark rectangles for bookmark on paper, then place paper on glass, cutting on marked lines using ruler and X-Acto knife. For bookmark front, cut one 2⅜" x 7⅝" rectangle. For bookmark back, cut one 2⅝" x 7⅞" rectangle. Use

scissors to rough-cut two pieces of laminating film, each measuring 3¼" x 8 ½".

2. *Create pressed flower arrangement on bookmark front.* Lay smaller rectangle on glass. Using tweezers, arrange pressed materials on surface. Lay down leaves and flowers with stems first, then lay down those without stems. Keep materials at least ¼" in from paper edges (*see* illustration A).

3. *Affix laminating film to interior rectangle.* To reduce static electricity, moisten tissue with a few drops of laundry softener and rub it onto front of acetate. Remove backing from acetate and lay, adhesive side down, on rectangle (illustration B); excess at edges will cling to glass. Rub acetate with fingers. Use ruler and X-Acto knife to trim excess acetate even with edges of rectangle (illustration C); peel up each piece off glass after you trim it. Enhance bond, if necessary, with heat by setting iron on low, laying dry press cloth on top, and pressing 2 or 3 seconds.

4. *Affix laminating film to bookmark back.* Lay larger rectangle on glass, peel backing from acetate, and lay it on top. Rub with fingers to adhere, then trim away excess acetate even with edges.

5. *Glue bookmark interior to back.* Lay back, acetate side down, on work surface. Lay interior face down on newsprint. Brush glue across back of interior and out beyond edges. Center interior glue side down on back and press to adhere (illustration D). Swab up any oozing glue with dry brush, then weight bookmark under heavy book overnight until dry. ◆

MAKING THE BOOKMARK

A. Use tweezers to arrange the dried flowers and leaves on the bookmark front.

B. Lay the acetate on the arrangement adhesive side down and rub to adhere.

C. Trim the excess acetate even with the bookmark edges.

D. Laminate the bookmark back in the same way, then glue both pieces together with the paper sides facing.

Foolproof Verdigris Finishing

The key: a patina antiquing kit that quickly and easily transforms a castoff into a treasure.

❧ BY FRANCOISE HARDY

MATERIALS

- Old metal object
- Modern Options Patina Antiquing Kit

You'll also need: newspapers or drop cloths; rags; goggles; rubber gloves; wood blocks; and disposable plastic cups.

Other items, if necessary: steel wool or stiff wire brush, naval jelly, Rust-Oleum, zinc chromate, or epoxy primer (to treat and/or prevent rust on iron, steel, aluminum, etc.); stiff wire brush and 220- to 400-grit sandpaper (to treat flaking paint).

WHEN LOOKING FOR A WAY to create a verdigris finish for a cast-off metal chair, I sidestepped techniques that use paints and glazes in favor of a kit that produces the real thing: a genuine oxidized patina.

Paints and glazes can produce extremely convincing faux patinas, but it takes an experienced hand to apply them. The Modern Options Patina Antiquing Kit offers more predictable and satisfying results with far less effort, particularly if you're tackling larger projects. (This kit is also used in "Folk Art Rooster," page 6.)

The kit contains almost everything you'll need, but you will have to supply rags and safety eye goggles and, if a metal project has or is prone to rust, a rust-proofing primer to treat the metal.

My chair featured a welded steel rod frame and woven steel seat. I treated it first with the kit's Copper Topper solution, and then with the Patina Green solution. The first signs of oxidation appeared in about thirty minutes, with the copper particles showing a hint of green. Full development took another hour. At that point, I recoated several nooks and crannies for added detail. I allowed three days' additional curing, and then sealed it to halt the patinating action and to protect the finish for outdoor use.

Francoise Hardy is an artisan and craftsperson living in Boston.

INSTRUCTIONS

Note: Set up work area in dry, well-ventilated space; lay down drop cloths. Read kit instructions thoroughly and wear rubber gloves and safety goggles during all steps. Pour solutions into plastic cups as needed. For easier access, elevate object on wood blocks. Proceed through steps 1 through 4, selecting those appropriate to your object. Finish your project with step 5.

1. *To treat and/or protect against surface rust:* Rub object with steel wool or wire brush to dislodge bits of flaking rust. If rusting is severe, chemically deoxidize with naval jelly. To prevent further rust, or to prevent future rust on new metal, brush on Rust-Oleum, zinc chromate, or epoxy primer. Follow manufacturer's instructions and safety precautions.

This steel chair has been coated with copper and then treated with a patina solution to produce a genuine verdigris finish.

2. *To treat flaking paint:* Rub object vigorously with wire brush to dislodge loose flakes. Where paint is firmly adhered, rub edges with 220- to 400-grit sandpaper. If surface defects prove insurmountable, have chair stripped chemically, then prime raw metal as in step 1.

3. *To treat copper, brass, or bronze:* Clean object thoroughly using Metal Master solution. Apply light coat of Patina Green with bristle brush. Rest object so coated areas are horizontal as solution dries; if object is large, coat it in sections that can be positioned horizontally. Blot drips at lower edges with brush to discourage pooling. Solution will dry in 20 to 30 minutes, and oxidation will begin. Let patina develop for 1 hour. To intensify patina, apply second and third coats, brushing perpendicular to previous coat. Let solution dry between coats.

4. *To treat all other metals:* Clean object thoroughly using Metal Master solution. Apply Primo Primer and Sealer

with foam brush; let dry 1 hour, apply second coat, and let dry again. Shake Copper Topper vigorously, then apply with foam brush. Let dry 1 or more hours; if object will be used outdoors, let dry 24 hours. Apply second coat of Copper Topper, brushing perpendicular to previous coat; work an area no larger than can be coated in 5 minutes. Before Copper Topper dries (5- to 10-minute window), use bristle brush to apply Patina Green. If object is large, repeat Copper Topper/Patina Green sequence until entire object is coated. Oxidation will begin in 10 to 25 minutes. To intensify patina, apply second and third coats of Patina Green, letting solution dry thoroughly between coats.

5. *To protect finish:* Let verdigris finish cure 3 to 4 days. If desired, wash object in warm soapy water, rinse well, and dry thoroughly. Apply one or two very light coats of Primo Primer and Sealer, letting dry at least 1 hour between coats. ◆

IMPORTANT SAFETY PRECAUTIONS

- Before starting, read all manufacturer's directions.
- Work in a well-ventilated room.
- Protect the work surface with newspaper.
- Wear protective eye goggles and rubber gloves.

COLOR PHOTOGRAPHY:
Carl Tremblay

Decorative Floorcloth with Faux Spanish Tiles

Apply simple painting techniques to a $7 piece of canvas to create a villa-style accent.

BY LILY FRANKLIN

COLOR PHOTOGRAPHY:
Carl Tremblay

ILLUSTRATION:
Michael Gellatly

STYLING:
Gabrielle Derrick dePapp/Team

MATERIALS

- **Primed artist's canvas, at least 30" x 42"**
- **Artist's acrylics: cadmium yellow deep, burnt sienna, burnt umber, titanium white, indigo blue, and black**
- **Clear acrylic glaze**
- **Acrylic matte varnish**
- **3½ yards light brown welting cord tape**

You'll also need:
1" flat, ¼" round, 1" stencil, and 2" foam brushes; 3" x 5" cellulose sponge; disposable plastic plates and craft sticks; paper towels; hot-glue gun; yardstick; T square; scissors; and pencil.

DESIGNER'S TIP

Gesso is a white liquid made from a fine white chalk and glue. To use it, you brush it onto a surface in layers. Sand lightly between layers.

You can create the warmth and beauty of terra-cotta tile using shades of tan, rust, and rose paint applied to artist's canvas.

SPANISH FLOOR TILES MADE OF fired terra-cotta are in high demand, and for good reason. The beautiful colors create a shifting geometric pattern of tan, rust, sand, and rose across a floor. It is this subtle variation, combined with an attractive diamond pattern, that makes terra-cotta floors so appealing.

To get this look, you don't necessarily have to buy and install tiles. Instead, using simple trompe l'oeil painting techniques, you can decorate a rectangle of canvas to create a floorcloth that imitates the characteristics of Spanish floor tile. All you need is common artist's canvas, paint, glaze, and sealer, all of which are sold at artist's supply stores.

Canvas is available by the yard both primed and unprimed. Primed canvas is coated with gesso, a white size that seals and preshrinks the surface so that it is firm and tight (*see* Designer's Tip, left). Some artists prefer to size their canvases themselves, but buying preprimed canvas allows you to immediately begin working on the floorcloth design.

Your first step is to draw a diamond pattern on the primed canvas, and then paint the diamonds in two colors checkerboard-style, using acrylic paint. Artist's acrylics come in tubes and are easy to use. They can be dispensed onto disposable plates and mixed together to create a variety of colors. Once you've drafted and painted the basic diagonal tiles, the color development begins.

The key to achieving a realistic tile look is to apply the paints and then the glazes in stages, treating each "tile" indi-

vidually. To suggest hand-molded clay tiles, each diamond is outlined with dark paint, and the corners are rounded off. Rubbing paint-tinted glazes into each marked diamond with a sponge creates a distinct patina and helps the individual tiles emerge.

After the painted tiles have dried, the entire floorcloth is varnished to protect it from wear. Varnish mediums come in plastic containers with screw-off lids and are available in various sizes. Because only a small amount is used on the floorcloth, you can save the remaining varnish for use on future projects. To finish the floorcloth, the raw edges of the canvas are folded to the wrong side, and hot-glued in place for a firm bond. Make sure the glue is very hot and press the flap down firmly before the glue begins to cool.

Lily Franklin is a designer living in Albuquerque, New Mexico. The floorcloth was designed by Ritch Holben, an architect from Nahant, Massachusetts.

INSTRUCTIONS
Marking the Canvas

1. *Draft floorcloth rectangle on canvas.* Using yardstick and T square, measure and mark 24" x 36" rectangle on center of canvas, allowing 3" border all around. Mark edges of rectangle in 6" increments, beginning 3" from corners (*see* illustration A, next page).

2. *Draft diamonds on rectangle.* Using yardstick and beginning at one corner, draft diagonal lines across rectangle to connect marks made in step 1. Draft perpendicular diagonal lines to complete diamonds (illustration B).

Painting the Canvas

Note: To use paints, squeeze small amounts as needed onto disposable plastic plates. To mix paints, use craft sticks.

1. *Paint diamonds.* Using 1" flat brush and burnt sienna paint, paint 20 triangles along edge of rectangle and 15 diamonds within rectangle that touch triangles and each other point to point (illustration C). Wash brush and blot on paper towel. Paint remaining 24 diamonds cadmium yellow deep

2. *Develop tile effect.* Using ¼" round brush and burnt umber paint, paint fine, dark lines between diamonds and triangles; round off all corners and triangle points to suggest handmade clay tiles. Paint outer edges of rectangle (illustration D).

3. *Glaze and intensify individual tiles.* Cut dampened sponge into two 2"-square pieces. Mix 1 tablespoon glaze, 1 drop yellow paint, and 1 drop titanium white paint, then rub into center of each yellow tile with sponge. Use 1" flat brush to apply same glaze mixture to yellow tile edges. Using second sponge piece, rub center of each burnt sienna tile with indigo blue paint. Mix 1 tablespoon glaze, 1 drop burnt sienna paint, and 1 drop white paint and brush along edges of burnt sienna tiles using flat brush (illustration D).

4. *Apply overall wash and spattering.* For wash, mix 2 tablespoons glaze and 2 drops white paint, then rub over entire surface with damp sponge. Blot excess with paper towel. For spattering, dilute white paint slightly with water until it reaches consistency of heavy cream. Work bristles of stencil brush into mixture, hold brush 6" above floorcloth surface, and run thumb across bristles to release fine spray. Spatter entire surface. Clean brush, then repeat spattering using black paint. Let surface dry at least one hour.

Finishing the Floorcloth

1. *Apply protective sealer coat.* Brush varnish across surface using foam brush. Let dry 1 hour.

2. *Finish edges.* Trim off corners diagonally (illustration E). Fold each edge to wrong side and hot-glue in place. Hot-glue welting cord tape around edge on wrong side, lapping ends at starting point and trimming off excess (illustration F). ◆

Making the Floorcloth

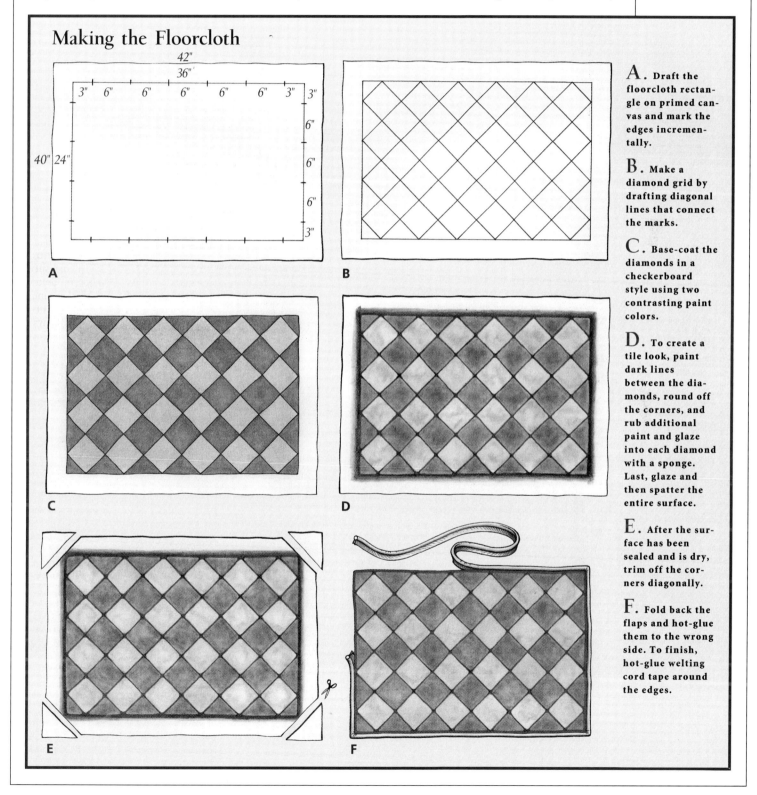

A. Draft the floorcloth rectangle on primed canvas and mark the edges incrementally.

B. Make a diamond grid by drafting diagonal lines that connect the marks.

C. Base-coat the diamonds in a checkerboard style using two contrasting paint colors.

D. To create a tile look, paint dark lines between the diamonds, round off the corners, and rub additional paint and glaze into each diamond with a sponge. Last, glaze and then spatter the entire surface.

E. After the surface has been sealed and is dry, trim off the corners diagonally.

F. Fold back the flaps and hot-glue them to the wrong side. To finish, hot-glue welting cord tape around the edges.

Fast and Fabulous Marbled Giftwrap

Create the look of traditional marbled paper in less than half the time with a size made from common gelatin.

❧ BY BOBBIE SULLIVAN

MATERIALS

- **Variety of oil and enamel paints**
- **White butcher paper**
- **1 envelope unflavored gelatin, such as Knox**
- **Odorless turpentine or paint thinner**

You'll also need:
13" x 17" x 4" pan or bin; large, plastic garbage bag; 5-quart pail; 2-cup measuring cup; scissors; old newspaper; plastic spoons; small plastic cups; and 1 latex glove.

Other items, if needed:
iron or heavy book (to minimize wrinkles).

DESIGNER'S TIP

For added accent, apply rubber stamp images on the butcher paper before you marble. Stamp the images using an oil-based stamp pad. The images will dry immediately and remain strong even after marbling.

ILLUSTRATION:
Nenad Jakesevic

COLOR PHOTOGRAPHY:
Carl Tremblay

You can transform plain butcher paper into this elegant giftwrap with just a few simple steps and materials you may already have on hand at home.

MARBLED PAPER CONVEYS A feeling of richness with its characteristic swirls and its beautiful color combinations. Now you can reproduce the look of traditional marbling on giftwrap, but without the time-consuming search for ingredients and the complicated preparation associated with it.

The traditional technique for marbling paper involves preparing a marbling bath, or size, of carrageenan (a pre-cooked, powdered seaweed) and tap water and letting it sit overnight. You prepare the paper by covering it with alum (aluminum sulfate) to improve paint adhesion and then air-dry it for one hour. When both the bath and paper are ready, you drop specks of paint onto the size. The paper is then placed into the size for a few seconds. You will pull it out with the paint adhered to it in a marble pattern.

My marbling method is similar to the traditional technique in principle but with two changes that accelerate the process. First, I use a kitchen staple—unflavored gelatin—instead of carrageenan. The gelatin and water create a size that is ready to use in only one hour and is similar in viscosity to soft, almost-jelled Jello. The surface of the gelatin supports the dropped paint so that the colors can float, mingle, and disperse into infinite patterns. Second, I don't pretreat the paper with alum because I prefer less color saturation. Skipping this step not only saves time but creates a marble design of pastel colors, which has a lighter, more delicate look than that of traditional marbled paper.

It's important to use a good-quality, medium-weight, white paper. I recommend butcher paper from a wholesale paper outlet; the paper comes in a roll thirteen hundred feet long and eighteen inches wide. You can also find it at art stores. The paper is uncoated and looks and feels like parchment. It dries fairly flat even though it retains quite a bit of moisture in the marbling process. If you can't find this paper, or prefer to use another kind, feel free to experiment. Any good-quality paper will work.

Less leeway exists with the paint. For this project, you must use oil-based paint. Small jars of enamel paint or tubes of oil paint come in many colors and can be found in any art supply store. Or search among your old paint cans. I did, and found Rust-Oleum and exterior oil paint, both of which worked well.

To prepare your paint, thin it with odorless turpentine or paint thinner to the consistency of light cream. Then use a spoon to transfer the paint to the size and create a swirling pattern. Don't be concerned if the pattern on the surface is difficult to see; it will appear on the paper. And don't worry about marking and cutting the paper exactly to size. You can rough-cut it into a basic size and shape as long as it's slightly smaller than the pan.

Experiment with paint colors and combinations. Adding white paint during the swirling stage will help the other colors to flow, and metallics, though finicky, are worth a try. I found that gold and silver enamels work best if they're dropped on first and swirled before adding any other colors. You can also create new colors by mixing paints before adding them to the size.

This method of marbling is very easy and forgiving. No two patterns are alike, and the more you do, the more you'll want to experiment with the colors. You can even change colors without preparing a new batch of sizing. If any paint residue is left behind from a previous print, simply take a new piece of paper and press it lightly on the surface. You will lift up the rest of the paint and end up with a pattern that is a much softer and more delicate version of the piece that came before. Once the gelatin size is free of paint, you can add a new color and begin again.

You can use marbled paper to accent a gift in several ways. It can make an elegant substitute for both the giftwrap outside and the tissue inside. Or it can be cut into strips and looped just like fabric ribbon. You can also coordinate the giftwrap on shower or wedding favors with the color of the bridesmaids' dresses or the table linen.

Marbled paper can be used for more than wrapping gifts; it is also a wonderful source of decorative paper for covering blank books and frames. You can marble the paper in a favorite color and use it to create a set of matching stationery items. For example, you can apply marbled paper to three small blank books, one for addresses, another for birthdays, and a third for a daily reminder. Keep the set for yourself, or bundle up the little books in a satin ribbon and present them as a gift.

One of the main appeals of marbling is the subtle color and delicate pattern that the method produces. The colors tend to be pale and lilting, which is perfect for making gifts and cards for baby showers or christenings, or for wedding-related events. To make a gift card, open up a small envelope and use it as a template to mark and cut an envelope from the marble paper. Fold the marbled paper to match the folds in the commercial envelope, then glue down the flaps. For the card, fold a piece of scrap paper in half and trim it until it fits the newly made envelope. Use the test card as a template for cutting the marbled paper. Decorate the front of the marbled card with an attractive stamp or sticker, or with a drawing done freehand using magic markers.

Bobbie Sullivan is a decorative artist and quilter living in Scituate, Massachusetts.

INSTRUCTIONS

1. *Prepare sizing.* Dissolve gelatin in 2 cups hot tap water (takes about 5 minutes). Pour into pail, add 3 quarts cold water, and let stand 1 hour.

2. *Prepare work area.* Cut open plastic bag to make large sheet. Line pan with plastic so it overhangs sides. Cut approximately 50 sheets of butcher paper 1" smaller all around than pan. (Size will allow creation of approximately 50 sheets before new solution needs to be prepared.)

3. *Marble paper.* After sizing has cured 1 hour, pour into pan and agitate to eliminate bubbles. Put on glove. Put small amount of paint into cup, dilute with thinner, and stir with spoon until mixture is consistency of light cream and no lumps

MARBLING THE PAPER

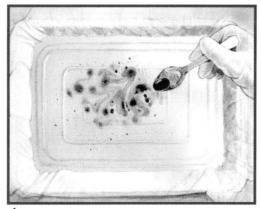

A. Use a spoon to drizzle diluted paint lightly across the sizing surface.

B. Draw the spoon across the surface to move the paint into swirling patterns.

C. To "print" the pattern, lay a sheet of paper on the surface and press gently.

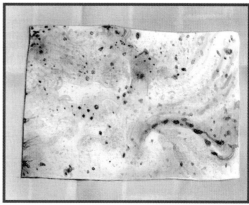

D. Lift up the paper immediately and lay it face up to dry on a sheet of newspaper.

remain. Drizzle paint lightly across sizing; paint will rest on surface (*see* illustration A). To create swirling marble pattern, draw spoon across sizing, dab surface, or stir gently (illustration B).

4. *"Print" pattern.* Gently and quickly lay sheet of paper on surface, pressing lightly to eliminate air bubbles (illustration C). Lift off immediately and lay face up on newspapers to dry (illustration D). Drying takes 1 to 24 hours, depending on humidity.

5. *Print additional sheets.* Follow same method as in step 3, drizzling new paint onto surface for each sheet. Try adding two or more separate colors, or mix colors before adding. Continue until paper is used up or paint no longer adheres. To clean up, empty size into sink, then fold up and discard plastic liner.

6. *Optional:* To minimize wrinkles, sandwich dry sheet between two more pieces of butcher paper (white only) and press with dry iron on low setting, or stack sheets and weight with heavy book for several days. ◆

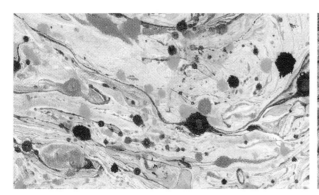

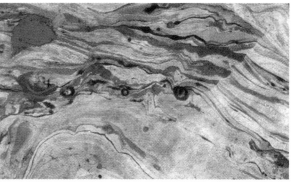

To make multicolored paper, such as the samples at left, add additional colors of paint during step 3.

Dried Rose Initial

You can make a garland using any letter from the alphabet.
All you need is wire, roses, and moss.

🐚 BY CAROL ENDLER STERBENZ

MATERIALS

- **Dried roses with leaves** (to determine size and quantity, see steps 1 and 2)
- **Sheet moss**
- **Fabric-covered florist stems**
- **Florist tape**
- **16-gauge stainless steel wire**
- **30-gauge wire**

You'll also need:
Alphabet design source; hot-glue gun; pruning shears; spray mister; needle-nose pliers; heavy-duty wire clippers; access to photocopier with enlargement capabilities *or* 12" x 18" sheet of newsprint; pencil; ruler or yardstick; masking tape; string; and scissors.

Other items, if necessary:
Small amounts dried plant material, such as pepperberry and hydrangea florets (to use as accents).

ILLUSTRATION:
Nenad Jakesevic

COLOR PHOTOGRAPHY:
Steven Mays

This eighteen-inch-high, S-shaped garland is covered with approximately seventy-five pink and yellow hybrid tea roses.

THIS INITIAL GARLAND, WHICH makes a beautiful accent for a door or wall, is quite simple to construct. The secret: using stainless steel wire for the garland's base, which is easily bent into any letter shape.

The directions here are written so that you can design a garland anywhere from eight to eighteen inches high. You'll have to measure your template to determine how many roses you'll need.

This is a good project for broken buds or flower heads left over from other projects, or you can use flowers you have dried yourself. If your buds have a small stem on them, all the better.

INSTRUCTIONS

1. *Make template.* Enlarge letter to desired size on photocopier, or draft rectangle in approximate size (8" to 18" high) on newsprint and sketch letter within the rectangle.

2. *Determine rose count.* Lay string along contours of letter, cut string, then stretch out string and measure length using ruler or yardstick (*see* illustration A). Double this figure to determine number of roses required. Select ½" to 1" blooms for letters up to 12" high, and 1" to 2" blooms for letters 12" to 18" high.

3. *Make armature.* Tape photocopy or newsprint template of letter to work surface. Unwind 16-gauge wire directly from coil without clipping. Lay wire on top of letter and bend it to match contours. Once basic letter is shaped, bend wire back on itself and retrace path in reverse (illustration B). Clip wire from coil. To add smaller pieces, such as crossbar on letter "A," repeat doubling-back method, twisting wire onto existing armature to hold it secure. Use pliers to curl all sharp wire tips inward.

4. *Pad armature with roses.* Adjust wires so space between them is about 1" on letters up to 12" high, and 2" on letters larger than 12". Wrap entire armature in florist tape. Lightly mist sheet moss. Tear off 2"-wide strips, wind around section of armature, and bind in place using 30-gauge wire (illustration C). Repeat to cover entire armature.

5. *Affix roses.* To decorate armature, snip a rose bloom from stem approximately ½" from base of rose using pruning shears. Apply hot glue to base and stem of rose, then press glued area into moss on top or sides of letter. Repeat to attach approximately half of roses (illustration D). Hot-glue leaves in between roses so leaf tips point out or up. To fill in remaining spaces, attach remaining roses and, if desired, dried materials.

6. *Attach tendrils.* Wind fabric-covered florist stems around pencil in tight spiral. Remove pencil and unwind stem slightly to relax spiral. Trim sections to desired length and hot-glue to garland (illustration E). ◆

MAKING THE GARLAND

A. Measure the letter with string.

B. Double the wire back on itself.

C. Pad the armature with moss.

D. Hot-glue roses to the moss surface.

E. Attach tendrils made from florist stems.

Decorating Frames with Wallpaper

Transform any flat frame using prepasted wallpaper borders and a special corner treatment.

❧ BY LILY FRANKLIN

COMMON WALLPAPER BORDERS can transform a plain frame into a decorative accessory that matches or complements your home's decor. You can use one border to decorate several frames of different sizes, or you can mix and match coordinated prints, plaids, stripes, and geometrics to relate several mismatched frames in one grouping. With the variety of wallpaper border designs and colors available today, the choices are almost limitless (*see* Field Guide, page 43).

For this project, you'll need to make two choices: the type of frame and the design of the wallpaper border. I recommend selecting a frame with flat, broad surfaces or, at the most, smooth and gentle troughs or crests that will still allow the wallpaper to lie flat. Frames with carved designs or deep contours will not work. When choosing a border pattern, look for one that can be hung easily in four different directions, such as geometrics, dots, stripes, or florals. A landscape pattern, for instance, might look odd hanging upside down.

You'll also need to consider the scale of the design: A wide frame can accommodate large-scale patterns, while a narrow frame will look more attractive with smaller prints. Patterns that include straight lines or bands of color on each side of the central design area can be used as guides for more accurate cutting and for neat placement on the frame. Some patterns have an interior design space bordered by two or more parallel stripes of color, which you can adapt to different frame widths. Stripes and straight lines can also be used to visually define the edges of the frame.

The frames shown at right were made with prepasted wallpaper borders. If you cannot find a prepasted border to your liking, you can use paper-backed borders, but you will need to purchase wallpaper paste. Follow the manufacturer's recommendations for the best results. For other design variations, consider using leftover scraps of wallpaper, textured wallcoverings, such as burlap or grasscloth, or cork, although the latter requires a special premixed adhesive.

To apply the wallpaper, cut the border to fit the frame, then miter and glue

You can cover plain, flat frames with a prepasted wallpaper border to create a decorative accessory for your home or as a gift for a friend.

down the corners. The trick is in the corner treatment. I recommend that you practice cutting forty-five-degree beveled pieces of border, then overlay them into the desired design. Two of the border pieces are angle-cut one-fourth inch larger to allow for an overlap at the mitered corners. You may have to slide the pattern back and forth to find the right pattern fit. If you can't arrange the design so it matches perfectly, select one motif and decoupage it on top of the seam to conceal the corners. You can trim the wallpaper border even with the edge of the frame, or if you prefer, fold the extra allowance onto the side of the frame, using hospital folds to finish the corners neatly.

Lily Franklin is a designer in Albuquerque, New Mexico. The frames were designed by Ritch Holben, an architect from Nahant, Massachusetts.

INSTRUCTIONS

1. *Test-fit border design.* Cut small piece of wallpaper border off end of roll for testing. Position test piece on flat section of frame, adjust design position, then crease at inner and outer frame edges (*see* illustration A, next page).

2. *Prepare border for cutting.* Unroll wallpaper border on cutting mat. Position top of frame face down on border design so inner and outer frame edges correspond to creases made in test piece from step 1. If design is symmetrical, adjust so designs visible to left and right of outer frame edges match. Run X-Acto knife blade from inner frame corners down to lower edge of border. Mark small dots on border at outer frame corners. Cut border from roll beyond marked area (illustration B) and label back as "top." Repeat to mark, cut, and label border sections for left side, bottom, and right side of frame.

MATERIALS

- ■ **Prepasted wall-paper border**
- ■ **Picture frame with flat, wide border**

You'll also need: X-Acto knife; self-healing cutting mat; steel straight-edge; clear plastic grid ruler; pencil; scissors; sponge; and waxed paper.

DESIGNER'S TIP

If a diagonal cut will slice through a design such as a flower, begin the cut as usual, but cut around the flower. Then, when gluing the border on the frame, overlap the extension onto the adjacent border.

ILLUSTRATION:
Mary Newell DePalma

COLOR PHOTOGRAPHY:
Carl Tremblay

3. *Miter-cut four border sections.* Lay two side sections of cut wallpaper border face up. At each end, draft diagonal line from end of slit through dot made in step 2 (illustration C). Lay top and bottom sections face up. At each end, lay ruler diagonally from end of slit through dot, then adjust ruler position down ¼" and draft line (illustration D). Using straightedge and X-Acto knife, cut on marked lines of all sections and discard excess.

4. *Trim excess from outer edge.* Lay each section of wallpaper border face up. Using straightedge and pencil, mark line corresponding to outer crease made in test piece from step 1. Using straightedge and X-Acto knife, cut on marked line of each section and discard excess (illustration E).

5. *Glue sections to frame.* Turn each section face down on waxed paper. Using moist sponge, wet entire back surface, going out beyond edges. Wet edges will curl; when they relax (1 to 2 min-utes), position section on frame so design placement at inner and outer frame edges corresponds to creases made in test piece from step 1. Fold excess at inner edge onto rabbet (the deep inside edge of a frame that holds a picture in place), then turn frame over and trim off any excess with X-Acto knife. Press firmly on right side with damp sponge to ensure adhesion and remove air bubbles. Glue bottom section in same way (illustration F), then glue sides (illustration G). ◆

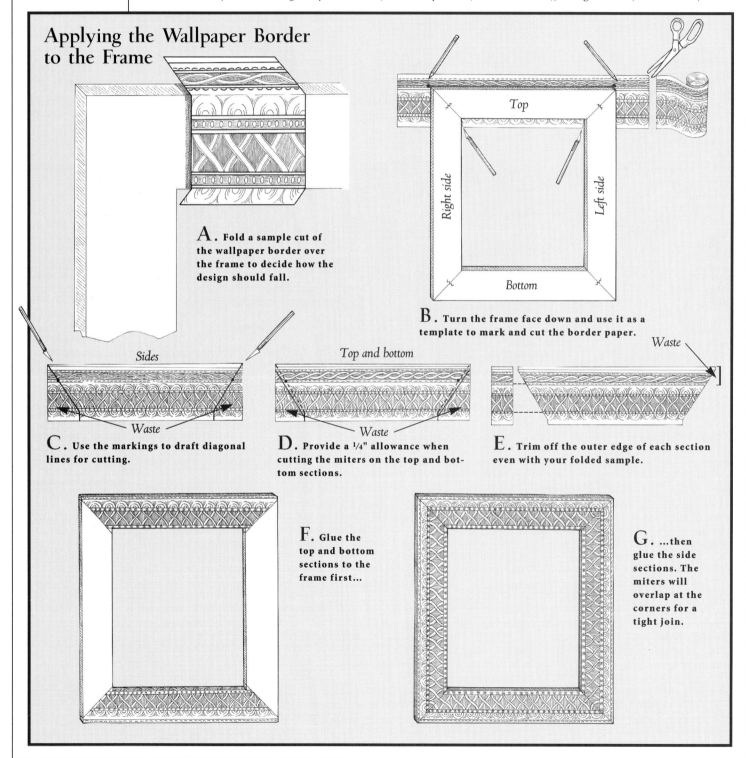

Applying the Wallpaper Border to the Frame

A. Fold a sample cut of the wallpaper border over the frame to decide how the design should fall.

B. Turn the frame face down and use it as a template to mark and cut the border paper.

Top

Right side

Left side

Bottom

Sides

Waste

C. Use the markings to draft diagonal lines for cutting.

Top and bottom

Waste

D. Provide a ¼" allowance when cutting the miters on the top and bottom sections.

Waste

E. Trim off the outer edge of each section even with your folded sample.

F. Glue the top and bottom sections to the frame first...

G. ...then glue the side sections. The miters will overlap at the corners for a tight join.

Field Guide

Easy-to-use wallpaper borders add flair to craft projects.

CREATIVE BORDERS

More and more, wallpaper is showing up on surfaces other than the wall. Crafters will find wallpaper, especially wallpaper borders, ideal as a covering for round or rectangular boxes, an accent strip for a wastebasket, or a decorative addition to giftwrap.

Wallpaper borders are particularly easy to use on projects because their designs are self-contained, and the border rolls are smaller and easier to handle than the full-size rolls. We used wallpaper borders to transform plain picture frames into decorative accents. (see "Decorating Frames with Wallpaper," page 41).

Wallpaper can accent almost any decor: traditional, neoclassical, country, romantic, or contemporary. You can match the wallpaper on your projects to the wallpaper in a room, or you can play off the existing wallpaper. For instance, you can decorate a project with floral wallpaper in colors that complement the striped wallpaper on the wall, or vice versa.

Today's wallpapers are not only easier to use than before—just wet the prepasted paper and apply (no more messy paste)—but the papers now come in an almost infinite variety of colors and designs and are available at many locations, including your local paint, hardware, or "super" home store. ◆

COLOR PHOTOGRAPHY:
Carl Tremblay

STYLING:
**Gabrielle Derrick
dePapp/Team**

Great Marriages

Pair your mismatched dishes with hand-painted glassware to create a new service.

DECORATIVE DINNERWARE

COLOR PHOTOGRAPHY:
Carl Tremblay

To extend the life of mismatched plates, bowls, and other dishes, pair them with inexpensive glass plates and tumblers that you have hand-painted with coordinating colors and patterns. You can create elaborate and serviceable place settings that include special dessert plates and bread plates, lemonade glasses, water glasses, or any other kind of glassware you desire by adding a matching dish or two.

To create the companion pieces, select a few paint colors that coordinate with the colors on your china. Then buy glass plates (about $2 each) and glass tumblers (about $1.50 each) in any number to augment your set. You will also need china paint, cotton swabs (unlike brushes, they don't leave streaks), a watercolor brush, and an oven.

Use the cotton swab to paint freehand dots, dashes, squiggles, stripes, or other designs on the outside surface of the tumblers and on the nonfood side of the plate rims. For the plates, use a watercolor brush to add a protective coat of paint in a coordinating background color over the painted design. Then place the plates and the tumblers in a cold oven, set it at 325 degrees, and bake for 35 minutes. Let the oven cool, then remove the items and let the paint set overnight. Hand-wash the glassware and use as desired. ◆

The Perfect Gift

Decorate a blank book and add personal mementos for a memorable gift.

KEEPSAKE BOOK

The perfect gift, by definition, is one that pleases and suits the recipient. It doesn't have to be expensive or time consuming to create. A personal keepsake book is in keeping with this philosophy. It simply commemorates a relationship or special event. It can be used to celebrate a friendship, the stages of a child's development (e.g., the toddler years), a birth or anniversary, or a new home or pet.

The book is part scrapbook and part photograph album, which allows both the giver and receiver to take part in its

continuing creation over the years. To start the book, the giver chooses items such as photographs, postcards, letters, pressed flowers, and small trinkets or coins, items that reflect the life of, or the giver's relationship to, the person receiving the book. The recipient can then continue to add special sentimental mementos of his or her own.

Start with any blank book with a sewn binding, and cover the front and back covers with giftwrap, marbled paper, or other art paper. You can glue or sew

small trinkets or coins directly onto a page, or sew on a one-eighth-inch-wide ribbon to create a band through which you can slip letters, postcards, and other memorabilia. Cover an old envelope with pretty giftwrap and glue it to the inside front or back cover of the book to hold other sentimental items. To make room for bulky photographs or larger items, cut several blank pages out of the book. As the book fills, slip a dressmaker's elastic band around the book's outer edge to keep the contents in place. ◆

COLOR PHOTOGRAPHY:
Carl Tremblay

Patterns for Projects in This Issue

Organdy Tablecloth
(see article, page 16)

Pattern 1

Pattern 2

ENLARGE PATTERNS 1 AND 2 SO EACH FILLS AN 11" X 17" SHEET OF PAPER.

How to Make a Fabric Covered Box
(see article, page 30)

LEGEND

Board

Waste

Right side
(fabric)

Wrong side
(fabric)

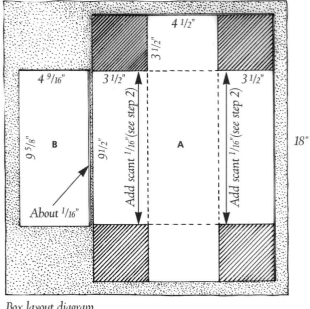

Box layout diagram

PATTERNS: **Roberta Frauwirth**

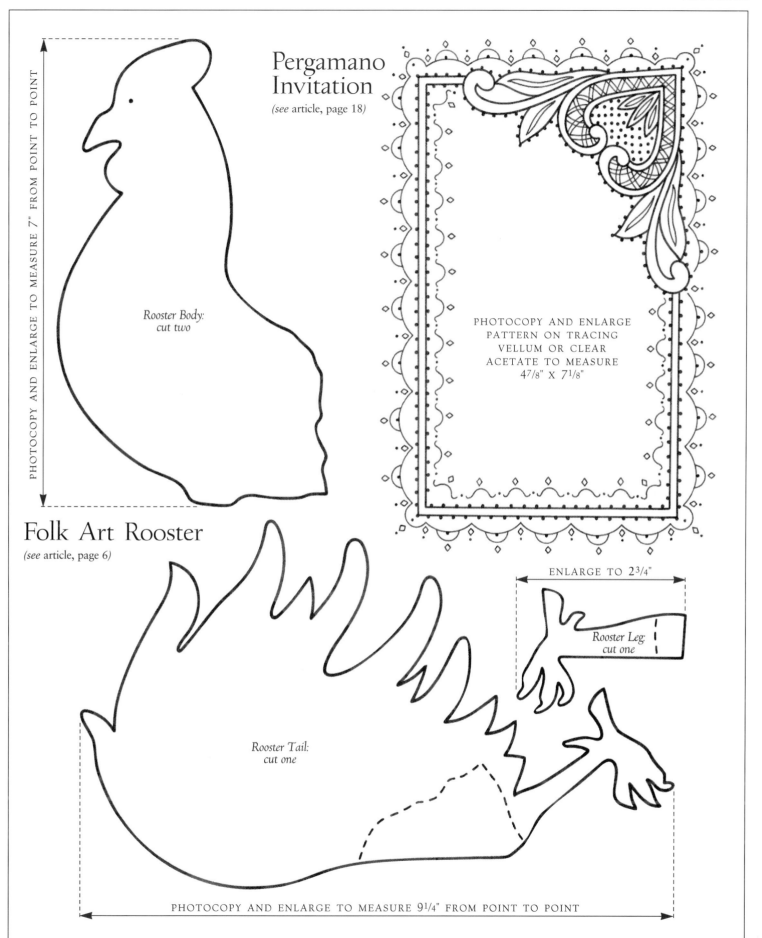

PHOTOCOPY AND ENLARGE TO MEASURE 7" FROM POINT TO POINT

Pergamano Invitation

(see article, page 18)

Rooster Body:
cut two

PHOTOCOPY AND ENLARGE
PATTERN ON TRACING
VELLUM OR CLEAR
ACETATE TO MEASURE
$4^{7/8}$" X $7^{1/8}$"

Folk Art Rooster

(see article, page 6)

ENLARGE TO $2^{3/4}$"

Rooster Leg:
cut one

Rooster Tail:
cut one

PHOTOCOPY AND ENLARGE TO MEASURE $9^{1/4}$" FROM POINT TO POINT

Sources & Resources

The following are specific mail-order sources for particular items, arranged by article.

Most of the materials necessary for the projects in this issue are available at your local craft supply store, florist's, fabric shop, or bead and jewelry supply. Generic craft supplies, such as scissors and glue, can be ordered from such catalogs as Calico Corners, Craft King, Dick Blick, Newark Dressmaker Supply, Pearl Paint, or Sunshine Discount Crafts. The following listings are specific mail-order sources for particular items, arranged by article. The suggested retail prices listed here were current at press time. Contact the suppliers directly to confirm prices and availability of products.

Folk Art Rooster, *page 6*
Antiquing kit for $25 and 2 ounces each of "Instant Rust" and "Instant Iron" for $10 from Modern Options. Copper sheets for $13.90 from Sax Arts & Crafts.

Pinafore Chair Cover, *page 10*
Fabric pictured—Mayfair from Hamil Textiles, Ltd. for $7.95 per yard from North End Fabrics.

Keepsake Box, *page 12*
Wooden box with lid for $11.25 from Viking Woodcrafts. Mushroom plugs (for legs) for $1.60 for package of fifty from The Woodworkers' Store. Robert Simmons Tolemaster liner brush #10/0 for $2.15 from Craft King.

Party Favor, *page 15*
Dried flowers from Mills Floral Company.

Organdy Tablecloth, *page 16*
Organdy (or organza) from $3.95 per yard and silk shantung from $19 per yard from North End Fabrics. Plaid fabric paint for 95¢ for 1.1 ounces from Sunshine Discount Crafts.

Lace Stationery, *page 18*
Parchment paper for 95¢ per sheet, single-needle perforating tool from $3.15, mapping pen for $5.95, ballpoint embossing tool from $5.25, piercing pad for $5, and embossing pad for $5.95, all from Kindred Spirit. White beeswax for 80¢ from Clotilde. White waterproof drawing ink from $2.40 per ounce and fifty sheets of acetate for $7.40 from Dick Blick.

Easy Ottoman, *page 22*
Fabric pictured—Tashkent in blue from Marvic Textiles—for $73 per yard from designers. High-loft batting from $12.10 from Atlanta Thread & Supply Co. Large unfinished wood finials from $6.25 and dome-headed upholstery tacks for $3.45 from Constantine's.

Scented Waters, *page 25*
Rose oil for $3.41 for 1/4 ounce, orange oil for $2.88 for 1/4 ounce, dried orange rind for $2.47 for 4 ounces, and $2.38 for 4 ounces of rose petals from A World of Plenty.

Gilded Monogram, *page 26*
Edible 23-carat gold leaf starting at $35.90 for twenty-five sheets from Dick Blick. Pastry bag for $2.25 for package of twelve, cake-decorating tips from 60¢, and coupler for 50¢ from Sweet Celebrations.

Country Dresser, *page 28*
Six-drawer jewelry chest #20-9986 for $62.99 from Viking Woodcrafts.

Pressed Flowers, *page 32*
Chipboard starting at $1 for two 22" x 28" sheets from Dick Blick. Transfer web starting at $1.50 per yard and Mountain Mist Wonderloft 100% polyester batting from $1.56 per yard from Atlanta Thread & Supply. Three 9" x 12" sheets of clear acetate laminating film for $2.10 from Dick Blick. Fine denier nylon tricot from $8.50 per yard from North End Fabrics.

Verdigris Finishing, *page 35*
Antiquing kit from Modern Options for $25.

Spanish Floorcloth, *page 36*
Three yards 53"-wide primed artist's canvas for $22.75 from Dick Blick.

Dried Rose Initial, *page 40*
Dried roses from $10.35 for twenty stems from Mills Floral Company.

The Perfect Gift, *page 45*
Blank books with sewn bindings start at $6.47 from Pearl Paint.

Great Marriages, *page 44*
China paint from $2.50 per ounce from Evan's Ceramic Supply.

Quick Projects, *page 49*
Unfinished birdhouses from $7.38 from Craft King. Wooden buttons and plugs for $1.60 and $1.65 for fifty each from The

Woodworkers' Store. Two ounces each of "Instant Rust" and "Instant Iron" for $10 from Modern Options.

Seat Cover, *back cover*
"Jester" fabric from Waverly Fabrics for $73 per yard.

🐦 🐦 🐦 🐦 🐦

The following companies are mentioned in the listings provided above. Contact each individually for a price list or catalog.

ATLANTA THREAD & SUPPLY
695 Red Oak Road, Stockbridge, GA 30281; 800-847-1001

CALICO CORNERS
203 Gale Lane, Kennett Square, PA 19348-1764; 800-777-9933

CLOTILDE INC.
2 Sew Smart Way B8031, Stevens Point, WI 54481-8031; 800-772-2891

CONSTANTINE'S
2050 Eastchester Road, Bronx, NY 10461-2297; 800-223-8087

CRAFT KING
P.O. Box 90637, Lakeland, FL 33804; 800-769-9494

DICK BLICK ART MATERIALS
P.O. Box 1267, Galesburg, IL 61402-1267; 800-447-8192

EVANS CERAMIC SUPPLY, INC.
1518 S. Washington St., Wichita, KS 67201; 800-927-2508

KINDRED SPIRIT
1714 Government Street, Victoria, British Columbia, Canada V8W 1Z5; 604-385-4567

MILLS FLORAL COMPANY
4550 Peachtree Lakes Drive, Duluth, GA 30316; 800-762-7939

MODERN OPTIONS
2325 Third Street #339, San Francisco, CA 94107; 415-252-5580

NEWARK DRESSMAKER SUPPLY
6473 Ruch Road, P.O. Box 20730, Lehigh

Valley, PA 18002-0730; 610-837-7500

NORTH ENDS FABRICS
31 Harrison Avenue, Boston, MA, 02111; 617-542-2763

PEARL PAINT CO., INC.
308 Canal Street, New York, NY 10013-2572; 800-221-6845, x2297

SAX ARTS & CRAFTS
Box 510710, New Berlin, WI 53151; 800-558-6696

SUNSHINE DISCOUNT CRAFTS
P.O. Box 301, Largo, FL 34649-0301; 800-729-2878

SWEET CELEBRATIONS
7009 Washington Avenue South, Edina, MN 55439; 800-328-6722

VIKING WOODCRAFTS, INC.
1317 8th Street S.E., Waseca, MN 56093; 800-328-0116

WAVERLY FABRICS
1325 Cooches Bridge Road, Newark, DE 19713; 800-423-5881

THE WOODWORKERS' STORE
4365 Willow Drive, Medina, MN 55340; 800-279-4441

A WORLD OF PLENTY
P.O. Box 1153, Hermantown, MN 55810-9724; 218-729-6761

CORRECTIONS:
In the Mail-Order Directory in the Winter issue, the phone number for Artex Manufacturing Company of Culver City, California, should have read 213-870-6000. Best Buy Floral Supply of Cedar Rapids, Iowa, also listed in the directory, sells only to businesses, not retail.

Retail orders from Lotus Design, Union City, California, require no minimum. Embossing Arts Company's address and telephone number have changed to P.O. Box 439, Tangent, Oregon, 98739; 541-928-9898.

Artist's Club, referenced on the Sources & Resources page in the Winter issue, has moved to P.O. Box 8940, Vancouver, WA 98668.

Quick Projects

Style your own wooden birdhouses using moss, metal, "rust," and paint.

A

B

C

D

FOUR FINISHES

A. Weathered
Paint the birdhouse exterior with yellow and ocher craft acrylics and let it dry. Then paint the roof and sill moss green, and the body barn red. Let the birdhouse dry overnight. Sand the surface lightly with coarse- to medium-grade sandpaper to wear away the red and green paints so some of the yellow base coat shows through.

B. Old and New Metal
Treat the surface of the birdhouse with Modern Options Instant Iron followed by Instant Rust. For the "tin" roof, mark and cut two rectangles from sheet metal joist panning to overhang the roof edges all around. (Use tin snips and wear gloves.) Secure the pieces to the roof using copper tacks. For ornamental gingerbread trim, wind 19-gauge silver wire around the end of needle-nose pliers in a continuous figure-eight design and hot-glue it to the roof edge. Twist more wire around a pencil to make a spiral perch. Drill a 1/16"-diameter hole just below the opening and glue the perch in position.

C. Faux Birch Bark
Base-coat the house with white acrylic paint tinged with yellow. Let it dry, then dab on very pale salmon and blue-green touches using a dry sponge. Simulate the birch bark texture by dragging a nail horizontally across the surface, making random scratches. Base-coat the roof and sill using brown and red paints. To make the thatch, hot-glue straw or dried grass to the roof in layers, then trim it evenly with pruning shears just below the roof edge. Hot-glue a contrasting reed across the thatch on each side 1" to 2" below the roof peak, and sheet moss around the base of the house. Use thin wire to attach a bittersweet branch to roof.

D. Wooden Plugs and Buttons
Using waterproof glue, affix 3/8" wooden buttons to the roof planes and sill, and 1/4" wooden plugs along the roof ridge and around the hole. Paint the house ocher and the roof blue. Brush contrasting paint across the buttons and plugs. ◆

COLOR PHOTOGRAPHY:
Carl Tremblay

Refurbished Harlequin Seat Cover

Dress up an old seat cover with new fabric. Remove seat from chair; trace around it on newsprint (plain). Cut and discard center of tracing, creating window template. Move template across fabric to "frame" desired pattern for seat. Place seat inside window and lift off template. Mark fabric 6" beyond seat edge all around and cut. Center cut fabric on seat, then turn both pieces over. Grasp opposite edges of fabric along lengthwise grain and pull them onto seat's underside, taut but not tight. Use staple gun to staple 1" from seat edge. Repeat along crosswise grain. Continue stapling at 1" intervals all around, alternating back and forth between sides to keep tension even. Trim fabric close to staples, then drop seat back into chair frame.

NUMBER THIRTEEN

FALL 1996

Handcraft
ILLUSTRATED

SPECIAL
Holiday
Gift Issue

Fast and Elegant
Plaster Pears
Use a Quick-Mold Mix to Cast
Your Own Decorative Pears

Velvet Candleshade
Dress Up a Plain Candlestick
in 30 Minutes

Gourmet Herb Vinegars
Last-Minute Gifts with
Vinegar and Fresh Herbs

Decorative Bottle
Stoppers
Harlequin-Style Tops
for Any Bottle

All-Season
Magnolia Wreath
Quick-Wire Leaves to an
Old Picture Frame

ALSO
Laminated Leaf Lampshade
Easy Beaded Ornaments
Mixed Media Greeting Cards
Copper Leaf Napkin Rings
Geometric Velvet Pillows
Roses from Sliced Apples
Italian Opera Dolls

$4.00 U.S./$4.95 CANADA

0 74470 83731 2

63 >

Contents

Transform an ordinary shade into a work of art. *See* article, page 8.

Decorative bottle
stoppers, page 10

Hand-cast plaster
fruit, page 16

Copper wire
garland, page 24

COVER PHOTOGRAPH:
Carl Tremblay

Handcraft
ILLUSTRATED

EDITOR
Carol Endler Sterbenz

EXECUTIVE EDITOR
Barbara Bourassa

ART DIRECTOR
Amy Klee

SENIOR EDITOR
Michio Ryan

MANAGING EDITOR
Keith Powers

EDITORIAL PROD. COORDINATOR
Karin L. Kaneps

DIRECTIONS EDITOR
Candie Frankel

COPY EDITOR
Gary Pfitzer

EDITORIAL ASSISTANT
Elizabeth Cameron
❧

PUBLISHER AND FOUNDER
Christopher Kimball

EDITORIAL CONSULTANT
John Kelsey

MARKETING DIRECTOR
Adrienne Kimball

CIRCULATION DIRECTOR
Carolyn Adams

FULFILLMENT MANAGER
Jamie Ayer

CIRCULATION COORDINATOR
Jonathan Venier

PRODUCTION DIRECTOR
James McCormack

PROJECT COORDINATOR
Sheila Datz

ADVERTISING PRODUCTION MANAGER
Pamela Slattery

SYSTEMS ADMINISTRATOR
Matt Frigo

PRODUCTION ARTIST
Kevin Moeller
❧

VICE PRESIDENT
Jeffrey Feingold

CONTROLLER
Lisa A. Carullo

ACCOUNTING ASSISTANT
Mandy Shito

OFFICE MANAGER
Tonya Estey

Handcraft Illustrated (ISSN 1072-0529) is published quarterly by Boston Common Press, P.O. Box 509, Brookline, MA 02147-0509. Copyright 1996 Boston Common Press Limited Partners. Periodical postage paid at Boston, MA, and additional mailing offices, USPS #011-895. For list rental information, please contact List Services Corporation, 6 Trowbridge Drive, Bethel, CT 06801; (203) 791-4148. Editorial office: P.O. Box 509, Brookline, MA 02147-0509; (617) 232-1000, FAX (617) 232-1572. Contributions should be sent to: Editor, *Handcraft Illustrated*. We cannot assume responsibility for manuscripts submitted to us. Submissions will be returned only if accompanied by a large, self-addressed stamped envelope. Subscription rates: $24.95 for one year; $45 for two years; $65 for three years. (Canada: add $6 per year; all other countries add $12 per year.) Postmaster: Send all new orders, subscription inquiries, and change of address notices to *Handcraft Illustrated*, P.O. Box 7448, Red Oak, IA 51591-0448. Single copies: $4 in U.S.; $4.95 in Canada and other countries. Back issues available for $5 each at the editorial office. PRINTED IN THE U.S.A.

Rather than put ™ in every occurrence of trademarked names, we here state that we are using the names only in an editorial fashion and to the benefit of the trademark owner, with no intention of infringement of the trademark.

Note to Readers: Every effort has been made to present the information in this publication in a clear, complete, and accurate manner. It is important that all instructions are followed carefully, as failure to do so could result in injury. Boston Common Press Limited Partners, the editors, and the authors disclaim any and all liability resulting therefrom.

From the Editor

ON THE SURFACE, CRAFTING IS CONCRETE, with prescribed processes yielding tangible objects. There is another dimension to crafting, however, which becomes an integral part of the creative experience. Even before we put brush to paper, scissor to fabric, or saw to wood, our personal connection to our materials will impact the shape and quality of the finished project as much as the processes we will use to transform those materials.

We know about this ethereal dimension to crafting from our own personal sensitivity to materials. It is this sensitivity that compels some of us to run our hands across a sheet of velvet, and others to raise just-sawn wood to their nose so they can breathe in the perfumed pitch of ancient forests.

Ask any crafter who works with fabric. I know. Recently, in the days before I started a sewing project, I looked at swaths of shimmering silk, pristine and perfect, draped over my dining room table. I thought about what I might make using these ravishing lengths, wondering what combinations I could put together. One length of silk was the color of crushed raspberries with a glow of lime green; a second was a streak of chartreuse with pools of iridescent amber. Another, colored cobalt blue, gave life to the pale gray cloth next to it. Last, there was a yellow so bright and clean that it reminded me of sliced lemons. I fingered the silks, pushed them into undulating folds, and tried out a variety of combinations. I didn't do anything else—I simply absorbed the beauty of the fabric.

Woodworkers speak in reverential tones of planks of bleached white sycamore or rock hard maple. And whether awaiting a carving chisel or a common table saw, each sample is completely appreciated in its virgin state. Painters understand the satisfying top note of turpentine and the slight bounce of the brush as it strokes a newly stretched canvas. Knitters talk about the gentle tug of the wool on their finger as they wrap a single strand around the needle, yielding not only a

Even before we put brush to paper, scissor to fabric, or saw to wood, our personal connection to our materials will impact the shape and quality of the finished project as much as the processes we will use to transform those materials.

row of perfect V-shaped stitches, but a sweater imbued with the knitter's spirit.

If we pause, these moments can be epiphanies that enhance our projects and our spirits. Crafting is more than the sum of the materials we use; it is a state of mind in which a strange yet welcome alchemy is at work, an alchemy that transforms the very expressions we set on paper, sew from cloth, or chisel from wood. This alchemy informs the process and gives the craft project, as well as the crafter, a richer identity.

The French have a term, *l'heure bleue* ("the blue hour"), which describes the brief moment between the black of night and the yellow of dawn. Lasting only seconds, the blue hour is a moment of absolute quiet, a parenthesis enclosing the moment between the sleeping and the awakened earth. It is a time to experience the fullness and immensity of life, if you allow the experience to fill you. You need only stop what you are doing.

The next time you can, stop and take time to fully examine your materials. It is from this very personal perspective that the very subtle truths of your materials will reveal themselves. You'll notice the fine threads that rise and fall in the weave of a damask, the honey- and chocolate-colored rivulets that course through a plank of wood, or the swirling patterns that form and reform as you dip a paint-laden brush in turpentine. You'll be transformed by the inexpressible truths of paint, or fabric, or wood. While on one level your observations will present a definite insight, on a second, unseen level, you'll interact with the truth as it flows from a deep level of awareness, and you'll experience the joy of the crafting process. In the end, this consciousness will ultimately separate a craft project that is only the ordered assembly of materials from one that is an artful expression of the human spirit.

Carol Endler Sterbenz

Notes from Readers

Learn how to restore an ornate picture frame, locate mail-order card stock and Japanese paper, mend torn book pages, and turn beach glass into ornaments.

Restoring an Ornate Picture Frame

I've inherited an ornate picture frame from my great-grandmother. It looks like the top layer of the frame is made from a plasterlike material that has been painted gold, but many pieces have broken off. I'd like to restore the sections that are missing. Here's my idea: Roll out a thin layer of clay, then press it down on an unbroken section of the frame to pick up a clear impression. Once it's dry, I'd pry it off the frame and fill the clay mold with plaster of Paris, let that harden, and then glue the new piece onto the frame and paint it gold. Will this work?

CAROLYN PARSHALL
LANSING, MI

Your hunch about filling in the missing pieces of frame with plaster is correct. You'll need the following materials: a latex or rubber mold medium such as InstaMold (this is more flexible than clay) and a casting material such as Hydrocal, which sets harder than plaster but is just as light. Both products are available at Pearl Paint: Twelve ounces of InstaMold retails for about $6.30; two pounds of Hydrocal retails for about $7.65.

Seal the broken surfaces with a light coat of varnish before you make the mold. InstaMold is gelatin-based, so it shouldn't stick to the original plaster, as long as you remove it as soon as it's set. Use a white glue to attach the cast pieces onto the frame, then mask the undamaged parts of the frame, seal the new pieces with a spray primer, and finish with the appropriate paint or gold leaf.

Writing with Flair

I'm decorating a paper toy chest with rubber stamps and would like to finish it with a painted border and my child's name, but I'm very clumsy with a paintbrush. Can you suggest a tool that will help me?

BOBBIE TERWILLIGER
SPRINGFIELD, OH

Try a suede pen, a flat, metal blade covered with synthetic suede and fitted into a wooden holder. Used by calligraphers and sign painters, a suede pen provides a combination nib/brush effect, holds ink exceptionally well, and delivers the ink to a vertical surface without danger of spills. Such a pen works better with dye-based inks because the suede will absorb the liquid in pigment inks. The suede is washable with both soap and water. John Neal Bookseller sells the pen in seven widths ranging from one-quarter inch to one and one-quarter inches for $8.95 plus $3.75 for shipping. Call or write the company at 1833 Spring Garden Street, Greensboro, NC 27403; 800-369-9598.

Stonewashed Velvet

I saw a photo of some stonewashed cotton velvet pillows in a catalog. How is velvet stonewashed? Can this be done at home?

KIM SHARMAN
SACRAMENTO, CA

The velvet probably isn't actually stonewashed but chemically faded and softened. Fabrics such as denim can survive stonewashing using actual stones (such as pumice), but velvet is much too fragile for this technique. You're better off leaving the chemical manipulation to professionals, says Ingrid Johnson, professor and chair of the Fashion Institute of Technology's textile development and marketing department in New York. "You'd need about three hundred yards of velvet to play with. It could be disastrous."

Card Stock for Greeting Cards

I would like to make my own greeting cards with both painted and pressed flower designs. Can you direct me to resources for card stock? Also, I've been searching without luck for a supplier of shadow boxes.

G. GRIFFIN
WINONA, MN

Card stock can be found at most stationery and craft stores in a wide variety of colors, textures, and weights. You might also try watercolor paper, which is very strong and resilient. Strathmore, a large manufacturer of artist's papers, makes prefolded blank notecards that come with matching envelopes (about $8.75 for a box of 20 seven-inch-by-five-inch cards and 20 envelopes; available at many stationery stores). A sample pack of watercolor papers is available from Daniel Smith, a mail-order catalog of artist's materials, for $9.85. Daniel Smith carries a variety of watercolor papers, starting with the inexpensive Strathmore 400 series ($1.29 per each twenty-two-inch-by-thirty-inch sheet or $2.17 for a pad of 12 five-and-one-half-by-eight-and-one-half-inch sheets). The minimum order is ten sheets. Call 800-426-7923 for a free catalog or write the company at P.O. Box 84268, Seattle, WA 98124-5568.

Pottery Barn carries shadow box frames in four sizes (five-by-seven, eight-by-ten, fifteen-by-six, and eleven-by-fourteen) from $19 to $39. Call Pottery Barn at 800-922-9934 or write to the company at P.O. Box 7044, San Francisco, CA 94120-7044.

Where to Find Japanese Paper

I am looking for Japanese washi paper, which I use to decoupage eggs, and Japanese rice paste or glue. Also, do you know of any sources for egg-decorating supplies?

ANNETTE C. PETERSON
PARK CITY, UT

Washi paper is made from the inner bark of three Japanese trees: the *kozo*, or paper mulberry; the *gampi*, or paper bush; and the *mattsumata*. Its long fibers make it flexible and strong. You can find washi at large art supply stores and Asian import stores. The Daniel Smith catalog carries many kinds of washi, including *kasuiri*, a hand-made paper flecked with pieces of kozo bark, for $2.14 for a twenty-four-by-thirty-six-inch sheet. Another paper suitable for decoupage is natural mulberry paper from Thailand, which Daniel Smith sells for $1.30 per twenty-by-thirty-inch sheet. You can also get a swatch pack of Daniel Smith's traditional Japanese papers for $9.85 or a swatch pack of the "Exotic and Decorative" line, which includes many beautiful handmade papers from Thailand, the Philippines, and India, for $14.50. Call or write for a free catalog: P.O. Box 84268, Seattle, WA 98124-5568; 800-426-7923. *Note:* The minimum paper order is ten sheets, which can be a combination of any papers. (For another idea on using washi paper, *see* "Laminated Leaf Lampshade," page 8.)

Rice paste can be mail-ordered from New York Central Art Supply; two ounces sells for $4.15. The company also carries many different kinds of Japanese and Thai paper at prices similar to Daniel Smith's. Call for a free catalog of the paper line at 800-950-6111 and ask about sample packs, which start at $2, or write to the company at 62 Third Avenue, New York, NY 10003.

If you're interested in using traditional Ukrainian egg dyes, check out the Ukrainian Gift Shop's free mail-order catalog. Call 612-788-2545 or write the company at 2422 Central Avenue NE, Minneapolis, MN 55418. The shop carries a full line of dyes, drawing tools, beeswax, and blown chicken, duck, and goose eggs.

Thanks for the Memories

Just before the holidays I attended a party at which we made the tulle-wrapped ornaments featured in your November/December 1995 issue. I took my ornaments home and hung them on my Christmas tree. The next evening my mom came over, very excited, with a little gift box for me. When I saw what was inside, my first thought was,

Oh no, another tulle-wrapped ornament—how can I hide the ones I made last night? Two seconds later that was all behind me as I saw that my mother had wrapped the ornament in a scrap of beautiful moss green silk organza—from the dress my grandmother had made for my senior prom in 1967. Needless to say, it was the featured ornament on our Christmas tree this year!

JUNE MELLINGER
SOMERSET, NJ

Mountain Rose Pinecones
I have been trying to find a particular kind of pinecone that I saw used in a wreath. It looks almost like a rose. Can you help?

ANN HALL
TORRANCE, CA

The Mountain Rose pinecone is offered by Grande Impressions Ltd. in Denver, Colorado. The company does not sell to the public, but the Beverly Fabrics chain in California carries the line. The store closest to you, in Santa Maria, California, offers a package of three Mountain Rose pinecones for $4.99. For other stores that carry this particular pinecone, call or write Grande Impressions Ltd. at 5303 East 47th Avenue, Denver, CO 80216; 303-377-9415.

Mending Torn Book Pages
How can I mend the torn pages of my treasured old books? Regular tape looks too shiny and thick.

EMMANUEL BALLMAN
ARLINGTON, MA

Librarians and archivists use products such as Filmoplast P, a very thin, transparent, self-adhesive paper tape that will not dry out or yellow with age. You just tear off a small portion of tape and apply it to one side of the page, then burnish the area with a burnishing tool (or back of a spoon) to ensure a good bond. Filmoplast P is available by mail from Charrette (31 Olympia Avenue, Woburn, MA 01888; 800-367-3729) for $29.35 for a 164-foot roll. The manufacturer, Neschen Corporation, makes a full line of bookbinding products; call 800-434-0293 or write the company at 4348 Lower Mountain Road, Lockport, NY 14094.

Source for Battenberg Lace Tape
I recently purchased a wonderful craft book full of projects such as pil-lowcases and sheets using Battenberg lace tape, but I am unable to find a source from which I can purchase the tape. Do you know where I might be able to order the tape through the mail?

ELIZABETH J. PRICE
SALISBURY, MD

Battenberg lace, a combination of machine-made lace tapes or braids and embroidery stitches, was immensely popular during the 1840s and 1850s. Working with tapes, a fabric or parchment pattern, and a simple buttonhole stitch, Victorian lace lovers could turn out intricate-looking designs such as fleur-de-lis and rosettes that were simpler and less delicate than net lace. It was sold under such names as Bruges, Duchesse, Renaissance, and Marie Antoinette. Royal Battenberg, made by Sarah Hadley, who owned a lace shop in New York and wrote for the lace-making section of a fashion and fine arts magazine, may have been named for the German royal family that merged with Queen Victoria's.

We found several mail-order sources for those seeking Battenberg lace tapes: Nancy's Notions (333 Beichl Avenue, P.O. Box 683, Beaver Dam, WI 53916-0683; 800-833-0690); Home-Sew (P.O. Box 4099, Bethlehem, PA 18018-0099; 610-867-3833); The Lacemaker (176 Sunset Avenue South, Edmonds, WA 98208); 206-670-1644); Lacis (2982 Adeline Street, Berkeley, CA 94703; 510-843-7178); and Van Sciver Bobbin Lace (130 Cascadilla Park, Ithaca, NY 14580; 607-277-0498).

Christmas Ornaments from Beads
I'm looking for a book showing how to string beads on wire to make Christmas ornaments.

HELEN CHAPPELL
HOMER CITY, PA

For starters, take a look at page 12 of this issue for three ornament designs involving beads. For additional inspiration, the experts we talked to recommend two books for basic techniques, although they don't specifically contain patterns for ornaments: *Bead Work* by Sara Withers (Chartwell Books, 1995; $7.95) and Elizabeth Ward's *Step by Step Guide to Professional Bead Stringing* (Elizabeth Ward & Co., 1990; $6.95).

Turning Beach Glass into Ornaments
I'd like to make Christmas ornaments out of colored beach glass. Any suggestions?

FELICIA HOBBS
SAN FRANCISCO, CA

That's a great idea. You might try wrapping individual chunks of glass with short lengths of 18- or 24-gauge gold, silver, or brass wire, then linking them like chandelier crystals, or wiring them into clusters or star shapes. If the pieces are heavy, you may need to alternate them singly with plain loops of wire. Attach a loop of wire or a standard tree ornament hook to hang the ornament. Beading wire is less strong but can be used to wrap a delicate belt around larger shards of glass, which you could then attach to a wreath with heavier wire. Or attach the shards to a bobeche (*see the Crystal Bead Drop Candlestick project on the back cover of the March/April 1995 issue*).

Desperately Seeking Bullion
Last year at a florist convention I saw a material called gold bullion that I have not been able to find at any craft store. Do you know how I can order some?

LOURDES TROCHE
MIAMI, FL

Gold bullion is a crimped wire, about one-sixty-fourth-inch wide, which unfolds into a long, delicate, flexible wire. The crimping gives gold bullion its light-catching texture; many crafters use it to add sparkle to flower arrangements, wreaths, giftwrap, or the like. You can mail-order gold bullion from Atlanta Puffections, P.O. Box 13524-BOU, Atlanta, GA 30324; 404-262-7437. A one-ounce package is $12, plus $1.50 for shipping. The company also carries iridescent silver bullion.

Making a Traditional Toothbrush Rug
While at a flea market a few weeks ago, I met a woman making a toothbrush rug. She explained that years ago women created these rugs using worn-out sheets and a toothbrush needle. I loved the look of her handwoven rug and got the woman's card, but now I can't find that card anywhere! Can you help?

LAURIE ROBERTS
VAN NUYS, CA

Toothbrush rugs use long strips of cloth (100 percent cotton is best) threaded through a hole in the end of a toothbrush handle. (The brush end is broken off and filed to a point to make a needle.) Phyllis Hause of Aunt Philly's Toothbrush Rugs sells nine different toothbrush rug patterns for $6 each, needles (not the actual toothbrush, but a preshaped plastic needle that is easier to hold) for $2, and a thirty-two-minute video that shows you how to make an oval rug ($24.95).

Write to Aunt Philly's Toothbrush Rugs, P.O. Box 33051, Northglenn, CO 88023 or call 303-280-2373. The Clotilde catalog also offers Aunt Philly's oval basket and oval rug patterns ($5 each) and the needle ($1.76). Contact Clotilde at 2 Sew Smart Way, Stevens Point, WI 54481-8031; 800-545-4002.

Wooden Spools
I need wooden spools for thread in order to complete a project. Can you help me locate a mail-order source for these items?

AMY THIESSEN
FAIRBORN, OH

Craft King sells thread spools in a variety of sizes, ranging from one-half inch to one and one-half inches in diameter, for 6¢ to 12¢ apiece. Call or write Craft King at P.O. Box 90637, Lakeland, FL 33804; 800-769-9494. ◆

Quick Tips

EASY FLOWER DRYING

To dry bunches of fresh herbs and flowers in a small space, Hannah Hurley of Portland, Oregon, attaches them to a folding wooden drying rack.

ATTENTION READERS

See Your Tip in Print

Do you have a craft technique you'd like to share with other readers? We'll give you a one-year complimentary subscription for each tip that we publish. Send your tip to:

Quick Tips
Handcraft Illustrated
17 Station Street
P.O. Box 509
Brookline Village, MA
02147-0509

Please include your name, address, and daytime phone number.

ILLUSTRATION:
Harry Davis

RIBBON STORAGE

To keep freshly pressed silk ribbons and threads free of tangles, Bonnie Cernosek of Hoffman Estates, Illinois, recommends a cardboard tube.

1. **Cut two slits at each end of the tube, then slip a rubber band through them.**

2. **Wind the ribbons around the tube, securing the ends under the rubber band.**

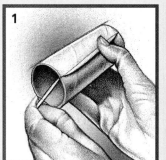
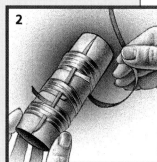

PICTURE-HANGING TIP

Shirley Carlson of Anacortes, Washington, shares this tip for hanging pictures over wallpaper. If you decide to take down the picture, just remove the hanger and glue down the flap.

1. **Mark the wall where the nail will go, then cut a small V in the wallpaper around the mark.**

2. **Lift the V-shaped flap to nail the picture hanger in place.**

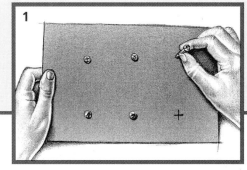
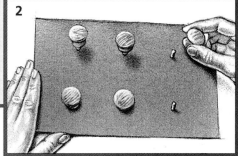

PAINTING KNOBS

To paint furniture knobs, Deb Gentile of Chula Vista, California, uses a corrugated cardboard stand.

1. **Cut an X for each knob, then push the knob's screw into the cardboard.**

2. **Screw on the knobs from the other side, but keep them up off the cardboard.**

3. **Now you can paint the entire knob, even the lower edge.**

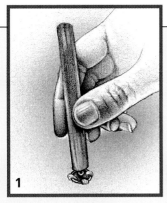
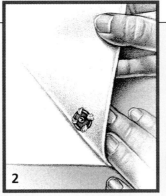
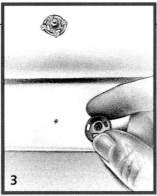

SNAP IN PLACE

Lois Mosher of South Windsor, Connecticut, recommends this easy technique for getting the two halves of sew-on snaps properly aligned.

1. Sew the male snap in position, then rub the nipple with chalk.

2. Position the male snap against the second fabric, and press the layers together.

3. Center the female snap over the mark and sew it in place.

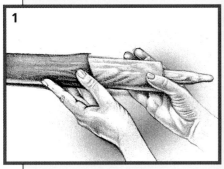
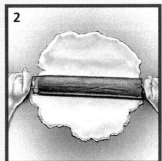

NO-STICK ROLLING PIN

To prevent dough from sticking to a rolling pin, Coleen Loughrey of Cortland, Ohio, uses pantyhose.

1. Cut a sleeve from an old, clean pantyhose leg and slip it onto the pin.

2. Roll out the dough as usual. You'll find you need less flour to prevent sticking.

SOLO KNOT TYING

You won't have to borrow a finger to tie a bow on a gift package if you follow this easy knot-tying tip.

1. Tie the ribbon in a single knot and pull the ends taut.

2. Hold down the knot, then slip one end of the ribbon around and under the taut ribbon.

3. Pull the end tight so a second knot forms around the first one.

4. Proceed to tie the bow.

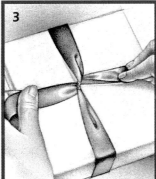

EFFICIENT SEED SOWING

To scatter-sow seeds, put them in a dry, clean container with a perforated shaker top. Tiny seeds such as lavender can be sprinkled from an old saltshaker while larger seeds like radish can go in a spice container that once held oregano.

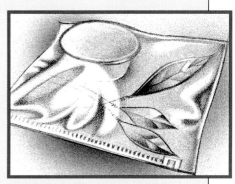

OVERNIGHT OXIDIZING

Ordinary ammonia can be used to oxidize unlacquered brass and copper, writes Gregory Gallardo of Reston, Virginia. Put a bowl of ammonia into a plastic bag, place the metal object alongside it, and seal. Let sit overnight. The ammonia fumes will produce a greenish patina.

NO-STICK CAPS

To keep screw caps on new paint and glue containers operating smoothly, rub a bit of petroleum jelly onto the threads. It creates a tight seal, and messy caps don't get permanently stuck. Diana Barbee of Olney, Illinois, shared this tip.

Great Marriages

Use a candleshade to transform a lone candlestick into a decorating accent.

MINIATURE CANDLESHADES

Using one basic pattern (*see* "Red Velvet Candleshade," page 36, for basic instructions), you can make an endless variety of candle lampshades. The resulting shades can then be mixed and matched with an assortment of candlesticks. Use a candleshade to turn a yard-sale find into an original centerpiece, or a pair of mismatched candlesticks into a sideboard or mantel decoration.

We paired a shade made from Anaglypta embossed paper with a glass candlestick base (center). As another possibility, a copper leaf shade (left) complements a blue star candlestick. For a coordinating detail on the copper leaf shade, we punched out tiny stars using a specialty hole puncher. For variation, use a hole puncher with clubs or diamonds; Pearl Paint offers a wide selection. The copper

leaf shade would also complement a verdigris candlestick.

For our third shade variation, we used a black diamond paper, then edged the shade with multicolored trim (right). This shade is festive when paired with a brass candlestick. For variation, consider a shade made from wallpaper, fabric, or handmade paper, or decoupage a variety of images to a paper backing. ◆

COLOR PHOTOGRAPHY:
Carl Tremblay

The Perfect Gift

Fill a set of test tubes with a custom selection of spices.

TEST TUBE SPICE RACK

We define the perfect gift as something that is created with a specific person in mind, but which isn't overly expensive or time-consuming to assemble. A custom selection of spices housed in a wooden rack is in keeping with this philosophy. We packaged a variety of freshly ground spices and herbs (which can be bought in bulk for less cost) in test tubes, then sealed the tops with melted beeswax. (The test tubes could also be filled with essential oils, bath salts, flavored oils, potpourri, beads, or other small, special items.)

The corked test tubes were ordered from a surgical supply company (*see* Sources & Resources, page 48). We used a paper cone to transfer the dry spices to the individual tubes, rolling a new cone for each spice so the flavors didn't get mixed. If you choose to fill the tubes with liquid, use a funnel for a neater transfer.

We varnished the rack, but you could also paint the rack, give it an antique, crackled finish, or use a product such as Modern Options' Instant Rust. If painting or staining, be sure to sand the rack

lightly and dust it with a tack cloth before proceeding.

Our labels are made from raffia and tin-edged, circular tags. We wrote the names of the spices on the tags, but you could rubber-stamp images, or number the spices to correspond with a special recipe. You can also write directly on the tube with a Pilot gold or silver marker.

If you decide to seal the tops, we recommend beeswax or canning wax. Follow the directions found in "Gourmet Herbal Vinegars," page 30. ◆

COLOR PHOTOGRAPHY:
Carl Tremblay

SPICE SET DESIGN:
Ritch Holben

Laminated Leaf Lampshade

Transform any plain, hardback lampshade into a work of art using leaves and a sheet of Japanese mulberry paper.

❧ BY MICHIO RYAN

MATERIALS

- **Translucent hard-back paper lamp-shade**
- **Fresh, dry, or synthetic leaves***
- **Japanese mulberry (unryû) paper***
- **½"- to ¾"-wide brown florist tape**
- **Yes Stikflat glue**

*See "Getting Started" for size and amount

You'll also need:
36"-wide kraft paper on roll; ruler; scissors; pencil; wooden burnisher (such as cuticle stick); clothespins; reusable putty adhesive (e.g., FunTak); 1" stencil brush; masking tape; newsprint; damp wash-cloth; and paper towels.

Other items, if necessary:
Telephone book and 3-pound weight (for pressing fresh leaves); iron and iron-ing board (for pressing dried or synthetic leaves).

For an extra-special lampshade, use flowers, herbs, or foliage you've pre-served yourself (*see* "Perfectly Pressed Flowers," Spring 1996).

COLOR PHOTOGRAPHY:
Carl Tremblay

ILLUSTRATION:
Nenad Jakesevic

THE BASIC IDEA BEHIND THIS PROJ-ect is quite simple: Start with a plain, paper-covered lampshade, glue on leaves or other foliage, then laminate a thin sheet of translucent paper, such as Japanese mulberry paper, on top. When the lamp is lit, the layers will unify into a glowing pattern.

I used a fairly plain hardback lamp-shade as the starting point. The paper covering my shade already had tiny flakes of bark, leaves, and flower petal frag-ments in it, but any matte paper shade is suitable. Don't use a shade with paper that's been covered with plastic or soaked in oil, or a cloth-covered shade, as glue won't stick to any of these surfaces.

You'll need an assortment of leaves. They can be fresh, dried, or synthetic (silk, for example), but they should be flat and fairly thin, or easy to flatten (*see* instructions for specifics on drying and/or flattening your leaves). If using fresh-picked leaves, avoid leathery, fleshy, heavily creased, or heavily veined speci-mens. You can also use the leaves of houseplants such as rabbit's-foot fern, but avoid Boston ferns, which have thick stems and are resistant to flattening. Adantium fern, another houseplant, also works well. Dried leaves, available from a florist or pressed yourself, can also be used, as can synthetic leaves, which you can purchase on boughs from variety store retailers. Look for leaves with little or no embossed veining texture or curl (ivy is not a good choice) and with as clean a cut edge as possible.

The overlay paper that holds the leaves in place must be fairly translucent or sheer. On the large shade (above, right), I used Japanese mulberry paper (*unryû*), which contains strands of silky heart-wood fibers. The overlay paper should be sturdy enough to hold the leaves in place when the glue is wet, yet sheer enough so

that the leaves will show through even when the lamp is not lit. At the same time, the paper needs to be thick enough for easy handling. On the smaller shade (left), I used a beige bark paper called *chirigami*.

The leaves and overlay paper should be affixed with a water-based adhesive because solvent-based glues such as Spray Mount and rubber cement are not only flammable but will ease under the heat of the lamp and will emit toxic (if low-level) fumes from prolonged heating. I settled on Yes Stikflat glue, which is a solid paste glue that is best applied with a one-inch stenciling brush. Because the glue has a low moisture content, it will not buckle delicate papers, and it will not stain. A wetter glue, on the other hand, such as PVC or wheat paste, might delaminate or warp the shade.

I used florist tape to finish the top and bottom edges of the shade. Florist tape is creped, which allows it to turn radially the way a flat tape cannot. Although it comes with an adhesive on the back, it is very low-tack, so the tape should be glued in place.

INSTRUCTIONS
Getting Started
1. *Make lampshade template.* Tape 36" square of kraft paper to work surface. Set lampshade on side so seam rests on paper. Roll shade along paper one full revolution until seam touches down again; if shade rolls off paper, try again until you find starting position that accommodates full arc of shade. To draft lampshade template, roll shade from starting point, running pencil point along lower edge of shade as it touches paper; extend arc 1" beyond point where seam touches down again, then stop (*see* illustration A, next page). Roll shade backwards from ending point, marking top edge, then remove shade. Draft straight lines to connect arcs at each end, then cut along marked lines. Test-fit tem-plate on lamp, clipping it with clothes-pins at top and bottom rims; straight edges should overlap by ½". When pur-chasing mulberry paper for overlay, select size of paper to accommodate this template, plus a ½" margin along each curved edge.

2. *Select and prepare leaves.* Choose fresh, dry, or synthetic leaves, figuring on approximately ten leaves up to 5" long for a small shade and twenty leaves up to 6" long for a larger shade. Vary leaf sizes and gather more than you need, for lay-out flexibility.

Fresh leaves: Select thin, unblemished specimens such as Japanese red maple, oak, red sumac, or rabbit's-foot fern. Trim back thick stems, then press leaves flat between paper towels in weighted telephone book (or other large book) for two weeks or until smooth and dry. Change paper towels every few days to prevent the leaves from molding. Discard moldy leaves.

Dried leaves: Choose thin specimens that are not too curled, brittle, or heavily veined, and trim back thick stems. To relax moderate curling, soak overnight in warm water, lay on paper towel over ironing board, and iron flat on both sides using cotton/linen setting. Use immediately after pressing to prevent recurling.

Synthetic leaves: Select thin cloth specimens that possess clean-cut edges, minimal curl, and minimal vein embossing. To flatten, pluck each leaf stem from its plastic or wire base, sandwich between paper towels, and steam-press on ironing board on both sides using rayon/synthetic setting.

Decorating the Shade

1. *Cut Japanese mulberry paper overlay.* Lay template on mulberry paper. Use pencil and ruler to mark straight edges, then draw curved edges ½" beyond template edges to allow for shifting when overlay is glued down (illustration B). Cut out along marked lines. Test-fit overlay on shade, then set aside.

2. *Plan leaf layout.* Work out leaf design on shade, using small pieces of putty adhesive to adhere and reposition leaves as desired. Intersperse large and small leaves, placing larger leaves near bottom rim of shade and smaller leaves toward top; let some leaves run beyond edge of lampshade. Avoid clumping same-color leaves together and make sure leaf tips point in different directions. Strive for free-spirited, random design (illustration C).

Note: To prevent unwanted glue from marring your project in steps 3 through 5, place newsprint under your work and replace it with fresh sheets as the old ones become sticky. Cover the glued leaves with a scrap of newsprint to soak up the excess glue while pressing them in place. Clean the glue from your fingers periodically using a damp washcloth.

3. *Glue down leaves.* Remove one leaf from shade and lay face down on newsprint. Leave putty on shade to mark position. Using stencil brush, apply glue to back of leaf from center out beyond edges. Remove putty, then work brush in circular motion on shade, overshooting leaf area by ½" (illustration D). Reposition leaf on shade and press firmly in place, using washcloth to keep fingertips clean. Repeat to glue down all leaves. Reglue any edges that curl up. Let set 15 minutes.

4. *Attach overlay.* On small shades, brush glue evenly over entire shade,

including leaves. Position straight edge of overlay ½" beyond lampshade seam; curved edges should extend ½" beyond top and bottom rims of lampshade. Press to adhere, then smooth overlay paper onto shade all around (illustration E). On large shades, work on one-quarter of the shade and overlay at a time to prevent premature drying of glue. To end off, apply light coat of glue to free edges and press down. Let dry 30 minutes, then trim excess paper, including overhanging leaves, even with top and bottom rims.

5. *Finish edges.* Turn shade upside down. Starting at seam, brush glue along

10" section of rim and adjacent paper. Press florist tape onto rim, stretching it as you go so tape conceals rim on inside of shade and extends about ¼" onto right side of shade (illustration F). If tape is not wide enough, cover outside part of rim only on this round, then use second pass of tape to cover inside edge of rim. Continue gluing and taping until you reach starting point; trim end neatly. Glue and tape top rim in same way, applying extra glue to inside edge of shade for good adhesion. Rub gently with wooden burnishing tool. Let dry overnight. ◆

MAKING THE LAMINATED LAMPSHADE

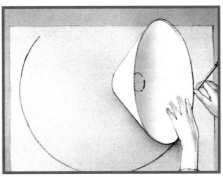

A. To draft a lampshade template, roll the shade one revolution on the kraft paper, tracing the edges as you go.

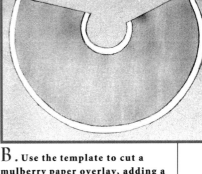

B. Use the template to cut a mulberry paper overlay, adding a ½" margin to each curved edge.

C. Arrange the flattened leaves on the shade in a free-spirited design, using FunTak for a temporary hold.

D. To affix the leaves, apply glue to the back of each leaf and to its spot on the shade.

E. When all the leaves are glued down, brush glue over the entire surface and apply the mulberry paper overlay.

F. Trim the top and bottom rims by gluing on brown florist tape.

Decorative Bottle Stoppers

Quickly sculpt a stopper from Fimo or Sculpey III to fit any bottle, then finish it with paint, glitter, or gold leaf.

❧ BY FRANCOISE HARDY

MATERIALS

Note: You will need one 2-ounce package for each Sculpey III color listed below.

Purple Helix
■ **Sculpey III, Purple (pearlescent)**
■ **Tulip Colorpoint fabric paint, Pearl Gold GD93**
■ **Sculpey Glaze #33 Gloss**

Glitter Star
■ **Sculpey III (any color)**
■ **Powderz micro glitter, Summer Sand**
■ **Sculpey Glaze #33 Gloss**

Lyre with Pearls
■ **Sculpey III, Lavender**
■ **Sculpey III, White**
■ **Sculpey III, Pearl**
■ **Sculpey III, Translucent**
■ **Sculpey Glaze #33 Gloss**
■ **Composition gold leaf**
■ **Japan size**
■ **Krazy glue**

You'll also need:
Bottle for fitting stopper; smooth, washable work surface; cookie sheet; ½" flat brushes; ruler; X-Acto knife; two small round brushes; kraft paper; and one sheet scrap paper.

COLOR PHOTOGRAPHY:
Carl Tremblay

ILLUSTRATION:
Michael Gellatly

STYLING:
Ritch Holben

Bottle stoppers can be molded—and custom-colored—to fit any size bottle. Left to right: Glitter star, purple helix, and lyre with pearls.

THESE DECORATIVE BOTTLE STOPpers—designed to replace missing or plain stoppers—are made from thermo-set resin clays such as Sculpey III and Fimo. Using these types of clay, you can design a stopper to fit any decorative bottle and, if desired, custom-mix the color to match the bottle. The clay's versatility allows such finishing details as dots of fabric paint, embedded glitter, or gilding. Best of all, the clays are easily molded with just your hands.

Sculpey III and Fimo are available in a wide range of colors, including pearlescent tones. Off-the-shelf colors are rather strong and not always suitable, however, so I custom-mixed my own colors. By blending Day-Glo or pearlescent clays with standard colors, you can create a more sophisticated palette. The lyre with pearls, for instance, uses a blend of Lavender and White Sculpey III for the stopper base and a blend of Pearl and Translucent Sculpey III for the pearls. One important note: The color names between different brand names of clay are not interchangeable. I used Sculpey III for all three bottle stoppers; if using Fimo or another brand name, you'll need to select your own colors.

The blended colors should be kneaded together thoroughly to avoid streaks. Kneading is necessary even for a single-color lump of clay, and blending colors takes no longer. Work on a washable surface such as a plastic cutting board; never work on unprotected furniture, as the clay can ruin the finish. For exact proportions, use a sharp X-Acto knife to cut off a pat of each color. When mixing colors, or when moving between colors, wash your hands frequently or the subsequent colors can become contaminated.

To form the stopper, I rolled a ball of clay, pulled out a rod, then pushed the rod into the top of the bottle. Because the thermo-set resin clays do not shrink during heat curing, the stopper should fit exactly after baking. If necessary, the clay can be easily shaved to adjust the fit.

All of my designs are composed symmetrically because they are baked in the oven standing upright on a cookie sheet. To stand upright, they need to balance properly. I don't advise baking them on their sides, as dents can result. Before heat-setting the stoppers, I stuck them firmly to the cookie sheet, then smoothed the surfaces with my fingertip to remove any dents, lumpiness, or fingerprints.

After heat-setting the stoppers, I lacquered the surfaces to even out the sheen. Without lacquer, the clay has a matte finish, which is not unattractive but which can show fingerprints and other surface defects. Three coats of glossy lacquer, however, leveled out the surface.

Both Fimo and Sculpey sell proprietary lacquers: Fimo's is called "Gloss Varnish" and Sculpey's, "Sculpey Glaze #33 Gloss." I preferred the latter because it is water-soluble, making it easier to clean up. At Pearl Paint, it was also half the cost: $2.28 for one ounce, versus $3.99 for 35 ml (just over one ounce).

Note: Do not use stoppers made from Sculpey III or other heat-set clays in bottles with edible contents. Such clays, even when baked, contain traces of chemicals that could contaminate food.

Francoise Hardy is a Boston-based artisan and craftsperson.

INSTRUCTIONS
Note: If making more than one stopper, bake them together and finish separately.

Purple Helix

1. *Mold stopper base.* Cut and knead 1 ounce (one-half package) Purple (pearlescent) Sculpey III into 1¼" ball. Draw out part of ball, mold into rod, and fit to bottle opening. Cinch above rod to form neck (*see* illustration A, next page).

2. *Create leaf helix.* Flatten compound above neck into leaf shape measuring approximately 1" x 3" x ⅜" thick (illustration B). Hold base firmly and twist leaf into helix, as if cranking a can opener (illustration C).

3. *Bake and finish stopper.* Double-check fit in bottle opening. Stand stopper upright on cookie sheet and bake in preheated 275-degree oven 15 to 20 minutes. Let cool in oven 1 hour. To finish, squeeze tiny dots of Tulip Colorpoint ¼" apart along curved edges (illustration D). Let dry 2 hours. Using flat brush, apply three coats glaze over entire surface from neck up, letting dry 20 minutes between coats; do not glaze rod. Retest fit, shaving rod with X-Acto knife if necessary until stopper fits snugly.

Glitter Star

1. *Mold stopper base.* Cut and knead 2 ounces (one package) any color Sculpey III into ball. Draw out part of ball, mold into rod, and fit to bottle opening. Cinch above rod to form neck (illustration E).

2. *Shape star.* Flatten compound above neck into ¾"-thick disk, then push thumb through center of disk and shape doughnut with ½" hole (illustration F). Pinch and pull out edge of doughnut to make six stubby points (illustration G).

3. *Affix glitter.* Fold scrap paper in half, open flat, and lay stopper on top. Sprinkle glitter over stopper, then press particles firmly into clay with fingertips. Turn stopper over and repeat to cover entire surface. Funnel excess glitter back into container.

4. *Bake and finish stopper.* Check fit in bottle opening. Stand stopper upright on cookie sheet and bake in preheated 275-degree oven 15 to 20 minutes. Let cool in oven 1 hour, then dust off loose glitter with any dry brush. Using flat brush, apply three coats glaze over entire surface from neck up, letting dry 20 minutes between coats; do not glaze rod. Retest fit, shaving rod with X-Acto knife if necessary until stopper fits snugly.

Lyre with Pearls

1. *Mold stopper base.* Cut and knead together ¼ ounce (one-eighth package) each Lavender and White Sculpey III until well blended, then mold into 1" ball. Taper to form rod and fit to bottle opening. Mold top into onion dome, trimming off any excess (illustration H).

2. *Shape lyre.* Knead 1 ounce (one-half package) Sculpey III (use any of the four colors) until very soft and pliable. Roll into 1¼" ball, then roll into 7"-long log, ½" thick at middle and tapering to ¼" at ends. Roll each end toward middle of log in tight spiral (illustration I), then bend up at middle of log to form lyre (illustration J).

3. *Make and attach pearls.* Knead together ¼ ounce (one-eighth package) each Pearl and Translucent Sculpey III until well blended. Shape into three pearls measuring approximately ⅞", ⅝", and ⅜" in diameter; set aside excess. To assemble stopper, press lyre onto onion dome, then stack graduated pearls on lyre and press until adhered (illustration K).

4. *Bake and gild stopper.* Double-check fit in bottle opening. Stand stopper upright on cookie sheet and bake in preheated 275-degree oven 15 to 20 minutes. Let cool in oven 1 hour. Rejoin any separated parts with glue and let dry 15 minutes. To gild stopper, brush glaze over lyre, let dry 20 minutes, then brush size on lyre. While size is reaching tack (10 to 15 minutes), lay down kraft paper, remove one sheet gold leaf from book, and tear into 1" pieces. Pick up leaf on tip of round brush, attach to tacky surface, and tamp down. Burnish surface and remove excess flakes of leaf with dry round brush. Using flat brush, apply three coats glaze over entire surface from neck up, letting dry 20 minutes between coats; do not glaze rod. Retest fit, shaving rod with X-Acto knife if necessary until stopper fits snugly. ◆

DESIGNER'S TIP

When you are working with thermo-set resin clays, kneading agents such as Mix Quick can make softening the clay much easier. With this project, on the other hand, I don't advise using such softeners. In my tests, clay that was kneaded with Mix Quick was too soft for the sculpturelike designs, and fingerprints were much more prevalent.

Sculpting the Stoppers

GLITTER STAR

LYRE WITH PEARLS

PURPLE HELIX

A. Roll a ball of clay, mold one end to fit the bottle opening, then cinch to form the stopper's neck.

B. Flatten and mold the clay above the neck into a leaf shape.

C. To create the helix, twist the leaf into a gentle spiral.

D. After baking, apply dots of fabric paint.

E. Roll a ball of clay, mold one end to fit the bottle opening, then cinch to form the stopper's neck.

F. Shape the clay above the neck into a thick doughnut.

G. Pinch and pull out six stubby points along the doughnut edges.

H. Mold a rod-shaped stopper base with an onion-dome top.

I. To make a lyre, roll a tapered cylinder and curl in the ends...

J. ...then bend it up at the middle.

K. To assemble the stopper, press the lyre onto the base, then top it with three graduated pearls.

Beaded Star Ornaments

Use these simple but elegant beaded ornaments to decorate your own home, or give the silvery trio as a special holiday gift.

🍂 BY MICHIO RYAN

Clockwise from top: Graduated Bead Star, 3¼" across; Teardrop Star, 5" across; and Circle Star, 5" across.

COLOR PHOTOGRAPHY:
Carl Tremblay

ILLUSTRATION:
Mary Newell DePalma

STYLING:
Ritch Holben

ALTHOUGH THESE DELICATE beaded star ornaments may look difficult, they're actually very easy to make. I started with a center core made from cork or a filigree bead, then inserted three wires through the respective centers to create the star's six arms. I finished the ornaments by threading a variety of faceted and round clear or mirrored beads on each arm.

For the overall six-arm construction technique to work, the center core needed to have six holes. I couldn't find a bead with this number of holes, however, and I didn't want to drill additional holes, so I used two different solutions. For the Teardrop Star ornament I used a three-quarter-inch cork bob; on the Graduated Bead Star ornament I used a three-quarter-inch filigree bead. (The two cores are interchangeable if you can't find one or the other.)

Cork bobs, available at fishing supply or tackle shops, can be covered with gold or silver micro glitter. If you choose this type of core, be sure to insert the wires into the cork first, then apply glue and sprinkle glitter on the ball. If you reverse the process, the glitter will rub off as you try to insert the wires. If you use a filigree bead, you may have trouble getting the second and third wires inserted past the first wire. To circumvent this problem, curve the ends of the last two wires slightly and their ends will bypass whatever wires are already present. For the Circle Star ornament, I used an 8mm filigree bead for the core.

Once the beads are threaded on the arms, they need to be secured. I considered gluing the end bead but then decided making a loop in the wire would be more secure. To display the ornament, slip an ornament hanger through this end loop.

INSTRUCTIONS
Making the Teardrop Star

1. *Make six-spoke core.* Fill precut holes in cork with putty using fingertip. Draw bisecting line around cork, then mark six dots evenly spaced on line (*see illustration A, next page*). To "drill" channels for wire, set brad point on each dot in turn and push in toward center of cork. Cut three 7" lengths of wire. Push end of one wire into channel so it emerges on opposite side. Insert second and third wires through remaining channels; adjust so ends are equal in length (illustration B).

2. *Coat cork with glitter.* Fold scrap paper in half, then open flat. Holding core by wires over scrap paper, brush core surface with glue. Sprinkle glitter over core, rotating it to coat entire surface. Lay on wax paper and let dry 1 hour. Funnel excess glitter back into container.

3. *String beads on spokes.* Working one spoke at a time, string beads in following order: one gold flat, one silver 6mm, one silver teardrop, one silver

10mm, and one silver 4mm (illustration C). To end off, slide beads toward cork to eliminate slack, bend wire at 45-degree angle using pliers, and clip ¼" from bend (illustration D). Grip short end with round-nose pliers and bend in opposite direction, forming small loop (illustration E). Repeat to string and finish remaining spokes (illustration F).

Making the Graduated Bead Star

1. *Make six-spoke core.* Cut three 6" lengths of wire. Push one wire into filigree bead so it emerges on opposite side. Insert second and third wires into bead on same plane, curving wire slightly to facilitate pass-through. Reposition wires if necessary to make six spokes equidistant from each other, then adjust so wire ends are equal in length (illustration G).

2. *Coat bead with glitter.* Proceed as for Teardrop Star, step 2.

3. *String beads on spokes.* Working one spoke at a time, string silver beads in following order: 12mm, 10mm, 6mm, 4mm (illustration H). End off as for Teardrop Star, step 3 (illustrations D and

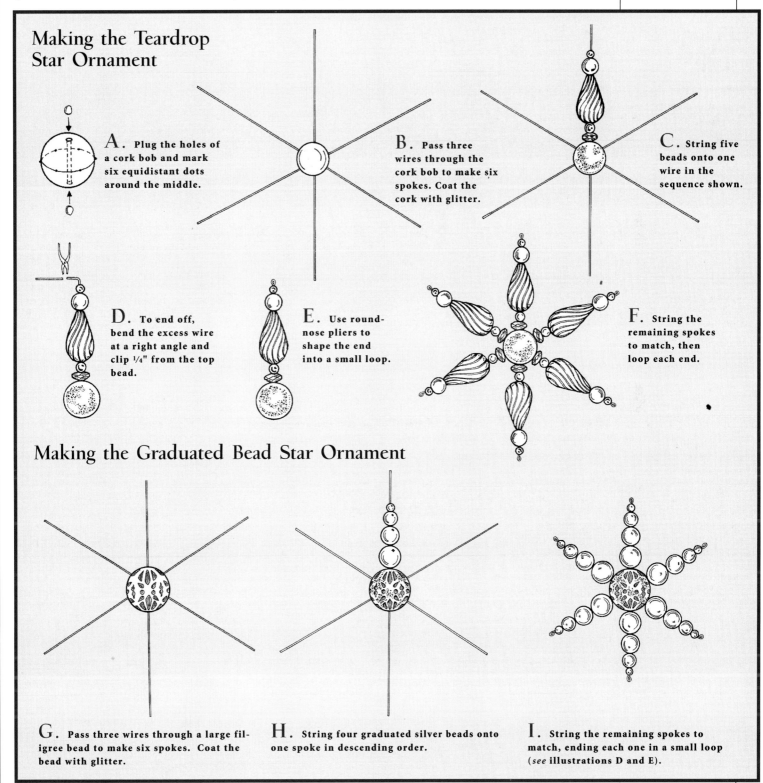

Making the Teardrop Star Ornament

A. Plug the holes of a cork bob and mark six equidistant dots around the middle.

B. Pass three wires through the cork bob to make six spokes. Coat the cork with glitter.

C. String five beads onto one wire in the sequence shown.

D. To end off, bend the excess wire at a right angle and clip ¼" from the top bead.

E. Use round-nose pliers to shape the end into a small loop.

F. String the remaining spokes to match, then loop each end.

Making the Graduated Bead Star Ornament

G. Pass three wires through a large filigree bead to make six spokes. Coat the bead with glitter.

H. String four graduated silver beads onto one spoke in descending order.

I. String the remaining spokes to match, ending each one in a small loop (*see* illustrations D and E).

E). Repeat to string remaining spokes (illustration I).

Making the Circle Star

1. *Make 6-spoke core.* Cut three 7" lengths of 20-gauge wire. Push one wire into filigree bead so it emerges on opposite side. Insert second and third wires into bead. Reposition wires if necessary to make six spokes equidistant from each other, then adjust so wire ends are equal in length.

2. *String beads on spokes.* Working one spoke at a time, string beads in following order: one 8mm bugle, one silver 6mm, one 8mm bugle, one bronze 3mm, one gold 5mm x 9mm flat, one silver 4mm, one pink 9mm x 8mm oval, one silver 4mm, one silver 7mm x 5mm oval,

and one silver 4mm (illustration J). End off as for Teardrop Star, step 3 (illustrations D and E). Repeat to string and finish remaining spokes (illustration K).

3. *Join and string circle of beads.* Cut 11" length of 28-gauge wire. Bend wire 1" from end, then wrap once around spoke and lodge between 8mm bugle bead and 3mm bronze bead. String on 7mm x 5mm oval bead, 12mm silver bead, and 7mm x 5mm oval bead (illustration L). Slide beads to spoke, bend wire at end bead, and wrap around adjacent spoke between 8mm bugle bead and 3mm bronze bead. Continue stringing between remaining sections in same way to create bead circle. To end off, twist wire ends together for ¼" and clip close to spoke (illustration M). ◆

Making the Circle Star Ornament

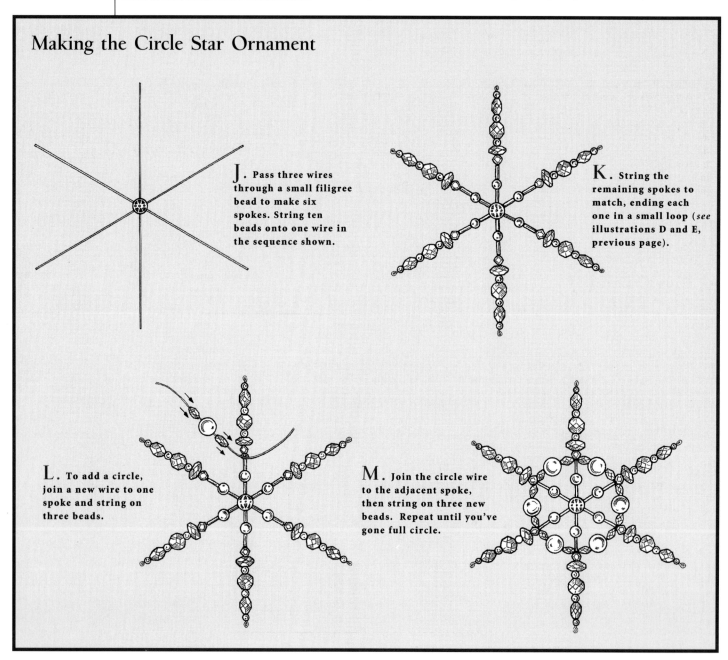

J. Pass three wires through a small filigree bead to make six spokes. String ten beads onto one wire in the sequence shown.

K. String the remaining spokes to match, ending each one in a small loop (*see illustrations D and E, previous page*).

L. To add a circle, join a new wire to one spoke and string on three beads.

M. Join the circle wire to the adjacent spoke, then string on three new beads. Repeat until you've gone full circle.

Copper Leaf Napkin Ring

Our quick-leaf technique transforms miniature oak leaves. Combine the leaves with pearls and wire to make an elegant tabletop accent.

🌿 BY FRANCOISE HARDY

MATERIALS
Yields one napkin ring

- ⁵/₈ yard 1"-wide copper gauze wire-edged ribbon
- Six 2" silk oak leaves
- Two 1" gold lamé leaves
- Five ¹/₂" baroque pearls
- 1 or 2 sheets copper leaf
- 28-gauge copper wire
- 24-gauge copper wire
- Brown florist tape
- Copper metallic enamel paint

You'll also need: newsprint; small paintbrush; soft brush or cotton balls (for burnishing); table knife; scissors; pencil; and needle-nose pliers with wire cutters.

FOR A FAST AND EASY WAY TO dress up your fall table, consider the copper leaf napkin ring. Using our quick-leafing technique, miniature oak leaves, pearls, and wire, you can make a set of napkin rings in about two hours. Use them yourself, or give them as a gift.

I chose copper leaf for this design, but you could also use silver or gold leaf with the same beautiful results. Instead of real oak leaves, which would be too large for a napkin ring, I started with burgundy-colored miniature leaves made from silk-like fabric. The burgundy color on the back of the leaves contrasts well with the copper leaf on the front of the leaves; if using silver or gold leaf, choose a color that offsets the metallic tone. If you can't find oak leaves, you can substitute miniature silk maple, birch, or ash leaves.

In keeping with our quick gild technique (*see* "Quick Gilded Autumn Leaves," September/October 1995), I used enamel paint to adhere the copper leaf to the oak leaf. You can substitute rubber cement or size, but these materials will take longer to reach their ready stages.

Francoise Hardy is a Boston-based artisan and craftsperson.

For variations on this design, use silver or gold leaf, different types of leaves, small wired acorns, or other preserved flowers.

INSTRUCTIONS

1. *Apply copper leaf to oak leaves.* Cover work surface with newsprint. Using knife, transfer one sheet copper leaf from book to work surface. Working one oak leaf at a time, brush enamel paint on face side of oak leaf, extending beyond edges. Immediately lay coated oak leaf face down on copper leaf, then press gently and evenly (*see* illustration A, right). Repeat process on remaining oak leaves. Let dry overnight. Gently separate oak leaves, turn over, and remove loose flakes of copper leaf along edges with soft brush. Burnish each oak leaf gently with cotton ball or soft brush.

2. *Attach wire stems to leaves.* Using 28-gauge wire directly from spool, hold wire parallel to leaf stem so ends match, then wind down from base of leaf, enclosing stem and wire in tight spiral (illustration B). Clip wire 4½" from base of leaf. Repeat to wire remaining copper leaf and gold lamé leaves.

3. *Attach stems to pearls.* Cut five 5¾" lengths of 24-gauge wire. Using pliers, bend down one end of wire about one pearl's length, slide pearl onto other end, then pull wire through hole so double thickness lodges inside (illustration C).

4. *Assemble bouquet and napkin ring.*

Gather eight leaf and five pearl stems together in bouquet, then bind with tape (illustration D). Wrap ribbon once around rolled napkin and tie single knot. Lay bouquet stem on knot and tie second knot. Fan out leaves and pearls. ◆

COLOR PHOTOGRAPHY:
Carl Tremblay

ILLUSTRATION:
Nenad Jakesevic

MAKING THE NAPKIN RINGS

A. Brush the oak leaf with paint, then press it onto a sheet of copper leaf.

B. Add a long stem to each leaf by spiraling a thin wire around the stem.

C. Add a stem to each pearl by bending the wire and wedging the doubled end inside the opening.

D. Gather the stems into a bouquet and bind with florist tape.

Elegant and Easy Hand-Cast Plaster Fruit

Use a quick-mold mix and artist's gouache to hand-cast and -color a set of plaster pears.

❧ BY NANCY OVERTON

MATERIALS

- **4 pounds plaster of Paris (makes 5 to 6 pears)**
- **2-ounce tubes Winsor & Newton gouache in the following colors: Golden Yellow, Yellow Ochre, Linden Green, and Van Dyke Brown***

*See paint samples, page 18, for additional colors

You'll also need:
fresh pear; two 12-ounce containers Insta-Mold; 1-quart glass or plastic bowl; handheld electric mixer; large mixing bowl; wet and dry measuring cups; rubber spatula; paring knife; pruning shears; 6 small containers (e.g., baby food jars or shot glasses); dinner plate; extra jars with water; sabeline brush #10 or #12; stenciling brush; damp sponge; 2 to 3 rubber bands; 400-grit wet-dry sandpaper; craft sticks or wooden coffee stirrers; ruler; newsprint; and disposable container(s).

Other items, if necessary:
titanium white tempera paint (for enhancing chalky effects).

COLOR PHOTOGRAPHY:
Carl Tremblay

ILLUSTRATION:
Nenad Jakesevic

COLOR SAMPLES:
Daniel van Ackere

PEAR COLORINGS:
Michio Ryan

STYLING:
Ritch Holben

Using a quick-mold compound and a selection of fresh fruits such as apples, plums, oranges, bananas, and pears, you can create an endless variety of plaster fruit centerpieces.

P LASTER CASTING HAS EVOLVED from an art form reserved for sculptors to an at-home, kitchen table craft. The advent of quick-mold compounds, which set up to make a flexible, rubbery mold in just a few minutes, has significantly simplified the casting process. In addition, creating a realistic painted finish on the cast objects no longer requires advanced freehand painting skills; even beginners can create lifelike effects quickly and easily using transparent color media such as gouache or watercolors.

For this project, I used Insta-Mold, a molding compound that mixes with water to create a rubbery mold in about two or three minutes. Although this article deals only with casting plaster pears, you can use Insta-Mold (and other quick-mold compounds) to cast cameos, doll heads, figurines, refrigerator magnets, even molded human hands. Items may be cast in plaster, craft casting mediums, wax, or resin. For the fruit shown here, I used plaster of Paris, which mixes easily with water, pours readily, sets in about thirty minutes, and hardens to a durable finish.

Rather than making half molds of like sides of the fruit, I made one mold of the bottom part of the fruit and one of the top, as this approach preserved the detail of the stem and bottom buds. Then I secured the two sides of the mold together with rubber bands and carved a pouring hole for the plaster. When you cast objects, some of the plaster escapes between the two sections and extends into the pouring hole. While the plaster is

"green," or freshly cast, however, you can easily trim off this excess plaster with a paring (or X-Acto) knife.

Painting the Pears

The pears should to be painted while they are still green. To create a frescolike effect, I used Winsor & Newton gouache. Gouache, although similar to watercolor paint, comes in a wider range of more subtle colors. The paint pigments in gouache are finely ground and contain only a small amount of binder, so they easily permeate the plaster to produce a color stain, rather than an opaque paint film, which sits on top of the plaster. For this reason, acrylic paints, which contain a high proportion of binders, are unsuitable. You can use thinned oil paints, but they are harder to clean up after, and the plaster must be completely dry before they can be applied.

I thinned each color of gouache with water until nearly transparent. Rather than mixing two colors together and applying them as one layer, I found it easier to apply two different colors in two coats in order to produce an intermediate color. Using two different washes also produced gradated or mottled effects, making the pears, in turn, appear more lifelike.

I considered using a spray bottle to apply the paint in order to eliminate any hard edges produced by brush strokes. When painting on green plaster, however, the paintbrush does not leave marks as it would on dry, absorbent plaster. I recommend a soft sable or sabeline round #10 brush.

For expediency, thin each color in a small container such as a baby food jar, and line up all the jars in a row when painting. The jars should have mouths large enough so that you can easily dip in the brush, because speed is essential in making the coats of color blend properly on the absorbent plaster. Keep a damp

MAKING THE MOLD

A. Submerge a pear partway in the mold mixture for 2 to 3 minutes until the mix gels.

B. Use the same container to mold the top half of the pear. Let mold mixture set several minutes.

C. To calibrate the two mold halves, remove the container and cut notches across the seam.

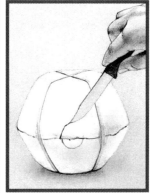

D. Remove the pear, reassemble the mold using rubber bands, then cut a pouring hole for the plaster.

sponge and several jars of water nearby for moistening the fruit, blending colors, removing some paint in order to create highlights, and/or rinsing your brush.

Cover the fruit completely with the first wash, working quickly to avoid bare spots. Immediately apply the next wash, working in a random way to mottle the colors. To simulate the sun-ripened shading found on some pears, apply the second wash heavier on one side and much lighter on the other. To create freckles, use a coarse brush (e.g., stenciling brush) to stipple the surface.

After the paint has dried completely, the pear's surface will appear chalky. This chalkiness derives from the plaster itself, because the gouache pigments are absorbed into it. You can enhance this weathered, stony effect by adding titanium white (such as Rich Art tempera) to the thinned gouache colors. When first applied, the gouache will appear somewhat milky, but the colors will fully emerge as the plaster dries.

I recommend purchasing one or two spatulas just for plaster work and using them to clean your mixing containers. For added ease, wipe your mixing containers with mineral or olive oil before mixing the plaster. Once the excess plaster has hardened, turn the container over a trash can; the mineral oil will cause the plaster to fall out easily. Take note: Plaster of Paris should never be washed down any drain, as it can harden and block your pipes.

Nancy Overton, a resident of Oakland, California, has designed products for the craft industry and written how-to books for more than twenty years.

INSTRUCTIONS
Making the Mold
1. *Make bottom half of mold.* Fill 1-quart bowl with cold water to within ¼" of rim, then measure and pour into large mixing bowl. Measure same amount dry Insta-Mold, add to water, and beat 30 seconds or until mixture resembles smooth oatmeal. Transfer mixture back to 1-quart bowl, then set bowl on plate to catch any spillover. Submerge bottom half of pear in Insta-Mold mixture, and hold steady 2 to 3 minutes or until mixture gels (*see* illustration A, above). Slide rubber spatula in between bowl and gelled mold, then carefully remove bowl without dislodging pear. Wash bowl and all utensils.

2. *Make top half of mold.* Snip pear stem to ¼". Mix new batch of mold mixture as in step 1 and transfer to 1-quart bowl. Turn previously gelled mold upside down and submerge exposed portion of pear in new mixture until gelled mold rests on new mixture (illustration B). Let set 2 to 3 minutes or until mixture gels. Hold two mold halves together and carefully remove bowl. Wash bowl and all utensils. To calibrate mold, cut four or five notches around seam; notches should extend across both halves of mold (illustration C).

3. *Prepare mold for casting.* Carefully separate mold halves and remove pear. Realign mold halves with notches matching and secure with rubber bands. Carve ¾"-diameter hole on seam for pouring plaster; hole should extend into pear-shaped cavity (illustration D). Remove rubber bands and take mold apart, rinse both halves to remove any debris, then reassemble mold.

Casting the Pears
Note: The plaster pears are cast one at a time and require about one-half hour of curing time each. To create the fresco effect, paint the pears as soon as possible after casting, while the plaster is still "green." If casting multiple pears, alternate between casting and painting, painting one pear while another pear is curing in the mold.

CASTING THE PLASTER PEAR

E. Fill the mold with plaster of Paris and let it cure for 30 minutes.

F. Separate the mold halves, then gently wiggle the pear free.

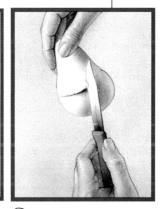

G. Shave off the seam ridge and sand any blemishes while the plaster is still green.

DESIGNER'S TIP

When working with plaster, always mix a bit more than you think you need. Trying to mix additional plaster while some has already been poured is hurried and often messy work.

1. *Pour plaster into mold.* Working at sink, fill mold with tap water up into pouring hole, then quickly pour out into 2-cup measuring cup. Measure twice as much dry plaster of Paris, add to water, and stir 3 to 4 minutes or until creamy and smooth. Pour into mold until liquid begins filling in pouring hole (illustration E). Pour any excess plaster into disposable container and discard later when hard; do not pour any plaster down sink drain. Rinse equipment promptly. As plaster cures in mold, it will heat up and then cool; let cure until cool to touch, about 30 minutes.

2. *Unmold and refine pear.* Remove rubber bands and separate mold halves (illustration F). Gently wiggle plaster pear free. Using paring or X-Acto knife, shave off plaster ridge along seam and pouring knob (illustration G). Smooth unwanted blemishes with wet-dry sandpaper.

Painting the Pears

Note: See paint samples, below, for ideas on what colors to use for the first wash, second wash, and accents.

1. *Set up painting work area.* Cover workspace with newsprint. Squeeze small amount of each gouache color into its own container and thin with water, stirring until nearly transparent. Set out damp sponge, jars of water, and paint brushes.

2. *Apply first color wash.* Dampen surface of pear with sponge. Cover entire surface with first color wash. To create highlights, dab off color with damp sponge.

3. *Apply second color wash.* Immediately apply second color wash in fast, loose strokes, working in a random way to mottle colors. To create shading, apply wash heavier on one side and lighter on the other. Reapply first and second washes as needed; note that colors will appear lighter once dry.

4. *Add color accents.* To further shade fruit, brush small amounts of accent color onto base of fruit and blend in. For freckles, moisten stenciling brush with Van Dyke Brown gouache, dab excess on paper towel until bristles are almost dry, then tamp on plaster surface where color is deepest. To add a subtle highlight, brush a contrasting wash or gouache color across the neck and blend in. Let pears harden overnight. ◆

COLOR OPTIONS

The following samples were created to show the breadth of effects you can create with Winsor & Newton gouache. Some of these effects are appropriate for pears, while others are designed for painting other types of plaster fruits or vegetables.
1. Red Delicious apple: Gold Ochre first wash with a second wash of Havannah Lake.
2. Peach: Chrome Yellow first wash with a second wash of Rose.
3. Persimmon/orange: Marigold Yellow first wash with a second wash of Gold Ochre.
4. Pear: Golden yellow first wash, Linden Green second wash.
5. Bosc pear: Yellow Ochre first wash, Linden Green second wash, Van Dyke Brown stipple spots.
6. Tomato/cherry: Rose first wash with a second wash of Spectrum Red.
7. Plum: Havannah Lake first wash with a second wash of Indigo Blue.
8. Plum: Purple Lake first wash with a second wash of Havannah Lake.

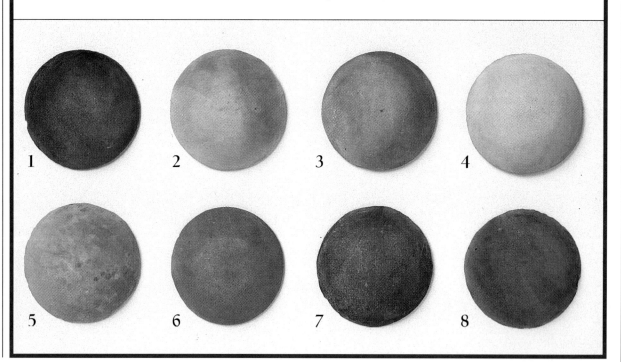

Curtain Finial Candlestick

This elegant candlestick, constructed from a curtain finial, a wooden base, and a candlecup, can be finished in a wide variety of ways.

❧ BY CANDIE FRANKEL

THOUGH THIS TEN-INCH CANDLEstick looks like one piece—molded from wood or resin—in reality it comprises four separate pieces: a drapery finial, a base constructed from two wooden blocks, and a wooden candlecup. All four pieces are glued together, with screws for reinforcement. You can finish the resulting candlestick using a wide variety of paints or patinas.

INSTRUCTIONS

1. *Make candlestick base.* Apply wood glue to top of 4½"-square block and bottom of 3½" baseplate, then press glued surfaces together (*see* illustration A, below). Let glue dry 15 minutes. If glue oozes beyond edges, let glue bead up and dry (1–2 hours), then pick off beaded glue using fingernail or small nail.

2. *Attach finial to base.* Measure and mark center on top of candlestick base (unless it has a predrilled hole). Select bit slightly smaller than diameter of screw found on bottom of finial. Drill hole at mark, through baseplate and two-thirds into rosette block. Screw finial into candlestick base until it rests snugly on top block (illustration B). Lightly trace outline of finial on base, then unscrew and remove finial. Apply wood glue to screw end of finial and circle area of base, then rescrew finial until tight. Let glue dry 15 minutes. If glue oozes beyond edges, repeat as above.

3. *Attach candlecup.* Saw off domed end of finial, then lightly sand sawed end. Measure and mark center of sawed end. Using ⅜" bit, drill ⅝"-deep hole at mark. Using illustration C as reference, drive 10 x 1½" screw through candlecup hole so ¼" tip emerges inside candlecup (to pierce base of candle) and ½" shows at bottom. To test-fit candlecup, insert screw headfirst into hole on sawed end of finial until candlecup rests firmly on finial; drill hole deeper if necessary. To attach candlecup permanently, remove it from hole, fill hole halfway with hot glue, then reinsert it (illustration C). Hold until set.

4. *Finish the candlestick.* Fill any cracks or gaps between joined pieces with putty following manufacturer's directions. Let dry overnight, then sand off excess putty. Apply desired finish and let dry following manufacturer's directions. Install brass candlecup insert before use. ◆

MATERIALS

- 7" wood or resin-cast finial
- 1⅜" x 1⁹⁄₁₆" wood candlecup
- Brass insert for candlecup
- 4½"-square rosette block
- 3½"-square fence post baseplate
- 10" x 1½" screw
- Wood glue
- Paint or finish of choice

You'll also need: drill and bits; small handsaw; screwdriver; sandpaper; hot-glue gun; ruler; and pencil.

Other items, if necessary: wood putty (to fill gaps); small nail (for removing glue beads).

The candlesticks (front to back) were finished using Modern Options' Instant Iron Kit, milk paint in Oyster White and Antique Crackle, and gold paint.

COLOR PHOTOGRAPHY:
Carl Tremblay

ILLUSTRATION:
Mary Newell DePalma

STYLING:
Ritch Holben

Making the Candlestick

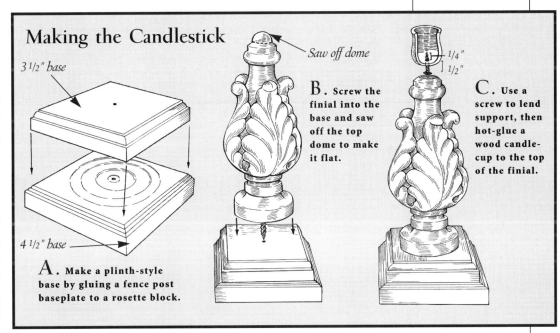

3 ½" base

4 ½" base

A. Make a plinth-style base by gluing a fence post baseplate to a rosette block.

Saw off dome

B. Screw the finial into the base and saw off the top dome to make it flat.

¼"
½"

C. Use a screw to lend support, then hot-glue a wood candlecup to the top of the finial.

Italian Opera Dolls

These quick-sew dolls feature faces sculpted from Sculpey III clay and clothing assembled from scraps of fabric.

❧ BY LINDA Y. KUNDLA

MATERIALS
(For 1 doll)

- **2-ounce package Sculpey III clay (any color)**
- **2-ounce acrylic paints: flesh tone, red, brown, black, and white**
- **Velvet, brocade, or damask in contrasting colors:**
  12" x 12" piece for suit
  6" x 7" piece for hat
- **Assorted metallic trims, cord, and buttons**
- **Small amount synthetic hair**
- **Fiberfill**
- **Thread to match fabrics**
- **Heavy-duty thread**

You'll also need:
hat and body part patterns (*see* pages 44 and 45); sewing machine; shears; hot-glue gun; large-eyed needle; access to photocopier; pins; chopstick; cookie sheet; wooden modeling tools; and small round and fine-tip paintbrushes.

Other items, if necessary:
6" to 8" length of 2"- to 3"-wide sheer or lace trim (for oversleeves); and mini tassel (for unstuffed cone hat).

COLOR PHOTOGRAPHY:
Carl Tremblay

SILHOUETTE PHOTOGRAPHY:
Daniel van Ackere

ILLUSTRATION:
Michael Gellatly

STYLING:
Ritch Holben

This version of the opera doll features a fiberfilled cone hat, lace oversleeves, and a more pointed nose. The finished doll measures about six inches high.

THESE LIGHTHEARTED DOLLS, reminiscent of the characters found in Italian operas, make wonderful gifts or tree ornaments. The face, hands, and feet are modeled from Sculpey III clay, while the simple bodies, arms, and legs can be fashioned from scraps of velvet or other lavish fabrics. Sort through your leftover sewing materials for the finishing trims, tassels, and buttons.

I modeled the dolls' faces using Sculpey III, a brand of thermo-set resin clay. There are two possible techniques for making the doll's face: by sculpting, an art form that lets you develop a unique face for each doll, or by using a push mold. This article only addresses sculpting; if you want to use a push mold, *see* the designer's tip, next page.

When selecting your fabric and trims, keep these points in mind. The doll's body should be sewn from rich fabrics such as velvet, brocade, or damask. The fabric for the hats should be crisp, not soft or prone to ravel. As for the trims, don't be afraid to pick something opulent. Trims that might look gaudy in large-scale use will look tasteful and appropriate on these dolls because you

need only a very small amount.

If you're making more than one doll, you may want to vary the hat styles. Two of the dolls feature a cone hat; one is stuffed with fiberfill for a more upright look, while the second is folded to the side and finished with a tassel. The second type of hat, which I call a pouf hat, is sewn from a four-inch circle of fabric, then finished with a band.

Linda Y. Kundla is a part-time sculptress living in Huntington, New York.

INSTRUCTIONS
Sculpting the Head, Hands, and Feet

1. *Make head blank for sculpting.* Knead 1½ ounces (three-quarters package) Sculpey III until soft. Form into ball, then pull down section ⅝" long x ¾" thick for neck (*see* illustration A, below).

2. *Model facial features.* Use fingers to rough in features: Pull out clay for nose and push in to form eye sockets. Push up toward sockets to form cheekbones. Shape chin, making sure overall head remains rounded and neck stays under head (illustration B). Refine features using wooden modeling tools. To make bulging eyeballs, take small bit of clay from neck, roll into ball, and set into eye socket. Shape lips using tools. Exaggerate nose so that it is round and bulbous or long and pointed (illustration C).

3. *Model hands and feet.* Divide remaining clay (one-quarter package) into four pieces. For each hand, roll 1"-long sausage, then flatten one end slightly to suggest fingers. Cut line into hand to divide thumb from remaining fingers, then curve fingers slightly. Make other hand in mirror image. For each foot, roll 1½"-long sausage, then bend middle at right angle and shape to form heel and ankle. Draw toe end into pointed tip to suggest stocking.

4. *Bake and paint pieces.* Bake pieces on cookie sheet in 275-degree oven 15 to 20 minutes. Let cool 1 hour in oven. Using round brush, paint face and hands fleshtone and feet white or black. Using

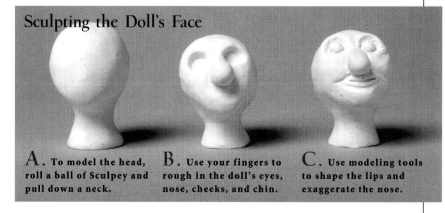

Sculpting the Doll's Face

A. To model the head, roll a ball of Sculpey and pull down a neck.

B. Use your fingers to rough in the doll's eyes, nose, cheeks, and chin.

C. Use modeling tools to shape the lips and exaggerate the nose.

Assembling the Doll

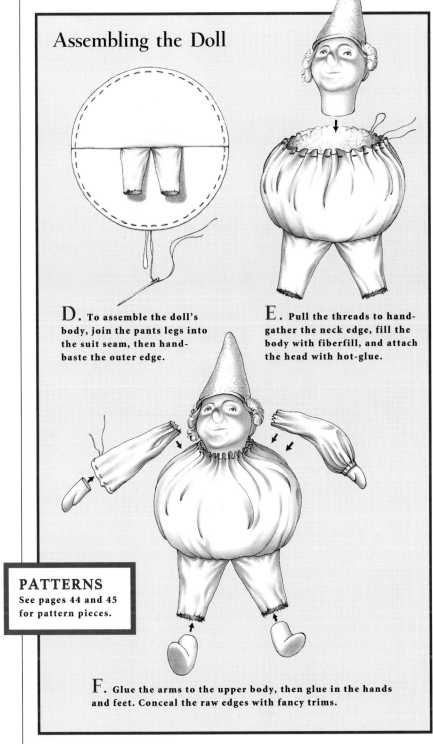

D. To assemble the doll's body, join the pants legs into the suit seam, then hand-baste the outer edge.

E. Pull the threads to hand-gather the neck edge, fill the body with fiberfill, and attach the head with hot-glue.

F. Glue the arms to the upper body, then glue in the hands and feet. Conceal the raw edges with fancy trims.

PATTERNS
See pages 44 and 45 for pattern pieces.

fine-tip brush, paint eyes white with brown or black irises; when dry, add white dot to iris for highlight. Paint eyelids and eyebrows brown. Tinge flesh paint with red and brush onto doll's cheeks and lips.

Assembling the Body

Note: Machine-stitch all seams ¼" from the edge.

1. *Cut fabrics for suit and hat.* Photocopy (*see* pages 44 and 45 for specific dimensions). Use patterns to cut two bodies, two sleeves, and two pant legs from "suit" fabric. Using contrasting fabric, cut one cone hat or one pouf hat circle and one pouf hat band.

2. *Finish doll head and hat.* Cut locks of doll hair and hot-glue to head, allowing curls to fall around face and neck.

Cone hat: Fold hat in half right side in and stitch long edges together. Test-fit on head and restitch seam for tighter fit if needed. Fold and hot-glue raw edge ¼" to wrong side. Clip point and turn right

side out. Tack mini tassel to tip of hat if desired or stuff hat lightly with fiberfill for upright look. Glue to head.

Pouf hat: Using doubled heavy-duty thread, hand-baste hat circle ¼" from edge all around. Gather to fit head, tie off threads when snug, and hot-glue to head. Fold band in half lengthwise, right side out, and stitch long edges. Trim seam ⅛" from stitching, then refold so seam is centered. With seam against head, test-fit band, concealing gathering stitches and raw edge of pouf hat. Hot-glue band to head so ends overlap at front center, then trim off excess.

3. *Sew doll's body.* Fold each leg in half right side in and stitch seam opposite fold; turn right side out. Lay one body piece right side up and pin legs to straight edge so seams face in. Place second body section face down on top, then stitch straight edge. Open body circle and lay flat, right side up. Using doubled heavy-duty thread, hand-baste ¼" from edge all around (illustration D).

4. *Join head to body.* Pull thread ends gently to draw body fabric into ball. Stuff with fiberfill until plump but not stiff. To join head, apply hot-glue to base of neck, then plunge neck down into fiberfill and hold until glue sets (illustration E). Draw thread ends tightly to gather body firmly around neck and tie off.

5. *Make and attach sleeves.* Fold each sleeve in half lengthwise, stitch seam opposite fold, and turn right side out. To make oversleeves, cut lace trim in half crosswise and stitch each piece as above. Slip sleeve inside oversleeve so seams and top edges match. To join sleeves to body, apply hot-glue to upper third of sleeve/oversleeve seam and press against body seam near neck; pinch top of sleeve to take in fullness (illustration F).

6. *Attach hands and feet.* For hands, hand-baste wrist edge of sleeve, hot-glue hand into wrist opening, and pull threads snug. For feet, poke fiberfill into ankle opening. Hot-glue foot into opening and crimp around ankle (illustration F).

7. *Glue on metallic trims.* Cut trim to fit wrists, ankles, and neck, then hot-glue in place, covering raw edges. Glue additional trims, cords, or buttons to body front. Glue trim to front of pouf hatband to cover raw edges. ◆

The soft cone hat on the doll at left includes a tassel at the end. The doll's pouf hat (right) is made with a four-inch circle of fabric.

Mixed Media Greeting Cards

Create one-of-a-kind cards using a simple folding technique, an embossed cutout window, and small trinkets or beads.

❧ BY LILY FRANKLIN

These five-by-six-inch cards use a variety of beads, buttons, and charms. For variation, consider matching the charms to the occasion: Santa Claus beads for Christmas cards, or a cake charm for birthday cards.

MATERIALS
Makes 3 cards

- **Assorted trinkets: buttons, pearls, charms, beads, and so forth**
- **28-gauge silver or gold wire**
- **1 sheet 18" x 24" 140-pound water-color paper**
- **1 sheet 15" x 20" 90-pound water-color paper**
- **Colored 75-pound drawing paper**
- **Thin metallic cord**
- **Double-sided tape**

You'll also need:
steel ruler; X-Acto knife; clear grid ruler; wood stylus; pencil; self-healing cutting mat; embroidery needle; wire cutters or old scissors; and graph paper.

COLOR PHOTOGRAPHY:
Carl Tremblay

ILLUSTRATION:
Mary Newell DePalma

STYLING:
Ritch Holben

THESE MIXED MEDIA CARDS ARE assembled by folding a cover and inside pages, cutting out a window in the cover, and suspending trinkets inside the window. You can hang any number of different items in the window, ranging from charms, buttons, and beads to found objects or jewelry you've taken apart. To further offset the suspended trinkets, you can use colored paper as a background behind the cutout window.

You have a number of choices for paper. The card's cover is made from 140-pound watercolor paper; the pages use 90-pound watercolor paper. I considered using bond paper (i.e., ordinary copy paper) for the pages but decided the cover stock would overwhelm the relatively light weight of bond paper. The stiff colored paper for the trinket's background can be colored 75-pound drawing paper. Other options include construction paper (less elegant and not colorfast) or individual sheets of stationery, such as those found in "paper by the pound" displays.

Two important notes with regard to mailing these cards. First, because the cards are a custom size, you'll need to make your own envelope, unless you alter the card's measurements to match an existing envelope (*see* "Making Your Own Envelopes," next page). Second, be sure to have the post office hand-stamp your cards, versus running them through a postage machine, to prevent the charms and/or beads from being crushed.

Lily Franklin is a designer living in Albuquerque, New Mexico.

INSTRUCTIONS
1. *Cut and fold paper pieces.* Working on self-healing cutting mat and using steel ruler and X-Acto knife, draft and cut the following pieces for each card: one 5" x 24" cover from 140-pound watercolor paper, one 5" x 11" page from 90-pound watercolor paper, and one 4 7/8" x 5 3/4" background from colored paper. Fold cover in fourths: First, fold in half crosswise, then unfold, lay flat, and fold each end to within 1/16" of middle fold (*see* illustration A, next page). Fold inside sheet in half crosswise.

2. *Cut window.* Draft 5" x 6" rectangle on graph paper to represent card cover. Using grid as guide, arrange one or more trinkets in center of rectangle, then draft smaller rectangle (no larger than 2" square) around them to represent window. Set graph paper rectangle on panel 3 of cover (illustration B), position both pieces of paper on self-healing cutting mat, then use steel ruler and X-Acto knife to cut out window through both layers.

3. *Emboss window, then wire trinkets to window.* Using wood stylus and grid ruler, emboss a border around window 3/16" beyond cut edges. Emboss border on right side for "valley" effect or on wrong side for raised effect. Wrap wire securely around trinket(s) or thread through holes, then position within window so wire ends extend at least 1" beyond opening. Clip off excess wire. Using embroidery needle, pierce hole on embossed border for each wire end, then thread wire through on right side (illustration C). Turn cover face down and tape wire ends on wrong side using double-sided tape (illustration D).

4. *Add pages and background.* Place folded sheet inside cover so folds butt, then unfold and lay flat. Using needle and ruler, pierce two holes along fold line 1¼" and 1¾" from each outside edge (for a total of four holes). Thread needle with 9" length of metallic cord. Starting at outside cover, sew cover and pages together (illustration E). Tie ends together in overhand knot and trim excess. Slip colored background between window panel and inside flap and press gently to adhere to tape (illustration F). ◆

DESIGNER'S TIP

For variations on these card designs, consider gilding the area behind the trinkets; making two embossed borders around the window; drawing freehand star or sunburst borders around the window using metallic markers; or personalizing the design to the event, such as using alphabet beads for baby announcements.

Making the Mixed Media Card

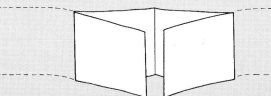

A. To make the card's cover, fold a strip of 140-pound watercolor paper in fourths.

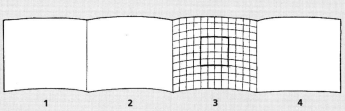

1 2 3 4

B. Use a graph paper template to cut a window opening in cover panel number 3.

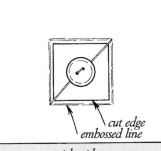

cut edge
embossed line

right side

C. Suspend a button or other trinkets in the cutout window using gold or silver wire.

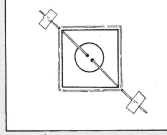

wrong side

D. Tape the wire ends down on the wrong side of the window with double-sided tape.

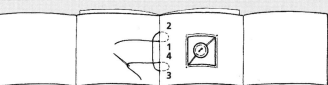

E. Make four holes along the folded spine and sew in the inside page using metallic thread.

F. Slip a colored paper insert behind the cutout window opening.

Making Your Own Envelopes

It's easy to make your own envelopes. Using illustration G as a reference, sketch out a similar shape about three-eighths inch larger all around than your cards (the extra space will allow for the card's thickness). Cut along the solid lines and fold along the dashed lines. To make the envelope, start by folding in the side flaps. Then put glue on the side edges of the bottom flap, fold it up, and stick it in place. To seal the envelope, turn down the top flap and adhere it with glue or double-sided tape.

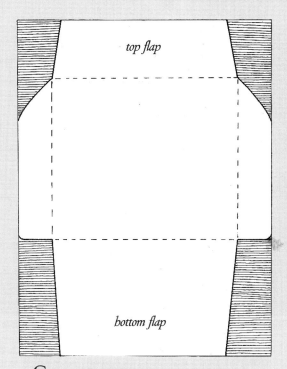

top flap

bottom flap

G. Cut along the solid lines and fold along the dashed lines.

Copper Wire Garland

Construct a sweeping leaf and berry garland using copper tooling foil, beads, and copper wire.

BY MICHIO RYAN

MATERIALS
(for 36" garland)

- **1 square foot (or equivalent) copper tooling foil**
- **8 matte silver ⅝" beads**
- **8 matte gold ⅝" beads**
- **10 shiny silver 10mm beads**
- **20-gauge copper wire**
- **24-gauge copper wire**
- **28-gauge copper wire**
- **Modern Options English Brown patinating solution**
- **Nevr-Dull wadding polish**
- **Wax-based liquid furniture polish (such as Vernax)**

You'll also need:
copper leaf patterns (*see page 46*); needle-nose pliers with wire cutters; extrafine (#0000) steel wool; wooden burnishing tool; 1"-wide foam brush; small disposable bristle brush; stiff brush (to spread glue); large disposable aluminum pan; denatured alcohol; cotton balls; scissors; fine-point permanent marker; pencil; ruler; tracing paper; clear glue; thin cardboard; computer mousepad; credit card; goggles; canvas gloves; and disposable latex gloves.

Other items, if necessary:
ball tool (for scoring veins).

COLOR PHOTOGRAPHY:
Carl Tremblay

ILLUSTRATION:
Nenad Jakesevic

Instead of dried or preserved foliage, this garland is constructed using copper tooling foil for leaves, copper wire for the stems, and beads for berries.

MANY GARLANDS ARE MADE from dried or preserved flowers. For a different look entirely, I decided to make a garland using copper tooling foil for leaves, copper wire for stems, and beads for berries. To tone down the new-penny color of the finished piece, I antiqued the leaves and stems with Modern Options' English Brown patinating solution.

For the garland's leaves, I chose copper tooling foil, which is available in craft and hobby shops. To begin, I used a fine-point, permanent, felt tip pen to trace the outlines of the leaves onto the copper so it would not leave dents. After cutting out the leaves using a pair of hardy scissors (tin snips proved too unwieldy), I cleaned the copper with denatured or rubbing alcohol to remove the pen lines and any oils from handling. (Make sure you dispose of any scraps of foil immediately and handle the cut leaves carefully, as the edges of the copper tooling foil can be sharp.)

In designing the garland, I tested several different types of wire. I needed a wire that would bend without springing out of shape. In the end, I chose copper wire. Brass wire was too springy, while steel wire was too stiff. In addition, wires made from steel, as well as from nickel and ferrous metals such as iron, will not patinate with commonly found solutions. And while silver-plated wire is available in jewelry and bead shops, it is more expensive than copper. Copper wire comes in a variety of gauges (thicknesses), meaning you can match it to any size bead. One important note: If you want to antique the garland, don't use lacquered copper wire or wire that is only copper-colored (versus made of copper), as both types will repel the patinating solution. For the same reason, lacquered copper, brass, or bronze beads cannot be patina-ted. Because unlacquered copper beads, which can be antiqued, are too expensive, I decided not to antique the berries and instead use plastic-core beads that had been painted a metallic color.

After assembling the garland, I wanted to make it look old. I considered a ragged paint finish but realized that it could crack or flake off as the leaves were bent. A patina, on the other hand, is an oxidized layer on the metal itself. I bought Modern Options' English Brown and Pewter Black solutions, thinking two different patinas combined on the same garland might be visually interesting. On copper, however, the difference in tone was minimal, so I settled for English Brown, which is a warm brownish black, over Pewter Black, a bluish gray black.

Keep in mind that patina solutions such as English Brown do not work instantaneously. It took ten to fifteen minutes for the full dark color to appear, and because the liquid can bead, run off, or dry up, it had to be rebrushed several times. Gently scrubbing the surface beforehand using extrafine (#0000) steel wool or a Scotchguard pad helped speed up the process.

Remove the garland from the solution when the copper has turned dark brown/black with pink copper showing only at the edges. Once washed and dried, the garland will be matte gray, but this color can be buffed out using Nevr-Dull wadding polish. Nevr-Dull is cotton wadding in a can of solvent-based cleaner with a trace of fine abrasive. It cuts through the dark color and polishes the metal to a sheen without scratching. (If you can't find Nevr-Dull, you can substitute Noxon 7 applied with steel wool.) Although Nevr-Dull leaves a trace of abrasive in the form of an ashy haze, you can remove this by polishing the garland with liquid furniture wax (I used Vernax). Make sure to use a liquid wax rather than oil polish, which may contain lemon oil but no wax.

INSTRUCTIONS
Making the Leaves and Berry Stems

1. *Cut out copper leaves.* Trace four leaf patterns (*see page 46*). Glue tracings to cardboard, let dry, and cut out. Using cardboard templates and marker, trace six large leaves, six medium leaves, eight small leaves, and six serrated leaves on copper foil. Cut out leaves just inside marked lines. Lay leaves on mousepad and burnish rough-cut edges with wooden burnisher. Rub cotton ball moistened with alcohol over leaves to clean leaves. If desired, use ball tool to lightly score veins.

2. *Attach wire stems to leaves.* For each

leaf, cut 4" stem from 20-gauge wire. Using pliers, make right-angle bend ⅜" from one end. Crease stem section of foil leaf by setting edge of credit card on it slightly off-center and bending foil up toward card. Set wire stem in crease with bent end near top of crease, then lay 28-gauge wire alongside it with its end near bottom of crease (see illustration A, right). Use pliers to fold and crimp foil around wires from both sides, then bend down and crimp bent end. Wind 28-gauge wire down around leaf stem in tight spiral, then clip off and crimp end (illustration B). Repeat on all remaining leaves.

A. Crease the foil leaf, then set the thick and thin wires against the crease.

B. Crimp the foil over the wires, then spiral the thin wire around the crimp.

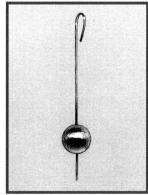

C. Loop one end of the stem wire, then slide a bead on the other end.

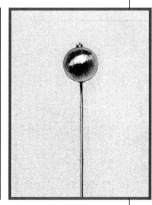

D. Pull the wire through the hole so the loop lodges inside.

3. *Attach wire stems to beads.* For each bead, cut 4" stem from 20-gauge wire. Using pliers, bend down end of wire about one bead's length so it almost touches main stem. Slide bead onto other end (illustration C). Pull wire through hole so double thickness lodges inside (illustration D). If doubled wire is too thick for bead opening, try again with 24-gauge wire. Reinforce with glue if beads feel loose.

Assembling the Garland

1. *Arrange pieces for assembly.* Sort all leaves and beads into seven groups as follows:

L	large leaf
M	medium leaf
S	small leaf
X	serrated leaf
g	gold berry
s	silver berry
ms	mini silver berry

Working from left to right, line up half of pieces on work surface in following order:

M, g, g, ms, X, L, s, s, X, S, S, L, g, s, L, ms, ms, X, M, g, s, M, ms, ms, S, S. Return to starting point and arrange remaining pieces in same order from right to left. The starting point marks the middle of the garland.

2. *Join pieces together.* Twist together two small (S) leaf stems from left side of lineup for ½". Add two mini silver (ms) berries and continue twisting so all stems travel in same direction. Make sure each stem gets twisted instead of simply spiraling one stem around another (illustration E). To grow garland, unroll a few feet of 20-gauge wire from spool and twist end in with stems. Working from left to right across lineup, add new leaves and berries to garland, spacing them ½" to 1½" apart and twisting their stems and wire together (illustration F). Occasionally twist two stems together and then join to wire. To end off, wind together last two leaves from lineup, enclosing spool wire within. Do not cut wire.

3. *Add stabilizing wire.* Wearing canvas gloves, reinforce garland by winding spool wire back around garland main stem in reverse spiral until you reach starting point (illustration G). Cut end, bend into loop, and crimp to main stem.

Patinating and Finishing the Garland

1. *Patinate copper leaves and wire.* Rubbing in one direction, abrade wires and front and back of each leaf with steel wool. Lay garland in aluminum pan, separate and flatten leaves, and point bead wires straight up and out of way. Follow Modern Options English Brown instructions and safety precautions. Make sure work area is well ventilated and put on latex gloves and goggles. Using foam brush for leaves and bristle brush for wire, apply solution to all surfaces. Dark patina will appear within several minutes; if it doesn't, brush on more solution in small amounts. When coppery pink sheen is no longer apparent and surface is somewhat blackened, wash garland in warm soapy water to stop patinating action, and dry thoroughly. Copper should appear matte gray.

2. *Style and burnish leaves.* Curl small and medium leaf tips individually by rolling them between forefinger and thumb. To enhance natural look, shape each large leaf so middle swells out and tip curls back, then twist entire leaf near stem so it curls around central vine. To bring out copper highlights on leaves, apply wadding polish (it comes with a cotton wad applicator) to all high surfaces and buff gently; leave low spots and backs of leaves dark. To remove lingering haze and bring up shine further, polish with liquid furniture wax. Curl serrated leaves. ◆

DESIGNER'S TIP

The copper garland can be used in a variety of ways. Use it to accent a mirror or small window, or place it around a bowl or the base of a vase to create a centerpiece. The garland can also be entwined around a pair of tall candlesticks, draped off a mantel or curtain finial, or used as a curtain tieback.

ASSEMBLING THE GARLAND

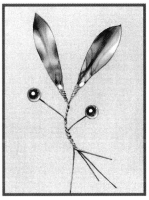

E. Twist two small leaf stems together for ½", then twist in two berries.

F. To grow the garland, twist in spooled wire along with the new stems.

G. Once complete, wind the wire back over the main stem in a reverse spiral.

PATTERNS
See page 46 for patterns.

Colorblock Velvet Pillows

Sew this colorful mix of slouchy-style pillows from two yards of velvet.

❧ BY MICHIO RYAN

COLOR PHOTOGRAPHY:
Carl Tremblay

ILLUSTRATION:
Mary Newell DePalma

SILHOUETTE PHOTOGRAPHY:
Daniel van Ackere

STYLING:
Ritch Holben

MATERIALS
Yields 4 pillows

- **60"-wide medium-weight cotton velvet:**
  - **¹/₂ yard gold**
  - **⁵/₈ yard green**
  - **¹/₂ yard red**
  - **³/₈ yard aubergine**
- **2 ivory 2" pom-poms**
- **4 ivory ³/₄" pom-poms with cord (clip from ball fringe)**
- **2 gold braid 1¹/₂" buttons**
- **4 monkey's fist buttons**
- **One 18", two 14", and one 10" pillow form**
- **Thread to match fabrics**
- **Button and carpet thread**

You'll also need:
sewing machine; rotary cutter; sewing shears; 5" doll-making needle; hand-sewing needle; scissors; pins; ruler; self-healing cutting mat; and seam ripper.

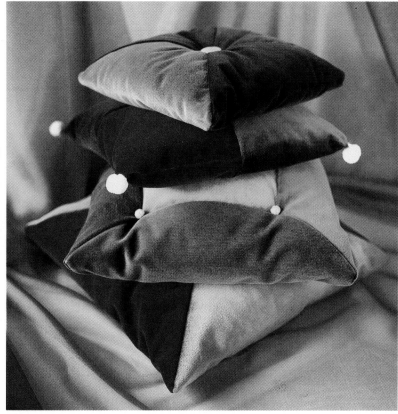

This collection of slouchy-style pillows were sewn using warm, autumnal shades of cotton velvet. For variation substitute a cool palette.

THIS ENTIRE COLLECTION OF COLOR block pillows was assembled from only two yards of cotton velvet. All the pillows are unique in design and size yet coordinate into a unified grouping through color and trim.

The overall harmony of the collection derives from the rich velvet fabrics, chosen for their saturated, off-key colors. The yellow velvet I selected has an orange-brown cast for a richer depth, the red has a slight orange-yellow cast to tone it down, and the aubergine is a grayer, more sophisticated version of purple. Although ordinarily a cool color, the green velvet I used is more yellow than blue, which warms it up and keys it to the other colors. I also excluded shades of blue because their cool tones didn't fit the warm overall cast of the other colors. Had the pillows been rendered in strident, primary colors or in pastel colors, they might have looked garish or tepid.

I considered varying the fabric textures for visual interest, for example, using a pleated velvet or a slubbed silk as a counterpoint to the panes of smooth cotton velvet. This approach made recombining the colors and textures into various layouts more complicated. For texture variation, I selected instead a variety of trims: monkey's fist buttons with their braided cord; spiral, braided cord buttons; and raffia pom-poms in pale colors with a matte sheen. Their colors and textures create a nice contrast with the strongly colored and lustrous velvet, resulting in a vivacious look.

For best results, use medium-weight cotton upholstery velvet, available in sixty-inch widths. Mohair is too coarse, thick, and expensive while rayon velvet is too limp and shows the weave. A velour of reasonable weight is an acceptable substitute if the sheen of the fabric is acceptable to your taste.

Sewing the Large and Small X-Square Pillows

A. Stitch one red A square to a gold A square along two adjacent edges.

backtack ½" from edge

Red A #1 (wrong side)

Gold A (right side)

B. Fold back the red A square diagonally.

Red A #1 (right side)

Gold A #1 (right side)

C. Lay a second red A square on top and stitch the two opposite edges.

Red A #1 (right side)

Red A #2 (wrong side)

D. Fold back the second red A square diagonally.

Red A #1 (right side)

Red A #2 (right side)

E. Sew the remaining gold A square to the two red A squares.

leave open for turning

Gold A #2 (wrong side)

F. Turn the cover right side out, insert the pillow form, and tack on a large pom-pom.

Green

Gold

Gold

Green

If you want to make just one or two of the pillow designs, find the pattern piece(s) that corresponds to the pillow in the pattern diagrams (*see* next page), then cut the required number of pieces and proceed as outlined in the instructions.

If this is your first sewing project or you need a refresher on sewing techniques, consult the "Glossary of Sewing Terms," previous page.

INSTRUCTIONS
Cutting the Fabric
Cut pattern pieces from velvet. Working one color at a time, lay velvet on cutting mat right side up. Follow pattern diagrams (*see* next page) for required measurements of pillow pieces. Follow layout diagrams (next page) for fitting patterns on each color of velvet. Using rotary cutter, cut following pieces, then stack them by shape in five groups.

> Green: 2 B, 1 C, 4 E (cut two on crosswise grain)
> Aubergine: 2 B, 1 C, 1 D
> Gold: 2 A, 1 C, 1 D
> Red: 2 A, 1 C

Assembling the Pillows
Note: Sew, stuff, and finish each pillow following the individual directions below; make one-half-inch seams.

Large X-Square Pillow
1. *Sew A squares together.* Lay one red A square on one gold A square, right sides together. Stitch two adjacent edges, backtacking ½" from edge at beginning and end and pivoting at corner; clip pivoted corner (*see* illustration A). Fold back free corner of red A square diagonally (illustration B). Lay second red A square right side down, stitch to two free gold edges in same manner as above and clip corner (illustration C). Fold back free corner of second red A square (illustration D). Lay second gold A square on top, right side down, and stitch remaining edges in same manner, flipping aside those sewn previously so they are not caught in seams. Leave 10" opening on final edge for turning cover inside out; clip corners (illustration E).

2. *Stuff pillow.* Turn cover right side out. Compress 18" pillow form, insert into opening, then slip stitch opening closed (illustration F).

3. *Attach pom-poms.* Plump pillow and adjust form. Using doll-making needle, draw button and carpet thread through center of pillow and back, catching opposite points of two gold squares on one side and two red squares on other. Pull thread ends to lightly cinch pillow, then tie off. Tack 2" pom-pom to center on each side (illustration F).

Small X-Square Pillow
1. *Sew B squares together.* Lay one aubergine B square on one green B square, right sides together. Proceed as for Large X-Square Pillow, step 1, until all four B pieces are joined; leave 7" opening for turning cover inside out.

2. *Stuff pillow.* Proceed as for Large X-Square Pillow, step 2, using 10" pillow form.

3. *Attach buttons.* Anchor center with button and carpet thread as for Large X-Square Pillow, step 3, then tack gold braid button to each side.

Four-Square Pillow
1. *Sew C rectangles.* Fold each C rectangle in half, right sides together. Stitch one edge perpendicular to fold, backtacking ⅛" from fold to leave small opening in seam for pom-pom cords. Press opposite edge of green rectangle ½" to wrong side; turn remaining pieces right side out (illus-

The finished Small X-Square Pillow (upper left) measures eleven inches wide. The finished Large X-Square Pillow (below) measures eighteen inches wide.

Pattern Diagrams

Use the measurements listed here to create a pattern for each pillow piece.

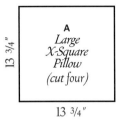
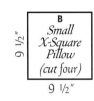
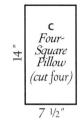
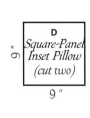
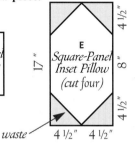

A
*Large
X-Square
Pillow*
(cut four)
13 3/4" × 13 3/4"

B
*Small
X-Square
Pillow*
(cut four)
9 1/2" × 9 1/2"

C
*Four-
Square
Pillow*
(cut four)
14" × 7 1/2"

D
*Square-Panel
Inset Pillow*
(cut two)
9" × 9"

E
*Square-Panel
Inset Pillow*
(cut four)
9" / 17" / 8" / 4 1/2" / 4 1/2" / 4 1/2" / 4 1/2"
waste

Layout Diagrams

Cut out the pieces for the pillows from four different-colored velvets. Use these diagrams in conjunction with the pattern diagrams (above) for assistance in fitting the various pillow piece shapes on the four different pieces of velvet.

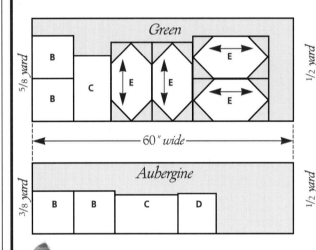

Green — 5/8 yard
B, B, C, E, E, E, E, E — 60" wide

Aubergine — 3/8 yard
B, B, C, D

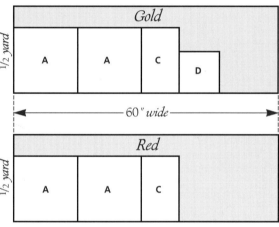

Gold — 1/2 yard
A, A, C, D — 60" wide

Red — 1/2 yard
A, A, C

Designer's Tip

The medium-weight velvet tends to slip during sewing, so be sure to pin the pieces before stitching. If the fabric still slips, you can use the sewing machine's walking foot.

The finished Four-Square Pillow (below) measures thirteen inches wide. The finished Square Panel Inset Pillow (lower right) measures fifteen inches wide.

Designer's Tip

To enhance the slouchy look of the pillows—made possible by velvet's soft, resilient texture—just omit pressing the seams.

tration G). Slip gold C piece inside green "pocket," right sides together, so seams butt folds and raw edges match. Stitch seam opposite green fold, backtacking ½" from edge at beginning and end (illustration H). Open wrong side out. Slip aubergine piece inside gold pocket so seams butt folds, and stitch seam opposite gold fold (illustration I). Open wrong side out, slip red piece inside aubergine pocket so seams butt folds, and stitch seam opposite aubergine fold. Clip corners diagonally (illustration J).

2. *Stuff pillow.* Turn cover right side out. Compress 14" pillow form and insert through opening. Overlap and pin pressed green edge over raw red edge, then slip-stitch closed (illustration K).

3. *Attach pom-poms.* Using seam ripper, poke tie cords of ¾" pom-pom into each corner opening, then tack by hand.

Square Panel Inset Pillow

1. *Sew E pieces together.* Arrange four green E pieces right side up in doughnut shape with nap running in same direction (illustration L). To join E pieces, lay one E piece face down on adjacent E. Stitch "arrow point" at one end, backtacking ¾" from edge at beginning and end and pivoting at point (illustration M). Repeat to join all four E pieces end to end, forming square border when laid flat; clip outside corners (illustration N).

2. *Add panel insets.* Pin aubergine D square to four E edges that form square, then stitch all around (illustration O). Turn over and press one inside E edge ½" to wrong side. Pin and stitch gold D square to three remaining E edges, leaving opening for turning (illustration P).

3. *Stuff pillow.* Turn cover right side out. Compress 14" pillow form and insert through opening. Overlap and pin pressed green edge over raw gold edge, then slip stitch closed.

4. *Attach monkey's fist buttons.* Using

doll-making needle, draw button and carpet thread through pillow and back at each inset corner. Pull thread ends to lightly cinch pillow, then tie off. Tack monkey's fist button at each aubergine inset corner (illustration Q). ◆

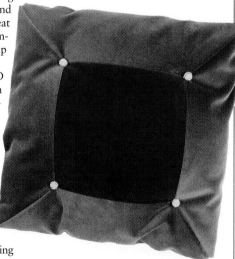

Sewing the Four-Square Pillow

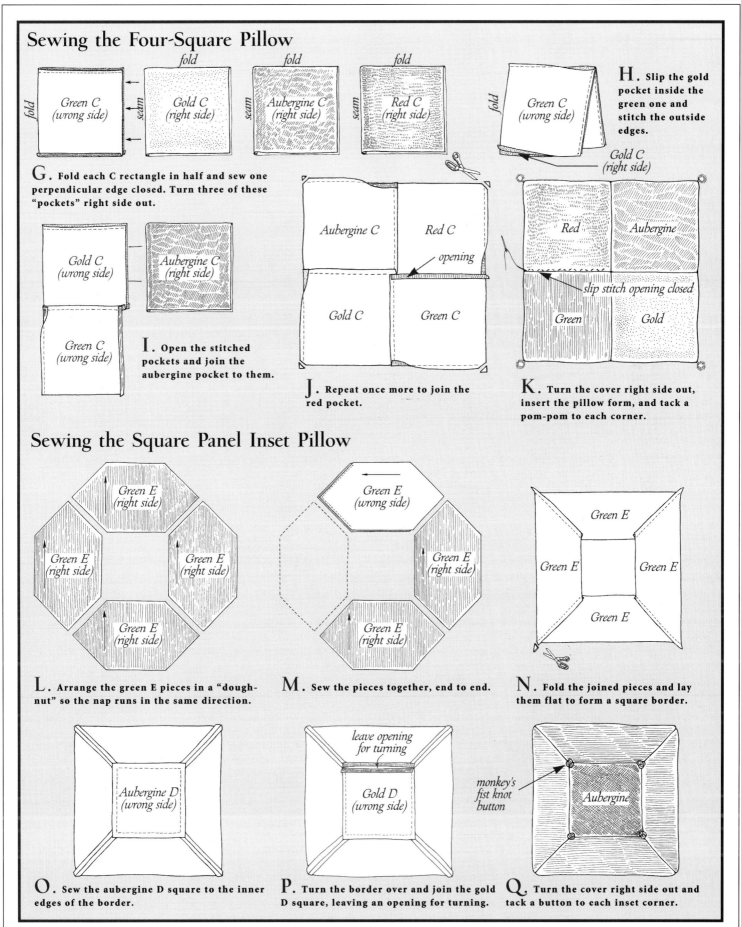

fold — Green C *(wrong side)* — *fold* / *seam*

Gold C *(right side)* — *fold* / *seam*

Aubergine C *(right side)* — *fold* / *seam*

Red C *(right side)* — *fold*

Green C *(wrong side)* — *fold*

H. Slip the gold pocket inside the green one and stitch the outside edges.

Gold C *(right side)*

G. Fold each C rectangle in half and sew one perpendicular edge closed. Turn three of these "pockets" right side out.

Gold C *(wrong side)* — Aubergine C *(right side)*

Green C *(wrong side)*

I. Open the stitched pockets and join the aubergine pocket to them.

Aubergine C — Red C — *opening* — Gold C — Green C

J. Repeat once more to join the red pocket.

Red — Aubergine — *slip stitch opening closed* — Green — Gold

K. Turn the cover right side out, insert the pillow form, and tack a pom-pom to each corner.

Sewing the Square Panel Inset Pillow

Green E *(right side)* — Green E *(right side)* — Green E *(right side)* — Green E *(right side)*

L. Arrange the green E pieces in a "doughnut" so the nap runs in the same direction.

Green E *(wrong side)* — Green E *(right side)* — Green E *(right side)*

M. Sew the pieces together, end to end.

Green E — Green E — Green E — Green E

N. Fold the joined pieces and lay them flat to form a square border.

Aubergine D *(wrong side)*

O. Sew the aubergine D square to the inner edges of the border.

leave opening for turning

Gold D *(wrong side)*

P. Turn the border over and join the gold D square, leaving an opening for turning.

monkey's fist knot button

Aubergine

Q. Turn the cover right side out and tack a button to each inset corner.

Gourmet Herbed Vinegars

Homemade flavored vinegars make an inexpensive but tasteful gift. The secret: red or white wine vinegar and fresh herbs.

❧ BY MELISSA SNYDER

MATERIALS

- **Decorative bottles with new corks**
- **¹/₂ pound beeswax**

Herb Garden Vinegar
- **Red wine vinegar**
- **Multicolored peppercorns**
- **Small garlic clove, peeled**
- **Long, thin red chile pepper**
- **Fresh sprigs of marjoram, sage, rosemary, and thyme**

Basil Vinegar
- **Red wine vinegar**
- **Small garlic clove, peeled**
- **Fresh basil sprigs**

Tarragon Vinegar
- **White wine vinegar**
- **Fresh tarragon sprigs**

You'll also need:
plastic funnel; wooden skewer or chopstick; small bowl; empty coffee can; 1-quart saucepan; cutting board; and knife.

Other items, if necessary:
crayon (for coloring beeswax) and self-stick labels (if not making homemade tags).

COLOR PHOTOGRAPHY:
Carl Tremblay

SILHOUETTE PHOTOGRAPHY:
Daniel van Ackere

ILLUSTRATION:
Nenad Jakesevic

The basil vinegar (above left) uses red wine vinegar and basil, while the tarragon vinegar (above right) blends tarragon with white wine vinegar. Herb garden vinegar (below right) calls for red wine vinegar and a chile pepper.

GOURMET VINEGARS—THOSE that include fruit, herbs, spices, vegetables, or blends of those ingredients—can be expensive. Using red or white wine vinegar as a base, fresh herbs, and a few other ingredients, however, you can easily make your own. These mixtures make a tasteful gift or a special condiment for your own kitchen.

My recipe is especially easy because you'll simultaneously combine and age the ingredients in the presentation bottle. There's no need to age the vinegar in a separate container and then decant it. In addition, although many vinegar recipes require several months of curing time, these simple vinegars will be ready to use in about two weeks.

For each vinegar mixture, you'll need a bottle and cork. Wash them with very hot water or run through the dishwasher. Be sure to use fresh herbs (I grow my own) and red or white *wine* vinegar. Plain white vinegar, commonly found in grocery stores, is too harsh and will overpower the subtle flavors of the herbs.

Although many recipes call for specific ratios of herbs (and other ingredients) to vinegar, I've never followed such a recipe. Just pack a pleasing amount of herbs in a jar and have enough vinegar on hand to fill whatever size bottle you're using. For more flavorful vinegar, use more herbs. For a more subtle taste, use less herbs.

Make sure the herbs are clean and dry, as water can cloud the finished vinegar. Remove any roots or large stems. Place the herbs in the bottle in a visually pleasing way, making adjustments with a wooden skewer or chopstick. Place delicate herbs like marjoram in the bottle first, followed by stronger-stemmed ones like rosemary and thyme. Then slowly pour in the vinegar through a plastic funnel. Hold the bottle up to the light to see

MORE ABOUT HERBED VINEGAR

As beautiful as herbal vinegars are, they are made to be used. The herb garden blend is ideal for salads and marinades, while the basil vinegar works well on tomatoes or with pasta salads and Italian dishes. The tarragon vinegar can be used for salads, chicken dishes, or homemade French-style mustard. If giving the vinegar as gifts, you can add this information to the back of each bottle's tag.

Once you've made these simple vinegars, try experimenting with other combinations, such as types of mint, lemony flavors, or my favorite, edible flower blossoms, which impart their colors to the vinegar.

Most vinegars remain clear, but some turn murky as they cure. While they're not as pretty to look at, murky vinegars are still edible. You may want to strain them before use, however.

how everything looks. When you are satisfied, cork the bottle tightly. Some people start this process in a large mayonnaise jar, let the vinegar age three to six weeks, then transfer it all to a decorative bottle and add fresh herb sprigs. I found this added step unnecessary because all my vinegars were flavorful after about two weeks. Some recipes also call for heating the vinegar to just boiling, but I've found it's too easy to look away just as the vinegar boils, which ruins it. In my tests the proper heating didn't make much difference in the flavor.

The vinegar will need to cure for at

least two weeks. I set the bottle on a sunny windowsill to let the flavors mingle. Once flavored, however, the vinegar should be stored in a cool, dark place.

If you're giving the vinegar as a gift, you should seal the corked tops with wax, as this will keep the vinegar fresh for a longer period of time and prevent leakage. I prefer beeswax because of its natural color, but canning wax will also do. Beeswax costs about $9 per pound, and you'll need to melt one-quarter to one-half pound in a can to get enough depth to submerge the cork. Melt the wax in a large tin can, such as an empty coffee container. You can store the leftover cooled wax right in the can and remelt it when you need it.

To renew the vinegar after a little use, pour in enough fresh vinegar to cover the herbs (the new vinegar will mix in with the original). This is important because any herb sprigs suspended above the top of the vinegar line can get moldy. Using this method, you can keep the same herbs for about one year. An unopened bottle will last for about three years.

Whether you're giving the vinegars as gifts or keeping them for your own use, you'll want to add labels to the bottles. *See* "Sealing Wax Tags," below, for ideas on how to do this.

Melissa Snyder sells herbs, vinegars, and dried flower arrangements from her farm, Barleywine Herb Farm, in Perkinsville, Vermont.

INSTRUCTIONS

1. *Arrange dry ingredients in bottles.* Wash bottles and corks in hot water and let drain overnight, or run through dishwasher; proceed when glass is thoroughly dry. For each recipe, place the dry ingredients into the bottle in the order listed in the materials box. Drop peppercorns through funnel slowly until they form single layer on bottom of bottle. Push garlic clove through bottle top. (Do not halve or quarter the clove, because cut garlic will disintegrate faster.) Use skewer or chopstick to poke chile and herbs (start with marjoram and sage and finish with rosemary and thyme) gently through bottle neck (*see* illustration A).

2. *Add vinegar and cure.* Using funnel, pour vinegar into bottles up to bottle neck (illustration B). Soften corks by soaking in small bowl of hot water, then insert cork tightly and set bottle on sunny windowsill for at least two weeks prior to storage in cool, dark place. Label vinegars using self-stick labels or homemade tags (*see* "Sealing Wax Tags," below).

3. *Seal corked tops with beeswax (optional).* Cut ¼ pound of the beeswax into slivers, place slivers in can, and set can in saucepan. Add water to saucepan until half full. Bring this double boiler setup to boil, then reduce to simmer. Using skewer or chopstick, stir wax occasionally until liquefied. Cut and drop in more wax slivers and melt until can is half full. If tinting wax, drop in bits of crayon and stir to mix in color. Turn off heat. When water stops simmering, invert bottle and dip end into hot liquid. Lift out and let cool, then repeat to add up to ten layers to each bottle, adding more wax to keep can half full (illustration C). ◆

DESIGNER'S TIP

Because of vinegar's corrosive nature, you should avoid metal utensils when working with it. Strainers and funnels should be made of plastic, all containers should be glass, and corks should be used in place of metal bottle caps.

MAKING THE HERBED VINEGARS

A. Start with a clean, dry bottle. Put in the herbs and seasonings first.

B. Funnel in the vinegar up to the bottle neck, then cork the top.

C. If sealing the bottles, dip them into melted beeswax up to ten times.

SEALING WAX TAGS

One easy way to identify homemade vinegars and to indicate what use they are best suited for is to make sealing wax tags (see photo, far left, previous page).

For each tag, you'll need some type of paper and string, and some kind of bead. You can recycle a variety of materials for paper, such as grocery or shopping bags, cards, or junk mail envelopes. Look for paper that is fairly sturdy and has subtle texture. For added interest, cut your tags using paper edgers, pinking shears, or other specialty scissors. For the string that hangs around the bottle's neck, consider twine, perle cotton, cord, or even raffia. The sliding object that keeps the tag tight on the bottle's neck can be a candlecup, a bead, or some other small item with a hole through it, such as a lucky stone or a button.

INSTRUCTIONS

1. *Cut out tags.* Working on cutting mat and using X-Acto knife and steel ruler, cut out one small (e.g., 1⅞" x 2⅝") rectangle from paper for each tag. If desired, recut tag using edged scissors.

2. *Thread twine through candlecup.* Cut two lengths of twine (or substitute), each equal to height of bottle to be tagged. Hold four ends together, then insert them through hole at base of candlecup and draw them through about 2". If twine is too thick, remove one length and try again or drill hole slightly larger. If hole is too large, add additional strand(s). Candlecup should slide up and down twine without resistance, yet not be loose.

3. *Seal twine ends to tag.* Lay twine ends down, overlapping edge of tag with clipped corners, and tape to work surface (do not tape tag). Light sealing wax wick and hold ½" above twine ends; let 10 to 20 drops of wax fall on ends. Blow out wick and set stick aside. Press head of screw (or substitute) into wet wax to seal twine and create imprint. Let cool about 15 seconds.

4. *Attach tag to bottle.* Inscribe name of vinegar on tag, then, if desired, add notes to back of tag. Slip looped end of twine around bottle neck and slide candlecup up.

MATERIALS

- Stiff paper
- Twine
- Wooden candlecup
- Sealing wax with built-in wick

You'll also need: large Phillips head screw, coin, or other decorative device; matches; steel ruler; X-Acto knife; scissors; tape; pencil or fancy marker; and self-healing cutting mat.

Other items, if necessary: drill with bit (for enlarging hole on sliding object) and paper edgers (for embellishing edges).

Jacob's Ladder Book

Unlike most books, this double-hinged folder opens from either side. Use it to hold stationery or postcards.

❧ BY LILY FRANKLIN

MATERIALS

- **Giftwrap paper(s)***
- **Grosgrain ribbon***
- **3-ply chipboard***
- **1-ply chipboard***
- **Yes Stickflat glue**
- **Double-sided tape**
- **Sample stationery (envelope, postcard, photo, etc.)**

For amounts, see steps 1 through 3.

You'll also need:
Scotch Magic Removable tape; stiff, flat brush (to spread glue); self-healing cutting mat; utility knife; steel ruler; pencil; heavy book; and newsprint.

You can cover this double-hinged book with homemade paper, fabric, giftwrap, wallpaper, or marbled paper. These books measure 5½" by 7¾".

MAKE A BOOK OF ANY SIZE

Panel-hinged edge	Ribbon width	Hinge distance from edge
3"	⅛"–⅜"	¾"
4"	⅛"–⅜"	⅞"
5"	⅜"–⅝"	1"
6"	⅜"–⅝"	1⅛"
7"	⅜"–⅝"	1¼"
8"	⅝"	1½"
9"	⅝"–⅞"	1¾"
10"	⅝"–⅞"	2"
11"	⅞"	2¼"
12"	⅞"	2½"

COLOR PHOTOGRAPHY:
Carl Tremblay

ILLUSTRATION:
Michael Gellatly

STYLING:
Ritch Holben

THOUGH THIS BOOK LOOKS LIKE an ordinary folder, its double ribbon hinges allow it to open completely from either side. The book's construction was inspired by a children's toy—blocks of wood hinged together with bands that allow the blocks to flop over on themselves without coming apart.

The book's size is determined by the item you store inside it (e.g., photographs, business cards, etc.). I've assembled two charts to assist with customizing the book's dimensions. The first lists a range of book sizes, the required ribbon width, and how far away to position the hinges from the book's top and bottom edges. The second chart tells you how much ribbon to purchase, depending on the book's dimensions.

Lily Franklin is a designer living in Albuquerque, New Mexico.

INSTRUCTIONS

1. *Cut four chipboard panels.* Measure stationery, jot down dimensions, and add ¾" to both length and width. Cut all pieces so chipboard grain runs lengthwise. Measure and mark two panels on 3-ply chipboard for covers and two on 1-ply chipboard for linings. Working on cutting mat, use utility knife and steel ruler to score and cut chipboard panels.

2. *Cut four giftwrap rectangles.* Add 2¾" to both length and width of stationery. Cut all pieces so paper grain runs crosswise. Cut two rectangles this size from giftwrap paper for cover and two from same or contrasting paper for lining.

3. *Cut ribbon hinges.* To determine ribbon width and yardage, *see* charts, right. From ribbon yardage, cut four "straight" hinges, each equal to panel width plus 2". Cut remaining ribbon into four equal pieces for "X" hinges.

4. Glue giftwrap to chipboard panels. Lay giftwrap rectangles face down on newsprint. For each rectangle, brush thin coat of glue on corresponding panel, then press glue side of panel down on giftwrap. Turn assembly over, smooth, then turn face down. Fold and glue down long edges (see illustration A). To miter corners, match fold at each corner to adjacent panel edge, then press flat to form triangle (illustrations B1 to B3). Trim excess from inner flaps to reduce bulk, then glue down outer flaps (illustration C).

5. *Tape hinges in position.* Lay four panels side by side, face up, so panel 1 is cover, 2 is lining, 3 is lining, and 4 is cover. Referring to chart at left and measuring from panels' top and bottom edges, make light tick marks on long panel edges for hinge placement (illustration D). Lay four "X" hinges in position on panels 1 and 3 so ribbon crosses edge just inside tick mark; secure with removable tape (illustration E). Position and tape four "straight" hinges on panels 2 and 4 so ribbon crosses edge just beyond tick mark. Tuck loose ribbon ends under adjacent panel (illustration F).

6. *Secure hinges on wrong side.* Fold panel 1 face down onto panel 2, and affix ribbon ends from panels 1 and 2 to back of panel 1 with double-coated tape. Fold panel 4 onto panel 3 and repeat process (illustration G). Unfold panels, refold in center (so panel 2 lies on panel 3, and panel 1 lies on panel 4), and tape ribbon ends to panel 2 (illustration H). Turn assembly over to tape ribbon ends to panel 3. Refold book so panels 2 and 3 face up, peel off removable tape, and slip stationery under ribbons; adjust ribbon tension on back of panels 2 and 3 if necessary (illustration I). To finish book, remove stationery, glue panels back to back in this position, and weight with heavy book at least 1 hour. ◆

RIBBON YARDAGE

Match your panel dimensions to the chart below to determine the ribbon yardage needed. Note that long, narrow panels are not suitable for this project (as marked by asterisks below).

		Ribbon required for nonhinged edges				
		3"	4"	5"	6"	7"
Hinged edges	3"	1¼	1⅜	**	**	**
	4"	1¼	1½	1⅝	**	**
	5"	1¼	1½	1¾	1⅞	**
	6"	**	1½	1¾	2	2¼
	7"	**	**	1¾	2	2¼
	8"	**	**	**	2	2¼
	9"	**	**	**	**	2¼

Assembling the Jacob's Ladder Book

A. Cover each chipboard panel with giftwrap, folding and gluing the long edges to the back.

B1. To miter the corners, fold the excess paper over...

B2. ...then push in the center portion...

B3. ...to create a flattened triangle.

C. Trim the inner triangles, then fold and glue down the top and bottom flaps.

cover *lining* *lining* *cover*

| 1 | 2 | 3 | 4 |

D. Lay the panels side by side and make tick marks for the ribbon hinge placement.

| 1 | 4 |

G. Fold the end panels onto the middle panels and stick down the loose ribbon ends with double-coated tape.

| 1 | 2 | 3 | 4 |

E. Use removable tape to temporarily affix the "X" hinges to panels 1 and 3.

| 2 | 1 |

H. Refold the book at the middle to stick down the remaining loose ends.

| 1 | 2 | 3 | 4 |

F. Tape the "straight" hinges to panels 2 and 4. Slip the ribbon ends under the adjacent panels

| 2 | 3 |

I. To finish, glue the panels back to back.

Block Print Fresco Garland

Create a mottled effect by combining several colors of paint on one printing pad.

❧ BY FRANCOISE HARDY

This garland uses five different colors of paint. For variety, block-print a garland using five different shades of one color.

COLOR PHOTOGRAPHY:
Carl Tremblay

ILLUSTRATION:
Nenad Jakesevic

MATERIALS

■ **2-ounce acrylic paints in the following colors: gold, burnt sienna, forest green, brown, and burgundy**

You'll also need:
leaf patterns (*see* page 46), computer mousepad; two-ply chipboard; Magic Rub eraser; ½" flat paintbrush; watercolor brushes size 5 and 8; paint palette; self-healing cutting mat; steel ruler; rubber cement; X-Acto knife; tracing paper; pencil; tape; chalk; newsprint; and small jar of water.

T O CREATE THE GARLAND PICtured above, I used multicolor block printing. This technique yields a mottled, frescolike design suitable for any painted surface, from a wall to a set of cabinets.

Multicolor block printing involves mixing several different colors on one printing pad. For this garland, I selected an autumnal palette of five colors—gold, burnt sienna, forest green, brown, and burgundy—although you can make your own substitutions. To get started, I cut a large leaf-shaped printing pad from a computer mousepad, then brushed three colors of paint onto the pad. I printed a cluster of

five leaves before reloading the pad with a different combination of colors. For the smaller leaves, I cut a printing pad from an eraser, then loaded the pad with two colors of paint. By using this technique and varying your paint colors, you can create an endless variety of foliage.

I printed my garland on top of a light gold and avocado green faux finish (*see* "The Best Shortcuts to Faux Fresco Painting," Spring 1996). You can re-create this effect on any painted surface—just prepare the surface accordingly.

Francoise Hardy is a Boston-based artisan and craftsperson.

INSTRUCTIONS
Cutting the Pads

1. *Cut out large leaf pad.* Trace large leaf pattern (*see* page 46). Tape tracing to fabric side of mousepad, then set on cutting mat. Using X-Acto knife, cut through paper to score leaf veins on surface of mousepad, then cut out entire leaf.

2. *Assemble large leaf pad.* Draft two rectangles measuring 3¼" x 1¾" on chipboard. Score and cut out rectangles. Brush rubber cement on facing sides of rectangles. Let cement get tacky, then press surfaces together, edges matching. Repeat to cement leaf to chipboard so fabric side of mousepad faces out.

3. *Cut out small leaf pad.* Trace small leaf pattern (page 46). Lay tracing face down on eraser, retrace lines with pencil, then remove tracing. Set eraser on cutting mat. Using X-Acto knife, cut shallow V-shaped troughs for leaf veins, then cut out entire leaf (*see* illustration A, below).

4. *Assemble small leaf pad.* Draft two 2¼" x 1½" rectangles on chipboard. Score and cut out rectangles, then glue together as in step 2. Cement leaf to chipboard as in step 2 so veined side faces out.

Printing the Garland

1. *Mark wall for printing.* Use chalk to sketch vine placement on wall.

2. *Print large leaf designs.* Squeeze small amount of each color on palette. Using paintbrush, apply any three colors to surface of large pad (illustration B). Press pad on newsprint to shed excess paint. Press pad on chalk line representing vine, then lift up. Without reloading paint, print leaves above and below this leaf, up to 5" from line (illustration C). Repeat using three different paints, printing clusters spaced 5" apart along line.

3. *Print small leaf designs.* Apply any two colors to eraser leaf stamp. Shed excess paint, then print leaves. Repeat, reloading stamp as needed.

4. *Paint vine and branches.* Dip size 8 brush in water, then load with green and/or brown paint. Run brush alongside chalk line path to paint vine. Repeat using size 5 brush to add smaller branches (illustration D). Let dry overnight. ◆

BLOCK-PRINTING THE GARLAND

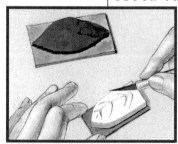

A. **Cut out two leaf-shaped printing pads.**

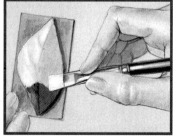

B. **Ink the pads with acrylic paint.**

C. **Print the large leaves first, then print the smaller leaves.**

D. **Paint in vines between the leaves.**

Golden Delicious Apple Roses

You can assemble this beautiful arrangement using a bag of apples and a paring knife or an electric food slicer.

🌸 BY LE SPEARMAN

THOUGH THIS CERAMIC PITCHER appears to be filled with fresh roses, these beautiful flowers were actually assembled from preserved apple slices. To give the roses a soft yellow tinge, I used Golden Delicious apples, although you can also use Red Delicious. Apple roses are perfect for decorating a wreath or in arrangements.

Le Spearman is a writer, photographer, and designer living in Sac City, Iowa.

INSTRUCTIONS
Slicing and Curing the Apples

1. *Slice apples.* Pour lemon juice into baking dish, add salt, and stir with spoon to dissolve. If using paring knife to cut slices, stand apple upright on cutting board, slice off and discard ¼" from end, then make very closely spaced parallel cuts, ⅛" thick or less, until you reach core. To prevent discoloration, immediately drop slices into salted lemon juice. Repeat to cut slices from opposite side. If using food slicer, use paring knife to slice out core, slice off and discard ¼" from end, then proceed following manufacturer's instructions and safety precautions.

2. *Cure apple slices.* Let apple slices soak 3 to 5 minutes. Cover flat surface with several layers of newsprint, then arrange slices on newsprint in single layer. After 1 hour, transfer slices to several layers of fresh, dry newsprint. Let slices cure a minimum of 24 hours, occasionally transferring them to fresh newsprint, until dry, velvety, and flexible.

Assembling the Rose

1. *Make rose core.* Sort apple slices by size into three groups of petals: small, medium, and large. Discard damaged or discolored slices. Using pliers, cut desired stem length from 18-gauge wire, then bend tip into small loop. Roll small petal snugly around stem, concealing loop. Select medium-size petal, position it on first petal to cover its vertical edge, and roll to each side. Roll two additional medium-size petals around core in same way, concealing vertical edge of petal underneath. For realistic shape, pinch petals at base as you go (*see* illustration A, right).

2. *Secure additional petals with wire.* Lay end of 30-gauge wire against stem for 3", then wind small portion of wire

The petals on these lifelike roses were made using the Golden Rose variety of Golden Delicious apples from Stemilt, an orchard in Washington State.

firmly around pinched base of petals (illustration B). Add between six and ten additional large petals to rose, winding wire around base of each petal as you go. To end off, spiral excess wire a few turns around stem and clip off.

3. *Attach calyx.* Photocopy pattern. Unfurl paper twist so it lies flat, lay pattern on top, and mark and cut one calyx. Wrap around rose stem, pinching it so leaves will be evenly spaced and flare out just below rose base. Unwrap, apply tacky glue to lower edge of calyx, and rewrap around stem. To finish, bind entire stem with florist tape, starting just below calyx leaves and working down (illustration C). To curl tips of leaves, wrap around pencil or wooden skewer. ◆

MATERIALS

- **Golden Delicious apples (allow 1 apple per rose)**
- **Green paper twist**
- **Green florist tape**
- **18-gauge florist wire**
- **30-gauge green fabric-covered florist wire (on spool)**
- **16 ounces undiluted lemon juice**
- **1 tablespoon salt**
- **Tacky glue**

You'll also need: calyx pattern (*see* page 46); access to photocopier; spoon; sharp paring knife and/or electric food slicer; cutting board; flat-bottomed glass baking dish; newsprint; pliers with built-in wire cutters; pencil and/or wooden skewer; ruler; and scissors.

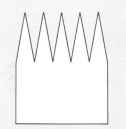

PATTERN
See page 46 for pattern.

COLOR PHOTOGRAPHY:
Lynn Neymeyer

ILLUSTRATION:
Judy Love

STYLING:
Le Spearman

ASSEMBLING THE APPLE ROSE

A. Form the core with a small petal, then add medium petals.

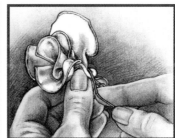

B. Wind the wire around the pinched base of the rose.

C. Wrap the calyx around the stem, then bind with the tape.

Red Velvet Candleshade

Transform an ordinary candlestick into a tabletop decoration with this quick and easy shade.

&❧ BY FRANCOISE HARDY

Wondering what to do with those fabric scraps? This candleshade requires only a twelve-inch-by-twelve-inch piece of fabric.

IF YOU'RE LOOKING FOR AN EASY WAY to dress up your dinner candles, consider this elegant red velvet candleshade. At first glance, a candleshade might seem like a fire hazard. When using a candle follower and a straight (*not* tapered) candle, however, it's possible to safely display a shade on a lit candle.

A candle follower comprises two parts: a ring and the harp (*see* illustration A, next page). The ring fits around the burning end of the candle; as the candle burns down, the ring lowers itself along the candle shaft. The harp has a collar on which the shade rests, lifting the shade safely above the flame. (But never leave a candle burning unattended.)

For this project I used Yes Stikflat glue instead of spray adhesive. The Stikflat glue, available in a one-pound, three-ounce tub for about $9, is spread with a thin brush. You can thin it with water to make it more spreadable, although for this project that isn't necessary. Because the shade is small, and the arc of paper needs to form a cone, it tends to spring apart easily, so the more "stick" you have, the better. I ended up putting craft sticks over the seam splint-style (to prevent marking the velvet) and using clothespins to hold the shade together as the glue dried.

For this project, and others like it, I recommend using newsprint rather than newspaper, because it protects your project as well as your work surface. Newsprint, available in large pads in art supply stores, does not feature ink, which can rub off onto the velvet shade. As your newsprint sheets get sticky from glue, simply tear off a new page, much like a disposable tablecloth.

Francoise Hardy is a Boston-based artisan and craftsperson.

INSTRUCTIONS
Making the Candleshade Arc

1. *Draft basic candleshade arc.* Measure harp height (a) and diameter (b) (*see* illustration A, next page). Following illustration B and working on bristol board, draft vertical line equal to harp height (a), then draft bisected perpendicular lines at each end, one equal to harp diameter (b) and one 6" long, or equal to diameter of lower shade (c). Draft two straight lines (d) through endpoints, extending them so they intersect at center point. Insert compass point at intersection and swing large and small arcs through endpoints. Multiply lower shade diameter (c) x 3.14 to determine lower shade circumference. Starting at outer edge, use tape measure to measure and mark this length around large arc (e). Draft straight line connecting length mark to center point (f). Draft parallel line ½" away for overlap (g).

2. *Add guidelines for beads.* Beginning at outer edge (d), measure and mark large arc in 1¼" increments (illustration C). Align ruler on each mark and center point to draft fifteen 3"-long radial spokes.

3. *Cut out arc template and lining.* Lay bristol board on cutting mat. Cut out arc, using X-Acto knife and steel ruler for straight edges and scissors for curved edges. Use arc as template to mark and cut lining from giftwrap paper; set lining aside.

Note: Glue is applied in several of the following steps. To prevent unwanted glue from marring your project, place newsprint under your work and replace it with fresh sheets as the old ones become sticky. Use scrap bristol board to press and adhere the glued pieces. Clean the glue from your hands frequently using a wet washcloth.

4. *Glue shade arc to velvet.* Lay velvet right side down. Lay arc template marked side down on newsprint. Brush template surface evenly with glue, going out beyond edges, then set arc glue side down on velvet and smooth to adhere. Trim excess velvet ½" from edge all around, trim corners diagonally, and trim overlap edge even with arc straight edge (illustration D). Using scissors, cut ¼" slits ⅛" apart on short curved edge; cut notches ½" apart along long curved edge. Brush glue onto each allowance, fold onto arc, and press to adhere (illustration E). Fold and glue down remaining straight edge allowance. Lay shade wrong side down on waxed paper, weight with heavy book, and let dry 1 hour.

Assembling the Shade

1. *Shape and glue shade.* Cut each of two craft sticks to equal shade height. Roll arc into shade shape so folded velvet edge overlaps trimmed edge by ½", hold

Making the Candleshade Arc

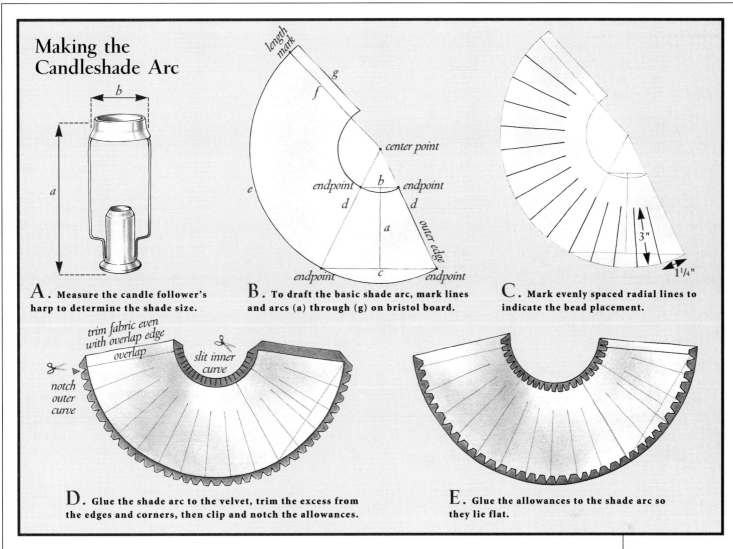

A. Measure the candle follower's harp to determine the shade size.

B. To draft the basic shade arc, mark lines and arcs (a) through (g) on bristol board.

C. Mark evenly spaced radial lines to indicate the bead placement.

D. Glue the shade arc to the velvet, trim the excess from the edges and corners, then clip and notch the allowances.

E. Glue the allowances to the shade arc so they lie flat.

firmly, and test-fit on follower. Using illustration F as reference, adjust width of overlap if needed, then sandwich overlapped section between splints and secure with clothespin at each end. Mark overlap edge on inside of shade. Undo clothespins, remove sticks, and let relax. Brush glue on overlap, reassemble, and reclip (illustration F). Let dry 2 hours.

2. *Attach beaded trim.* Insert pearl-head pin into black bead, then push pin-point into shade rim even with radial line so shaft lodges within bristol board and black bead touches rim. Repeat to attach remaining beads evenly spaced all around (illustration G).

3. *Glue in lining.* Turn shade upside down. Test-roll lining and fit inside shade

so straight edges align. Remove and trim curved edges if necessary. Stand shade upside down and brush glue inside top and bottom rims. Roll lining slightly tighter than necessary, insert it inside shade, then slowly unroll, pressing it against glue at each rim edge (illustration H). When you near starting point, brush glue on overlap and press down to adhere. ◆

ASSEMBLING THE SHADE

F. Glue the shade seam, apply a wooden "splint," and secure the shade with clothespins until dry.

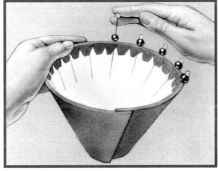

G. Attach the beads with the pearl-head pins so the shaft lodges between the plies of the bristol board.

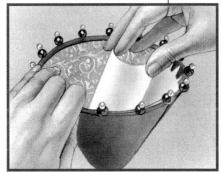

H. Insert the rolled lining inside the shade, then slowly unfurl it and press to adhere.

Floral Fan Topiary

Cover a fan-shaped section of chipboard with tiers of dried flowers to create this elegant topiary.

❧ BY CAROL ENDLER STERBENZ

PHOTOGRAPH REPRINTED WITH PERMISSION FROM DECORATING WITH WREATHS, GARLANDS, TOPIARIES, AND BOUQUETS BY CAROL ENDLER STERBENZ (RIZZOLI INTERNATIONAL, 1993).

MATERIALS

Note: Actual number of flowers needed to fill fan may differ slightly.

- 2"- to 3"-diameter container (for base)
- 26 stems cream cockscomb
- 24 stems golden yarrow
- 24 stems yellow tansy
- 24 stems magenta cockscomb
- 20 stems purple statice
- 24 pink tea roses
- 6 yellow tea roses
- Sheet moss
- ½ yard 1"-wide chartreuse ribbon
- Florist foam
- 1-ply chipboard
- ⅜"-diameter dowel

You'll also need:
scissors; pruning shears; small handsaw; hot-glue gun; compass; ruler; triangle; pencil; and table knife.

COLOR PHOTOGRAPHY:
Steven Mays

ILLUSTRATION:
Mary Newell DePalma

This 20"-tall fan topiary makes a lovely accent for a sideboard or mantel. For holiday decorating, substitute a variety of greens, roses, and pepperberries.

INSTRUCTIONS
Assemble Chipboard Fans

1. *Mark and cut two chipboard fans.* Draft 10" line on section of 1-ply chipboard and label it *x*. Using triangle and ruler, draft perpendicular 10" line to bisect first line and label second line *y*. Place compass point at intersection of two lines and draft circle with 4½" radius (*see* illustration A, next page). Draft seven additional concentric circles, decreasing radius by ½" for each one. Then draft two lines connecting inner circle/line *x* to outer circle/line *y* (illustration B). Cut out fan using scissors, then number rings 1 to 9, with number 1 on outermost tier (illustration C). Mark and cut second chipboard fan to match first chipboard fan.

2. *Glue flowers to fans.* Clip all flower stems close to bloom or cluster. Set aside eight stems magenta cockscomb. Sort all remaining stems by type into seven groups. Divide cream cockscomb into two groups of fourteen and twelve stems each. Lay chipboard fans on work surface, numbered sections facing upwards. Referring to illustration D and working with one group of flowers at a time, hot-glue the stems to each ring of the fan, blooms facing outwards, as follows:

Ring #1 magenta cockscomb
     #2 golden yarrow
     #3 cream cockscomb (7 stems)
     #4 purple statice
     #5 pink tea roses
     #6 cream cockscomb(6 stems)
     #7 yellow tea roses
          (cluster near center)
     #8 yellow tansy (use to fill out remainder of ring #7)

Assemble Topiary

1. *Join chipboard fans to stem.* Measure and saw dowel to equal container height plus 8". Gently set one fan with flowers facing down on work surface. Apply hot-glue to end of dowel for 2", then press glued section of dowel gently against center of fan (illustration E). Run bead of glue just inside curved edge of fan and upper 2" portion of dowel, then affix second chipboard fan back-to-back on top of first fan with edges matching (illustration F).

2. *Assemble topiary.* Using table knife, cut block of florist foam slightly larger than container. Lodge florist foam inside container, shaving edges to fit if necessary. Plunge end of dowel straight down into center of florist foam so topiary stands upright. Wind ribbon around dowel stem, folding under raw edges, then secure at top and bottom with glue. Hot-glue reserved magenta cockscomb to fan edges to conceal open spaces. Arrange moss in container to conceal foam. ◆

M ANY DRIED FLOWER TOPI-aries are based on a globe design, in which a foam ball is covered with dried, fresh, or preserved material. This fan-shaped topiary, on the other hand, is constructed using two pieces of chipboard, which are cut into a fan shape, then sandwiched around a dowel stem. The fan-shaped piece of chipboard is then covered with arching tiers of magenta cockscomb, golden yarrow, cream cockscomb, purple statice, pink and yellow tea roses, and yellow tansy.

Using this one basic topiary construction technique, you can create a variety of design interpretations. Arrange the dried flowers in a different pattern, change their order of placement, or mix two types of roses, for example, within one row. You can also substitute other dried or preserved flowers, as long as the material is in proper scale to the other flowers, and to the size of the fan. You could substitute pink strawflowers for the roses, for example, or create a striped pattern using yellow and red roses.

The finished topiary pictured above measures about twenty inches high; the fan is nine inches wide at the bottom. A small-scale topiary such as this one works well on a mantel or shelf.

Making the Fan Topiary

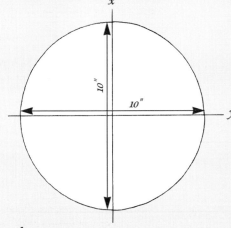

A. Draft two perpendicular lines and a circle on the chipboard.

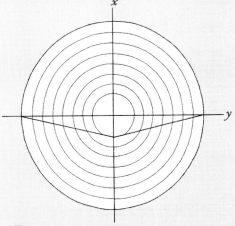

B. Draft inner concentric circles for the fan rings and straight lines for the lower edges.

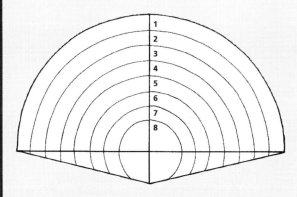

C. Cut out the fan and number the rings. Make a second fan to match.

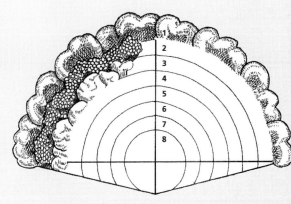

D. For each fan, glue the dried flower stems to the rings in a prearranged order.

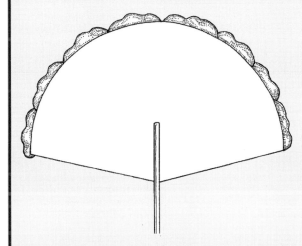

E. Glue a dowel to the back of one fan.

F. Glue the second fan to the first fan with the dowel in between.

FLOWER IDENTIFICATION

1. **Magenta cockscomb**
2. **Golden yarrow**
3. **Cream cockscomb (7 stems)**
4. **Purple statice**
5. **Pink tea roses**
6. **Cream cockscomb (6 stems)**
7. **Yellow tea roses (cluster near center)**
8. **Yellow tansy (fill out rest of ring #7, too)**

Flapdown Sewing Box

This four-sided box opens flat to reveal its contents. Fill it with sewing, embroidery, or craft supplies for a special gift.

🐚 BY CANDIE FRANKEL

MATERIALS
Yields 2 boxes

- **32" x 40" 2-ply museum board**
- **45"-wide cotton/linen woven fabric:**
  - **³/₈ yard print**
  - **¾ yard stripe**
  - **¼ yard solid**
- **Thin batting**
- **Yes Stikflat glue**
- **Fray preventer**

You'll also need:
utility knife; steel ruler; pencil; waxed paper; heavy books or other objects (for weight); stiff, flat brushes ¼" to 1" wide; newsprint; scissors; rotary cutter; self-healing cutting mat; and tape.

COLOR PHOTOGRAPHY:
Carl Tremblay

ILLUSTRATION:
Mary Newell DePalma

The large version of the flapdown box (open) measures eight and one-half inches high and six inches across. The smaller box (upper left) measures six and one-half inches high and three and one-half inches across.

T HE DESIGN OF THIS BOX MAKES it the perfect gift for craft, sewing, or embroidery enthusiasts. When closed, the four sides are held in place by the edged lid; when the lid is removed, the four sides lie flat to reveal the box's contents, such as embroidery thread, scissors, or other supplies.

Although it may look complicated, the construction of the box is actually very logical. Each side of the box comprises two panels—an inside panel and an outside panel—made from museum board. Museum board, available in art supply and craft stores, is used for mounting exhibits. Although strong, it can be scored and cut with a utility knife. The museum board panels are covered with fabric, then glued back to back to one another to conceal the unfinished edges. Before covering the inside panel with fabric, I glued in a layer of batting (for stor-

ing needles or pins) and added a strap to hold items like scissors or embroidery thread in place.

The box's four sides are joined at the bottom edges to a base; when closed, the sides are held in place with a lid. The lid features two crisscrossed straps on its top, and a tab, which is used to open the box.

I made two versions of the box—a large one measuring eight and one-half inches high and six inches across, and a smaller box measuring six and one-half inches high and three and one-half inches across. I used a "scenic" print cotton/linen blend for the outside of the large box and a striped cotton/linen weave for the inside panels and lid. To coordinate the two boxes, I covered the outside of the small box and the inside straps and base with the same striped fabric. (*See* Sources & Resources, page 48, for more information.) If you only want

to make the large box, buy the fabric yardages listed. If you'd rather make the small box, omit the print fabric and purchase one-half yard of the striped fabric and one-quarter yard of the solid fabric.

The flapdown box was designed by Ritch Holben, an architect and designer living in Nahant, Massachusetts.

INSTRUCTIONS
Getting Started

1. *Cut box pieces from museum board.* Referring to diagrams for required measurements (*see* illustration A, next page), draft pieces for each box on museum board as follows: four outside panels, four inside panels, one lid, one outside lid, one inside lid, one outside base, and one inside base. Label each piece lightly with pencil. Score and cut out pieces using utility knife and steel edge ruler. Score lid flaps as indicated by dashed lines in illustration A.

2. *Cut and glue inside straps.* Using rotary cutter, cut two strips along lengthwise grain of striped fabric, with stripe design centered on strip, as follows (strip widths listed here are suggested widths and can be varied as needed to accommodate stripe design): Large box: one 1½" x 31" piece. Small box: one 2" x 21" piece. To make straps, lay each piece right side down on newsprint and brush glue over entire surface. Fold long edges to middle so raw edges butt, and press to adhere. Cut each piece into four equal lengths, then sandwich all pieces (eight total) between sheets of waxed paper and weight with heavy book for 1 hour.

3. *Cut lid straps, tab, and lid edge strips.* Using rotary cutter, cut five strips along lengthwise grain of striped fabric, with stripe design centered on strip, as follows: Large box: two 4" x 8" lid straps, each with different color stripe; one 2" x 6" tab (match width to central stripe of one lid strap); and one 2¾" x 26" lid rim strip.

Large and Small Box Diagrams

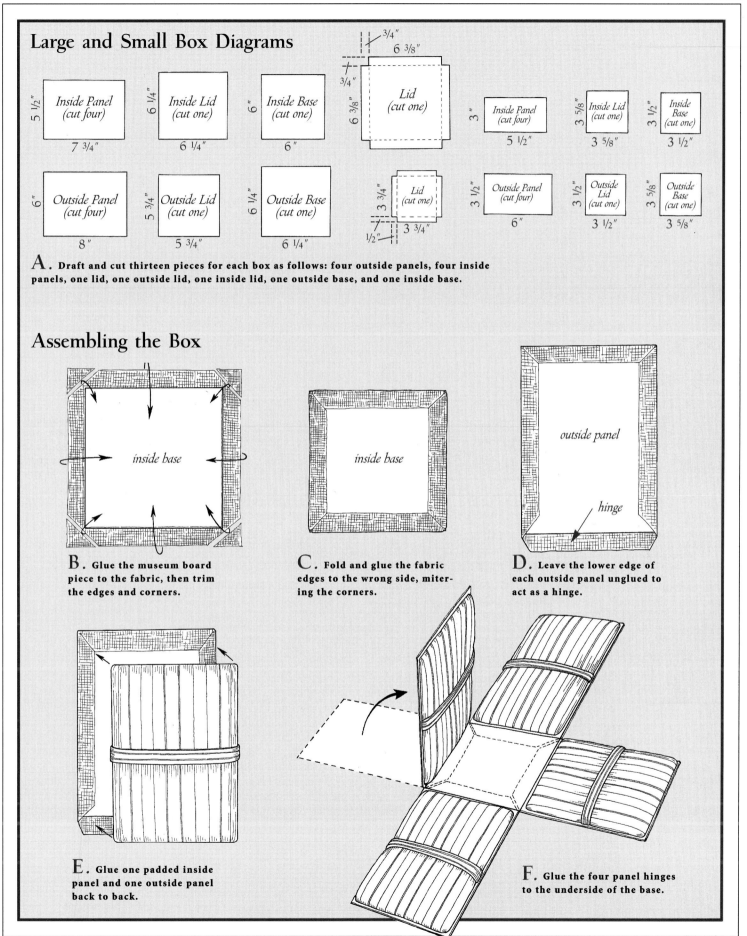

Inside Panel (cut four) — 5 1/2″ × 7 3/4″

Inside Lid (cut one) — 6 1/4″ × 6 1/4″

Inside Base (cut one) — 6″ × 6″

Lid (cut one) — 3/4″ · 6 3/8″ · 3/4″ · 6 3/8″

Inside Panel (cut four) — 3″ × 5 1/2″

Inside Lid (cut one) — 3 5/8″ × 3 5/8″

Inside Base (cut one) — 3 1/2″ × 3 1/2″

Outside Panel (cut four) — 6″ × 8″

Outside Lid (cut one) — 5 3/4″ × 5 3/4″

Outside Base (cut one) — 6 1/4″ × 6 1/4″

Lid (cut one) — 3 3/4″ · 1/2″ · 3 3/4″

Outside Panel (cut four) — 3 1/2″ × 6″

Outside Lid (cut one) — 3 1/2″ × 3 1/2″

Outside Base (cut one) — 3 5/8″ × 3 5/8″

A. Draft and cut thirteen pieces for each box as follows: four outside panels, four inside panels, one lid, one outside lid, one inside lid, one outside base, and one inside base.

Assembling the Box

inside base

B. Glue the museum board piece to the fabric, then trim the edges and corners.

inside base

C. Fold and glue the fabric edges to the wrong side, mitering the corners.

outside panel

hinge

D. Leave the lower edge of each outside panel unglued to act as a hinge.

E. Glue one padded inside panel and one outside panel back to back.

F. Glue the four panel hinges to the underside of the base.

Small box: one 2½" x 16" lid rim strip.

4. *Glue lid straps.* To make lid straps, lay each piece right side down on newsprint and brush glue over entire surface. Fold long edges to middle so raw edges butt, and press to adhere. Set aside tab and lid rim strips; they will be used in "Assembling the Boxes and Lids," steps 3 and 4.

Gluing the Fabric

1. *Cover unpadded pieces with fabric.* Lay solid fabric face down. Working on newsprint, brush thin, even coat of glue onto inside base for large box. Press piece glue side down on fabric so at least ¾" of

for lid) with appropriate fabric. Position pieces so stripes and printed designs are centered. Leave short lower edge of each outside panel unglued for hinge (illustration D.) Interleave finished panels with sheets of waxed paper and weight under heavy book for 1 hour.

2. *Cover padded pieces with fabric.* Brush thin, even coat of glue on each remaining piece of museum board (excluding lid), press face down onto batting, and smooth to adhere. Trim batting even with edge. Referring to Fabric Selection chart below, set padded piece batting side down on appropriate fabric, then trim and glue in place as in step 1.

2. *Join panels to base.* For each box, arrange four panels in plus sign, padded sides up, with hinge ends facing toward center. Brush glue onto each hinge, then press inside base, fabric side up, onto hinges (illustration F). Lift each panel one by one at right angle to base to make sure it can move freely. Protect with waxed paper and weight with heavy book for 1 hour. When dry, turn over and glue outside base to bottom of each box.

3. *Cover lid with fabric.* Fold large box lid along score lines and tape ends together to form shallow box. Brush outer edge with glue, then starting at middle of one side, press lid rim strip (from "Getting

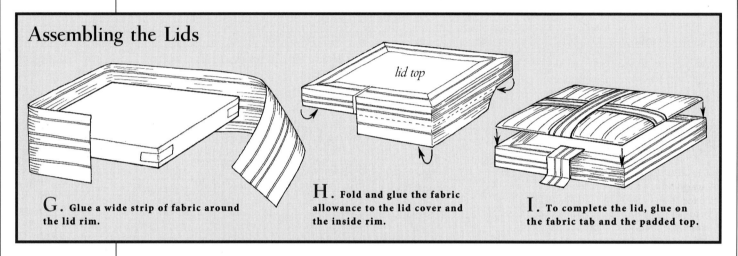

Assembling the Lids

G. Glue a wide strip of fabric around the lid rim.

H. Fold and glue the fabric allowance to the lid cover and the inside rim.

I. To complete the lid, glue on the fabric tab and the padded top.

fabric extends on all sides; turn over, rub gently to bond, then turn face down again. Using scissors, trim fabric ¾" beyond edge all around, then trim corners diagonally, passing a scant ³⁄₁₆" from tip of corner (illustration B). Brush 1" band of glue around edges of museum board piece, then brush glue onto diagonal cuts of fabric. Fold fabric allowances onto glued area all around, forming miters at corners and pressing cut edge onto tip of corner (illustration C). Referring to Fabric Selection chart below, repeat process to cover remaining unpadded pieces (except

3. *Reinforce raw edges.* To discourage fraying, use small flat brush to apply fray preventer to raw fabric edges at corners and near edges of all pieces; also brush long raw edges of straps. Let dry 24 hours.

Assembling the Boxes and Lids

1. *Glue inside and outside panels.* For each box, lay inside strap across middle of inside panel, fold back extensions to wrong side, and glue in place (illustration E). Glue inside and outside panels back to back and centered; leave ⅜" free at lower edge of small box to accommodate padded base.

Started," step 3) around rim, leaving 1" allowance extending evenly at top and bottom (illustration G). Glue top allowance to top lid, folding and mitering corners as you go, as if wrapping a package (illustration H). Then fold and glue bottom allowance onto inside rim and interior lid, trimming out excess bulk so fabric lies smoothly against interior corners (illustration H). Repeat process to cover small box lid, except overlap ends of lid rim strip at one corner instead of butting them at middle.

4. *Assemble lid pieces.* For large box lid, arrange lid straps on padded outside lid in plus sign, with stripes that match tab stripes on top (illustration I). Fold back extensions to wrong side and glue in place. To glue tab to lid, brush glue on wrong side of tab, then position tab on top of lid so one short end conceals butted edges of lid fabric. Bring tab down onto rim of lid, then fold it back on itself and onto inside rim of lid, leaving ¾" overhang for tab handle (illustration I). Glue padded outside lid to top of lid so matching stripes align. Glue in inside lid panel. Apply fray preventer to raw tab edges. For small box lid, glue on padded outside lid and flat inside lid. Draw up box sides, put on lids, and let dry 24 hours before using. ◆

FABRIC SELECTION

This chart lists the pieces that make up each box and the fabrics needed to cover them.

	LARGE BOX	SMALL BOX
INSIDE BASE	solid	stripe; padded
OUTSIDE BASE	solid	stripe
INSIDE LID	stripe	solid
OUTSIDE LID	solid; padded	solid; padded
4 INSIDE PANELS	stripe; padded	solid; padded
4 OUTSIDE PANELS	print	stripe
LID	stripe	stripe

Magnolia Leaf Wreath

Combine magnolia leaves and an old picture frame to make this dramatic two-toned wreath.

❧ BY FRANCOISE HARDY

MATERIALS

- **Approximately 40 fresh *Magnolia grandiflora* branches, varying from 6" to 12" long, with 5 to 10 leaves per branch**
- **19" x 21" picture frame**
- **Fabric-covered spool wire**

You'll also need: pruning shears and wire cutters.

I WANTED TO MAKE A VERY SIMPLE wreath that would maximize the strong visual appeal of *Magnolia grandiflora* leaves, which are a high-gloss bottle-green color on one side and a rust color with a velvet texture on the other side.

Depending on the region of the country where you live, the term "magnolia" can refer to several different varieties of deciduous and evergreen shrubs and trees. I used the leaves of the *Magnolia grandiflora*, a tree found predominantly in the South. Individual branches can be purchased at a florist shop.

After experimenting with several sizes and types of wreath bases, I ended up using a rectangular oak picture frame. The nineteen-by-twenty-one-inch frame I selected was strong enough to support the weight of the branches, was the right scale for the leaves (which measure from four to ten inches in length), and was an interesting variation on the traditional round wreath.

I attached the magnolia leaves to the frame while fresh and let them dry on the frame. The leaves maintain their color when dry, although they do become fragile, so avoid moving the wreath after it has been hung.

I tested two types of wire for binding the branches: medium-gauge spool wire and fabric-covered spool wire. I prefer the latter, as the fabric covering seems to grab the branches better.

Francoise Hardy is a Boston-based artisan and craftsperson.

INSTRUCTIONS

1. *Prepare branches.* Sort and prune branches by average leaf size into three groups: small, medium, and large.

2. *Wire branches onto frame.* Wrap wire twice around frame at one inside corner and twist end securely. Select one branch from each pile—small, medium, and large—and lay together on frame with largest leaves toward back and smallest leaves toward front. Wrap wire around leafy sections, spacing wraps 1" apart. As you approach a less leafy section, lay new stems over the previously laid stems and continue maneuvering wire around and under leaves to maintain 1" spacing (*see* illustration A, at right). Continue until you reach corner.

The large scale of this wreath requires an appropriate space for hanging, such as over a fireplace or on a large open wall.

3. *Attach leaves at corner.* To round corner, gather three short-stemmed branches, one from each size pile, into one group and wire onto corner. Repeat two additional times, clustering groups tightly to make corner extra full and leafy (illustration B).

4. *Finish the wreath.* Repeat to wrap remaining edges and corners. To end off, slip a few stems under starting loop of wire, then fill in bare spots and wrap with wire. Slip final stems under leaves of starting bouquet, wire securely, and twist and clip wire ends (illustration C). ◆

COLOR PHOTOGRAPHY:
Carl Tremblay

ILLUSTRATION:
Mary Newell DePalma

STYLING:
Ritch Holben

Making the Wreath

A. Select several branches and wire them to the frame.

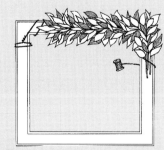

B. Cluster groups of short stems together for full corners.

C. Anchor the final stems under the starting loop.

Patterns for Projects in This Issue

Italian Opera Dolls

(*see* article, page 20)

Note: Photocopy all pattern pieces for this article at 100 percent.

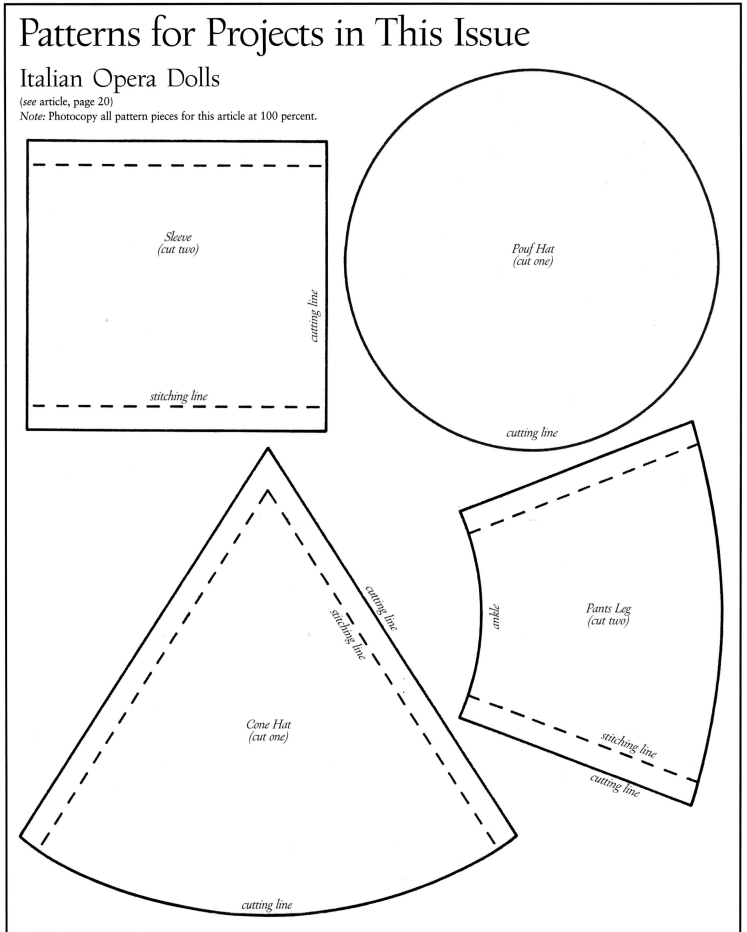

Sleeve
(cut two)

cutting line

stitching line

Pouf Hat
(cut one)

cutting line

Cone Hat
(cut one)

cutting line

stitching line

cutting line

Pants Leg
(cut two)

ankle

stitching line

cutting line

PATTERNS: **Roberta Frauwirth**

Italian Opera Dolls

(*see* article, page 20)

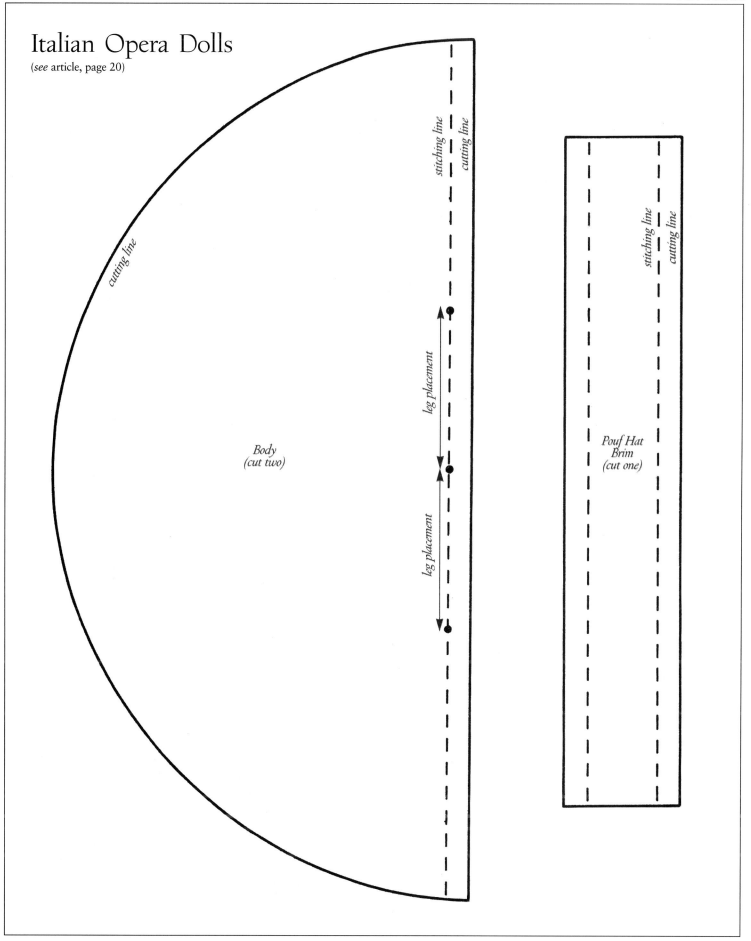

cutting line

stitching line

cutting line

leg placement

Body
(cut two)

leg placement

stitching line

cutting line

Pouf Hat
Brim
(cut one)

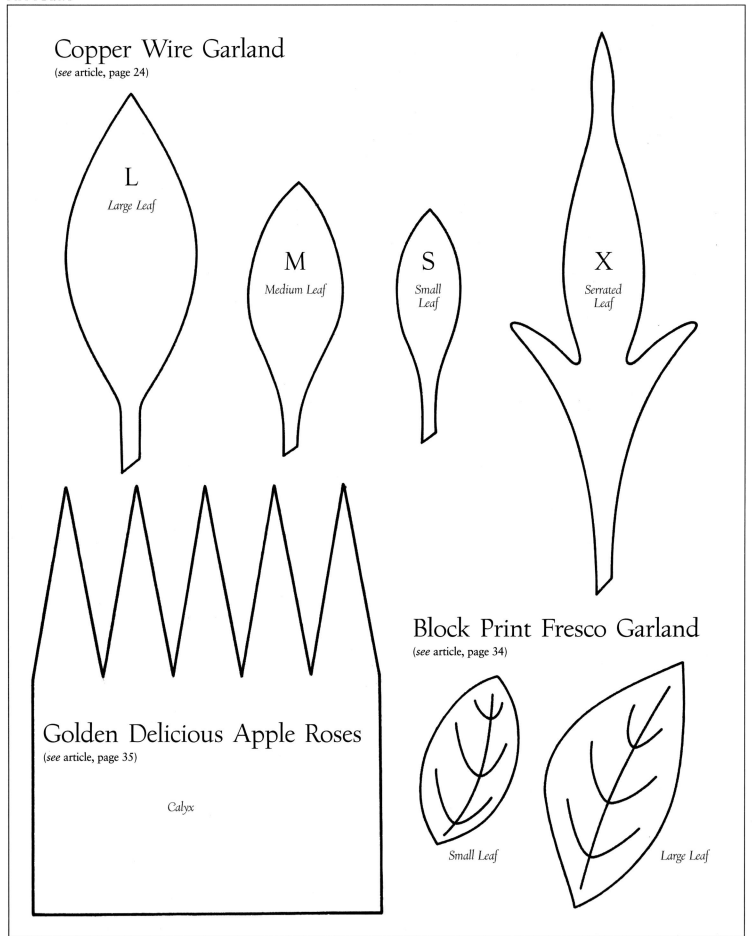

Copper Wire Garland
(*see* article, page 24)

L
Large Leaf

M
Medium Leaf

S
Small Leaf

X
Serrated Leaf

Golden Delicious Apple Roses
(*see* article, page 35)

Calyx

Block Print Fresco Garland
(*see* article, page 34)

Small Leaf

Large Leaf

CORRECTION:
How to Make a Covered Box

(see page 30, Spring 1996)

The four diagrams found at the top of this page were inadvertently left out of the "How to Make a Covered Box" article in the Spring 1996 issue. All the diagrams presented here provide the necessary dimensions for making the box.

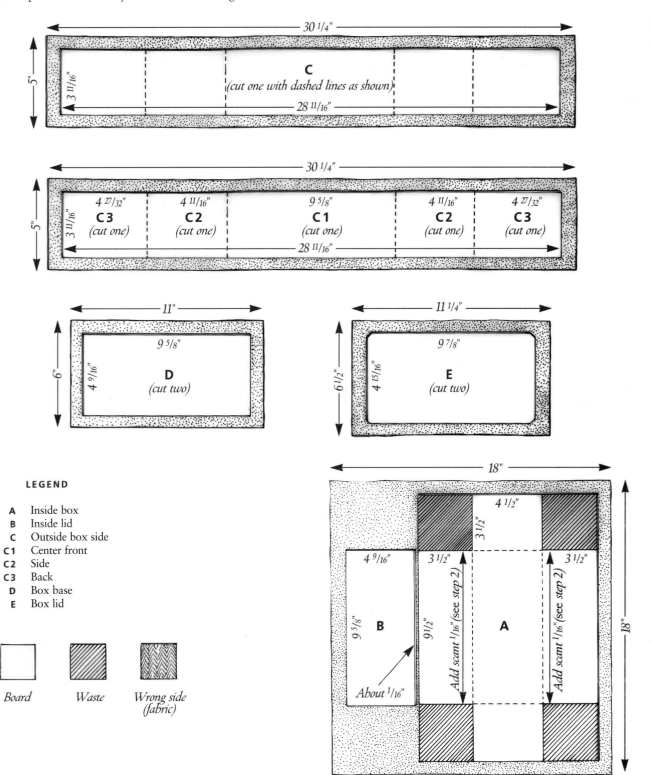

LEGEND

A	Inside box
B	Inside lid
C	Outside box side
C1	Center front
C2	Side
C3	Back
D	Box base
E	Box lid

Board   *Waste*   *Wrong side (fabric)*

Sources & Resources

The following are specific sources for particular items, arranged by article.

Most of the materials necessary for the projects in this issue are available at your local craft supply store, florist's, fabric shop, hardware store, or bead and jewelry supply. Generic craft supplies can be ordered from such catalogs as Craft King, Dick Blick Art Materials, Newark Dressmaker Supply, Pearl Paint Company, Inc., or Sunshine Discount Crafts. The following are specific sources for harder-to-find items, arranged by article. The suggested retail prices listed here were current at press time. Contact the suppliers directly to confirm prices and availability of products.

Great Marriages, *page 6*
Anaglypta embossed paper from $5.75 per sheet from Rug Road Paper Company. Copper leaf for $8.30 per book from Dick Blick. Specialty hole puncher from $6.79 from Texas Art Supply.

The Perfect Gift, *page 7*
Test tube rack for $15.50 and corked test tubes for $5 per dozen from Arista Surgical Supply. Tin-edged tags from $5.38 for fifty from Texas Art Supply. Beeswax from $8.99 per pound from Sunshine Discount Crafts.

Leaf Lampshade, *page 8*
Paper lampshade from $18 from Kate's Paperie. Japanese papers starting at $1.50 per sheet from Kate's Paperie. Brown florist tape for $1.69 from A World of Plenty. Yes Stikflat glue for $9.25 for 19 ounces from New York Central Art Supply.

Bottle Stoppers, *page 10*
Set of ten colors of Sculpey III clay for $12.68, 1 ounce of Sculpey Glaze for $2.57, ½ pint of Japan size for $4.09, book of composition gold leaf for $27.68, and .07 ounces of Krazy Glue for $2.39, all from Texas Art Supply. Tulip Colorpoint fabric paint for $10.15 for ten colors from NASCO. Powderz micro glitter from $1.88 for 2.5 ounces from Pearl Paint's main store.

Beaded Ornaments, *page 12*
Cork fishing bobs by mail order from L. L. Bean's main store for 20¢ each. Silver wire from $2.50 from Munro Corporation. Powderz micro glitter from $1.88 for 2.5 ounces from Pearl Paint's main store. Beads from Ornamental Resources.

Napkin Ring, *page 15*
Copper leaf for $8.30 per book from Dick Blick. Metallic enamel paint from $6.64 for 4 ounces from Pearl Paint. Wire from $2.50 from Munro Corporation. Brown florist tape for $1.69 from A World of Plenty.

Plaster Fruit, *page 16*
Insta-Mold from $6.90 for 12 ounces and plaster of Paris for $2.95 for 4 pounds from Dick Blick. Winsor & Newton gouache from $6 for 2 ounces from Pearl Paint.

Finial Candlestick, *page 19*
Finial from $29.95 from S & S Products. Candlecup (twelve for $4.09) and brass insert for candlecup (twelve for $2.49) from Viking Woodcrafts.

Italian Opera Dolls, *page 20*
Push molds from $3.90 and Sculpey III clay from $1.40 for 2 ounces from Dick Blick. Synthetic hair from $1.29 for 14 grams from Sunshine Discount Crafts.

Copper Leaf Garland, *page 24*
Copper tooling foil for $20.75 for a 10-foot roll and English Brown patinating solution for $14.40 for 16 ounces from Dick Blick. Wire from $2.50 from Munro Corporation. Beads from $2.10 for ten from Ornamental Resources.

Velvet Pillows, *page 26*
Variety of trim and notions available from Tinsel Trading.

Herbed Vinegars, *page 30*
Potted herbs starting from $3 from Tinmouth Channel Farm. Beeswax from $8.99 per pound from Sunshine Discount Crafts.

Jacob's Ladder Book, *page 32*
Grosgrain ribbon from $1.35 for 5 yards from Newark Dressmaker Supply. Yes Stikflat glue for $9.25 for 19 ounces from New York Central Art Supply.

Apple Roses, *page 35*
Apples from $19.99 for twenty apples from Walnut Acres Organic Farms. Paper twist from 99¢ for 6 yards from Sunshine Discount Crafts.

Candleshade, *page 36*
Candle follower for $11.25 from Viking Woodcrafts. Glass beads from $8 for 100 from Ornamental Resources. Pearl-head pins

from $3.50 for 144 from Sunshine Discount Crafts. Yes Stikflat glue for $9.25 for 19 ounces from New York Central Art Supply.

Floral Fan Topiary, *page 38*
Dried flowers from $4.10 per bunch from Mills Floral Company.

Flapdown Box, *page 40*
Portfolio (village scenes) cotton/linen blend from $18.95 per yard and Braemore cotton stripe for $13.95 per yard from Zimman's. Yes Stikflat glue for $9.25 for 19 ounces from New York Central Art Supply.

Quick Projects, *page 49*
Papers available from Kate's Paperie and Pearl Paint. Micro glitter from $1.88 for 2.5 ounces from Pearl Paint's main store.

🐛 🐛 🐛 🐛 🐛

The following companies are mentioned in the listings provided above. Contact each individually for a price list or catalog.

ARISTA SURGICAL SUPPLY COMPANY INC.
67 Lexington Avenue, New York, NY 10010; 800-223-1984

A WORLD OF PLENTY
P.O. Box 1153, Hermantown, MN 55810-9724; 218-729-6761

CRAFT KING
P.O. Box 90637, Lakeland, FL 33804; 800-769-9494

DICK BLICK ART MATERIALS
P.O. Box 1267, Galesburg, IL 61402-1267; 800-447-8192

KATE'S PAPERIE
561 Broadway, New York, NY 10012; 212-941-9816

L. L. BEAN (MAIN STORE)
Freeport, ME 04033; 800-341-4341

MILLS FLORAL COMPANY
4550 Peachtree Lakes Drive, Duluth, GA 30316; 800-762-7939

MUNRO CORPORATION
3954 West 12 Mile Road, Berkley, MI 48072; 800-638-0543

NASCO ARTS & CRAFTS
901 Janesville Avenue, P.O. Box 901, Fort Atkinson, WI 53538-0901; 800-558-9595

NEWARK DRESSMAKER SUPPLY
6473 Ruch Road, P.O. Box 20730, Lehigh Valley, PA 18002-0730; 610-837-7500

NEW YORK CENTRAL ART SUPPLY
62 Third Avenue, New York, NY 10003; 800-950-6111

ORNAMENTAL RESOURCES, INC.
Box 3010, 1427 Miner Street, Idaho Springs, CO 80452; 800-876-6762

PEARL PAINT COMPANY, INC.
308 Canal Street, New York, NY 10013-2572; 800-451-7325 (catalog) or 800-221-6845 x2297 (main store)

RUG ROAD PAPER COMPANY
105 Charles Street, Boston, MA 02114; 617-742-0002

S & S PRODUCTS
6576A I-85 Court, Norcross, GA 30093-1178; 800-701-0903

SUNSHINE DISCOUNT CRAFTS
P.O. Box 301, Largo, FL 34649-0301; 800-729-2878

TEXAS ART SUPPLY COMPANY
P.O. Box 66328, Houston, TX 77266-6328; 800-888-9278

TINMOUTH CHANNEL FARM
Box 428B, Town Highway 19, Tinmouth, VT 05773; 802-446-2812

TINSEL TRADING
47 West 38th Street, New York, NY 10018; 212-730-1030

VIKING WOODCRAFTS, INC.
1317 8th Street S.E., Waseca, MN 56093; 800-328-0116

WALNUT ACRES ORGANIC FARMS
Penns Creek, PA 17862; 800-433-3998

ZIMMAN'S
76-88 Market Street, Lynn, MA 01901; 617-598-9432

Quick Projects

Design your own giftwrap using our simple paper-cutting and layering techniques.

MAKE-AT-HOME GIFTWRAP

You can turn inexpensive art store papers and butcher wrap into designer giftwraps with these easy cutting and layering techniques. The papers will be easier to decorate, with less waste, if you cut them to size first. Wrap the paper once around the gift box, allowing a three-quarter-inch overlap, and trim off the rest. Trim each end to overhang the box depth by two-thirds.

A. Gold Glitter Spirals
Draw snail-shaped spirals on butcher paper with high-tack glue to form an allover arabesque pattern. Immediately sprinkle fine glitter over the paper, shake to distribute, and tap off any excess. To add an overlay, spray white lace paper lightly with adhesive. Pick up the lace paper, holding the corners together in pairs, adhesive facing outwards. Lower the lace paper until the adhesive side touches down on the middle of the glittered paper. Continue lowering the lace paper so both halves come down flat,

then tamp lightly to bond in place. Finish the package with gold ribbon.

B. Leaf Cutouts
Sketch leaves on opaque paper, then add a few lines, stencil-style, to represent the veins and a stem. Cut out the shapes using an X-Acto knife. One cutout at a time, spray the area around each opening with adhesive, then press a square of tissue paper over the opening. Turn over the paper to see the leaf cutouts. Finish the package with matching ribbon.

C. Rose Petals
Wrap the gift box with white butcher's paper, then spray the top and four sides with adhesive. Gently press dried rose petals and a few small preserved leaves onto the surface. Turn the box upside down on a sheet of gossamer sheer lace paper, and wrap, pressing the lace paper into place where there is adhesive. Tape the overlap and ends, and finish with pearlescent wire-edged ribbon.

D. Harlequin
Use this design on gift boxes with four equal sides. Wrap the box with white paper, then cut four diamonds in a contrasting color, each one the height and width of one box side. Crease each diamond vertically, spray it with adhesive, and then press it against the box so that the crease hugs the box edge. Tie on a ribbon as shown. Cinch the ribbon with thread at each diamond join, then hot-glue a pom-pom to conceal the thread.

E. Torn Paper Polka Dots
Cut white butcher paper and white lace paper to size for the gift box. Tear two contrasting, vividly colored tissue papers into "polka dots" measuring 1" to 3" across. Spray the dots with adhesive, then press them at random onto the lace paper. Layer the butcher and lace paper so the dots are sandwiched between and wrap the box as usual. Finish the package with ribbon of your choice. ◆

COLOR PHOTOGRAPHY:
Carl Tremblay

GIFTWRAP DESIGN:
Michio Ryan

Glitter Ornaments

Create these glittery ornaments in just a few minutes using this shortcut: "Glue" glitter to any color glass ball using transparent double-sided tape. To cut the tape into narrow $1/4"$ widths, lay it on a gridded self-healing mat and slice off sections using a craft knife and a steel-edged ruler. Wrap the tape around the circumference of the ball, then roll the sticky sections in fine glitter until it adheres. Apply new tape strips to add second or third colors.

NUMBER FOURTEEN

CHRISTMAS 1996

Handcraft

ILLUSTRATED

50 NEW IDEAS FOR CHRISTMAS

Fast and Easy Holiday Wreath
Pin Lemon Leaves to a Straw Base

Beaded Christmas Tree
Create a Miniature Evergreen with Glass Beads

Antique Cherub Plaque
Foolproof Casting with Liquid Latex

Gilded Glitter Village
Dramatic Townscape from Chipboard and Glitter

Holiday Velvet Runner
Block-Print a Shimmering Filigree Pattern

Embossed Ornaments
Lustrous Jewel Tones with Glass Paint

ALSO
Appliqué Wool Stocking

Classic Carriage Clock

Secrets of Making Soap at Home

Faux Limoges Boxes

Reversible Table Wreath

$4.00 U.S. / $4.95 CANADA

Contents

Appliqué stocking, page 8

Teddy bear sweaters, page 14

Antique cherub plaque, page 22

Embossed velvet runner, page 26

COVER PHOTOGRAPH:
Carl Tremblay

STYLING:
Ritch Holben

This elegant Christmas tree features branches made of green seed beads. *See* **page 20.**

Handcraft
ILLUSTRATED

EDITOR
Carol Endler Sterbenz

EXECUTIVE EDITOR
Barbara Bourassa

ART DIRECTOR
Amy Klee

SENIOR EDITOR
Michio Ryan

MANAGING EDITOR
Keith Powers

DIRECTIONS EDITOR
Candie Frankel

COPY EDITOR
Gary Pfitzer

EDITORIAL ASSISTANT
Elizabeth Cameron

EDITORIAL INTERN
Jennifer Putnam

❧

PUBLISHER AND FOUNDER
Christopher Kimball

EDITORIAL CONSULTANT
John Kelsey

MARKETING DIRECTOR
Adrienne Kimball

CIRCULATION DIRECTOR
Carolyn Adams

FULFILLMENT MANAGER
Jamie Ayer

CIRCULATION COORDINATOR
Jonathan Venier

❧

VICE PRESIDENT PRODUCTION AND TECHONOLOGY
James McCormack

EDITORIAL PRODUCTION MANAGER
Sheila Datz

ADVERTISING PRODUCTION MANAGER
Pamela Slattery

SYSTEMS ADMINISTRATOR
Micah Benson

PRODUCTION ARTIST
Kevin Moeller

EDITORIAL PRODUCTION ASSISTANT
Robert Parsons

ADVERTISING PRODUCTION ASSISTANT
Daniel Frey

❧

VICE PRESIDENT
Jeffrey Feingold

CONTROLLER
Lisa A. Carullo

ACCOUNTING ASSISTANT
Mandy Shito

OFFICE MANAGER
Tonya Estey

Handcraft Illustrated (ISSN 1072-0529) is published quarterly by Boston Common Press, P.O. Box 509, Brookline, MA 02147-0509. Copyright 1996 Boston Common Press Limited Partners. Periodical postage paid at Boston, MA, and additional mailing offices, USPS #011-895. For list rental information, please contact List Services Corporation, 6 Trowbridge Drive, Bethel, CT 06801; (203) 791-4148. Editorial office: P.O. Box 509, Brookline, MA 02147-0509; (617) 232-1000, FAX (617) 232-1572, e-mail: hndcftill@aol.com. Editorial contributions should be sent or e-mailed to: Editor, *Handcraft Illustrated*. We cannot assume responsibility for manuscripts submitted to us. Submissions will be returned only if accompanied by a large, self-addressed stamped envelope. Subscription rates: $24.95 for one year; $45 for two years; $65 for three years. (Canada: add $6 per year; all other countries add $12 per year.) Postmaster: Send all new orders, subscription inquiries, and change of address notices to *Handcraft Illustrated*, P.O. Box 7448, Red Oak, IA 51591-0448. Single copies: $4 in U.S.; $4.95 in Canada and other countries. Back issues available for $5 each at the editorial office. PRINTED IN THE U.S.A.

Rather than put ™ in every occurrence of trademarked names, we state that we are using the names only in an editorial fashion and to the benefit of the trademark owner, with no intention of infringement of the trademark.

Note to Readers: Every effort has been made to present the information in this publication in a clear, complete, and accurate manner. It is important that all instructions are followed carefully, as failure to do so could result in injury. Boston Common Press, the editors, and the authors disclaim any and all liability resulting therefrom.

From the Editor

I LOVED THE HOUSE THE FIRST TIME I SAW IT. Passing on foot along the lower road, I could see its immaculate details through the bare branches of a hundred-year-old elm tree. The house's white clapboard front boasted eight pairs of French doors and a porch stretching along its full length.

I stopped to stare at the house, imagining what it looked like inside: velvet couches, mantles with ticking clocks, and a chandelier, glacial and sparkling in the foyer. I imagined what a wonderful place this would be to raise our children, then six, ten, and twelve, and what the house would look like at Christmastime.

For a year, I only knew the house from the outside. Then one evening all that changed. The house was for sale. The owners who had raised their sons there were moving to a smaller house. I climbed the front steps, leaving deep footprints in the loaves of snow rising high on the stairs. I stepped into the foyer and looked into the expanse of the living room. To my surprise, the room held an ice blue velvet Empire couch. I strained to hear the notes of a Handel composition that must have echoed in this room at some time. I climbed the bridal staircase to the second floor and was surprised at how easily I found my way through the rooms. It felt like home.

Over the next few months, I took the entire family to see the house several times, and even invited along our parents, who thought us impetuous and said so. We silently wondered if they were right, but presented our first offer anyway. By the time the elm was filled with young shoots, the owners had accepted our offer. They were sad to leave, they said, and we promised that they could visit anytime. We moved in, and the kids found their way to their rooms, the kitchen, and the bus stop. John and I looked at each other like we were being moved along by some heavenly plan.

By Christmastime, we had taken over the house as if we had never lived anywhere else in the world. We put up a tree in the foyer that was so tall we had to tilt our heads back to see its top, which rose past the crys-

Now, as I look back, I am more trusting than ever in the divine order of life and the sweet gifts that come from that trust, gifts that we carry inside for all time.

tal chandelier. We baked a wobbly version of our new house in gingerbread while listening to the strains of Handel playing triumphantly on the stereo in the living room. On Christmas day, we cooked a goose with all the trimmings, and the whole family joined in the celebration, along with French friends who brought a bûche de Noël and a brand new baby who played the role of Jesus in our traditional skit about the Christmas miracle. By midnight, after everyone had left and we had settled in for our very first Christmas night in the house, we were filled with the joy of family life, grateful for our blessings, and curious (but thankful) at the number of coincidences that had moved us into this very special home.

Many Christmases passed after that, and one day, the oldest son of the previous owners visited us. Before he left, he went outside to take a picture of the house. Later, he sent us a copy, which I slipped into our album, thinking my view of the house would naturally be from inside. And it was, but not in the way I believed at that moment. For the day came when it was time for us to leave our Christmas house. On moving day, I placed a photograph of the house on the mantel for the new owners; they promised that we could visit anytime we wanted.

Recently, I walked the lower road again and looked at the house in the glow of an evening sunset. I knew that the house was one part of our lives, as well as an apt metaphor for the circle of life, always mysterious, and more often than not, joyous and full. Now, as I look back, I am more trusting than ever in the divine order of life and the sweet gifts that come from that trust, gifts that we carry inside for all time.

From all of us at *Handcraft Illustrated*, have a joyful holiday season. May there be peace on this good earth for all.

Carol Endler Sterbenz

Notes from Readers

Learn how to clean up an old teddy bear, wire your own lamp, locate tinware for decoupage, and eliminate hot-glue strings.

Christmas Decorations from Cookie Dough

In 1950 or 1951, my children and I made Christmas decorations out of a material that resembled cookie dough. I don't remember whether the dough came as a powder that I added water to or whether it came ready to use, but we rolled the material out, cut it out like cookies, and baked it in the oven. The finished result looked like gingerbread. The dough also came with paints that looked like chocolate and vanilla icing. I would like to relocate this material or a recipe to make it myself. For some reason, the name "Hazel Pearson" comes to mind. Can you help?

SHIRLEY BUMPOUS
LUBBOCK, TX

Hazel Pearson, a California-based company that is no longer in business, manufactured crafts products many years ago. It's entirely possible that they sold a kit such as you have described. Unfortunately, we were unable to locate another product like it at this time.

We came up with several possible alternatives, however. Arm & Hammer (as in Arm & Hammer Baking Soda), offers a formula for PlayClay, a bakeable dough made of baking soda, corn starch, oil, and cold water. The clay can be decorated with markers, acrylic paint, watercolors, glitter, and decorative glues. For a free booklet on PlayClay and its uses, write or call PlayClay, Church & Dwight Co., Inc., Arm & Hammer, P.O. Box 826, Spring House, PA 19477; 800-524-1328. Morton International Inc. (makers of Morton Salt) offers a similar recipe for a salt-and-flour dough that can be decorated in the same manner. For a free booklet on this dough, write Morton International Inc., Dept. PR, 100 North Riverside Plaza, Chicago, IL 60606.

Although they do not brown like dough, heat-set resin clays, such as Fimo and Sculpey III, are great for making ornaments. Such clays, available in a wide variety of colors, are inexpensive and easy to roll out, cut, and mold. You can use the different colors to add various details to your ornaments, but if you want to create a cookie look-alike, you should use a white or brown heat-set resin clay, then decorate it with white or brown acrylic paint. You can then seal the paint with an acrylic sealer. You might also want to try using glue as a substitute for the painted icing. Piped on the cookie directly from the bottle, glue is a tidy and effortless way to create a three-dimensional effect. For colored icing, use one of the many decorative glues on the market today. Elmer's, for example, makes a range of solid-color and glitter glues.

Building a Library of Cross-Stitch Patterns

Laurie Linnes-Bagnley, a reader from Minneapolis, Minnesota, suggests this tip for cross-stitchers. She was having trouble finding graphic cross-stitch designs that weren't too childish or too detailed, so she uses knitting patterns instead. The patterns are marked out stitch by stitch just like cross-stitch, so they're easy to follow and adapt.

Teddy Bear Cleanup

Help me save my eleven-year-old teddy bear! Because he is well loved, his fur has become matted and attracts dust. How can I clean him up without damaging him forever?

JODY HALL
MANHATTAN, KS

A. Christian Revi, editor-at-large of *Teddy Bear Review* (717-637-1463), suggests lightly vacuuming your teddy with a hand vacuum such as a Dustbuster and giving him a sponge bath. Use a diluted mild liquid dish detergent such as Ivory or Joy (spot-test it first), being careful not to saturate the bear. Rinse the fur with a damp sponge and let it dry (or use a blow-dryer). Brush it lightly with a not-too-stiff bristle brush (no wire bristles) to raise the nap. Don't wash very fragile stuffed animals and don't wash the whole body at once.

For general bear maintenance, keep it away from direct sun, dust it regularly with a hand vacuum, and keep it in a constant temperature away from humidity. If moths, fleas, silverfish, or ticks are a problem, keep a cedar block near the bear. Bear Clawset sells a package of four cedar blocks for $3.50. Write or call the company at 27 Palermo Walk, Long Beach, CA 90803; 310-434-8077.

Locating Cotton Beads

Can you help me find pressed cotton beads? A beading book I bought has instructions that call for ball- and pear-shaped pressed cotton beads.

DEE SCHULTZ
FRESNO, CA

Pressed cotton beads are available by mail from Ornamental Resources, which specializes in unusual decorative materials for jewelry, clothing, and costumes. (The staff of this mail-order bead supplier also offers design assistance for specific projects and special searches for items not in their stock.) The company offers the pear-shaped beads your book mentions in a variety of colors, sizes, and prices. Phone the company at 800-876-6762 or 303-279-2102 or write: Box 3010, 1427 Miner Street, Idaho Springs, CO 80452.

Freeze-Dried Flowers

I would like to know how freeze-dried flowers are "freeze-dried." Is this something I can do at home? If not, where can I buy freeze-dried flowers for crafts?

LESLIE SHONKA
LAKE CHARLES, LA

Freeze-drying flowers isn't a home project. It requires a special machine, the smaller versions of which measure about ten feet long and cost $30,000 to $40,000, explains Joe Zucker of J&T Imports in Solana Beach, California. Freeze-dried flowers, which are very close to the color of the fresh flower, can be mail-ordered. They are more expensive than silk or dried flowers, however. J&T Imports offers a variety of freeze-dried roses; phone the company at 619-481-9781.

Lamp Making at Home

I would like to know where I can order supplies to make lamps out of household objects. I have been able to purchase the wiring supplies, but have difficulty obtaining the parts necessary to cap off the top of a vase or the ends of a hurricane globe.

TOM MOORE
VIA E-MAIL

Call or write Lamp Specialties, P.O. Box 240, Westville, NJ 08093; 800-225-5526. Their catalog costs $5, which is refundable after your first order.

Looking for a Bottle Cutter

I would like to recycle some bottles by cutting them and turning them into glasses and vases, etc. I'm unable to find bottle cutters, the types that were around in the early to mid-'70s. Is there a source for such a thing anymore?

GARY HAINES
BUCKINGHAM, PA

We couldn't find a bottle cutter either, but a technical rep at Delphi Stained Glass in Lansing, Michigan, recommends the following technique for cutting bottles (try it out on a junk bottle first, and be sure to wear safety glasses). Start by scoring the bottle very lightly with a glass cutter where you want to cut it. Hold the bottle in a dishcloth or with oven mitts and heat the scored area over a candle flame for about a minute, slowly rotating it. (If the glass turns black, you can easily clean it up with alcohol.) Remove the glass from the heat and run an ice cube around the score, then tap it gently with a small hammer. The glass should break cleanly.

Glass cutters, priced from $2 to $30, are available at most stained glass or arts and crafts stores. Delphi Stained Glass also offers glass cutters; call them at 800-248-2048. Their catalog is $5, and you will receive a 25 percent discount on your first order.

Tinware for Painting and Decoupage

I would appreciate your help in locating a source for old-fashioned metal wastebaskets, oval metal letter holders, pencil tins, etc. that could be hand-painted, decoupaged, or embellished to match various decors. It seems that all wastebaskets today are made of plastic. I remember that my grandmother had a round metal wastebasket painted black with a beautiful pink rose hand-painted on the side. I own and have restored a Victorian home and would love to add some of these items to my decor.

DALE O'DAY ROBISON
SAN DIEGO, CA

Tinware is scarce these days, mostly because of a lack of tinsmiths, says Ann Patsis, a crafter from Ellsworth, Maine, who specializes in painted tinware and tole. Patsis paints and sells custom-made tinware as well as pieces she's found at antique stores and flea markets. She didn't have any wastebaskets or desk accessories on hand when we contacted her, but she may be able to come up with some. Write her at Ann's Tole House, 25 West Main Street, Ellsworth, ME 04605.

One mail-order source for unpainted tinware is Master Pieces, 11A Loudoun Street S.W., Leesburg, VA 20175; 703-771-1303. Kraft Klub Floral and Craft Supply, in Chino, California, carries galvanized tin watering cans, milk cans, pitchers, and planters (12395 Mills Avenue #12, Chino, CA 91710; 909-590-0880). Hardware stores sometimes sell galvanized buckets or coal bins, and tinware often turns up at swap meets and antique fairs. For finished pieces, try Montana Country, a vintage furnishings store in Santa Monica, California. When we spoke with them, they had several turn-of-the-century painted wastebaskets on hand, at prices from $45 to $89.

Preserving Autumn Leaves

Will colorful fall leaves last if you press them with an iron between waxed paper? Or is there a better way to preserve them?

DAWN WEBER
VIA E-MAIL

Autumn leaves will last longer if you dry and press them. Trim any thick stems, then press the leaves flat between paper towels in a weighted telephone book for two weeks, or until smooth and dry. Change the paper towels every few days to prevent mold, and discard any moldy leaves. For a project that uses dried leaves to decorate a lampshade, see "Laminated Leaf Lampshade" in the Fall 1996 issue.

Christmastime Wooden Figurines

I am looking for a source for small wooden figures to use with old-world Santas and/or Christmas scenes, such as fir trees, sleds, baskets, rocking horses, etc.

KALETA LANE
FLONA, IL

Craft King carries many inexpensive wooden miniatures, including fir trees (with and without snow), Nativity scenes, wrapped "packages," angels, and baskets. You can contact the company at P.O. Box 90637, Lakeland, FL 33804; 800-769-9494.

Locating Musical Christmas Buttons

Do you know of a source for musical Christmas buttons?

VADE FORRESTER
VIA E-MAIL

These battery-powered buttons, which play a tune at the touch of a finger, are available by mail from Sunshine Discount Crafts, P.O. Box 301, Largo, FL 33770; 800-729-2878 or 813-538-2878. Songs available include "Joy to the World," "Silent Night," "White Christmas," and several Christmas medleys.

Make Your Own Furniture Cleaner and Polish

To clean wood furniture pieces that are in good shape (not cracked or discolored) but could use some perking up, I mix equal parts vinegar, linseed oil, and turpentine. Rub the mixture briskly into wood with #0000 (finest) steel wool, then wipe clean with a soft cloth. (Stir mixture frequently while using.) For polish, mix together two parts linseed oil, one part rubbing alcohol, and one part vinegar. Apply with a cloth and wipe off with a clean, soft cloth for a gentle luster.

DOLORES SKROUT
SUMMERHILL, PA

We tried these formulas on a dark-finished cabinet with some scratches. We noticed that the scratches were diminished somewhat and the wood looked cleaner and brighter. The cleaning mixture did leave a film on the wood, but this residue was easily removed with polishing. Be sure to work in a well-ventilated room and wear gloves when using turpentine.

Eliminating Hot-Glue Strings

Eliminating the "strings" is a problem familiar to anyone who uses a hot-glue gun. Three readers share their methods. Diana Barbee of Olney, Illinois, and Lillian Sibbersen of Kalamazoo, Michigan, recommend this technique: After applying the glue, lift the nozzle from the surface and rotate your wrist several times, as if you were drawing a circle in the air. After completing the project, Janet Garner of Mesa, Arizona, sets a handheld hair dryer on high, and aims it at any remaining strings, allowing the heat to dissolve them.

Doll Maker's Resource

In your March/April 1995 Notes from Readers, Annette Le Chaux from New Orleans, Louisiana, asked about flesh-colored fabric. Readers may want to contact Gloria "Mimi" Winer, who publishes a newsletter called "Let's Talk About Dollmaking." The newsletter includes a variety of sources (in the United States and abroad) for the best doll-making supplies, including patterns and materials. Write Winer at P.O. Box 662, Point Pleasant, NJ 08742, or call 908-899-0804.

HELEN DANNATT
NEWTON, NJ

Unfinished Birdhouses

Since I decorated my kitchen with a grouping of front-only birdhouses, many of my friends and family would like me to do groupings for them—but I can't find any more unpainted birdhouses. Can you help me locate a source?

GWEN ROTA
BETHPAGE, TN

Unfinished birdhouses are available from Provo Crafts, 295 West Center Street, Provo, UT 84601; 800-563-8679. Fax orders to 801-373-1446. The company carries solid pine one-hole and three-hole birdhouses that you can decorate with wind chimes, stencils, paint, or wooden cutouts. The company also offers books of projects for all skill levels.

Quick and Easy Candlesticks

I'd like to make candles for holiday decorating, but I don't enjoy the messy process of melting and molding. Do you have any suggestions?

LUCINDA CHESTER
COMMERCE, GA

Try making taper candles from sheets of beeswax, which is pliable enough to work at room temperature. You simply roll the beeswax tightly around a length of wicking to form the taper; you can then roll the finished candle in glitter or sequins, which will adhere to the wax without glue.

You can order beeswax sheets by mail from Honey Wax, a division of Mann Lake Ltd., at P.O. Box 370, Hackensack, MN 56452; 800-880-7694. The company offers sheets of 100 percent beeswax, made with organic, nontoxic dyes, as well as molds, wicks, and other candle-making supplies. A ten-pack of sheets (which makes up to twenty tapers and includes wicks and instructions) costs $18.25, and a fifty-pack is $57.50. Call the company for a list of available colors or a color brochure. ◆

Quick Tips

REMOVING ADHESIVE

When the price sticker affixed to glass does not peel up easily, Dolores Prichard of Greeley, Colorado, uses nail polish remover to dissolve the persistent adhesive.

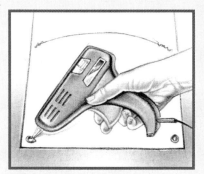

NONSKID PICTURE HANGING

To prevent wall-hung pictures from going askew, add stabilizing feet using a hot-glue gun. Squeeze a blob of hot glue on each lower back corner of the frame. The rubbery surface on each glue blob will touch the wall and prevent the frame from slipping, without permanently adhering the frame to the wall.

ERASER STAMPING

Instead of painting tiny hearts, stars, and checkerboard squares one by one, Missi Boyer of Schuylkill Haven, Pennsylvania, has devised an easy way to stamp them using the eraser end of a pencil.

1. **Sketch the image on the eraser tip and cut out the shape with an X-Acto knife.**

2. **Dip the stamp in paint, dab off the excess, and print the image.**

COLORED SUGAR

Colored sugar, used for decorating Christmas cookies, can be expensive. You can make your own using red or green food coloring and white sugar.

1. **Sprinkle white sugar into a pie plate, then add five drops food coloring.**

2. **Mix the color into the sugar using a spoon. To dry the sugar, set the plate in a 200-degree oven for 10 minutes.**

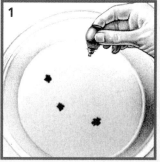 

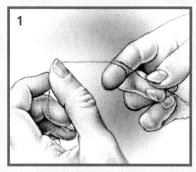 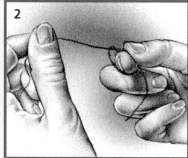

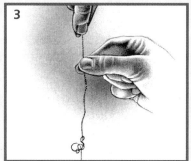 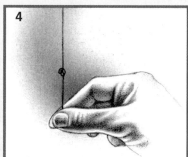

QUICK KNOT TYING

Here's a trick for knotting a basting thread. The entire sequence, once you get the knack of it, takes just a few seconds. First thread the needle, then proceed as follows:

1. **Wind the end of the thread once around the tip of your index finger.**

2. **Roll the thread off your finger with your thumb so the thread loop twists together.**

3. **Slide your fingers rapidly down the thread past the twisted loop...**

4. **....to form an instant knot.**

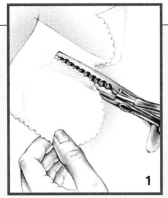

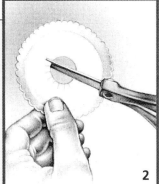

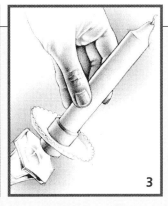

PLASTIC BOBECHES

Jean Watt of Shreveport, Louisiana, makes candle bobeches using empty plastic gallon milk jugs.

1. **Rough-cut the recessed circular section (or any flat area** on the sides) of the jug with an X-Acto knife. Then, trim the circle using pinking or scalloping shears for a decorative edge.

2. **Cut a nickel-sized opening** in the center using scissors, then cut slits around the edge of the opening.

3. **Slip the bobeche onto the candle and adjust.**

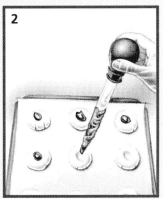

FILLING JAM COOKIES

To fill jam cookies neatly and quickly, Kit Carson of Chicago, Illinois, uses a turkey baster.

1. **Set the baster in the jam jar, then depress and release the bulb to load the tube.**

2. **Dispense the jam onto each cookie, using the bulb to control the flow.**

MAKE-AT-HOME GIFT TAGS

You can make your own gift tags easily and quickly using last year's Christmas cards and eight-by-five-inch unlined index cards. Thanks to Barbara Thacher of Brooklyn, New York, for this tip.

1. **Cut out small rectangular vignettes or pictures from used holiday cards.**

2. **Apply glue stick to the back, then affix the picture to a folded index card.**

3. **Trim the card for an even white border all around.**

4. **Slip the card onto the package ribbon.**

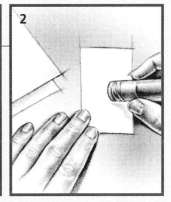

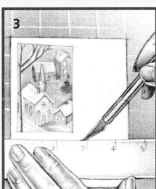

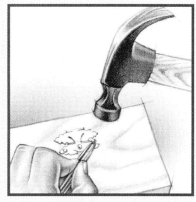

HAMMERING TINY NAILS

When a nail is too small for your fingers to hold upright during hammering, try using needle-nose pliers or tweezers, says Leila Smith of Birmingham, Alabama. The same tools work with tiny screws.

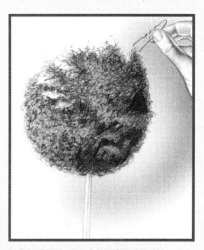

LONGER FLORIST PINS

When commercial florist pins aren't long enough to provide a sure hold, Candie Takacs of Kettering, Ohio, substitutes old-fashioned hairpins. They're perfect for securing moss to foam.

PAINTING FINE LINES

Alana Chandler of Brewster, New York, recommends a single-edged razor blade as a guide for painting fine lines. Set the blade on its sharp edge and run the paintbrush against it.

Great Marriages

Use your favorite collection to create one-of-a-kind holiday decorations.

COLLECTIBLE WREATHS

For a fresh approach to holiday decorating, consider using your favorite collection as a starting point. The basic idea is simple: using collectibles—keys or spoons, for instance—to decorate a tree, wreath, garland, window, chandelier, or the like. To make the decorations more Christmaslike, use fresh greens, strings of miniature lights, or brightly colored ribbons with the collectibles.

In the photo shown above, we used florist wire to attach a collection of antique souvenir spoons to a wreath made of privet. For variation, the spoons could be hung from tree branches using tiny red ribbons or attached to a garland by weaving a ribbon throughout.

We made a "Baby's First Christmas" wreath by attaching a tiny blue teacup, two silver rattles, a blue plastic doll, and a miniature silver picture frame to a wreath of dried baby's breath. For the "Farmer's Christmas" wreath, we wired miniature green tractors to a willow branch wreath base, then attached red wooden apples. We filled in the gaps with wheat sheaves.

Other collectibles to consider: napkin rings, thimbles, small silver items, earrings, fishing lures, china dogs, and so forth. ◆

COLOR PHOTOGRAPHY:
Carl Tremblay

STYLING:
Ritch Holben

The Perfect Gift

Use the lid of a box to stamp out perfect-fit cookies.

CUSTOM-FIT COOKIES

We define the perfect gift as something that is created with a specific person in mind but that isn't overly expensive or time-consuming to assemble. A decorative box, filled with cookies baked especially to fit that box, is in keeping with this philosophy.

Start by finding the decorative box—it might be a brass cannister, a ceramic cookie jar, or a tin candy box—that suits your special person. Look for a box that is worth saving and reusing, versus an ordinary gift box. If you're feeling especially creative, buy a plain cardboard box and decorate it yourself with giftwrap, ribbon, decoupage, color photocopies, or the like.

Select your favorite sugar cookie, gingerbread, or graham cracker recipe, mix it up, and roll out the dough. Then use either the box lid or bottom (whichever is smaller) as a cookie cutter. To protect paper or other delicate boxes, cover the lid or bottom with clear plastic wrap before stamping out the cookies. After baking, the cut cookies should fit inside the box exactly. *Note*: This technique works best with doughs that don't expand horizontally during baking, such as those mentioned above. ◆

COLOR PHOTOGRAPHY:
Carl Tremblay

STYLING:
Ritch Holben

Appliqué Wool Stocking

Topstitch mistletoe leaf and berry designs to a boiled wool stocking, then add decorative embroidered stitches.

✍ BY FRANCOISE HARDY

PATTERNS

See page 44 for patterns and enlargement instructions.

COLOR PHOTOGRAPHY:
Carl Tremblay

ILLUSTRATION:
Judy Love

STYLING:
Ritch Holben

This sixteen-inch stocking uses mistletoe leaves and berries for its motif. For variation, sketch or photocopy a holly, evergreen, or poinsettia pattern.

MATERIALS

■ **Medium-weight wool fabric in the following sizes and colors:**
  18" x 26" piece of cranberry red
  9" x 18" piece of ivory
  9" x 12" piece of dark green
  Scraps of tan
■ **½ yard 45"-wide cotton or muslin lining fabric**
■ **Size 3 pearl cotton in the following colors:**
  2 skeins gold
  1 skein yellow
  1 skein brown
■ **½ yard 1" yellow moss fringe**
■ **⅓ yard ½" green upholstery braid**
■ **3 wooden large-hole ³/₈" beads**
■ **Sewing thread to match fabrics**
■ **Scrap of batting**

You'll also need:
stocking and cuff patterns (*see* page 44); 8-quart pot; 4-quart bowl; tongs or wooden spoon; ice; dryer; iron; access to photocopier with enlarger; tracing paper; spray fixative; transparent tape; sewing machine; sharp sewing shears; embroidery or manicure scissors; tweezers; straight pins; crewel needle; old bath towel; and size 4 crochet hook.

THIS COLORFUL CHRISTMAS stocking combines the homespun appeal of boiled wool with contemporary materials like moss fringe on the cuff and pearl cotton for the embroidered stitches. The simple mistletoe leaf and berry shapes make it a traditional yet tasteful holiday accent for a door or mantel.

Boiled wool is easy to make at home using wool from a bolt of fabric, a remnant, or even a piece of used clothing such as a woman's wool skirt. Because I had trouble finding the right shades of wool, I ended up using three different sources for my fabric. I found the cranberry wool for the stocking body at a fabric store. For the ivory, green, and tan shades, I bought an ivory-colored wool skirt at the Salvation Army thrift store. I used the skirt material as is for the cuff and dyed it green and tan for the mistletoe leaves and berries, respectively. If you

decide to purchase wool and dye it, follow the guidelines in "Dyeing Your Own Wool," page 10. As a last resort, the stocking, cuff, and/or the appliquéed leaves and berries can be made from synthetic felt, but I found the color selection was too bright for my taste. Synthetic felt also has less of a homespun feel.

Once the wool is selected, it is submerged in boiling water, one color at a time, boiled for about ten minutes, then removed and placed in ice water. If any color comes out in the boiling water, you'll need to start with fresh water for the next color. After all the pieces of wool have been boiled, squeeze out as much water as you can, and machine-dry them on the hot setting for fifteen to twenty minutes. This process shrinks and felts the wool so it won't ravel or fray when you cut it, much the way felt behaves. The nap will be slightly raised and fluffy, which adds to the fabric's appeal. To

remove any wrinkles, steam-press the fabric from the wrong side before you begin sewing.

Once the stocking is complete, I used two simple embroidery stitches for the finishing touches. For an easy, foolproof way to keep the blanket stitching around the stocking's edge neat and uniform, use the machine stitching as a built-in guide. Blanket stitches should be spaced about one-quarter inch apart. Set your machine for twelve stitches per inch, which means you'll insert the needle for the blanket stitch every third machine stitch.

INSTRUCTIONS

1. *Boil and shrink wool fabrics.* Fill 4-quart bowl with ice water. Fill 8-quart pot halfway with water, bring to boil, and drop in ivory and tan wool. Let boil 10 minutes, swishing occasionally with tongs or wooden spoon, then lift out and plunge in ice water for a few minutes. Remove from ice water and rinse in cold water until water runs clear. Wring fabric, roll in towel, and squeeze out excess moisture. Repeat process to shrink green and red fabrics individually, starting with fresh water if hot bath becomes discolored. Put all fabrics in dryer and tumble dry on hot (high) setting 15 to 20 minutes or until dry. Steam-press on wrong side.

2. *Make tracing patterns.* Photocopy

Making the Stocking

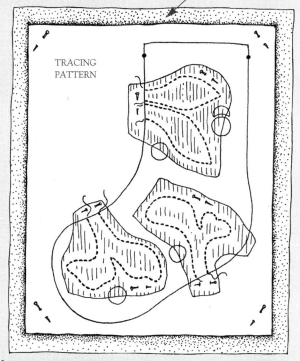

red wool (right side)

TRACING PATTERN

A. Sandwich the green wool between the red wool and the tracing pattern, and stitch along the leaf outlines.

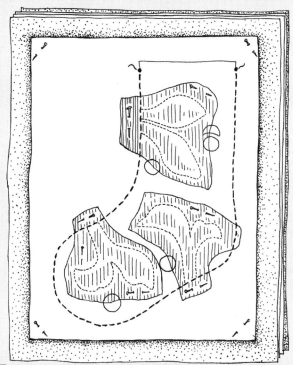

B. Stack the wool and lining fabrics together and stitch along the stocking outline.

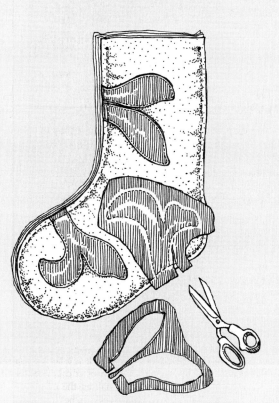

C. Tear off the tracing pattern. Cut out the stocking ¼" beyond the stitching. Trim the excess green wool close to the stitching.

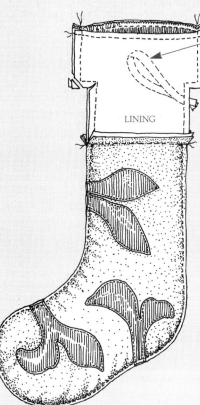

hanging loop

LINING

D. Sew the cuff pieces to the stocking top, then stitch the sides together and add a hanging loop and fringe.

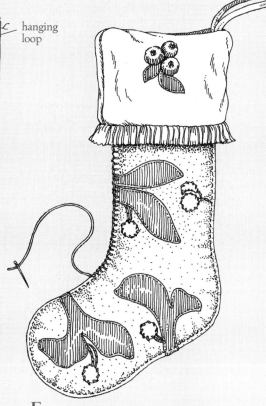

E. With the cuff folded down, add a blanket stitch edging, couching, and wooden berries (*see* page 10 for stitch close-ups).

stocking and cuff patterns onto tracing paper, enlarging 200% or until top edge of stocking measures 6" across. Tape sections of photocopied stocking pattern together, if necessary, but do not cut out. Photocopy leaf and berry patterns, enlarging by 200 percent. To prevent smearing, apply spray fixative to stocking pattern pieces.

3. *Pin and sew leaf appliqués.* Cut red wool in half to yield two 13" x 18" pieces. Lay one piece right side up on flat surface, then position stocking tracing pattern on top. From green wool, cut three pieces ½" larger all around than each leaf cluster. Slip green pieces right side up into position between pattern and red wool, adjust and/or trim them so they clear each other, and secure with straight pins. Using green thread, slowly machine-stitch leaves along leaf pattern outlines through all layers. Take your time when topstitching to prevent errors. Do not remove tracing (*see* illustration A, page 9).

4. Sew stocking body with lining. Cut two 13" x 18" pieces from lining fabric. On flat surface, stack the following pieces: plain red wool wrong side up; one lining right side up; one lining wrong side up; red wool from step 3, tracing paper face up. Pin all layers together. Using cranberry thread and beginning and ending at dots, machine-stitch stocking outline; leave top edge open (illustration B). Peel away tracing pattern. To cut out stocking, trim ¼" beyond stitching all around through all layers. Trim top edge along marked line. To reduce bulk, spread seam with fingers and use embroidery or manicure scissors to trim lining fabric close to seam. Using shears, trim excess green wool leaf fabric a scant ¹⁄₁₆" beyond stitching (illustration C). Use tweezers to remove any paper or fibers

that remain trapped under stitching.

5. *Attach stocking cuff.* Cut two cuffs from ivory wool and two cuffs from lining fabric. Pair each wool cuff with lining, wrong sides together. Pin one pair to front of stocking and second pair to back, wool cuff against stocking lining and edges matching. Machine-stitch ¼" from stocking's top edge. Press seams toward cuff. Sew cuffs together at sides, enclosing upholstery braid in right seam for hanging loop. Sew fringe around top edge, right sides facing. Clip outside corners diagonally and clip into inside corners (illustration D).

6. *Add berries and blanket stitching.* Fold down cuff. From tan wool, cut three berries and one half berry. Pin berries to stocking right side up (*see* original pattern, page 44, for placement). Using yellow pearl cotton and crewel needle, work blanket (buttonhole) or straight stitch around each berry (illustrations E and F), taking care to sew through wool layer only. To make berries three-dimensional, insert small wad of batting under each one as you complete stitching. Embroider straight stitch stems to join berries to leaves (*see* original pattern for placement). Using gold pearl cotton and crewel needle, work blanket stitch around edge of stocking, inserting needle every third machine stitch for even placement. Using yellow pearl cotton and crewel needle, add couching (illustration G) to leaves (*see* original pattern for placement).

7. *Add berries to cuff.* Using size 4 crochet hook and gold pearl cotton, work single crochet around each bead until fully covered. From green wool, cut two green leaves for cuff. Using brown pearl cotton and crewel needle, tack leaves and berries to front cuff. ◆

DYEING YOUR OWN WOOL

If you can't find the right color of wool for your stocking, consider buying white or ivory wool and dyeing it at home. Because the fabric has to be boiled anyway, you can easily add a dye bath to the process, followed by a thorough washing in a washing machine to rinse out the excess dye.

I tested a number of dyes—including Sennelier and Procion—and in the end settled on DEKA's Series "L" Lightfast Batik & Textile dye. This brand of dye can be used in a hot water bath and is set with vinegar, which gets added to the dye bath. Follow the manufacturer's instructions carefully. I found that fifteen minutes in boiling hot water, with frequent stirring, was sufficient to both set the color and shrink the fabric to create the boiled effect. Rinse the dyed fabric in cold running water and then run it through a hot cycle on your washing machine, which will not only rinse out excess dye but also soften up the fabric. Tumble dry on hot as with the undyed boiled wool.

Before dyeing and washing the wool, rough-cut the dimensions as called for in the materials list, but leave at least two to three inches around each shape to allow for shrinkage. Keep in mind, however, that fabrics shrink to different degrees. Heavier-weight wools with larger yarns will shrink more and acquire a heavier texture than thinner-weight wools with a thinner weave. If you're not sure, simply dye the entire piece and go from there.

Before dyeing, I recommend trying to verify the fabric's fiber content. While 100 percent wool fabric will take color the best, you can also use a 50 percent wool/50 percent fabric blend. Avoid 100 percent polyester and acrylic felts or knits, as these do not take color or shrink.

Decorative Embroidery Stitches

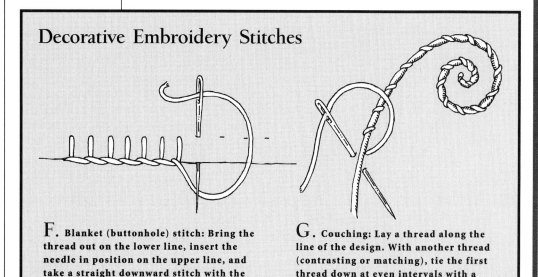

F. Blanket (buttonhole) stitch: Bring the thread out on the lower line, insert the needle in position on the upper line, and take a straight downward stitch with the thread under the needle point. Pull up the stitch to form a loop and repeat.

G. Couching: Lay a thread along the line of the design. With another thread (contrasting or matching), tie the first thread down at even intervals with a small stitch into the fabric.

Empire-Style Door Wreath

Construct this handsome holiday wreath using fresh lemon leaves and a bulked-up straw wreath base.

❧ BY CAROL ENDLER STERBENZ

MATERIALS

- 550 to 600 fresh lemon leaves
- 18"-diameter straw wreath base
- 4½ yards 2¾"-wide green velvet wire-edged ribbon
- 1 yard gold metallic twisted cord
- Bright gold metallic spray paint
- 10 to 15 white plastic 13-gallon trash bags
- 30-gauge green spool wire
- Florist pins

You'll also need: newspaper; wire cutters; permanent marker; and scissors.

AROUND THE BUSY HOLIDAY season, the ideal door wreath looks elegant, is easy to assemble, and uses materials that are readily available. This classic Empire-style wreath meets all three criteria.

I used only one type of foliage—lemon leaves—to cover the wreath base. Lemon leaves can be purchased by the branch in floral shops. Half the leaves are painted gold while half are left green. I bulked up a simple straw wreath base to enlarge the display surface by wrapping it with plastic garbage bags. Then I pinned tiers of lemon leaves to the wreath base using florist pins. To give the wreath greater visual interest, the leaves radiate downwards from the twelve o'clock position and meet at the bottom of the wreath in a soft flare.

INSTRUCTIONS

1. *Paint leaves gold.* Spread newspaper flat in well-ventilated work area. Lay approximately three hundred lemon leaves face up on newspaper and spray with gold metallic paint following manufacturer's instructions. Let dry at least 1 hour, preferably overnight, before handling.

2. *Wrap and mark wreath.* Wrap plastic bag around wreath, concealing straw. Cover adjacent section of wreath with second bag, wrapping in same direction (*see illustration A, below*). Continue until all straw is concealed, then add one or two more bag layers to build up wreath bulk. To secure bags, bind entire wreath with wire. For leaf placement, visualize wreath as a clock face and use permanent marker to draw lines at two, five, six, seven, ten, and twelve o'clock positions (illustration B).

3. *Pin leaves to wreath in tiers.* Position several gold leaves horizontally across six o'clock line; to secure, push florist pins through leaf tips. Repeat to cover entire six o'clock line. Working toward right, position tier of gold leaves around wreath so lower tips overlap and conceal previously inserted pins. Secure with pins. Repeat to attach two or three additional tiers, or enough to conceal five o'clock line (illustration C). Each tier should con-

This elegant door wreath uses fresh lemon leaves, which will dry on their own. Once the leaves have dried, handle the wreath carefully to prevent damage.

ceal previous tier's pins. Repeat to add gold tiers up left side to reach seven o'clock line. Pin approximately ten tiers of green leaves up each side to reach two and ten o'clock lines (illustration D). Finish with approximately seven tiers of gold leaves on each side to reach twelve o'clock line.

4. *Add ribbon and cord.* To finish, wrap green ribbon around wreath at twelve o'clock position and tie into four-loop bow. Shape streamers to dangle into center of wreath and notch ends. Loop gold cord into 4"-diameter circle with two 12"-long streamers, knot ends to prevent raveling, and wire to bow knot. ◆

COLOR PHOTOGRAPHY:
Carl Tremblay

ILLUSTRATION:
Judy Love

STYLING:
Ritch Holben

Making the Wreath

A. Wrap a wreath base with plastic bags.

B. Mark the wreath for the leaf placement.

C. Attach gold lemon leaves in layers with florist pins.

D. Continue pinning leaves up the sides of the wreath.

Embossed Tree Ornaments

Cut out fruit and vegetable designs from aluminum, then color them with glass paints to make this trio of lustrous ornaments.

🌰 BY MICHIO RYAN

MATERIALS
Yields 3 ornaments

- **36-gauge aluminum embossing foil**
- **16-gauge aluminum armature wire**
- **24-gauge silver wire**
- **⅔ ounce Deka Transparent glass paints in the following colors: light red, light green, violet, lemon, and colorless**
- **Micro glitter in the following colors: silver, pale gold, and green**
- **Fine elastic cord**
- **Matte acrylic spray**
- **Stick glue**

You'll also need:
fruit and vegetable patterns (*see* page 43); #2 graphite pencil with blunt point and add-on eraser tip; 1/16"-thick foam pad; denatured alcohol; #10 sableine brush; sturdy utility scissors; manicure scissors; 3/4 ounce Deka Thinner #37; wire cutters or pliers with wire-cutting ability; steel nail file; orange stick; circle drafting template; access to photocopier; unopened #10 tin can; craft sticks; baby food jars; paper towels; cotton swabs; wood slats; newsprint; tape; sheet of typing paper; and stainless steel teaspoon.

COLOR PHOTOGRAPHY:
Carl Tremblay

ILLUSTRATION:
Nenad Jakesevic

STYLING:
Ritch Holben

To create a frosty, lustrous effect on these fruit and vegetable ornaments, we applied glass paint to cut aluminum.

RE-CREATING THE LOOK OF handblown frosted glass using a two-dimensional material is easier than you think. I cut these fruit and vegetable shapes from a thin sheet of aluminum, then embossed them from the reverse side, which gave them three-dimensionality. Then I painted the ornaments with glass paint, followed by a matte overcoat. The finished look is soft and satiny like a handblown glass ornament.

Although I tested a number of different metals for this project, including tin and stainless steel, I found that aluminum is ideal. It's lightweight, can be cut with scissors, and is shiny enough to reflect light back through the glass paint. Embossing the ornaments, and thus improving on their flat, two-dimensional design, proved particularly easy with aluminum by applying a pencil eraser to the wrong side of the metal.

Then I began my search for paint. The ideal paint would produce an effect very much like mirrored glass, of which blown ornaments are made, where the tinted glass is backed with a thin coating of mercury. The paint thus needed to be a transparent medium but with dyes in it to produce different colors, and also able to build up a nice film, preferably in a single coat. Glass paint, used to make light catchers and faux stained glass, met all these criteria. The paint is transparent, available in a range of colors, and dries within minutes.

Glass paint usually comes with a transparent extender, essentially a clear lacquer, which can be used to thin out the colors and to add shading effects. I found this product essential for creating the right effect on my ornaments. Because glass paints are meant to be applied to glass, held against light, and seen through, the darker colors are more saturated. Intending to apply the paints directly to metal, however, I used a large amount of the extender to lighten the violet paint. The paint should be applied in a very thin coat, which allows some of the aluminum's silvery shine to show through. A thin coat of color will also show through the final coat of ordinary matte spray (sold in hardware stores and used to "frost" windows).

For the finishing effect, I added glitter to the stems of the grapes and peas and to the greenery at the top of the tomato. This relatively small amount of texture and additional color doesn't overpower the delicate embossing but instead provides a necessary contrast.

INSTRUCTIONS
Making the Ornaments

1. *Transfer patterns to foil.* Photocopy patterns, then rough-cut ½" beyond pattern outlines all around. Tape patterns, right side up, to aluminum, then slip foam pad underneath aluminum. Trace all circles and arcs with blunt pencil, using heavy pressure to indent aluminum as follows: For tomato, align tin can on pattern and trace around can rim, skipping over stem area. For pea pods (make two), use circle template to draw various-sized peas. For grapes, use circle template to draw whole grape at center and arcs clustered around it (*see* illustration A, next page). Rest aluminum on hard surface and lightly trace grape leaf and all remaining lines including dashed stem lines. Untape and remove patterns. Slip pad back under aluminum and deepen all freehand lines except stem lines by retracing.

2. *Emboss foil from wrong side.* Turn foil face down on foam pad. Rub areas within traced lines in circular motion using eraser end of pencil, pressing down and hollowing out foil in back to create raised, gently rounded surface on right side (illustration B). Work several rounds in succession to stretch and shape foil gradually, versus trying to achieve full depth in one particular area at once. For tomato, use pointed end of orange stick to push out tips on stem, then run back of teaspoon against broad lower bowl to smooth out bumps and create full, swelling shape. For pea pods, sweep eraser down edges to create gentle rippling, then emboss individual peas. Emboss grapes so those at middle protrude more than those at sides. When done, turn each piece right side up on hard surface and run pencil point back over any lines that have lost clarity.

3. *Cut out embossed ornaments.* Rough-cut each ornament ¼" beyond outlines using utility scissors. Use manicure scissors to trim off allowance just outside pencil lines and along stem lines (illustration C). Cut into deep "V"s first,

TRACING AND EMBOSSING THE ORNAMENTS

A. Transfer the fruit or vegetable design to aluminum. Use a circle template for perfect circles and arcs.

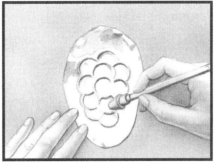

B. Emboss the design from the back using a pencil with an add-on eraser.

C. Trim the ornament with manicure scissors along the edge of the recessed outline.

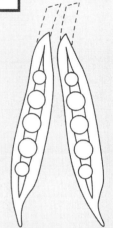

trim out excess, then cut rounded parts. Cut tips of pea pods so they are blunt and rounded versus sharp. Smooth cut edges by running steel nail file against edges at 45-degree angle from both sides. Gently push out and swell center of grapes and tomato using thumb.

4. *Add stems to grape leaf and pea pods.* Cut 14" length from armature wire using wire cutters or pliers. Set wire against wrong side of grape leaf stem so ½" extends into leaf area (illustration D). Lay 24-gauge wire alongside stem wire so end is even with bottom of leaf stem. Using pliers, roll foil stem around both wires from both sides, then crimp aluminum stem around wires (illustration E). Wind 24-gauge wire down around entire leaf stem in tight spiral, clip off end, and crimp securely (illustration F). Add 8" stem to each pea pod in same way.

Painting the Ornaments

1. *Prepare ornaments for painting.* Work in well-ventilated room and cover work surface with newsprint. Clean each ornament with denatured alcohol and paper towel. Use cotton swab dipped in alcohol to clean crevices. To prevent painted ornaments from adhering to newsprint, lay two wood slats parallel to each other on newsprint, then lay ornaments across them, spanning space in between (illustration G).

2. *Apply glass paints.* Using sabeline brush, apply thin coat of paint to each outlined section of ornaments as noted below. To mix colors, use craft sticks and baby food jars. Clean brush with thinner between colors. Apply paint as follows:
   a) Light green paint to tomato stem and grape leaf.
   b) 2 parts lemon + 1 part light green to outer area of pea pods (do not paint peas).
   c) Light red to tomato.
   d) 1 part violet + 2 parts colorless to grapes.
Let ornaments dry overnight. Holding can 18" above work surface, apply matte

spray to ornaments, then let dry 1 hour. To restore shine on peas, paint individual peas using lemon paint.

Finishing the Ornaments

1. *Glue glitter to stems.* Working over sheet of typing paper, brush colorless paint onto tomato stem, then sprinkle with green micro glitter. Shake off excess glitter onto paper and funnel back into container. For peas, twist wire stems together in free-form curlicue or twist around pencil. Brush stems with colorless paint and sprinkle with silver micro glitter as above. For grape leaf, curl portion of

stem nearest leaf into ½" loop and wind remaining portion around pencil to form tight spiral (illustration H). Brush entire stem with colorless paint and sprinkle with pale gold micro glitter as above. Let dry ½ hour. Use dry brush to whisk off excess glitter from ornaments.

2. *Add hanging loops.* Using stick glue, affix loop of grape leaf stem to top back of grape cluster (illustration H). Let dry overnight. Cut three 8" lengths of elastic cord and knot ends of each together. Glue one to back of tomato for hanger. Let dry overnight. Loop remaining two around pea and grape stems. ◆

PATTERNS
See page 43 for patterns and enlargement instructions.

FINISHING THE ORNAMENTS

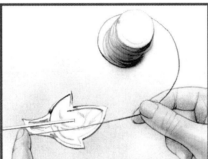

D. To create a stem for the grape leaf, lay armature wire and 24-gauge wire side by side.

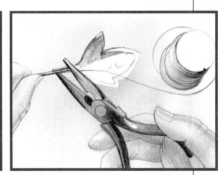

E. Wrap the foil around both wires, then crimp down on them using the pliers.

F. Use the 24-gauge wire to bind the entire length of the stem.

G. To prevent the ornaments from adhering to the newsprint during painting,

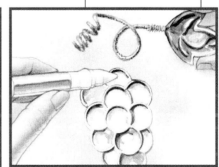

H. Coat the wire stem with fine glitter, then glue it to the back of the ornament.

Custom-Fit Teddy Bear Sweaters

Knit a snug wool sweater for any size bear using five quick measurements.

❧ BY ALYSON PRESTON

KNITTING KEY

GAUGE:
4 stitches=1"
6 rows=1"
(larger needles)

KEY:
dp = double-pointed
p = pearl
k = knit
ss = stockinette stitch
st = stitch
sts = stitches

COLOR PHOTOGRAPHY:
Carl Tremblay

ILLUSTRATION:
Michael Gellatly

STYLING:
Ritch Holben

Beginning knitters should knit the solid-color red sweater (left); intermediate knitters may want to tackle the green and white striped sweater (right).

T HESE HANDSOME HAND-KNIT sweaters are the perfect holiday accessory for any teddy bear. Using five quick measurements and a series of simple calculations, you can create a sweater to fit any size bear. Use the sweaters to personalize a gift or to turn a collection of bears into a decorative Christmas display.

Customizing the sweater to fit your bear is easier than it sounds. Start by measuring the bear, then use the measurements to calculate the specific stitch and inch amounts required. To simplify the process, use a calculator and record the results on a schematic, or flat drawing of the sweater (*see* page 15). Once you've prepared the schematic, the actual knitting should take two to five hours from start to finish, depending on the size of the bear. The instructions follow conventional format and are keyed to the schematic; just plug in your custom numbers as you go along.

I designed two versions of the sweater: a solid red version for beginning knitters and a green and white striped version for intermediate knitters. *Note:* This article will not teach you how to knit. The sweaters presented here are designed for crafters with basic knitting experience. If you don't know how to knit and would like to learn how, *see* "Knitting Resources," next page, for ideas.

For both sweaters, front and back are knitted separately, then joined at the shoulders. The sleeves are knitted on after the front and back are sewn together. For the striped sweater, work two rows green, two rows white throughout.

Alyson Preston is a professional knitter living in Swampscott, Massachusetts.

INSTRUCTIONS
Note: Knit test swatch and check gauge before you begin.

Knitting the Red Sweater

1. *Create custom schematic. See* page 15.

2. *Knit back and front.* Referring to schematic and using smaller needles, cast on (a) sts for back. Work in k1, p1 ribbing for ½" (or desired depth); end wrong side. Change to larger needles. Work in ss until piece measures (b) inches from ribbing edge; end wrong side. Bind off loosely. Work front same as back.

3. *Join back to front at shoulders.* Using tapestry needle and yarn, sew back to front in duplicate st for (d) sts at each shoulder. Mark back and front armhole edges (g) inches from ribbing edge.

4. *Knit sleeves.* From right side, with larger needles, pick up (e) sts evenly spaced between armhole markers. Work in ss for (h) inches minus ½" (or ribbing depth established in step 2); end wrong side. Change to smaller needles and work in k1, p1 ribbing for ½" (or established ribbing depth). Bind off. Work second sleeve to match on opposite side.

5. *Knit neck ribbing.* With dp needles, pick up (c) sts evenly around neck edge. Work k1, p1 ribbing in round for ½". Bind off loosely.

6. *Sew side and sleeve seams.* Using tapestry needle and yarn and with right sides together, backstitch arm and side seams on one side. Repeat to join opposite side.

Knitting the Striped Sweater

1. *Create custom schematic.* Same as Red Sweater, step 1.

2. *Knit back and front.* Referring to schematic and using smaller needles and green yarn, cast on (a) sts for back. Work in k1, p1 ribbing for ½" (or desired depth); end wrong side. Change to larger needles and white yarn. Work two rows ss in white yarn, two in green yarn, continuing until entire piece measures (b) from ribbing edge; end wrong side. Bind off loosely. Work front same as back.

3. *Join back to front.* See Red Sweater, step 3.

4. *Knit sleeves.* From right side, with larger needles and white yarn, pick up (e) sts evenly spaced between armhole markers. Work two rows ss in white yarn, two in green yarn, continuing until piece measures approximately (h) minus ½" (or ribbing depth established in step 2); end wrong side white row. Change to smaller needles and green yarn and work in k1, p1 ribbing for ½" (or established ribbing depth). Bind off. Work second sleeve to match on opposite side.

5. *Knit neck ribbing.* With dp needles and white yarn, pick up (c) sts evenly around neck edge. Work k1, p1 ribbing in round for ½" (or established ribbing depth). Bind off loosely.

6. *Sew side and sleeve seams.* Same as Red Sweater, step 6. ◆

Creating a Custom Schematic

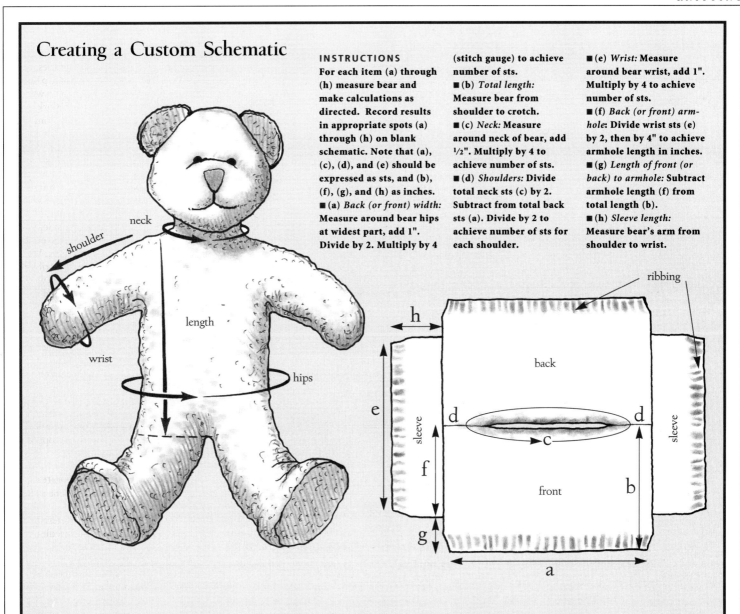

INSTRUCTIONS

INSTRUCTIONS

For each item (a) through (h) measure bear and make calculations as directed. Record results in appropriate spots (a) through (h) on blank schematic. Note that (a), (c), (d), and (e) should be expressed as sts, and (b), (f), (g), and (h) as inches.

■ **(a)** *Back (or front) width:* Measure around bear hips at widest part, add 1". Divide by 2. Multiply by 4

(stitch gauge) to achieve number of sts.

■ **(b)** *Total length:* Measure bear from shoulder to crotch.

■ **(c)** *Neck:* Measure around neck of bear, add ½". Multiply by 4 to achieve number of sts.

■ **(d)** *Shoulders:* Divide total neck sts (c) by 2. Subtract from total back sts (a). Divide by 2 to achieve number of sts for each shoulder.

■ **(e)** *Wrist:* Measure around bear wrist, add 1". Multiply by 4 to achieve number of sts.

■ **(f)** *Back (or front) arm-hole:* Divide wrist sts (e) by 2, then by 4" to achieve armhole length in inches.

■ **(g)** *Length of front (or back) to armhole:* Subtract armhole length (f) from total length (b).

■ **(h)** *Sleeve length:* Measure bear's arm from shoulder to wrist.

KNITTING RESOURCES
by Jennifer Putnam

Want to learn how to knit? The knitting experts I spoke to recommend the first set of titles for learning the basics, and the second set of titles for experienced knitters who want to learn more about design, color, or yarn types. *Note:* Some of these titles may be difficult to locate in bookstores. Contact your local yarn and knit shops or look in your public library. Many knitting shops also offer knitting instruction,

and if you find written instructions hard to follow, demonstration may be the best way to learn.

LEARNING TO KNIT
■ **The All New Teach Yourself to Knit,** by Evie Rosen (Leisure Arts, Inc., 1992)

■ **The Harmony Guide to Knitting: Techniques and Stitches,** edited by Beryl Kempner (Harmony Books, 1992)

■ **Reader's Digest Knitter's Handbook,** by Stanley Montse (Reader's Digest Association, 1993)

■ **Vogue Guide to Knitting** (Galahad Books, 1972)

LEARNING ABOUT DESIGN, COLOR, OR YARN TYPES
■ **Knitting the New Classics: 60 Exquisite Sweaters from Elite,** by Kristin Nicholas (Sterling Publishing Co., Inc., 1995)

■ **The Knitter's Design Sourcebook: 127 Chartered Motifs to Use in Your Own Original Designs,** by Helene Rush (Down East Books, 1991)

■ **Knitting in the Old Way,** by Priscilla A. Gibson-Roberts (Interweave Press, 1985)

■ **Sweater Design in Plain English,** by Maggie Righetti (St. Martin's Press, 1990)

Gilded Glitter Village

Build this tiny townscape from chipboard, then transform it into a shimmering village using fabric paint, glitter, and beads.

BY MICHIO RYAN

The gilded glitter village includes the house (left), the cathedral (center), and the cottage (right). The church is shown on page 18.

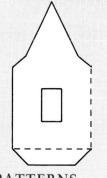
THIS SHIMMERING VILLAGE townscape, which includes a house, a cottage, a church, and a cathedral, started out as plain chipboard. Once assembled, the buildings are painted gold and coated with glitter, then accented with decorative details such as windowpanes, bells, and beads. The village can be displayed on a mantel, set in a windowsill, used as a centerpiece, or grouped under a Christmas tree.

Building the village breaks down into four main tasks: 1) cutting the chipboard forms; 2) assembling the buildings; 3) painting the buildings and covering them with glitter; and 4) adding the decorative details. Of the four steps, the first is clearly the most time-intensive. I found that spreading the cutting process out over a few days is very helpful. The second step, assembling the buildings, goes very quickly. The pieces fit together intuitively, much like a children's jigsaw puzzle. You'll need a few hours for painting and adding the glitter to the buildings before

proceeding to my favorite step: adding the finishing details.

All of the village pieces are cut from one- or three-ply chipboard. For efficient cutting, work on a cutting mat and use a utility knife and a steel ruler. Following the patterns on pages 45 to 47, score all the dashed lines (which represent folds) and cut clear through the solid lines (except for the building bases).

When all the pieces are cut out, you should have three pieces for the cottage (base, cottage, and roof); five pieces for the house (base, house, roof, and two shutters); five pieces for the church (base, church, tower, roof, and spire); and fifteen pieces for the cathedral (base, bell tower base, cathedral, door A, door B, tower A, tower B, roof, bell tower, two spires, and four flying buttresses). Based on the intricacy and the number of pieces, it should be clear that the cottage and house are faster and easier to assemble than the church. Furthermore, all three buildings are less time-consuming than

the cathedral. You can design a village made up entirely of houses or build only the cathedral as a dramatic holiday focal point. You can also convert the village into tree ornaments (*see* "Glitter Village Tree Ornaments," next page.)

Painting the Village

Once the buildings are cut from chipboard, they are assembled and glued together with hot glue, then covered with gold fabric paint. I used Tulip's Colorpoint pearlescent fabric paint in Antique Gold.

Once the fabric paint has dried, you can coat the buildings with glue, then cover them with glitter. For this project you'll need a fine grade of glitter, sometimes referred to as micro or ultrafine glitter. I used two shades of gold and one shade of silver: a fine grade of Glitterix for the darker gold glitter, Powderz's Summer Sand for the pale gold, and Powderz's Silver.

MATERIALS

- 20" x 30" piece one-ply chipboard
- 9" x 12" piece three-ply chipboard
- 2 ounces fine Glitterix dark gold glitter
- 2/5 ounce Powderz's Summer Sand (CAK994) pale gold glitter
- 2/5 ounce Powderz's Silver (CAK993) glitter
- 4 ounces Tulip Colorpoint pearlescent/Antique Gold (GD95) fabric paint
- Spray adhesive
- Krylon Crystal Clear spray fixative
- White craft glue
- Two 1/2" gold bells
- Six 4mm silver beads
- Three 3/16"-diameter gold crimped beads
- Three 3/16"-diameter gold filigree beads
- 3/16" x 3/16" x 36" balsa stick
- 9" x 12" sheet plastic needle-point canvas
- 1 1/2"-diameter metal filigree finding or paper doily with filigree center
- Fine-gauge wire
- 6 straight pins

You'll also need:
building patterns (*see* pages 45 to 47); access to photocopier with enlarger; utility knife; X-Acto knife; straight-edge steel ruler; self-healing cutting mat; hot-glue gun; newsprint; several sheets plain white paper; pencil; 1/2" flat brush; 1/4" stiff stencil brush; tape; scissors; and needle.

Other items, if necessary:
paper stiffener (if using cut paper doily for cathedral rose window).

If you've worked with glitter before, you know that it can flake off, leaving tiny specks everywhere. To prevent this, I recommend adding two spray coats of Krylon Crystal Clear.

Adding the Details

Now comes the fun part: adding the final trims. One note: Although I've included windowpanes in the list of decorative details, these are actually added while the buildings are still flat.

I considered a number of materials for the windows, including plastic needlepoint canvas, aluminum grating from a hardware store, and architectural model

appropriate product before gluing them in place (I recommend Plaid's Stiffen).

To further decorate the church and cathedral, I added beads at the pinnacles and bells inside the towers. I also used dots of fabric paint to decorate the towers. The roofs can also be dressed up by attaching crimped and filigree beads with ordinary straight pins and a dot of glue.

INSTRUCTIONS

1. *Affix patterns to chipboard.* Photocopy patterns, enlarging all pieces by 200 percent. Tape together any enlargements that span two sheets. Rough-cut each pattern 1/2" beyond outlines. Spray light coat of

tabs and short edges, and finally long straight lines. Peel off template paper as you go. Turn roofs face down to mark and score lines from wrong side as indicated. Sort pieces into four groups and lightly label each piece using pencil:

Cottage: base, cottage, roof.

House: base, house, roof, 2 shutters.

Church: base, church, tower, roof, spire.

Cathedral: base, bell tower base, cathedral, door A, door B, tower A, tower B, roof, bell tower, 2 spires, 4 flying buttresses.

3. *Add windowpanes.* Turn house, church, and cathedral face down. Cut three plastic canvas rectangles slightly

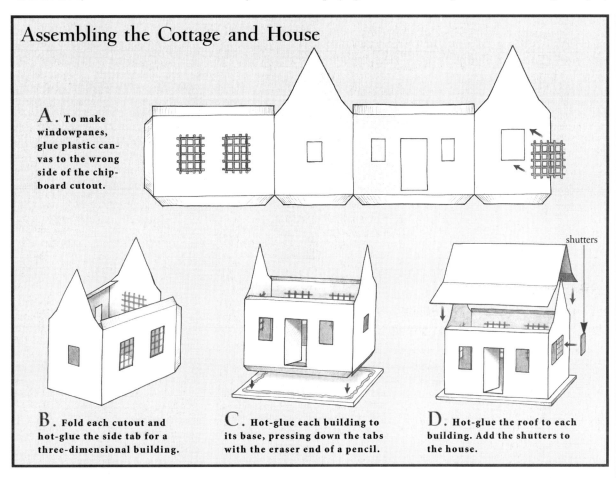

Assembling the Cottage and House

A. To make windowpanes, glue plastic canvas to the wrong side of the chipboard cutout.

B. Fold each cutout and hot-glue the side tab for a three-dimensional building.

C. Hot-glue each building to its base, pressing down the tabs with the eraser end of a pencil.

D. Hot-glue the roof to each building. Add the shutters to the house.

shutters

screen material. Ultimately, I chose the plastic canvas, as it is inexpensive, cuts easily with scissors, and takes paint, glue, and glitter. The canvas can be used two ways: vertically, to represent windowpanes (on the house), or diagonally, to represent the leading of stained glass windows (on the cathedral and church).

The cathedral also features a round rose window above the door. I found a round metal finding about one and one-half inches in diameter, with a filigree design, for this decorative accent. If you can't find such an item, you can substitute the center from a paper doily. The paper doily should be stiffened with an

adhesive on back. Press five base patterns onto three-ply chipboard. Press remaining patterns onto one-ply chipboard with grain arrow running parallel to chipboard grain (where indicated).

2. *Score and cut out patterns.* Lay chipboard on cutting mat. Use utility knife and ruler to cut all straight edges. Use X-Acto knife to cut all rounded lines including church, cathedral, and tower windows; spires; flying buttresses; bell tower; and cathedral doors. Cut clear through all solid lines and score all dashed lines; mark dashed lines on base pieces with pencil rather than scoring them. Cut windows and doors first (do curves freehand), then

larger than three largest house windows. Hot-glue canvas over window openings (*see* illustration A, previous page). For church and cathedral, cut rectangles on diagonal grid (for diamond panes) large enough to cover each wall of Gothic windows (identified in illustrations F and G), then hot-glue in place. For cathedral rose window (illustration G), hot-glue metal finding within circle opening. If using cut paper or fabric doily, spray or coat with stiffener following manufacturer's instructions, then hot-glue in place over opening from back. Glue doors A and B behind cathedral door opening to recess opening.

4. *Fold and glue main pieces.* Fold cottage, house, church, and cathedral on score lines so scoring faces out. Lap free end over tab to form box and hot-glue in place (illustration B). Fold and glue sides of three towers in same way. To add bell to church tower, pierce hole in tower top with needle, string bell on wire, and thread wire through hole. Adjust wire so bell is suspended inside belfry, then glue wire at top to prevent slipping. Fold each tower top, then tuck in and glue tabs (illustration E). Fold and glue spires (identified in illustrations F and G) to form tall pyramids. Fold all roofs on score lines.

5. *Add base pieces and roofs.* For each building, apply hot-glue generously to base within penciled outline, then immediately set structure in position (illustration C). Press inside tabs firmly against base with eraser end of pencil. Test-fit roof, apply hot glue to remaining tabs and gables, and press roof in position. Glue house shutters by end window on left side of house (illustration D). *Note:* This step concludes assembly of cottage and house. Follow steps 6 and 7 to complete church and cathedral, then proceed for all structures to step 8.

6. *Complete church assembly.* Referring to illustration F, hot-glue remaining church components as follows: 1) Apply glue within tower outline of church base and to side of church, then press tower into position; 2) Glue spire to tower; 3) Using utility knife, cut 1¼" length from balsa stick and glue to church base to form step at foot of door.

7. *Complete cathedral assembly.* Referring to illustration G, hot-glue remaining cathedral components as follows: 1) Glue towers A and B to cathedral and base as for church tower in step 6; 2) Glue bell tower base to top of tower A; 3) Fold bell tower, glue edges together, and add bell as for church tower, step 4, then glue bell tower to its base; 4) Glue two spires in position; 5) Glue flying buttresses between Gothic windows, spanning from base to upper wall; 6) Cut three 2⅝" lengths from balsa stick. Stack balsa and glue to base to form two-tier step between towers.

8. *Paint all structures.* Apply gold fabric paint to all exposed surfaces with ½" flat brush. Use straight, overlapping strokes for flat surfaces and circular motion to work paint into crevices and under eaves. To fill noticeable gaps, apply paint directly from dispenser tip, as if caulking. Let paint dry 1 hour, then apply second coat. Let dry 2 hours.

9. *Apply glitter to all structures.* Cover work surface with newsprint. Fold sheets of white paper in half, then unfold and set aside. Use sheets as needed to catch excess glitter and funnel it back into containers for reuse. Using ¼" stencil brush, apply white craft glue to all portions of each structure designated to receive pale gold glitter (as indicated below). Sprinkle glitter liberally over glued area, shake structure from side to side to distribute flakes, then tap off excess. Continue until pale gold color is applied to all structures, let dry at least 10 minutes, then glue and glitter remaining areas one color at a time.

Pale gold glitter: Bases, roofs, spires, house shutters, and cathedral buttresses.
Silver glitter: Doors, window grilles, and rose window.
Dark gold glitter: All other surfaces.
Let dry overnight. To prevent flaking, spray two light coats Crystal Clear in quick succession. Let dry 10 minutes.

10. *Trim spires and roofs.* Apply dots of gold fabric paint directly from dispenser tip along edges of cathedral spires. Insert straight pin through silver and gold filigree beads and glue to top of each spire (illustration H). Attach remaining silver and gold beads to each end of church roof peak and back of cathedral roof peak. ◆

Assembling the Church and Cathedral

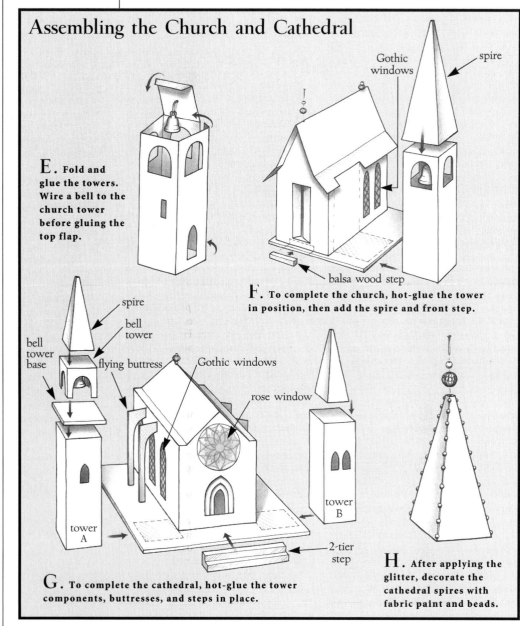

E. Fold and glue the towers. Wire a bell to the church tower before gluing the top flap.

F. To complete the church, hot-glue the tower in position, then add the spire and front step.

G. To complete the cathedral, hot-glue the tower components, buttresses, and steps in place.

H. After applying the glitter, decorate the cathedral spires with fabric paint and beads.

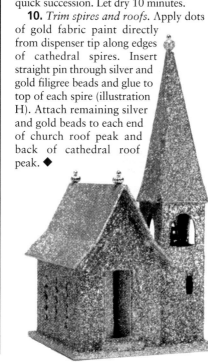

Dipped Appliqué Candles

Transform plain pillar candles into festive decorating accents using tissue paper, melted wax, and a fast coating technique.

❧ BY LILY FRANKLIN

MATERIALS

- 1 package (20 sheets) multi-colored tissue paper
- 3" x 6" white dripless paraffin pillar candle(s)
- 1 pound (4 bricks) household paraffin

You'll also need:
14" x 9½" x 2" stainless steel roasting pan with rack; 11¾" x 9¼" x 1½" disposable foil pan; corncob holders; toilet tissue; Turpenoid or other odorless turpentine substitute; very sharp scissors; paring knife; three to four flat trivets or large heat-proof cutting board (for use as work surface); newsprint; and 2"- and 1¾"-diameter jar lids or bottle caps (for cutting doughnut shapes).

Other items, if necessary: candle and matches (if using electric stove).

WORKING WITH COLORED tissue paper and paraffin wax, you can easily turn a plain white pillar candle into a unique holiday accent. When the candle is lit, the colored tissue shapes on the surface appear to glow from within.

Lily Franklin is a designer living in Albuquerque, New Mexico.

INSTRUCTIONS

1. *Cut tissue paper appliqués.* Cut shapes with scissors following directions below. Cut identical shapes from same color, layering up to 12 sheets to make multiples.

Doughnuts and circles: Layer three 3" squares of tissue and fold in quarters. Hold folded corner against center of 2"-diameter jar lid with thumb, and cut quarter arc following lid edge (*see* illustration A). Remove lid, cut second arc about ⅝" in from first, and open paper to reveal doughnuts. Cut three doughnuts using 1¾" bottle cap. Cut seven ½"-diameter circles freehand.

Square grid: Cut twelve squares each from three colors in following sizes: 1¼", ⅝", and ¼".

Vertical waves and lozenges: Cut five strips measuring 6" x 1½", then cut long edges into wavy curves. Cut twelve lozenges from three different colors.

2. *Apply tissue shapes to candle.* Protect work surface with newsprint. Moisten small wad of toilet tissue with Turpenoid (or substitute), then rub over

candle. Rewet tissue and dab onto surface until gummy. Press appliqués onto surface, then rub gently with fingertip to adhere (illustration B).

3. *Melt paraffin in double boiler.* Fill stainless steel roasting pan halfway with water so rack is covered, then set foil pan on rack. Place four paraffin bricks

in foil pan. Place double boiler across two stove burners, set burners to low, and heat 10 minutes.

4. *Roll candle in melted paraffin.* Turn off stove, then carefully remove double boiler and set on trivets. Heat corncob holder prongs for a few seconds, then push hot prongs into candle near wick and center of base. Hold candle by prongs above melted wax at back of pan. Roll candle toward you, skimming it across wax surface in one continuous motion. Coat entire circumference with wax (illustration C), then quickly hold upright for 30 seconds. Repeat entire rolling sequence. Hold candle upright for 30 seconds, then remove prongs.

5. *Finish candle.* Set candle on 2½" jar lid to elevate base off surface. Immediately smooth any rippling at lower edge with paring knife. Let set 5 minutes. To smooth over bumps and fill in holes from corn holder at top edge (near wick), dip and roll top of candle in liquid wax, then stand candle upright. Let cool at least 5 minutes more before handling. ◆

DESIGNER'S TIP

If you decide to mix and match colors, I recommend limiting the number of colors on one candle to three. More colors become difficult to coordinate successfully.

MAKING THE CANDLES

A. Cut multiples of each shape from colored paper.

B. Arrange the designs on the candle surface.

C. Hold the candle by the corncob holders and roll it in the melted wax.

COLOR PHOTOGRAPHY:
Carl Tremblay

ILLUSTRATION:
Nenad Jakesevic

STYLING:
Ritch Holben

Beaded Christmas Tree

Build this delicate evergreen using glass seed beads, then decorate it with miniature candles, candy canes, and ornaments.

❧ BY CAROL ENDLER STERBENZ

MATERIALS
Yields one 5" tree

- 2 ounces (or 260") strung size 11 green glass seed beads
- 1 ounce (or 22") strung size 11 gold glass seed beads
- 1 ounce (or 13") size 11 red glass seed beads
- 1 ounce (or 10") size 11 white glass seed beads
- 40 silver 5mm beads
- 20 silver filigree 8mm beads
- 20 white bugle beads
- 20 gold sequins
- 20 gold filigree 6mm cap beads
- 20 gold filigree 6mm cone-shaped cap beads
- ¹/₂"-high gold star
- 16-gauge stem wire
- 28-gauge spool wire
- 34-gauge beading wire
- 2"-tall plastic flower pot
- Brown florist tape
- Plaster of Paris
- Fray preventer
- White glue

You'll also need:
needle-nose pliers with built-in wire cutters; light-colored flannel or wool scrap (about 14" square); Popsicle stick; scissors; ruler; soft rag; rubbing alcohol; and small paper cup.

COLOR PHOTOGRAPHY:
Carl Tremblay

ILLUSTRATION:
Judy Love

STYLING:
Ritch Holben

This five-inch-high beaded tree is decorated with a garland and ornaments. For variation, design your own ornaments using your favorite beads.

OVER THE YEARS, I'VE SEEN beautiful Christmas trees designed from a wide range of materials including wood, fabric, and live foliage. For a fresh take on this traditional holiday icon, I decided to make a miniature five-inch tree using beads.

The tree's branches are made with glass seed beads, while the decorations—candles, candy canes, and ornaments—use assorted seed, silver, filigree, bugle, and cap beads as well as sequins. The resulting design is delicate and translucent and works equally well accompanied by miniature packages and toys or as a stand-alone decoration on a shelf or mantel.

For this project I used size 11 seed beads, which measure approximately 16 beads to the inch. Most bead stores sell seed beads by the ounce (or pound), with one ounce containing approximately 2,700 beads. The tree branches require 260 inches of strung green beads, or approximately 4,160 beads. For this project I've listed both weight and length in the materials list in case your bead store only offers the beads one way or the other. If buying the beads by weight, be sure to purchase them already strung, or you'll have to spend a great deal of time threading them on wire.

INSTRUCTIONS
Making the Beaded Branches
1. *String beads on spool wire.* Lay flannel or wool scrap on work surface to prevent loose beads from rolling. Unwind about 20" of 28-gauge wire from spool but do not cut. Transfer approximately 7" (about 112 beads) of green beads to wire, 1" to 2" at a time (*see* illustration A, next page).
2. *Make twenty-six beaded loop pieces.* Lay ruler on scrap. Press thumbnail against wire 2" from end, slide beads against it, and measure 1" segment of beads (approximately sixteen beads)

(illustration B). Bend this section back on itself to form loop, then twist twice at base to secure. Slide loose beads up to base, count off five beads, set thumbnail against wire, and measure second 1" segment (illustration C). Bend this segment into loop and twist once to secure (illustration D). Repeat process to form five loops. To secure end loop, twist twice, then use needle-nose pliers or wire cutters to clip wire 2" from twisted base (illustration E). Repeat process to make 7 additional five-loop pieces, 6 seven-loop pieces, 6 nine-loop pieces, and 6 eleven-loop pieces. For seven-loop pieces, transfer 9" (144) beads at start; for nine-loop pieces, transfer 12" (192) beads at start; for eleven-loop pieces, transfer 16" (256) beads at start.

3. *Shape branches.* For each piece, bring wire ends together, then bend entire piece in half, so middle loop forms branch tip. Grip both wire ends with pliers, twist in tight spiral, then wrap with florist tape. Do not let adhesive from tape touch beads (illustration F). To finish, give branch a half twist between each pair of loops (illustration G).

Assembling the Tree
1. *Attach branches.* Lay twenty-six completed branches on clean surface in order of size. Cut 5" length of 16-gauge stem wire and wrap with florist tape. Place five-loop branch at one end of stem wire, with wrapped stems touching, and bind with florist tape to make tree top (illustration H). Cluster 3 five-loop branches around stem ¹/₈" below first branch and bind in place with tape (illustration I). Cluster 4 five-loop branches around stem another ¹/₈" down and bind on with tape. Repeat process to bind remaining branches to stem in downward spiral about ¹/₈" apart, increasing branch size as you descend. Leave 2" of stem free at bottom (illustration J).
2. *Stand tree in base.* Mix water and plaster in paper cup following manufacturer's directions. Stir with Popsicle stick. Transfer plaster to flower pot, set tree stem in plaster, and prop until set (10 minutes). If desired, clean beads with soft rag and rubbing alcohol.

Decorating the Tree
1. *Make twenty silver filigree ball ornaments.* Use illustration K as reference. For each ornament, cut 3" length of 34-gauge beading wire. Bend wire into hairpin shape, then insert one end into stringing hole of filigree 8mm bead and second end into adjacent filigree opening. Draw both wires out opposite stringing hole, grip ends together with needle-nose pliers, and twist into tight spiral. Using needle-nose pliers or wire cutters, clip wire ¾" from top of bead and bend into hanging hook.

2. *Make forty silver bead ornaments.* Use illustration L as reference. For each ornament, cut 3" length of beading wire. Slip red or gold seed bead to middle of wire, then bend wire in half. Slip silver 5mm bead onto both wires and slide snug against seed bead. Slip gold filigree 6mm cap or cone-shaped cap onto wires, concave side down, snug against silver bead. Grip wire ends together with needle-nose pliers and twist into tight spiral. Clip ¾" from top of bead and bend into hanging hook.

3. *Make twenty candles.* Use illustration M as reference. For each candle, cut 1¾" length from spool wire. Slip red seed bead to middle of wire, then bend wire in half. Slip white bugle bead onto both wires and slide snug against red bead. Slip gold sequin onto wires, concave side first, snug against bugle bead. Separate wires, press them flat against sequin, and clip excess even with sequin edge.

4. *Make twenty candy canes.* Use illustration N as reference. For each candy cane, thread eight red and eight white seed beads alternately on spool wire; do not cut. Make L-shaped bend ½" from end, slide nearest bead into crook, then bend end parallel to main wire. Slide remaining beads over both wires, snug against first bead. At other end, wind free wire once tightly between two end beads and clip off excess. Bend into candy cane shape.

5. *Hang ornaments on tree.* Use three to four strands of gold seed beads to decorate tree. On each strand, knot both threads snug against end beads, seal with fray preventer, and let dry 24 hours. Clip excess string close to knot. Drape or glue gold strands on tree branches for garlands. Glue candles to tips of branches. Hang remaining ornaments on branches at random. Glue star to top of tree. ◆

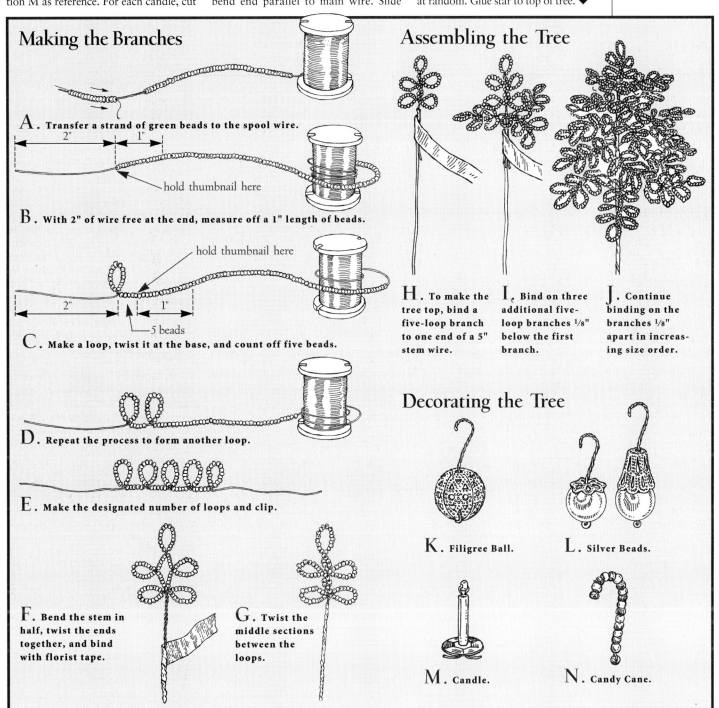

Making the Branches

A. Transfer a strand of green beads to the spool wire.

B. With 2" of wire free at the end, measure off a 1" length of beads.

hold thumbnail here

C. Make a loop, twist it at the base, and count off five beads.

5 beads

hold thumbnail here

D. Repeat the process to form another loop.

E. Make the designated number of loops and clip.

F. Bend the stem in half, twist the ends together, and bind with florist tape.

G. Twist the middle sections between the loops.

Assembling the Tree

H. To make the tree top, bind a five-loop branch to one end of a 5" stem wire.

I. Bind on three additional five-loop branches ⅛" below the first branch.

J. Continue binding on the branches ⅛" apart in increasing size order.

Decorating the Tree

K. Filigree Ball.

L. Silver Beads.

M. Candle.

N. Candy Cane.

Antique Cherub Plaque

Create your own work of art in two simple steps:
Make a mold with brush-on liquid latex, then cast your
items using a plaster substitute.

❧ BY NANCY OVERTON

MATERIALS

- **1 pair flat-backed decorative cherubs, approximately 7" across**
- **28 ounces Permastone Extra Strong Casting Medium**
- **2-ounce Deco Art Heavenly Hues Transparent Wash in any 2 shades**
- **Matte spray sealer**

You'll also need:
16 ounces ETI Mold Builder liquid latex rubber; oval disposable aluminum baking pan with bottom measuring approximately 10½" x 15½"; shallow corrugated cardboard box measuring approximately 10" x 20"; corrugated cardboard scraps; 12" x 22" piece of masonite (or other smooth-surfaced and portable panel); #10 sabeline brush; surgical gauze; scissors; 1" flat brush; aluminum foil; splash goggles; paper towels; rubber dishwashing gloves; disposable quart containers; spoon; spatula; talcum powder; vegetable oil; utility knife; masking tape; paring knife; pencil; and 1-cup wet and dry measuring cups.

COLOR PHOTOGRAPHY:
Carl Tremblay

ILLUSTRATION:
Nenad Jakesevic

STYLING:
Ritch Holben

This beautiful plaque was cast from a pair of decorative cherubs designed for use as curtain tiebacks. To create your own version of the plaque, substitute your own favorite flat-backed objects.

THIS BEAUTIFUL BAS-RELIEF PLAQUE resembles those found in antique stores or museums. I made my own version at home in just a few days using liquid latex rubber and a plaster substitute. To create an aged, antique effect on the finished plaque, I coated it with a transparent wash.

The first step in making this plaque (or any other molded frieze) involves selecting the right item for casting. I found two seven-inch cherubs in a drapery store, where they were being sold as decorative curtain tiebacks. I could have substituted a variety of other objects, but I find flat-backed objects easier to cast and easier to incorporate into a flat-backed plaque.

To make a mold from the cherubs, I used liquid latex rubber, which is excellent for picking up very small details. Using liquid latex, I can cast complex objects without worrying about how to remove the object from the newly formed mold. Once dry, the latex is very flexible and easily peeled away from the cast object.

To make the mold, I brushed liquid latex rubber over the cherub. It is important to extend the latex approximately two inches beyond the cherub in order to create a flange. When the mold is then inserted in its cardboard holder, the flange rests on the surface and gives the mold stability. Although I needed to apply ten layers of the latex rubber—with eight to ten hours of drying time in between each layer—the resulting mold can be cast many times with repeated success. (It's possible to use a hair dryer with some brands of liquid latex rubber in order to accelerate the drying time. Check the label carefully.)

Once the molds are complete, you can begin casting. I found that Permastone Extra Strong Casting Medium is stronger than plaster of Paris or Faster Plaster. Items cast from Permastone are also weatherproof in case you want to hang the plaque outdoors. If you cannot find Permastone, I've also had success with plaster substitutes such as Hydrocal.

Even with the stronger Permastone molding compound, take care when unmolding the plaster, as it is easy for delicate, protruding features such as hands or feet to break off. If this happens, you can glue them back in place using white glue. Although my instinct during the unmolding process was to handle the cherub more roughly and be more gentle with the latex mold, in reality the reverse is better. Handle the molded cherub with care and be more aggressive with the latex, as it will stretch as you move it and then spring back when released. Take care not to damage the molded cherub, as it dominates the finished plaque.

To create the plaque that surrounds the cherubs, I used a baking pan. The cast cherubs are elevated on pedestals built from cardboard squares. The pedestals lift the cherubs just high enough so that one-half inch of plaster can run beneath them, which creates their oval-shaped background.

Nancy Overton, a resident of Oakland, California, has designed products for the craft industry and written how-to books for more than twenty years.

INSTRUCTIONS

1. *Make latex molds.* Cover masonite (or substitute) with aluminum foil. Set cherubs on foil at least 5" apart. Make sure room is well ventilated and put on goggles and rubber gloves. Using flat brush, cover each cherub with thin coat liquid latex, extending onto foil for 2" all around to create flange (*see* illustration A, next page). Let dry 8 to 10 hours. Clean brush in water. Repeat to add second layer liquid latex. Let dry. Repeat process over a few days to add ten layers total, making each successive layer thicker. For final layer, lay strips of surgical gauze into latex while still wet (illustration B). Let dry 24 hours. Clean brush in water. Using dry flat brush, dust surface of each mold with talcum powder to prevent it from sticking to itself during removal. Carefully peel mold from cherub original (illustration C).

2. *Mount molds on cardboard.* Lay each cherub on floor of corrugated cardboard box and trace outline. Using a utility knife, cut out silhouette ¼" beyond traced line. Turn box over and fit each cherub mold into opening from outside of box (illustration D). Tape down flange to outside of box (illustration E).

3. *Make Permastone castings from molds.* Fill measuring cup with water. To determine mold volume, pour water from cup into mold. Repeat to fill mold to capacity. Subtract amount left in cup from the number of cups it took to fill the mold. To make two castings, mix double this amount of water with Permastone powder in disposable quart container following manufacturer's ratio and instructions. Spoon liquid Permastone into molds (illustration F) and scrape out excess with spatula. Tap box around edges of each mold to release trapped air bubbles. Let dry 1

hour, or until hard. To release castings, gently push them out of molds from underside (illustration G).

4. *Cast plaque with cherubs in relief.* Fill baking pan with water to depth of ½", then pour off and measure water. Dry pan, then grease bottom and sides with vegetable oil. Cut four or six 1" squares from corrugated scraps and stack them in pan to make two ½"-high pedestals. Position cast cherubs on pedestals, side by side in mirror image (illustration H). Using pan water measurement from above, mix Permastone in disposable quart container following manfacturer's ratio and instructions.

Spoon liquid Permastone into pan evenly all around so it just covers edges of cherubs (illustration I). Let dry 1 hour, or until hard, then carefully unmold plaque from pan. Trim edges of plaque with paring knife and remove any bumps or lumps. Let dry overnight.

5. *Apply finishes.* Using sabeline brush, cover entire plaque with transparent wash, then wipe off some color with paper towels to leave pigment in crevices. Continue adding and subtracting color in this way to achieve desired finish. Let dry 24 hours, then spray with two coats matte sealer following manufacturer's instructions and drying time. ◆

MAKING THE PLAQUE

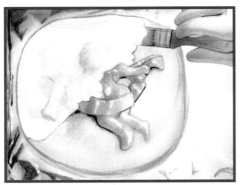

A. Brush liquid latex onto the cherub, adding layers over a period of days.

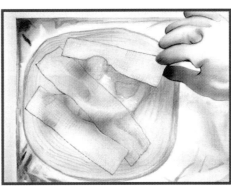

B. Stabilize the mold by pressing strips of gauze into the final latex layer.

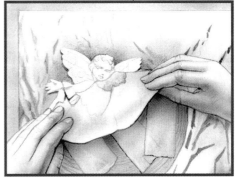

C. Let the molded latex cure for 24 hours, then peel it from the cherub.

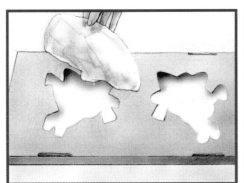

D. Insert the molds into openings cut in a shallow cardboard box.

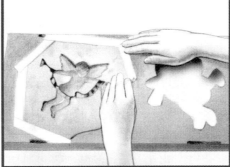

E. Tape down the mold's flange on the underside of the box.

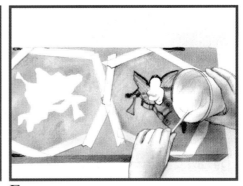

F. Spoon the molding compound into each latex mold.

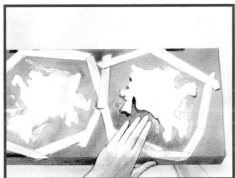

G. To release a casting, push up from the underside as you stretch the latex.

H. Elevate the cast cherubs off the floor of an oval pan using cardboard squares.

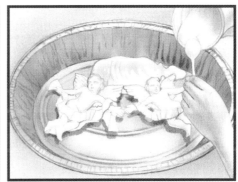

I. To create the plaque, surround the cast cherubs with molding compound.

Laminated Greeting Cards

Assemble these elegant greeting cards quickly and easily using just four basic materials.

☙ BY LILY FRANKLIN

MATERIALS
**Embossed Star
Greeting Card**
*Yields twenty 5" x 7"
cards with envelopes*

- **20 sheets 8½" x 11"
  ecru letter paper,
  plus extra sheets
  for testing**
- **20 size A-7 (5¼" x
  7¼") taupe
  envelopes**
- **1 sheet 24" x 36"
  textured white lace
  paper**
- **Spray adhesive**

You'll also need:
access to photocopier;
Season's Greetings type
(*see* next page); deckle-
edging scissors; rubber
stamp with 2½" star
motif; stamp pad with gold
ink; gold embossing pow-
der; toaster or toaster oven;
self-healing gridded cutting
mat; clear grid ruler; steel
ruler; X-Acto knife; glue
stick; pencil; scissors; newsprint; and 1 sheet 8½" x
11" plain white paper.

The skeleton card (left) uses a gold-flecked paper overlay, while the Season's Greetings version (right) lays white lace paper over an embossed gold star.

COLOR PHOTOGRAPHY:
Carl Tremblay

ILLUSTRATION:
Michael Gellatly

STYLING:
Ritch Holben

BOTH OF THESE CARDS USE VERY basic types of paper, which, on their own, are rather ordinary. When these same materials are chosen to offset one another, then layered together, however, the resulting design is both elegant and distinctive.

For both cards, I started with a stiff paper onto which I photocopied a holiday message. I next added a decorative motif such as an embossed gold star or a skeleton leaf. Last, I layered a piece of sheer paper over the greeting and the motif to unite the entire design. Changing the look and feel of the card is as simple as varying one or more of the materials.

For the Season's Greetings card, I printed and embossed a gold star on paper, then covered it with a white lace paper overlay. The metallic star glimmers through the filigree overlay, creating a subtle but tasteful effect. For the Happy New Year! card, I combined off-white paper and a skeleton leaf. The overlay, a gold-flecked paper, lets the finely veined silhouette of the leaf show through.

Although it sounds backwards, the best place to start this project is by selecting the card's envelope. The envelope size, in turn, determines the folded card size. (For the best fit, the card should measure at least one-eighth inch smaller all around than the envelope. For instance, the Embossed Star card's standard A-7 envelope measures five and one-quarter inches by seven and one-quarter inches; the finished card measures five inches by seven inches.)

After purchasing the envelope, select the decorative image, as this determines the choice of overlay paper. The skeleton leaf, for example, has a delicate and pale presence. I chose a very thin overlay paper so as not to obscure its laciness. I purchased my skeleton leaf at the wholesale flower market; in craft stores

they are seasonal, available in early fall, in sizes ranging from two to four inches. Rubber stamps are available at paper specialty stores, graphic art suppliers, and the like. If you select a rubber stamp to print your central motif, it should measure about three inches in diameter. Look for a rubber stamp with a strong, well-defined pattern, as this type of image will be legible under a textured overlay.

The easiest way to print the greeting is by running the card paper through a photocopier. To avoid excess fiddling with the copier, I recommend purchasing paper that already measures eight and one-half by eleven inches. Ecru and white papers are widely available in this size. Vellum and other more unusual papers, however, usually come in a nine-inch by twelve-inch pad form and may require trimming to fit the copier bed. If possible, test the paper in a photocopier before you purchase a large quantity. The ideal paper is stiff, yet not so thick that it cannot pass easily through the copier. Make sure the surface picks up the copier's toner and does not smear; I experimented with frosted Mylar, but it would not take the photocopier's toner.

Both of the stylized greetings used on my cards can be found on the next page. You can generate your own text, however, using a computer or by recycling text from other cards, magazine pages, or books. Although it is easiest to use complete messages that have already been typeset, you can also paste separate letters onto white paper, along the lines of a ransom note, in order to create a different look.

Lily Franklin is a designer living in Albuquerque, New Mexico.

Embossed Star Greeting Card
INSTRUCTIONS
1. *Create 5" x 7" card template.* To make card template to fit size A-7 envelope, fold sheet of 8½" x 11" paper in half crosswise, lay flat with fold at left, and lightly draft perpendicular lines 5" from folded edge and 7" from top edge, or ¼" smaller than envelope dimensions (*see* illustration A, next page). Photocopy, then cut Season's Greetings type in two pieces with X-Acto knife. Using glue stick and clear grid ruler, affix "Season's" 1¼" below top edge and "Greetings" 1¼" above bottom penciled edge (illustration B).

2. *Print cards.* Unfold template, lay face down on photocopier, and load 8½" x 11" letter paper, including extras, into paper tray. Print one copy on standard setting. If edge of message shows up as shadow, change to lighter setting and reprint until clear. When setting is correct, print twenty copies.

3. *Fold and cut cards.* Fold each printed sheet in half, type facing out, as

Printing the Cards

A. On a folded sheet of typing paper, draft a card outline 1/4" smaller than the envelope.

B. Affix the greeting type within the card area using a glue stick.

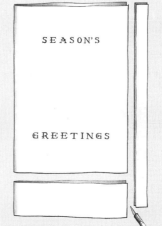

C. Photocopy twenty cards onto blank stationery, then fold each card in half and trim the edges.

Embossed Star Card

D. Use a rubber stamp and embossing powder to create a raised star on the card's front.

E. Use a light coat of spray adhesive to affix the lace paper over the star.

Skeleton Leaf Card

F. Use spray adhesive to affix a skeletonized leaf and a lace paper overlay to the card's front.

MATERIALS
Skeleton Leaf Greeting Card
Yields twenty 5¼" x 7¾" cards with envelopes

- 20 sheets 8½" x 11" off-white laid linen letter paper, plus extra sheets for testing
- 20 size A-8 (5½" x 8") parchment envelopes
- 1 sheet 24" x 36" gold-flecked mulberry lace paper
- 20 skeleton leaves approximately 3½" x 5"
- Spray adhesive

You'll also need:
access to photocopier; Happy New Year! type (*see below*); deckle-edging scissors; self-healing gridded cutting mat; clear grid ruler with centering bar; steel ruler; X-Acto knife; glue stick; pencil; scissors; newsprint; and 1 sheet 8½" x 11" plain white paper.

---

for template. With gridded mat underneath as guide, use steel ruler and X-Acto knife to trim off side and bottom edges of each card through both layers as marked (illustration C). Use deckle-edging scissors to trim right edge of each card front.

4. *Stamp and emboss star.* Emboss cards in assembly line style, first stamping star design on center of each card, then sprinkling embossing powder on top while ink is still wet (illustration D). Hold each card over heated toaster or toaster oven to activate embossing powder.

5. *Affix lace paper overlay.* Using steel ruler and X-Acto knife, cut twenty 4" x 6" overlays from lace paper. Working in well-ventilated work area, lay overlays flat on newsprint so edges do not touch, then position additional newsprint around to catch overspray. Spray overlays lightly. Affix overlays to cards by touching down one short edge so corners are square, then lower remainder of overlay onto face of card and press gently (do

not rub) with palm (illustration E).

Skeleton Leaf Greeting Card
INSTRUCTIONS
1. *Create 5¼" x 7¾" card template.* To mark card outline, fold sheet of typing paper in half crosswise, lay flat with fold at left, and lightly draft perpendicular lines 5¼" from folded edge and 7¾" from top edge. Photocopy, then cut out Happy New Year! type using X-Acto knife. Using glue stick and clear grid ruler affix type to card template 1¼" from top edge (refer to illustration A).

2. *Print cards.* Follow Embossed Star card instructions, step 2, except substitute 8½" x 11" off-white laid linen paper.

3. *Fold and cut cards.* Follow Embossed Star card instructions, step 3.

4. *Affix skeleton leaves to cards.* Lay skeleton leaves face down on newsprint and spray

lightly with adhesive, as in Embossed Star card instructions, step 5. To affix each leaf to card front, hold it in position ½" above card and touch down on surface.

5. *Affix lace paper overlay.* Using steel ruler and X-Acto knife, cut twenty 5" x 6¾" overlays from mulberry lace paper. Lay overlays flat on fresh newsprint and spray lightly with adhesive; in order to affix overlays to cards, touch down one short edge so corners are square, then lower remainder of overlay onto face of card and press gently with palm (illustration F). ◆

H A P P Y   N E W   Y E A R !
S E A S O N ' S
G R E E T I N G S

Hand-Blocked Velvet Runner

Create the look of Fortuny velvet using metallic fabric paints and a linoleum printing block.

🙠 BY JEANNE BEUTEL

MATERIALS

- **1-oz. Lumiere metallic fabric paints in the following colors: gold, silver, copper, bronze, and pearl white**
- **2 yards 44"-wide deep red rayon/silk velvet**
- **2 yards 44"-wide washable gold silk or synthetic lining fabric**
- **2 gold metallic 3" tassels**
- **Silk thread to match velvet**
- **Pattern** (*see* page 43, or substitute one of your own)

You'll also need:
4" x 6" linoleum block (or size to accommodate pattern); Speedball cutter set or handle and blades; rubber brayer; access to photocopier; carbon paper; #2 pencil; colored pencil; fine-tip permanent pen; chalk; old toothbrush; aluminum foil; cutting board; Popsicle sticks; old measuring spoons or teaspoon; mild laundry detergent; rotary cutter and cutting mat; cotton swabs; iron; cotton pressing clothes; paper towels; scissors; masking tape; sewing machine with walking foot; pins; chopstick or knitting needle; contrasting thread for basting; hand-sewing needle; and large plastic drop cloths.

COLOR PHOTOGRAPHY:
Carl Tremblay

ILLUSTRATION:
Naned Jakesevic

DIAGRAMS:
Michael Gellatly

STYLING:
Ritch Holben

I used my hand-blocked velvet to sew a 16"-x-60" table runner, though the fabric can also be used for pillow shams, shawls, or other accent pieces.

THIS ELEGANT HOLIDAY RUNNER was inspired by hand-blocked Fortuny velvet, which sells for hundreds of dollars per yard. You can simulate the look and feel of such exotic fabric for a fraction of the cost using metallic fabric paints and a linoleum printing block.

The beauty of this runner stems from two important factors: the choice of rayon/silk velvet and the use of several different metallic paint colors, which are applied randomly. Rayon/silk velvet is more expensive than most other velvets (about $20 per yard, versus $6 to $10 per yard for nylon velvet), but it shimmers and drapes more beautifully. By printing the design with multiple colors— I used gold, silver, copper, bronze, and pearl white paints—I achieved an iridescent pattern that continually changes tone as the fabric is draped, arranged, and viewed from different angles.

The process for hand blocking velvet breaks into five stages: transferring the printing design to a block of linoleum, carving the design into the block, coating the block with metallic paint, printing the design onto the fabric, and heat-setting the fabric. Once the fabric is complete, the runner can be sewn in about two hours.

The pattern I used to create the printed velvet is included on page 43. This design fits on a four-by-six-inch linoleum block. Blocks come in a wide range of sizes, ranging from two-by-two-inches (around 50¢) to nine-by-twelve inches (about $4.50), to accommodate just about any size design you might choose. If you want to substitute your own design, look in books featuring copyright-free designs. Many of these would make handsome prints and are easily adapted to linoleum block cutting.

To begin, the design lines are transferred to the block using a pencil and car-bon paper, then retraced with a fine-point permanent pen to safeguard against smearing. It's critical to determine which areas of the design will remain solid, or uncarved (these areas pick up ink), and which sections will be carved away. To keep things straight, color in the areas that will be cut away with a colored pencil. Don't skip this step—it's too easy, once you start cutting, to lose track of the overall design and cut into the wrong area by accident.

To carve my linoleum block, I purchased a Speedball cutter set for about $6. The set includes a handle and five different blades which fit into the handle. You can also purchase the handle and blades separately. When carving the block, always cut with the point of the tool facing away from your body. Use your free hand to hold the block steady, but make sure it is to the side of the blade. If the blade accidently slips and springs forward, you don't want your hand to be in its path.

Before you can print with your newly cut linoleum block, you'll need to wash and dry the velvet. (Fabric paint adheres better to fabrics whose sizing has been removed.) Use a gentle cycle, warm water, and mild laundry detergent (e.g., Ivory Snow). After washing, place the fabric in the dryer on a low heat or air-only setting for about one-half hour. The velvet may bleed, so don't wash it with any lighter fabrics, and it will shrink by about 4 percent, though I've compensated for this amount in the materials list. If desired, you can create a partial panne (crushed or flattened) effect by pressing the almost-dry velvet on the wrong side and then the right side using a pressing cloth.

For this runner, I tested two different types of "ink": Speedball water-soluble block printing inks and Lumiere metallic fabric paints. I prefer the Lumiere fabric paints, as they are available in a wider metallic color range and appear more intense on the fabric. The Speedball inks perform well technically, but the resulting colors are flatter and less exciting. In addition, the block-printing ink cannot be heat-set, which means the finished velvet cannot be washed or dry-cleaned.

It's possible to create a variety of printed effects, depending on how the paint is loaded onto the roller, or brayer. To create an ombré effect (one color fading into another), squeeze two or three paint colors side by side onto your work surface, load the brayer, and rotate the block 180 degrees after each print to change the color placement. To create color nuances or shadowy effects, make a print with a single color, then reload the block with a new color and reprint the same area. You can also use this technique to intensify an area that printed too light the first time.

Once you have printed the entire design and let the paint air-cure for twenty-four hours, you should heat-set the paints. Heat setting, usually done with an iron or a dryer, bonds the paint to the fabric permanently. All fabric paints differ slightly in their heat-setting procedures, so follow the manufacturer's instructions.

A few notes about sewing the runner: The runner's lining can be made from silk or a synthetic fabric. I used a lustrous polyester charmeuse with a silky drape. Both the lining and velvet are extremely slippery, especially when placed against one another, which makes for difficult sewing. I recommend pinning, then hand-basting, and finally machine-stitching over the basting stitches using a long stitch. If your sewing machine has a walking foot, that can also be used to discourage slipping.

Jeanne Beutel is a designer from Glen Cove, New York.

INSTRUCTIONS
Cutting the Linoleum Block

1. *Transfer pattern to linoleum block.* Photocopy pattern (page 43), then cut out along rectangular outline. Cut same size sheet from carbon paper. Lay carbon face down on linoleum block, set photocopy on top, and tape down edges. Trace all design lines with sharp #2 pencil, then remove papers. Retrace pencil lines and mark placement guideline at middle of each block edge using permanent pen.

2. *Cut design outline.* Using colored pencil and referring to pattern, color in all areas to be cut away (*see* illustration A, below). To make initial cuts, hold block steady on firm, flat surface and run cutter fitted with fine V-shaped blade along all marked lines (illustration B). To prevent paint from collecting in crevices during printing, slant blade away from uncut

Printing the Velvet

1. *Wash and press fabrics.* Machine-wash velvet on gentle cycle with mild detergent. Machine-dry on low or air-only setting 20 to 30 minutes, or until almost dry. To create panne effect, press almost-dry velvet with steam iron on wool setting, first on wrong side and then, with cotton pressing cloth, on right side. Hand-wash lining fabric, then press on appropriate iron setting.

2. *Prepare velvet for printing.* Using rotary cutter and cutting mat, cut 20" x 67" rectangle from velvet, with 67" edge parallel to selvage. (Set aside excess velvet

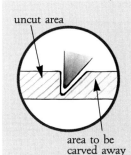

FIGURE 1
Slant the blade away from the uncut design area.

PREPARING THE LINOLEUM BLOCK

A. **Transfer the design to the linoleum block, and fill in the areas to be cut away.**

B. **Use a fine V-shaped blade to cut all the marked lines.**

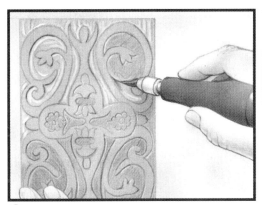

C. **Scoop out the colored pencil areas using a larger blade.**

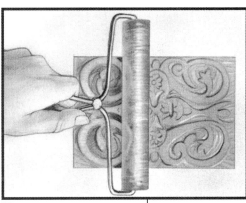

D. **Roll the paint onto the block using a rubber brayer.**

design area so that its "wall" is vertical versus sloped (figure 1). To maintain control, strive for long, slow, shallow cuts. To make corners sharp, cut into them from both directions.

3. *Cut away colored pencil areas.* Switch to larger V- or U-shaped gouge blade, then scoop out colored pencil areas, cutting deep into linoleum so no ridges remain (illustration C). Go back over design outline with larger V-gouge blade to ensure walls are deep and vertical. Whisk away any loose particles using old toothbrush.

for practicing block printing technique in step 4). Tape plastic drop cloth to work surface. Lay velvet horizontally on plastic right side up, pull it taut, and tape down edges. (Note: If large work surface is not available, tape down and print velvet in sections.) To indicate print area, mark two parallel chalk lines 16" apart along length of velvet 2" in from long edges (refer to illustration E, next page). Draw perpendicular line 2" from left edge using chalk.

3. *Load linoleum block with paint.* Lay sheet of aluminum foil across cutting

PATTERN
See page 43 for pattern.

board and fold ends to underside. Stir any color paint with Popsicle stick (or substitute), then transfer approximately 1 teaspoon to surface of aluminum foil. Roll brayer back and forth through paint until it is fully and evenly coated, then roll brayer across block surface until all raised areas are coated (illustration D, previous page). Remove any paint that runs into negative areas of cutout with cotton swabs.

4. *Print block design on velvet. Note:*

Printing the Runner

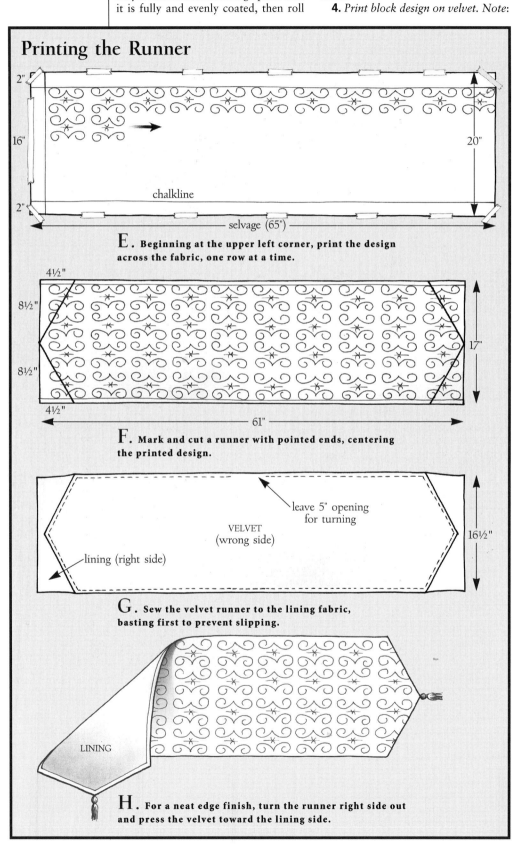

E. **Beginning at the upper left corner, print the design across the fabric, one row at a time.**

F. **Mark and cut a runner with pointed ends, centering the printed design.**

G. **Sew the velvet runner to the lining fabric, basting first to prevent slipping.**

leave 5" opening for turning

VELVET (wrong side)

lining (right side)

H. **For a neat edge finish, turn the runner right side out and press the velvet toward the lining side.**

LINING

Practice the following technique on a piece of excess velvet before printing the actual runner. Position block inside upper left chalked corner, then lower it onto velvet, apply firm even pressure to center and edges, and lift to reveal print. To make adjacent print, move block one space to right, with left edge abutting but not overlapping first print. Use guideline on edge of block to aid in centering. To vary colors, use either or both of the following methods: (a) Apply two or three paint colors side by side on aluminum foil, then load brayer and run brayer across block as usual. Rotate block 180 degrees after each print. (b) Make single-color prints, then reload block with new color and reprint same area.

Continue printing along chalk line axis to end of first row, reloading brayer with paint every two to three prints or as desired. When first row is printed, return to starting point and print adjacent row (illustration E); continue row by row until area between chalk lines is filled. When finished, wash block and brayer in warm soapy water, rinse well, and pat block crevices dry with paper towel. Clean up other paint surfaces with water.

5. *Heat-set paints.* Let printed velvet dry 24 hours. Dust off any lingering chalk lines with hand. Sandwich velvet between two cotton cloths. Using dry iron at cotton/linen setting, iron for 30 seconds on each side.

Sewing the Runner

1. *Cut runner and lining fabrics.* Using rotary cutter, cut 17" x 61" rectangle from printed velvet, with printed design centered. Mark middle of each short end, mark 4½" from corners on long edges, then cut diagonally between marks to make point at each end (illustration F). Cut 16½" x 63" rectangle from lining fabric.

2. *Assemble runner and lining.* Lay velvet and lining flat, right sides facing, and pin long edges together. Pin pointed ends of runner to lining, easing to fit. Hand-baste ½" from edge all around. Load machine with silk thread to match velvet, then machine-stitch ½" from edge all around using long stitch. Leave 5" opening on one long edge for turning runner right side out. Trim excess lining fabric even with velvet, and clip corners and points (illustration G).

3. *Finish the runner.* Turn runner right side out, and poke out corners and points using chopstick or knitting needle. Press runner on wrong side with dry iron on low setting, rolling velvet ⅛" toward lining side along each long edge (illustration H). Using silk thread, slip-stitch opening closed, then tack tassel to each point. ◆

Reversible Table Wreath

Spiral foliage around a wreath base, then suspend the wreath inside a pair of picture frames. The resulting design is viewable from either side.

✿ BY FRANCOISE HARDY

TRADITIONAL HOLIDAY WREATHS are usually displayed on a door or a wall. This wreath, in contrast, is designed for viewing from either side. It can be used in place of a centerpiece on a table or can be set on any surface that is looked at from both sides.

To make this design viewable from either side, I bound bouquets of foliage to a wreath base in a spiral pattern, concealing the base completely. To give the wreath a double-sided, boxlike border, I glued two wooden frames back to back, then suspended the wreath inside them.

I covered the seven-and-one-half-inch-diameter wreath shown here with variegated pitt. The miniature scale of the pitt leaves matches the small scale of the wreath. In addition, pitt leaves look good whether fresh or dried. This is an important consideration for a wreath such as this one, which does not contain a water supply, such as water-soaked foam. Other suitable choices include boxwood, rose leaves, eucalyptus, miniature holly, cedar, lemon leaves, and caspia.

Francoise Hardy is a Boston-based artisan and craftsperson.

INSTRUCTIONS

1. *Make wreath base.* Wind 18-gauge wire three times around container (*see* illustration A, right). Slide wire circle off container, clip wire from spool, and bind entire circle with florist tape.

2. *Assemble bouquets.* Cut pitt sprigs approximately 3" long. Gather five or six sprigs into bouquet and bind lower ½" of stems with florist tape. Repeat to make twenty-five to thirty bouquets.

3. *Bind bouquets to base.* Lay one bouquet against wreath base, then bind stem to base with 28-gauge florist wire. Position second bouquet on base so foliage overlaps stem of first bouquet, then bind stem to base (illustration B). Continue binding bouquets to base, concealing previous bouquet's stem with foliage of new bouquet. For a full, rounded wreath, spiral bouquets around base as you go. When you reach starting point, slip final bouquet's stem under foliage of first bouquet, bind securely, and clip wire.

4. *Attach wreath to frame.* Paint each frame with two coats white paint; let dry 20 minutes between coats. Cut two 7" lengths brass wire. Loop middle of wires once

For variation on this design, make several versions. You can mix and match the foliage on each wreath, or line the interior of the frames with matching giftwrap.

around wreath at top and bottom, letting free ends of wire extend. Lay one frame face down, and center wreath inside it. Staple free wire ends to outside edge of frame, pulling wire taut so wreath is suspended (illustration C). To conceal staples, glue frames back to back with wood glue. Let dry overnight before displaying. ◆

COLOR PHOTOGRAPHY:
Carl Tremblay

ILLUSTRATION:
Mary Newell DePalma

STYLING:
Ritch Holben

MATERIALS

- 150 fresh variegated pitt sprigs
- Two 10" x 10" x 1³⁄₈" wooden box-style frames
- 18-gauge florist wire
- 28-gauge florist wire
- 24-gauge brass wire
- Green florist tape
- White acrylic paint
- Wood glue

You'll also need:
4"- to 5"-diameter container (e.g., coffee can); lightweight pruning shears; wire cutters; staple gun; 1" flat brush; and ruler.

DESIGNER'S TIP

There are a few ways to prolong the display life of a wreath assembled from fresh foliage. Spritz it daily with water, taking care to protect the display surface. Avoid moving or bumping the dry wreath or exposing it to direct sunlight.

Making the Wreath

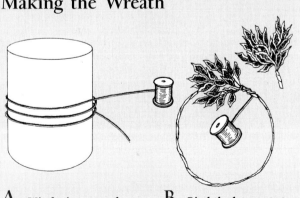

A. Wind wire around a can to shape the wreath base.

B. Bind the bouquets to the wreath base.

C. Suspend the wreath inside a pair of wooden frames.

Classic Carriage Clock

Make your own 1920s-style clock using a hinged basswood box, classic brass hardware, and faux sharkskin paper.

☙ BY MICHIO RYAN

MATERIALS

■ **26" x 40" green sha-green paper (shark-skin)**
■ **3" x 5" x 6½" bass-wood box (Walnut Hollow #3219)**
■ **2⅞" Roman clock face and works (Klockit 15134)**
■ **1.5-volt battery**
■ **Brass bail pull (Klockit 38206)**
■ **4 brass feet (Klockit 38240)**
■ **Small brass latch**
■ **Ivory spray paint**
■ **Yes glue**

You'll also need:
drill and bits; coping saw; 180-grit sandpaper; 400-grit wet-dry sandpaper; sanding block; scrap wood blocks; steel ruler; X-Acto knife with new blade; self-healing gridded cutting mat; scissors; ¾" stencil brush; newsprint; pencil; compass; tape; paper towels; spray mister; full laundry detergent bottle; thick rubber band; table knife; hammer; and screwdriver.

COLOR PHOTOGRAPHY:
Carl Tremblay

ILLUSTRATION:
Mary Newell DePalma

This classic carriage clock uses a hinged basswood box for its clock case. The box is then covered with faux sharkskin paper.

THE DESIGN OF THIS CARRIAGE clock pays homage to its early 1900s inspiration, then adds a modern twist.

The clock case is made from a hinged basswood box. I added a classic clock face with Roman numerals, and brass hardware. To update the design, I covered the clock body with faux shagreen, or sharkskin, paper. This choice is in keeping with the clock's 1920s look: During the early 1900s, genuine shagreen was dyed in many colors and veneered onto small items such as matchboxes and desk sets. The finished clock is sleek and clean, making it work with any number of decorating styles.

In designing the clock case, I needed a way to enclose the clock's quartz movement completely, both for aesthetics and to protect the clock mechanism. A basic hinged box is the least complicated and tidiest solution. I drilled a hole into the bottom (which becomes the front of the clock), then fit the back of the quartz movement into the hole.

I considered several different solutions for the clock's surface decoration. In the end, I decided on a printed sharkskin pattern. Because the sharkskin I selected is deeply embossed and has a satiny semi-gloss finish, it both complements and offsets the smooth face of the clock.

Faux sharkskin paper has a random pattern, so it can be cut anywhere and easily fitted onto panels. Before applying the sharkskin, the box must be painted. This coating (I chose ivory spray paint) protects the wood, forms a smooth surface onto which the paper can be evenly glued, and provides the pinstriping color at the edge.

INSTRUCTIONS
Marking and Cutting the Box
1. *Mark hardware position on box.* For clock face, lay box face down with hinges at right. Draft very light pencil line 2⅝" from top edge, mark midpoint, then set compass point at midpoint and scribe 2¼"-diameter circle or to match radius at back of clock face (*see* illustration A, next page). For bail pull, stand box on end with circle near top. Lightly draft centered perpendicular lines across both halves of box top surface, dividing box top into quarters. Center bail pull on longer line (on the portion of the box that will contain the clock face) and mark position with two dots. For feet, turn box over so opposite end faces up. Mark line ½" in from each edge at corners.

2. *Drill holes at markings.* To prevent wood from splitting, open box and support drilling area from behind with blocks of scrap wood. For circle, drill ½"-diameter starter hole at center using either bit, then use coping saw to saw along marked line. Drill bail pull holes with ⅛" bit and feet holes with ³⁄₃₂" bit.

Painting the Box
1. *Prepare surface for painting.* Using 180-grit sandpaper on sanding block, lightly sand all surfaces of box with grain, taking care not to round corners. Remove dust with lightly misted paper towel.

2. *Spray-paint box ivory.* Follow spray paint manufacturer's recommendations to set up painting area. Prop open box on laundry detergent bottle. Spray two to three coats ivory paint across entire outside surface and inside rims. Allow 5 to 10 minutes drying time between coats. Let dry overnight. Sand lightly with 400-grit wet-dry sandpaper on sanding block. Apply two final coats of spray paint, concentrating on edges for smooth, even finish. Let dry overnight.

Papering the Box
1. *Cut sharkskin panels.* Using ruler, X-Acto knife with new blade, and cutting mat, cut 6" x 40" strip of sharkskin, then make perpendicular cuts (at precise right angles) to yield five 6" x 8" panels. In steps that follow, position each panel so right-angle cut fits into box corner.

2. *Glue and trim back panel.* Lay one sharkskin panel face down on newsprint. Using stencil brush, apply glue in circular motion across back of panel and out beyond edges. Lay box so clock face opening faces down. Set sharkskin panel glue side down onto surface and ease into position until right-angle cut is ¹⁄₁₆" from box edges, revealing thin white band along two edges. Press sharkskin panel into position and smooth with palm. Trim opposite corner diagonally with scissors to expose sliver of white box corner beneath (illustration B). Lay steel ruler on box, aligning it ¹⁄₁₆" in from exposed corners at each end, and trim off excess side panel with X-Acto knife (illustration

B). Repeat to trim bottom edge. Wipe glue from surface and edges with lightly misted paper towel.

3. *Glue and trim top panels.* Open box and stand upright. Cut one panel in half lengthwise, then glue one piece to bail pull section, exposing thin white band around two edges as in step 2 (illustration C). Carefully poke nail tip through predrilled holes for bail pull. Turn box over, run table knife blade against box rim to lightly crease panel underside, then cut ½" beyond crease with scissors. Turn box right side up. Crease flap against inside rim, close box against flap, and secure with rubber band (illustration D). Trim panel edge as in step 2 to expose ¹⁄₁₆" white trim. Open box, clip flap corners diagonally with scissors as shown in illustration E, then glue flap onto rim and inside box. Repeat process to trim and glue second piece of sharkskin to remaining box top area.

4. *Glue and trim unhinged side panels.* Stand box hinged side down. Cut one panel in half lengthwise. Trim and glue pieces to unhinged side of box, as for top panels in step 3.

5. *Glue and trim hinged side panels.* Stand box hinged side up. Cut one panel in half lengthwise and glue one piece in position as in step 2. Trim excess ½" beyond box spine with scissors. To make cutouts around hinges, clip into flap until you reach hinge ends (a total of four clips), then run X-Acto knife along hinge barrel to connect clips. Remove cutouts, press panel flat against box, and trim remaining panel edge (illustration F). Open box, clip flap corners, slip exposed flaps to inside, and glue to box rim and interior as in step 3. Trim and glue other piece to remaining area in same way (illustration G).

6. *Glue and trim front panel.* Glue and trim front panel as for back panel, step 2. Open box, lay it face down on mat, and use X-Acto knife to cut panel to within ¼" of circumference of circle cutout. Notch this allowance every ¼" all around, then press tabs onto cutout rim. Apply additional glue to flaps if necessary. Let dry 3 hours.

Fitting the Hardware

1. *Attach latch, feet, and bail pull.* Hold box closed with rubber band, and stand so painted surface (bottom of clock) faces up. Position closed latch on box so it straddles seam, and tape down. Tap in nails to secure, then remove tape. Screw in feet at predrilled holes. Turn clock right side up and attach bail pull using nuts provided. Metal rods should extend down into box.

2. *Install clock face.* Install battery behind clock face and push clock face into circle cutout (illustration H). ◆

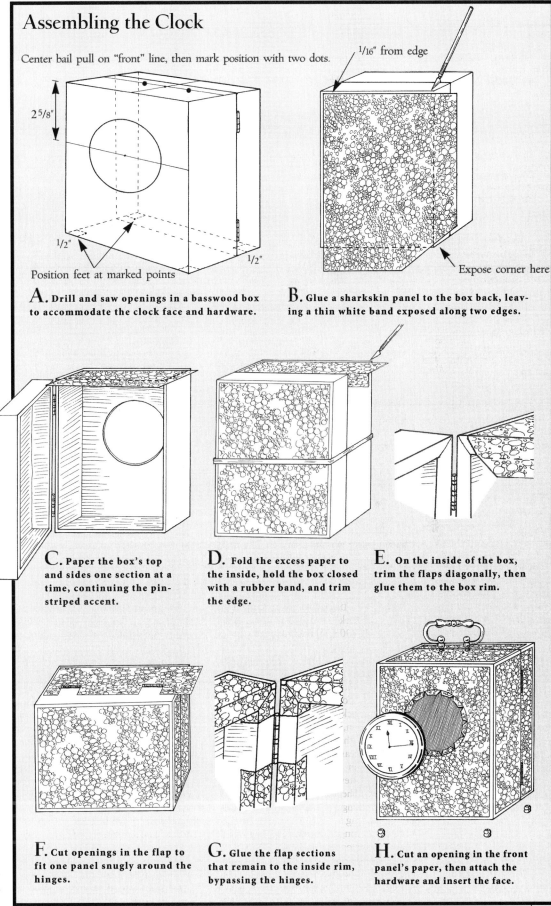

Assembling the Clock

Center bail pull on "front" line, then mark position with two dots.

2 ⁵⁄₈"

½"

½"

Position feet at marked points

A. Drill and saw openings in a basswood box to accommodate the clock face and hardware.

¹⁄₁₆" from edge

Expose corner here

B. Glue a sharkskin panel to the box back, leaving a thin white band exposed along two edges.

C. Paper the box's top and sides one section at a time, continuing the pinstriped accent.

D. Fold the excess paper to the inside, hold the box closed with a rubber band, and trim the edge.

E. On the inside of the box, trim the flaps diagonally, then glue them to the box rim.

F. Cut openings in the flap to fit one panel snugly around the hinges.

G. Glue the flap sections that remain to the inside rim, bypassing the hinges.

H. Cut an opening in the front panel's paper, then attach the hardware and insert the face.

Secrets of Making Soap at Home

Use one basic recipe and our simple technique to create your own special blends of homemade soap.

❧ BY AMY JENNER

MATERIALS
Yields about 8 pounds

Basic Recipe
- **38 ounces vegetable shortening**
- **24 ounces coconut oil**
- **24 ounces olive oil, plus 2 ounces for superfatting**
- **12 ounces lye**
- **32 ounces rain-water or distilled water**
- **4 ounces essential oil or fragrance oil**
- **Herbs, grains, nuts, flowers, spices, and dyes for color and/or texture**

You'll also need:
2 stainless steel or glass meat, dairy, or darkroom thermometers (should measure in the range of 95 to 100 degrees Fahrenheit in 2-degree delineations); 2 basins or sinks; kitchen scale (should delineate to the half ounce and go up to 3 pounds); 5-quart or larger stainless steel pot; large plastic bowl; small bowl; 2-cup glass measuring cup; 2-quart wide-mouth glass jar with cover; 2 long-handled wooden or stainless steel spoons; knife; rubber gloves; apron; newspaper; safety goggles; two coat hangers; wire cutters; large insulated picnic cooler; large cardboard shoebox; vinegar (for neutralizing lye in case of spill); small kitchen garbage bag; and cutting board.

COLOR PHOTOGRAPHY:
Carl Tremblay

ILLUSTRATION:
Nenad Jakesevic

STYLING:
Ritch Holben

To create checkerboard-style soap blocks, cut small pieces of two or more colors of soap, then layer them together and tie them with raffia.

HOMEMADE SOAP, LIKE HOME-baked bread, makes a wonderful holiday gift. A soap maker, like a cook, starts with a master "dough" recipe, then adds a variety of ingredients to change the "flavor" of the soap. To create variations on my basic white soap, I add essential oils, fragrance oils, textures, and colorants. Using this simple technique, you can replicate my tried-and-true soap recipes, or create your own special blends.

Soap has three main ingredients: water, chemicals known as alkalis (such as lye), and fats (such as vegetable shortening). The lye is dissolved in water, then combined with the fats and stirred. This activity triggers a chemical reaction called saponification, producing a mixture of soap and glycerin. The natural glycerin found in homemade soap is one of the reasons it is so soothing to the skin. Most commercial soaps do not contain it, as it is removed and sold to other industries.

To get started, you need water and lye. Because the various chemical reactions that take place during soap making are sensitive and can be affected by minerals found in hard water, I use rainwater (you can substitute distilled water). Lye, also known as sodium hydroxide or caustic soda, is available in hardware stores or by mail order from soap-making suppliers. *Lye must be used with great caution.* Although it is stable when dry, it can cause burns when mixed with water. Always wear safety glasses and rubber gloves. If you should accidentally splash yourself with lye, simply rinse in cool running water.

When the lye is dissolved in water, a chemical reaction takes place, heating the solution up to about 200 degrees. Before you can proceed with the soap-making process, this solution must be cooled to around 95 degrees. In order to cool the lye for soap making, I dissolve it in water the night before.

The soap-making process also requires fat. For my basic recipe, I use vegetable shortening, coconut oil, and olive oil. Each of these oils gives the resulting soap certain properties. Vegetable shortening produces a fine, soft variety of soap. Coconut oil (available at health foods stores) gives the soap a creamy, thick lather, and olive oil gives it moisturizing qualities.

Before the lye solution and fats are combined, the temperatures of both ingredients need to be brought simultaneously to the same temperature between 95 and 98 degrees. You'll need a pair of meat, dairy, or darkroom thermometers for this process. In order to prevent false readings, the thermometer should be suspended with a length of coat hanger in such a way that it doesn't touch the sides or bottom of the container.

Saponification (and constant stirring) turn the mixture into a creamy, yogurtlike consistency. This is the point at which the soap is "flavored," which is my favorite part of the process. For scent you can add essential oils or fragrance oil; for color you can add herbs or spices (e.g., dill, rosemary, cinnamon, clove, or turmeric) or synthetic dyes; and for texture you can add oatmeal, cornmeal, ground nuts, herbs, or broken flower parts and buds.

In addition to these ingredients, I also add extra olive oil to the soap. This technique, called superfatting, gives the soap added moisturizing qualities. The extra oil becomes suspended in the soap, making it especially rich, while at the same time mild enough for use on babies. Once complete, the soap is poured into a mold, allowed to cure, then cut into bars, squares, or other shapes.

Amy Jenner makes soap at Stoney Hill Soap Works in Groton, Massachusetts, with the help of husband Dana and three-year-old twins Blaise and Olin.

INSTRUCTIONS
Note: It is very important in soap making that all measurements are done by weight.

1. *Mix lye the night before making soap.* Set jar on scale and zero scale to subtract weight of jar. Add rainwater or distilled water to jar until scale reads 32 ounces (*see* illustration A, next page). Put on gloves, goggles, and apron. Use same method to weigh 12 ounces lye in measuring cup. Set jar with water in sink or basin. Slowly and carefully add lye to water, stir quickly to dissolve (avoid breathing fumes) with long-handled spoon, then cover quickly. Let solution stand overnight.

2. *Set up work area.* On soap-making

VARIATIONS ON THE BASIC RECIPE

LAVENDER: This mild, creamy white soap makes a good antibacterial soap for children. Add:
- 4 ounces lavender essential oil
- Small handful of lavender buds

BAY SPICE: A beautiful, dark brown, speckled variety. Add:
- 2 ounces bay essential oil
- 1½ ounces cinnamon essential oil
- ½ ounce clove essential oil
- 1 tablespoon ground cinnamon (colorant)

BAY ROSE: This recipe produces an unexpected spicy rose scent in an off-white soap. Add:
- 2 ounces bay essential oil
- 2 ounces rose fragrance oil

ALMOND AND OATMEAL COMPLEXION BAR:
I made this off-white, speckled soap in response to a request for a soap that would remove makeup. Add:
- 4 ounces almond fragrance oil
- 1 ounce ground almonds
- 1 ounce ground oatmeal
For superfatting, use 1½ ounces olive oil and ½ ounce vitamin E oil.

APHRODITE'S SPICY LOVE SOAP:
Patchouli's reputation as an aphrodisiac inspired this light brown, speckled soap. Add:
- 2 ounces patchouli essential oil
- 1 ounce Peru balsam essential oil
- 1 ounce clove essential oil
- 1 tablespoon ground clove (colorant)

CLEOPATRA'S SECRET:
This soap is creamy white with speckles. Add:
- 1 ounce noninstant milk powder
- 1 ounce honey
Mix ingredients together with superfatting olive oil in small bowl, then add 1 cup of soap from pot to mixture and blend thoroughly. Add resulting mixture back into soap.

ROSEMARY REFRESHER:
This is a beautiful green soap with the invigorating and clarifying properties of rosemary. Add:
- 4 ounces rosemary essential oil
- 2 ounces each dill weed and ground rosemary (colorants)

day, layer newspaper on kitchen counter and floor. Line shoebox with garbage bag, then set box in cooler.

3. *Test temperature of lye solution.* Put on gloves, goggles, and apron. Fill sink or basin with hot water to 4" level, set lye jar in it, and remove cover. Bend coat hanger into holder shape and use it to suspend thermometer in lye solution so that thermometer does not touch any sides of container (illustration B). Stir lye while checking thermometer reading periodically until final temperature reads between 95 and 98 degrees.

4. *Melt fats.* Weigh 38 ounces shortening in large plastic bowl using method from step 1. Place shortening in pot and heat on low setting until melted, then remove from heat. Using same technique, weigh and stir in 24 ounces coconut oil. Once coconut oil is melted, weigh and stir in 24 ounces olive oil. During final stirring, test temperature, making a wire holder as in step 3 to suspend thermometer away from all sides of pot. While being stirred, the fat's temperature should read between 95 and 98 degrees. To lower temperature, set pot in sink or basin with cool water bath. To raise temperature, set pot in hot water bath.

5. *Combine lye and fats.* Continue adjusting both temperatures until they

match exactly within 95- to 98-degree range (e.g., both read 97 degrees). Set pot with fats into empty sink or basin and put on gloves, apron, and goggles. Slowly pour lye solution into fats, stirring constantly with long-handled spoon (illustration C). Stir until solution takes on thicker, creamier quality, at least 10 minutes.

6. *Add fragrance, colorant, texture, and superfat.* Weigh 4 ounces of essential or fragrance oil and add to soap mixture. To add color or texture, remove 2 cups soap to small bowl and mix in colorant or textural ingredients. If using synthetic dye, follow manufacturer's directions. Mix colored and/or textured soap back into main pot. Stir until mixture takes on a light puddinglike consistency (illustration D), then weigh and stir in 2 additional ounces of olive oil. *Note:* Some essential oils act as a catalyst to saponification, making the soap thicken quickly. This is especially true with the spice essential oils such as bay.

7. *Mold and cure soap.* Pour mixture into shoebox (illustration E), close lid of cooler, and let cure 18 to 24 hours. Unmold finished soap onto cutting board. Turn upright and scrape soda ash from surface with knife. Cut block into cubes, bars, or sticks or hand-mold into balls as desired (illustration F). ◆

DESIGNER'S TIP

Before starting the soap-making process, it's worthwhile to check and calibrate your thermometers. To do this, fill a large glass with ice. Add water to the top of the ice and stir. Put both thermometers in the ice bath and keep stirring. They should both read 32 degrees. *Note:* Some thermometers are adjustable. After purchasing a new thermometer, I made thirty pounds of bad soap before realizing it was off by 2 degrees.

MAKING THE SOAP

A. Use a scale to measure the liquids by weight.

B. Make a coat hanger holder to check the temperature.

C. Melt the fats in a large pot, then add the lye.

D. Stir the mixture until it resembles pudding.

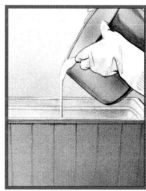
E. To mold the soap, pour it into a shoebox within a cooler.

F. Cut the soap block into individual bars.

Tasseled Ball Pillows

Assemble an endless assortment of ball-shaped pillows using one simple pattern.

❧ BY CANDIE FRANKEL

MATERIALS
Yields 3 pillows

- ¾ yard 60"-wide fabric
- 6 coordinating fabrics, 14" x 18" each
- Six 4" tassels
- 18 ounces fiberfill
- Thread to match fabrics
- Button and carpet thread

You'll also need:
ball pillow pattern (*see* page 44); access to photocopier with enlarger; sewing machine; rotary cutter; self-healing cutting mat; scissors; ruler; needle, 5" doll-making needle; seam ripper; and pins.

COLOR PHOTOGRAPHY:
Carl Tremblay

ILLUSTRATION:
Mary Newell DePalma

STYLING:
Ritch Holben

To coordinate this trio of pillows, we used a tan polka dot fabric on four panels. The remaining four panels were cut from other fabrics.

THE CONSTRUCTION OF THIS PILlow is very simple: It is sewn from eight lozenge-shaped panels that are cut using one pattern. The design's versatility comes in mixing and matching the fabrics.

For each pillow shown above, I bought three fabrics in total. For four of the eight panels I used a tan polka-dot sateen. For the four remaining panels, I selected two contrasting decorator-weight fabrics. I purposely varied the color, pattern, and texture of each pillow's fabrics. On one pillow, for example, soft graphic images are positioned side by side with the polka dot sateen. By pairing off like panels, I was able to create large blocks of color in a beach ball style.

For a busier effect with these same fabrics, I could have alternated the eight panels so that no two like fabrics ended up side by side. For less variation, I could have used similar textures, a single fabric

design in several different colors, or assorted patterns that share the same color tone. You could also mix three highly contrasting solid-colored fabrics or choose eight coordinating fabrics and cut one panel from each. Moving in a different direction, imagine the pillow sewn from a solid-colored fabric, such as a plush velvet, with contrasting tassels. With this one-panel technique, the design configurations are virtually endless.

To ensure that my pillows worked together as a set, I made the tan polka-dot fabric a constant in all three. There are other ways to coordinate the pillows: You could use the same tassels or repeat different colors of a patterned fabric.

No matter what fabric configuration you choose, most ball pillow designs require that the panels be cut on the bias. This cutting direction allows more all-around give, or stretch, along the seams, which enhances the rounded, globelike

form. You may find, however, that certain fabrics need to be cut on the straight grain in order to present the pattern a certain way. The harlequin diamonds used on one of my pillows, for instance, presented this problem. The diamonds are more dramatic viewed straight on, meaning the panels could not be cut on the bias. You can still make your pillow using this type of fabric, but be aware that the straight grain pieces will not have the same give as those cut on the bias, and the pillow will not have the same overall roundness. On the harlequin pillow, the diamond fabric "bumps out" slightly near the ends whereas the bias-cut pieces lie flatter and smoother. To mask this slight tendency, I ran button and carpet thread through the pillow and back, cinching the entire ball and lightly dimpling the ends.

INSTRUCTIONS

1. *Prepare ball pillow pattern.* Photocopy pattern (*see* page 44), enlarging it to measure 14" from tip to tip. (When enlarged, the pattern should fit diagonally on an 8½" x 14" piece of paper). Cut out pattern with scissors.

2. *Cut and sort fabric pieces.* Lay main fabric yardage face up on cutting mat. Following layout diagram (*see* next page), pin pattern to fabric on bias and cut out with rotary cutter. Repeat to cut twelve pieces total. Then repeat to cut two pieces from each of six coordinating fabrics. Divide main fabric pieces into three groups of four. To complete palette for each pillow, select and add two pairs of coordinating fabrics (four pieces) to each group for a total of eight pieces.

3. *Sew pairs together.* For each pillow, staystitch any two matching pieces ½" from one curved edge between dots (*see* illustration A, next page). Stack pieces right sides together so staystitching matches, then stitch from dots out to ends. Reinforce these short seams by stitching again ⅜" from edge (illustration B). Stack remaining pieces in pairs and staystitch ½" from one edge, then stitch again ⅜" from edge (illustration C).

4. *Assemble pillow.* For each pillow, sew four pairs together so fabrics alternate beach ball–style. Stitch and reinforce seams, as in step 3 (illustration D).

5. *Insert fiberfill.* Turn pillow cover right side out. Insert fiberfill through opening until ball is well rounded. Slipstitch opening closed (illustration E).

6. *Cinch pillow and attach tassels.* Using doll-making needle, draw button and carpet thread through center of pillow and back (illustration F). Pull thread ends lightly to cinch pillow, then tie off. Use seam ripper to poke tassel cord into each dimpled end, then hand-tack to secure (illustration G). ◆

Layout Diagram

grain

60"

27"

Sewing the Ball Pillow

A. Staystitch two matching pieces between the dots.

B. Sew the pieces together, but leave the staystitched section open. Reinforce the seams.

C. Join the three remaining pairs and staystitch along one edge. Then add a second row of stitching for reinforcement.

D. Sew all four pairs together beach ball–style.

E. Turn the pillow right side out, stuff it with fiberfill, and sew the pillow closed.

F. Draw carpet thread through the ball and back, pull it lightly to cinch, and tie it off.

G. Tack a tassel to each dimpled end.

STAYSTITCH DEFINED

A row of directional machine stitching, usually placed just inside the seam line, to prevent curved or sloped fabric edges from stretching out of shape. In the ball pillow, the staystitching also helps you keep a neat edge when slip-stitching the pillow closed.

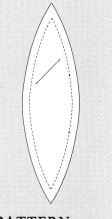

PATTERN

See **page 44** for pattern and enlargement instructions.

DESIGNER'S TIP

This is a good project for using up leftover fabric from larger decorating projects. Fabric left over from sewing draperies may not be sufficient to make a full pillow, for instance, but you might be able to work your scraps into a ball pillow.

Faux Limoges Hinged Boxes

Create your own Limoges reproductions using heat-set modeling clay and china paints. Finishing details, such as hinges and metal rims, complete the illusion.

&❧ BY LILY FRANKLIN

COLOR PHOTOGRAPHY:
Carl Tremblay

ILLUSTRATION:
Mary Newell DePalma

STYLING:
Ritch Holben

These Limoges reproductions can be used as tiny keepsake boxes, much in the same way authentic Limoges boxes are used.

MATERIALS

■ **Sculpey Promat (about 2 ounces per fruit)**
■ **1 ounce Duncan non-firing acrylic stains in the following colors*:**
Lime:
  Green Olive NT 040
  Medium Green OS 463
  Cinnamon OS 481
Peach:
  French Vanilla OS 485
  Pumpkin NT 063
  Boysenberry NT 027
  Cinnamon OS 481
Pear:
  Yellow Haze NT 061
  Camel NT 034
  Cocoa Brown NT 019

■ **Sculpey Glaze #33 Gloss**
■ **½" x ½" brass hinge(s)**
■ **Narrow flat brass wire or metallic cord (about 6" per fruit)**

* **OS numbers are opaque stains; NT numbers are "natural touch drybrushing acrylic."**

You'll also need:
1¼"-diameter wooden balls (one per fruit); cookie sheet; clay sculpting tools; needle-nose pliers; metal nail file; 400-grit wet-dry emery paper; X-Acto knife; nylon round, stippling, and fine-tipped brushes; old toothbrush; plastic palette; paper towels; cellulose sponge; dinner plate; granulated sugar; dark-colored polyester thread; cyanoacrylic glue; and laundry detergent bottle.

Other items, if necessary:
broomstick (to preshape brass wire).

P URCHASED IN THIS COUNTRY, AN authentic porcelain Limoges box might cost upwards of $200. Inspired by their design, I created these fruit reproductions using heat-set resin clay and china paints. Though the pear, lime, and peach designs could never pass for real Limoges, their lifelike coloring, hinged cavities, and wire-trimmed edges make them an easy make-at-home reproduction.

To mimic the look and feel of Limoges effectively, I needed a thermo-set resin polymer clay resembling porcelain, and a type of paint to create the effect of hand-painted china. After testing a number of different products, I chose Sculpey Promat modeling clay, which is a brilliant white color but warm in tone, most like bone china. For the painting steps, I settled on Duncan non-firing acrylic stains.

The design of the hinged fruit was a bit more complicated. Although it was fairly easy to form a solid clay fruit shape using Promat, it was very hard to render a hollow shape out of the clay, which is extremely soft. It was also nearly impossible to line up the rims without deforming the shape beyond recognition, and I would have had to file or sand them after heat setting for an accurate fit. I also tried using a small plastic piece of fruit as a press-mold, but the clay stuck to the plastic. In the end, I molded each fruit around a solid wooden ball, then shaped it individually. After heat setting, the ball is removed, leaving a hollow vacancy. (The fruit can be baked with the wooden core still inside because resin clay shrinks very little, if at all, and sets at a relatively low temperature as compared to ceramic clay. Do not substitute a plastic ball for the

wooden one, or it will melt during the heat-setting process.)

Once the fruit shapes are formed around the core, they need to be cut into two halves, which become the box's lid and base. I first tried using a sharp knife to circumscribe the shape around the equator of the fruit, but it was nearly impossible to make a perfectly level cut. Instead, I wrapped a thread around the waist of the fruit one and a half times, then pulled it taut for a clean and precise cut. This is best done shortly after the fruit is formed, while the clay is still soft.

To attach the two halves of the fruit, I used a tiny metal hinge, such as those sold with box-making supplies. The hinge is best installed when the clay is still soft, as this approach requires less work. Once the fruits have been heat-set—a simple process that takes place in your oven—and allowed to cool, the surfaces can be sanded and filed to remove any dents or fingerprints. The transparent china paints will show every surface defect, so be sure to prepare the surface carefully.

A few tips on working with Sculpey Promat. Work on a smooth surface when rolling and pressing the clay. I used an acrylic cutting board, but you could also use a dinner plate or a smooth countertop. It is very important that the surface, and your hands, be very clean. Otherwise, spots of trapped dirt or other material will discolor the white clay. To minimize dents while forming the shapes, hold the fruit loosely in the palm of one hand while using the fingers of the other hand or a separate tool.

The key to creating a realistic effect is to layer the colors of paint, applying them with different textural methods. The techniques I used include sponging and ragging, which leaves mottled patterns, and stippling, which leaves tiny flecks, such as the spots on a pear. I also used some detail painting with a fine-tipped brush to accent the stems.

The metal rim and clasp found on authentic Limoge boxes were difficult to reproduce. In the originals such parts are made of finely wrought metal, which is difficult to simulate, and then soldered together, which is not an option for at-

INSTRUCTIONS

1. *Make basic clay ball.* Knead 2 ounces Sculpey Promat until soft. Roll clay into 1½"-diameter ball, then press thumb into ball to form bowl. Insert wooden ball into bowl and manipulate clay until ball is completely covered with clay (*see* illustration A, below).

2. *Form fruit.* Model each fruit individually as directed below, then proceed right to steps 3 and 4 while clay is still soft. Bake all fruits together (step 5).

Lime: Pinch opposite ends of ball (illustration B) to make two points, then press points against palm to dull and

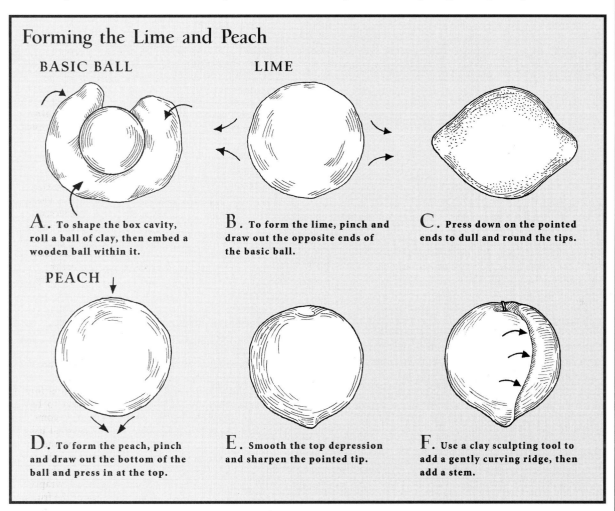

Forming the Lime and Peach

BASIC BALL

A. To shape the box cavity, roll a ball of clay, then embed a wooden ball within it.

LIME

B. To form the lime, pinch and draw out the opposite ends of the basic ball.

C. Press down on the pointed ends to dull and round the tips.

PEACH

D. To form the peach, pinch and draw out the bottom of the ball and press in at the top.

E. Smooth the top depression and sharpen the pointed tip.

F. Use a clay sculpting tool to add a gently curving ridge, then add a stem.

Painting and Finishing the Fruit

The secret to simulating the look of hand-painted china lies in the transparency of acrylic china stains. The paint is not thinned before application, but rather applied full strength and then selectively removed. Because the surface of thermo-set clay is nearly impervious, applying thinned paint only produces runoff, as opposed to the nice transparent wash color you could create by applying thinned paint to plaster of Paris.

Each fruit has a different color story.

home crafts. In the end, I left off the clasp and settled for a rim made of narrow flat brass wire attached with cyano-acrylic glue (Super Glue). You could also use metallic cord. I considered embedding the wire rims in the soft clay before heat-setting, just as with the hinges. This proved too difficult, however, because the wire cut into the soft clay too easily while being positioned, destroying the delicate rim.

Lily Franklin is a designer living in Albuquerque, New Mexico.

swell tips (illustration C). Carefully press lime against plate at 45-degree angle to flatten one side for base. Use fingers to press ⅛"-thick layer of granulated sugar into surface to create dimpled texture.

Peach: Pinch bottom of ball, then press in on opposite end to form dimple (illustration D). Smooth dimple so rim curves gently into sides of fruit and sharpen point so overall fruit resembles a peach (illustration E). Using flat-edged sculpting tool, imprint arching crease from top dimple down side of fruit, ending in whorling dent at bottom tip. To accentuate crease, press in along one side so edge swells out, then smooth ridges to round out swells. Roll small bit of clay to resemble rice grain and press into dimple for stem (illustration F).

Pear: Knead and roll ½"-diameter ball until very soft, then press onto basic clay ball (illustration G). Smooth join, and taper and tilt appendage slightly to one side to form pear shape (illustration H). Taper bottom half of pear, then press thumb into cone point to create dimple about ½" wide and ⅛" deep. Press dim-

through slowly until it comes clean.

4. *Embed hinge in fruit.* Mark hinge position at back of fruit along sliced line. Carefully lift up top hemisphere of fruit, leaving wooden ball lodged in bottom half of fruit. Open hinge 60 degrees and push lower half of hinge into bottom hemisphere of fruit at 30-degree angle until hinge spine lodges against rim of fruit. Push top hemisphere onto other half of hinge, then lower top hemisphere of fruit back onto ball. Smooth clay around hinge flanges (illustration K).

6. *Paint individual fruits.* Using nylon brushes, apply Duncan china paints/stains to fruit surface, then sponge off or manipulate colors as directed below. Prop each fruit open on laundry detergent bottle for initial coats but close it for final sponging or stippling across crack. Mix colors in plastic palette.

To create loose stippled effect, moisten stippling brush with paint, dab excess on paper towel until bristles are almost dry, then tamp on fruit surface. For coarse stippling, load stippling brush or toothbrush (for more extreme effect) with paint, then draw fingertip across bristles to spatter paint onto fruit. When done, let paints dry 30 minutes.

Lime: Using round brush, paint entire surface and inside rims with Medium Green, then blot with damp sponge to lighten texture. Apply loose stipple with Green Olive paint and stippling brush, then blot lightly. Using fine-tipped brush, mix 1 drop each Green Olive and Cinnamon, then paint five-pointed star at top for stem nub.

Peach: Using round brush, paint entire surface and inside rims with French Vanilla. To suggest sun ripening, apply Pumpkin in coarse stipple over fruit surface using stippling brush, then use damp sponge to blot up Pumpkin and expose French Vanilla on "shade" side of fruit. Mix 1 drop each Boysenberry and Cinnamon and brush over sun-exposed side. Smooth and blend edges with sponge, then streak off color by running dry crumpled paper towel across wet surface. Repeat to intensify blush.

Pear: Using round brush, paint entire surface and inside rims with Yellow Haze, then blot with sponge for soft mottling. To suggest sun ripening, brush Camel on one side of fruit, from bottom to crown. Feather edges with dry brush, then dab with dry crumpled paper towel to soften and blend color. Apply coarse stippling using stippling brush or toothbrush and Cocoa Brown as desired. While paint is still wet, press sponge onto surface to soften stipples. Using fine-tipped brush and Cocoa Brown, paint stem and five-pointed star at base.

7. *Apply glaze.* Prop fruit open on detergent bottle. Using round brush, apply two thin coats Sculpey Glaze to outer surface, working each half separately. Let dry 20 minutes between coats.

8. *Apply rims.* If using wire, preshape it by winding it tightly around broomstick, then let it spring open. For each fruit, cut two wire or cord lengths to fit around each rim, beginning and ending at hinge. Bend wire by hand to fit curves of each fruit's two rims. Use needle-nose pliers to crease peach rim to match crease. Following manufacturer's instructions, affix wire or cord to rim using cyanoacrylic glue. ◆

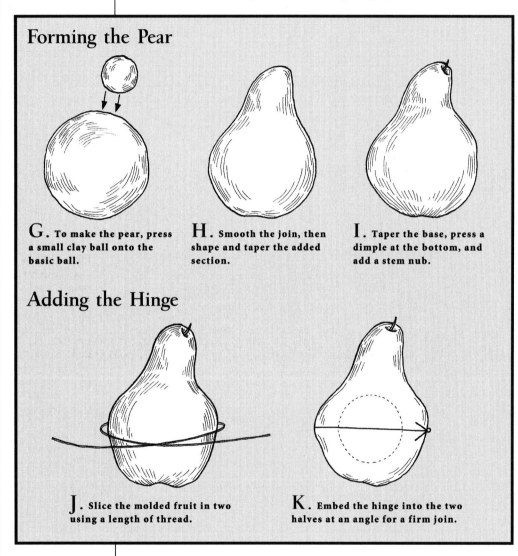

Forming the Pear

G. To make the pear, press a small clay ball onto the basic ball.

H. Smooth the join, then shape and taper the added section.

I. Taper the base, press a dimple at the bottom, and add a stem nub.

Adding the Hinge

J. Slice the molded fruit in two using a length of thread.

K. Embed the hinge into the two halves at an angle for a firm join.

pled end onto plate to flatten base so pear stands upright. Use round-pointed sculpting tool to make small dimple in very top appendage. Roll small bit of clay to resemble rice grain and set into dimple for stem (illustration I).

3. *Slice fruits with thread.* Wrap length of polyester thread around waist of each fruit one and one-half times, then pull thread ends gently in opposite directions, cinching through clay until you reach wood core (illustration J). To remove thread, release one end and pull other end

5. *Bake fruit in oven.* Preheat oven to 275 degrees. Place fruit on cookie sheet, set in oven, and bake 30 to 45 minutes. Remove from oven. Let cool 20 to 30 minutes, or until moderately warm. Gently separate two halves of fruit, slicing through stuck areas with X-Acto knife. Take care not to twist or distort the fruit. Check hinge operation and trim or file clay that prevents easy movement. When completely cool, sand or file off fingerprints and blemishes. If hinge is loose, inject cyanoacrylic glue into join from inside box.

Festive Country Stripe Cupboard

Turn an ordinary wooden shelf into a distinctive holiday decoration with painted red stripes and subtle gold accents.

❧ BY FRANCOISE HARDY

MATERIALS

- **Wooden cupboard or shelf**
- **2-ounce containers acrylic paint: 3 containers in base coat color 1 container in stripe color**
- **Sanding sealer**

You'll also need:
¾"-wide masking tape; 1½"-wide paintbrush; 1"-wide flat bristle brush; 150-grit sandpaper; saucer or plastic lid; ruler, tape measure, or yardstick; scissors; wide craft stick; gold marker; pencil; paper towel; and plant mister.

Other items, if necessary: screwdriver and wood glue (for removing and re-attaching knobs/pegs).

ONE OF MY FAVORITE TRADItions at Christmastime involves unpacking the special decorations that get used only once a year. In the same spirit, I decided to create a striped cupboard that can be used during the holidays.

The cupboard I purchased had a distressed green finish. (You can also use unfinished pieces for this project.) I used strips of masking tape to add red stripes, then looked for a way to further decorate the piece. In the end, I opted for very thin gold stripes, applied with a gold marker. The finished cupboard is neat but not fussy with a festive folk art charm.

Francoise Hardy is a Boston-based artisan and craftsperson.

INSTRUCTIONS

1. *Prepare cupboard surface.* Sand cupboard, pegs, and knobs with 150-grit sandpaper and wipe with lightly misted paper towel. Apply one coat sanding sealer using 1½"-wide brush and let dry overnight. Sand lightly and wipe. Repeat two more times, for three sealer coats total.

2. *Paint base coat.* Remove all knobs and pegs or protect with tape. Squeeze small amount base coat paint in saucer or lid as needed. Using 1"-wide brush, apply paint evenly over entire surface of cupboard, brushing with grain. Paint knobs and pegs. Let all pieces dry 1 hour. Apply second coat to all pieces. Let dry 24 hours. Clean up brush and paint supplies in water.

3. *Apply tape for striping.* Mask off horizontal front edge of cupboard top with long strip of tape. Mark middle of horizontal front edge, then make two additional marks ⅜" to each side of middle mark. Lay strip of tape between marks so it crosses top from front to back. Mark and lay more tape along middle of shelf/drawer facade, then along peg board. Apply new tape alongside middle strip so edges align. Repeat to tape remaining cupboard and other sections (*see* illustration A, right).

4. *Expose area for painting.* On each section of cupboard, peel up and discard middle strip of tape. Remove every other strip of tape until stripe

This wall-mounted shelf features a weathered green finish. The red stripes were added using DecoArt Americana cadmium red acrylic paint.

pattern emerges (illustration B). Using craft stick, press down edges of all remaining strips of tape. Mask off any areas (e.g., cupboard rims and side edges) that will not have stripes.

5. *Paint stripes.* Squeeze small amount of stripe paint in saucer as needed. Using 1"-wide brush, brush paint onto exposed areas between tape strips (illustration C).

Let dry 5 minutes, then apply second coat. Let dry 10 minutes, then peel up tape (illustration D). Let cupboard dry 24 hours. Clean up brush and paint supplies in water.

6. *Add finishing touches.* Add thin gold stripes between larger stripes using marker. Reattach knobs and pegs using screwdriver and/or wood glue. ◆

DESIGNER'S TIP

If you want very crisp lines on your stripes, use an X-Acto knife and a steel-edge ruler to cut a shallow groove along the tape's edge. The groove will prevent the paint from seeping under the tape.

COLOR PHOTOGRAPHY:
Carl Tremblay

ILLUSTRATION:
Nenad Jakesevic

STYLING:
Ritch Holben

PAINTING THE CUPBOARD

A. Cover the entire cupboard with tape.

B. Peel up every other strip of tape.

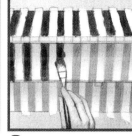

C. Paint the areas between the tape strips.

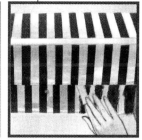

D. Peel up all the remaining pieces of tape.

Framed Shadow Box

This sophisticated display case uses a molded picture frame for its outside edge and a swath of metallic fabric to create a three-dimensional backdrop.

❧ BY MICHIO RYAN

COLOR PHOTOGRAPHY:
Carl Tremblay

ILLUSTRATION:
Michael Gellatly

STYLING:
Ritch Holben

To suspend hanging items such as ornaments in your shadow box, tie each one with a colorful ribbon, then hang them from a screw eye attached to the box's interior.

S HADOW BOXES COME IN MANY styles and sizes. To create this sophisticated version, I used a molded gold picture frame on the front and lined the box's interior with metallic voile. The frame's decorative molding gives the box a dressy feel, and the gauzy, lightweight fabric creates a three-dimensional backdrop for my collection of glass ornaments.

You can build this shadow box with minimal carpentry skills. The picture frame is attached to the box using Velcro strips. The box's sides and back are built from basswood and chipboard, respectively. You can assemble the entire box in a day's time.

My ready-made picture frame measures eleven by fourteen inches and costs about $28. This medium-size frame is appropriate for any number of col-

lectibles. The size of the frame (and the resulting box) can be easily adjusted, however, to suit a specific collection. The frame I selected features two-inch-wide molding. The width is important not only for its visual impact but because it makes the frame and the shadow box sturdier. To make a box with different dimensions, adjust the frame molding size accordingly and follow the instructions in "Making the Box," step 1.

To complete the box, I needed sides and a back. You can use a wooden tray, an unused drawer, an existing box, or even a ready-made shadow box with a plain frame. Whatever you choose, the box should be rigid, have four smooth rims, and be deep enough to hold your collection without crowding it. For a four-by-six-inch frame, a cigar box is probably sturdy enough, but for an

eleven-by-fourteen-inch frame, the side panels should be at least one-quarter inch thick. Given these requirements, I could not find exactly what I needed, so I decided to build a basic butt-joined box. If you find a ready-made item that meets the above-mentioned criteria, simply skip the box-building steps.

Basswood, which I selected for the box sides, is used for building architectural models. It is precisely cut, resin-free, smooth-grained, and soft enough to cut and sand by hand. Although it is more expensive than pine, this project calls for relatively small pieces, making the extra expense minimal. Basswood can be found on model-making and craft store shelves next to balsa wood, which is extremely light and fragile and should *not* be used for this project.

Basswood is available in a range of thicknesses at one-eighth-inch increments. I used three-eighths-inch-thick pieces for this project. A frame that is any larger than eleven by fourteen inches should use one-half-inch-thick pieces, and ones smaller than six by eight inches should use wood that is one-quarter inch thick. If you plan to display heavy objects, such as clocks or large porcelain items, I recommend using five-eighths-inch-thick (or thicker) basswood or one-half-inch-thick pine.

For the back of the box, I chose three-ply chipboard. Unlike plywood, which must be cut with a saw, chipboard can be cut with a utility knife. It is also less expensive than plywood and available in large sheets, which basswood is not.

Finishing the Box

To make the basic box more sophisticated, I painted it gold with alkyd spray paint. Because alkyd spray paint does not contain water, it will not warp the wood, a good reason to avoid brush-on acrylics. It also forms a better bonding surface for the self-stick Velcro strips, which are used to attach the picture frame to the sides of the box.

Next, I covered a piece of foamcore with green moiré and inserted it into the

back of the box. This addition gives the box's interior a finished, upholstered feel. It also doubles as a place to pin lighter-weight items such as letters, photographs, or textiles. If you want to suspend items such as ornaments, as I did, you'll also need to twist small screw eyes into the box's inside upper wall.

Last, I purchased a three-quarters-yard length of metallic voile. I draped this gauzy, lightweight fabric inside the box to give it a three-dimensional backdrop. The fabric also unifies the design by creating a smooth transition from the frame to the collection. You can select voile that matches the color of the shadow box for a unified and seamless design or use a complementary color. A very light, metallic color will reflect light back out onto the displayed items; a very dark color, on the other hand, will create a floating shadow box effect. The shadow box can

be "restyled" easily (e.g., if the display is being changed) by inserting a different color of gauzy fabric.

The glass that comes with the picture frame protects the shadow box contents. Inset the glass into the frame's rabbet and tack it in place with three-quarters-inch brads or glazier points.

INSTRUCTIONS
Making the Box

1. *Cut box sides, back, and foamcore insert.* Remove glass, if any, from frame and set aside. Lay frame face down, measure length (L) and width (W) extending across flat surface of frame back, and jot down figures (*see* illustration A, below). Use those figures to make the following calculations: Mark and saw two basswood sides for box where length equals L minus ½" and two sides where length equals W minus 1¼". On chipboard,

Making the Shadow Box

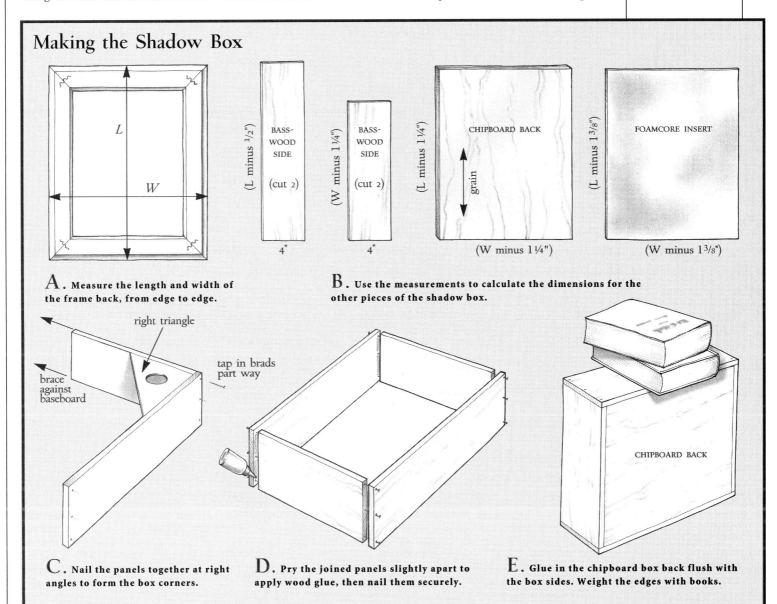

A. Measure the length and width of the frame back, from edge to edge.

B. Use the measurements to calculate the dimensions for the other pieces of the shadow box.

C. Nail the panels together at right angles to form the box corners.

D. Pry the joined panels slightly apart to apply wood glue, then nail them securely.

E. Glue in the chipboard box back flush with the box sides. Weight the edges with books.

ADDING SHELVES TO THE SHADOW BOX

Although this shadow box was not designed with shelves, it is not difficult to add them. To make the shelves, use basswood that is anywhere from one-half inch to three-quarters inch narrower than that of the box's sides; this will set the shelves back somewhat from the face of the box, as in a glass-fronted cabinet. The shelves should be cut exactly the same length as the top and bottom pieces of the box, as they will be butt-jointed in the same manner, much like rungs on a ladder.

Mark the shelves' locations with pencil on the side pieces before assembling the box. Construct the box first, including the chipboard backing, then insert the shelf pieces and nail them into place both at their ends (through the side walls of the box) and through their back edge (through the chipboard backing).

draft box back measuring (L minus 1¼") x (W minus 1¼"); run longer edge along grain. On foamcore, draft insert measuring (L minus 1⅜") x (W minus 1⅜"). Use utility knife and ruler to score and cut out chipboard back and foamcore insert (illustration B).

2. *Assemble box sides.* Lay longer basswood box sides flat and hammer three brads partway into each end (illustration C, previous page). Working on floor, stand

joints apart slightly, apply bead of wood glue along each exposed edge, then hammer brads through to join panels securely (illustration D). Countersink nailheads, then wipe oozing glue with damp sponge.

3. *Glue in chipboard back.* Stand box upright on one long side. Apply bead of tacky glue to inside back edge of box and outer edge of chipboard back. Carefully set chipboard in position, flush with box rim. Make sure rim touches chipboard all around, then weight evenly from above with two lightweight books. Let set ½ hour (illustration E).

4. *Spray-paint box.* Sand box sides lightly with 180-grit sandpaper, then wipe off dust using damp paper towel. Raise box off work surface by placing four small blocks under corners. Following manufacturer's instructions, apply spray primer inside and out, and let dry. Resand box sides very lightly with 220-grit wet-dry sandpaper. Apply two gold spray finish coats, letting paint dry between coats per manufacturer's recommendations. If necessary, prime and spray frame to match box. Let all pieces dry overnight.

Lining and Filling the Box

1. *Cover foamcore insert.* Press moiré to remove wrinkles, then lay face down. Set foamcore insert on top, then cut moiré 2" beyond edges all around. Apply bead of

down, center box face down on frame, and trace around box rim with pencil. Set box face up. Press Velcro "hook" and "loop" tapes together, cut in half lengthwise with scissors, then cut four lengths to fit around box rim. For each length, pull tape halves apart and remove adhesive backing. Affix hook tape to box rim and loop tape to corresponding area on back of frame, along marked rim line (illustration F).

3. *Add insert and voile.* Set insert, fabric side up, into box and press down against box back. Lay voile flat, set box on top, and cut voile 3" beyond box edges all around. Press voile lightly to remove wrinkles, then set it face up inside box. Lift and press one edge at a time onto a few Velcro "hooks" of box rim, overhanging it by 1"; manipulate edge into loose folds to finesse fit. When all edges are attached, trim off excess allowance even with box rim (illustration G). Rumple loose fabric to distribute it inside box.

4. *Add glass and mounting hardware.* Set frame face down, insert glass panel into rabbet, and bend down prongs to hold it in place. If no prongs are present, use needle-nose pliers to insert eight glazier points 3" in from each corner. Attach two serrated picture hangers to back of box 2" to 3" from top corners. Anchor corresponding screws in wall.

Lining and Filling the Box

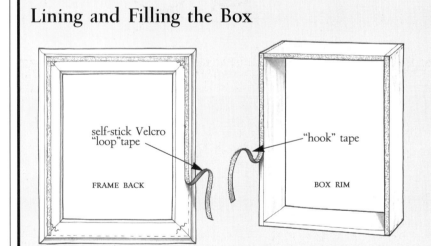

self-stick Velcro "loop" tape

FRAME BACK

"hook" tape

BOX RIM

F. Affix self-stick Velcro "loop" tape to the back of the frame and "hook" tape to the box rim.

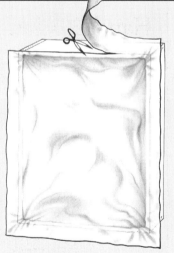

G. Pad the inside back of the box with fabric-covered foamcore, then drape voile on top.

one short and one long basswood side on edge, perpendicular to floor and each other, to form L shape. Brace free end of shorter box side against baseboard, then tap brads partway into opposite end (illustration C). Double-check angle with right triangle and adjust if necessary. Join remaining short panel, then remaining long panel in same way to form box sides. Pry

tacky glue ¼" in from foamcore edges all around and smooth with fingertip. Fold corners of fabric diagonally onto foamcore, tape down, then fold over and tape sides. Turn foamcore over and examine moiré; fabric should be taut and firm. Adjust tape on back if necessary. Weight and let dry ½ hour; do not remove tape.

2. *Attach Velcro strips.* Lay frame face

5. *Set up display.* Work with box mounted on wall or flat on tabletop, whichever is easier. Arrange collection collage-style, using pins to secure items to foamcore insert, or hang items from cords and twist small screw eyes into inside upper wall. When arrangement is complete, press frame into place so Velcro strips bond. ◆

Christmas 1996 Patterns

Embossed Tree Ornaments

(*see* article, page 12)

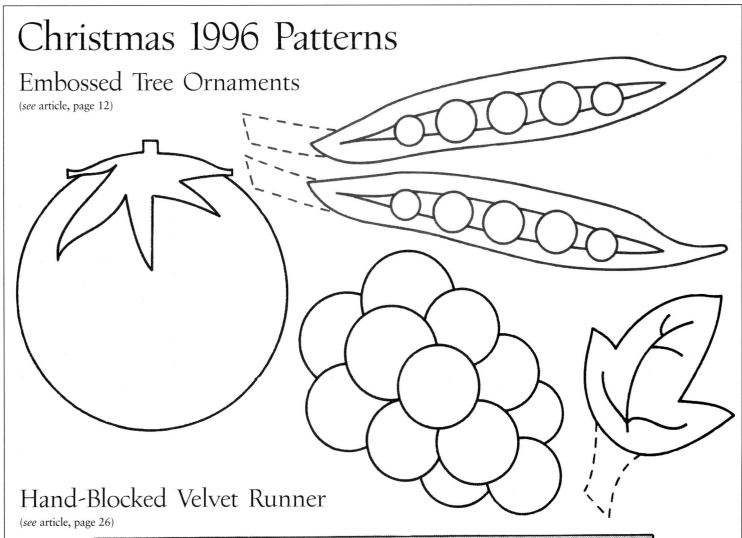

Hand-Blocked Velvet Runner

(*see* article, page 26)

Tasseled Ball Pillow

(see article, page 34)

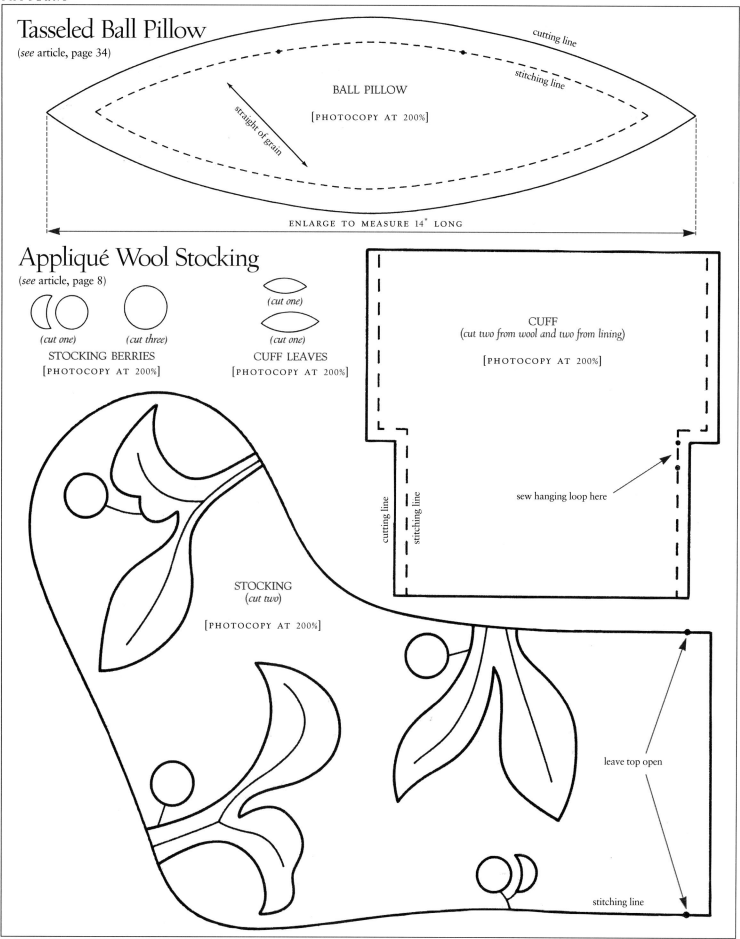

cutting line

stitching line

BALL PILLOW

[PHOTOCOPY AT 200%]

straight of grain

ENLARGE TO MEASURE 14" LONG

Appliqué Wool Stocking

(see article, page 8)

(cut one)   *(cut three)*

STOCKING BERRIES
[PHOTOCOPY AT 200%]

(cut one)

(cut one)

CUFF LEAVES
[PHOTOCOPY AT 200%]

CUFF
(cut two from wool and two from lining)

[PHOTOCOPY AT 200%]

cutting line

stitching line

sew hanging loop here

STOCKING
(cut two)

[PHOTOCOPY AT 200%]

leave top open

stitching line

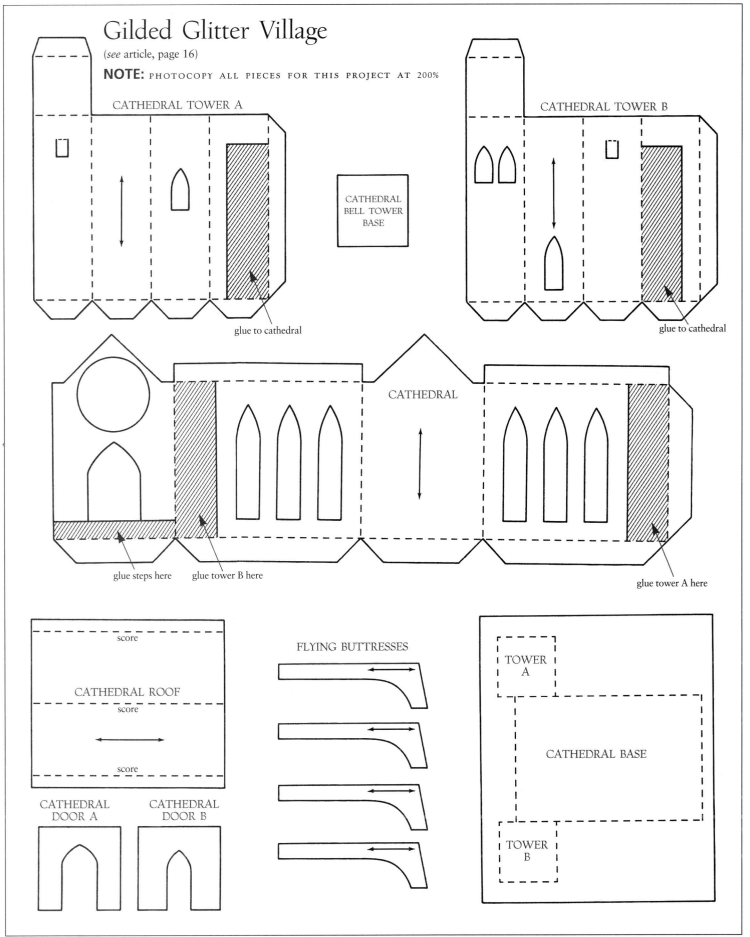

Gilded Glitter Village

(*see* article, page 16)

NOTE: PHOTOCOPY ALL PIECES FOR THIS PROJECT AT 200%

CATHEDRAL TOWER A

CATHEDRAL TOWER B

CATHEDRAL
BELL TOWER
BASE

glue to cathedral

glue to cathedral

CATHEDRAL

glue steps here

glue tower B here

glue tower A here

score

CATHEDRAL ROOF

score

score

CATHEDRAL
DOOR A

CATHEDRAL
DOOR B

FLYING BUTTRESSES

TOWER
A

CATHEDRAL BASE

TOWER
B

Gilded Glitter Village

(*see* article, page 16)

NOTE: PHOTOCOPY ALL PIECES FOR THIS PROJECT AT 200%

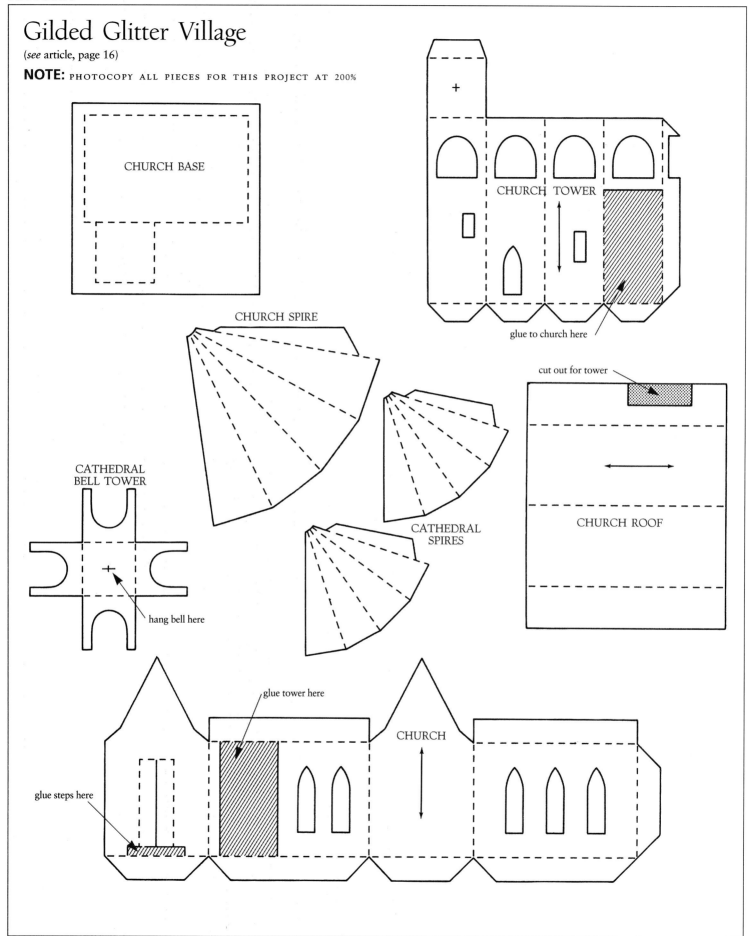

CHURCH BASE

CHURCH TOWER

glue to church here

CHURCH SPIRE

cut out for tower

CATHEDRAL
BELL TOWER

CATHEDRAL
SPIRES

CHURCH ROOF

hang bell here

glue tower here

CHURCH

glue steps here

Sources & Resources

The following are specific mail-order sources for particular items, arranged by article.

Most of the materials used in this issue are available at your local craft supply store, florist, fabric shop, hardware store, or bead and jewelry supply. Generic craft supplies can be ordered from such catalogs as Craft King, Dick Blick Art Materials, Newark Dressmaker Supply, Pearl Paint Company, Inc., or Sunshine Discount Crafts. The following are specific sources for harder-to-find items, arranged by article. The suggested retail prices listed here were current at press time. Contact the suppliers directly to confirm prices and availability.

Appliqué Stocking, *page 8*
Wool from $4.99 per yard, muslin lining from 99¢ per yard, fringe from $2.99 per yard, and green upholstery braid for 59¢ per yard, all from Zimman's.

Embossed Ornaments, *page 12*
Aluminum foil for $2.95 for 5 feet, and armature wire for $6.50 for 10 feet from Sax Arts & Crafts. Deka Transparent Glass Paint from $3.08 for 2/3 ounces from Texas Art Supply.

Teddy Bear Sweater, *page 14*
Yarn starting at $5.10 for a 4-ounce skein from Halcyon Yarn.

Gilded Village, *page 16*
Single-ply chipboard from $1.16 per sheet, gold glitter for $6.97 per pound, micro glitter for $1.88 per 2.5-ounce vial, pearlescent fabric paint for $4 for 4 ounces, balsa rods for 42¢ each, all from Pearl Paint.

Appliqué Candle, *page 19*
Household paraffin wax for $1.59 per pound from Craft King. Multicolored Spectra Art Tissue for $2.56 for twenty sheets from Pearl Paint. White pillar candle for $9.50 from Yankee Candle Company.

Beaded Tree, *page 20*
Green seed beads (strung upon request) from $6.90 for 1/4 pound from Ornamental Resources. Other colors of seed beads for 39¢ for 8 grams and bugle beads for 45¢ for 8 grams from Craft King. Filigree beads from $1.66 from Pearl Paint. Gold sequins for 59¢ from Munro Corporation.

Antique Plaque, *page 22*
Angel motifs for $16.98 per pair from Daisy Kingdom. Deco Art Heavenly Hues Transparent Wash for $1.99 for 2 ounces from Viking Woodcrafts. Permastone from $4.05 for 28 ounces, ETI Mold Builder Liquid Rubber for $7.93 per pint, all from Texas Art Supply.

Greeting Cards, *page 24*
Lace papers starting at $6.65 per sheet and card base for 80¢ per sheet from Kate's Paperie. Gold embossing powder for $3.27 per ounce, gold ink stamp pad for $5.51, embossing pad for $5.52, and star motif stamp for $5.24, all from Pearl Paint.

Embossed Runner, *page 26*
Velvet from $20.60 per yard and gold silk for $13.80 per yard from Thai Silks. Lumiere metallic paint for $2.80 per ounce from Dharma Trading Company. Linoleum block for $2.30, rubber brayer starting at $5.95, and linoleum cutter set for $8.75, all from Sax Arts & Crafts.

Classic Clock, *page 30*
Walnut Hollow Farms' "Classic" box for $9.62 from Pearl Paint. Clock insert starting at $7.90, feet, bail pull, and latches, all from Klockit. Sharkskin paper for $5 per sheet from New York Central Art Supply.

Handmade Soap, *page 32*
Lye for $29.95 for 10 pounds from Sugar Plum Sundries. Essential and fragrance oils starting at $16 for 4 ounces and coconut oil from $5.95 for 2 pounds from Sunfeather Herbal Soap Company.

Ball Pillow, *page 34*
Fabrics from Zimman's: Mini Harlequin Chenille at $41.95 per yard, Mini Dot (Camel) at $28.95 per yard, Quilted Silk Dupion (Taupe) at $29.95 per yard, Citadel Chenille (Red) at $41.95 per yard, and Cherubs (Olive) at $18.95 per yard.

Faux Limoges Fruit, *page 36*
Sculpey Promat polymer clay for $10.39 per pound from Pearl Paint. Sculpey Glaze #33 Gloss for $2.34, modeling tool set for $2.67, and 1-inch diameter wooden balls for 14¢ each, all from Craft King. Brass hinges from $1.79 for four from Viking Woodcrafts. One-ounce Duncan non-firing stains for $1.30 from Ceramic Supply of New York and New Jersey, Inc.

Shadow Box Frame, *page 40*
Basswood for $9.65 for two 38" x 4" x 24" strips from Charette. Moiré starting at $6.99 per yard and voile from $14.95 per yard from Zimman's.

🐦 🐦 🐦 🐦 🐦 🐦

The following companies are mentioned in the listing above. Contact each individually for a price list or catalog.

CERAMIC SUPPLY OF NEW YORK AND NEW JERSEY, INC.
#7 Route 46 West, Lodi, NJ 07644; 800-723-7264

CHARRETTE
P.O. Box 4010, Woburn, MA 01888-4010; 800-367-3729

CRAFT KING
P.O. Box 90637, Lakeland, FL 33804; 800-769-9494

DAISY KINGDOM
3720 NW Yeon Avenue, Portland, OR 97210; 800-234-6688

DHARMA TRADING COMPANY
P.O. Box 150916, San Rafael, CA 94915; 800-542-5227

DICK BLICK ART MATERIALS
P.O. Box 1267, Galesburg, IL 61402-1267; 800-447-8192

HALCYON YARN
12 School Street, Bath, ME 04530-2542; 800-341-0282

KATE'S PAPERIE
561 Broadway, New York, NY 10012; 212-941-9816

KLOCKIT
P.O. Box 636, Lake Geneva, WI 53147; 800-556-2548

MUNRO CORPORATION
3954 West 12 Mile Road, Berkley, MI 48072; 800-638-0543

NEWARK DRESSMAKER SUPPLY
6473 Ruch Road, P.O. Box 20730, Lehigh Valley, PA 18002-0730; 610-837-7500

NEW YORK CENTRAL ART SUPPLY
62 Third Avenue, New York, NY 10003; 800-950-6111

ORNAMENTAL RESOURCES
Box 3010, 1427 Miner Street, Idaho Springs, CO 80452; 800-876-6762

PEARL PAINT COMPANY, INC.
308 Canal Street, New York, NY 10013-2572; 800-221-6845 x2297

SAX ARTS & CRAFTS
P.O. Box 510710, New Berlin, WI 53151-0710; 800-558-6696

SUGAR PLUM SUNDRIES
5152 Fair Forest Drive, Stone Mountain, GA 30088; 404-297-0158

SUNFEATHER HERBAL SOAP COMPANY, INC.
1551 State Highway 72, Potsdam, NY 13676; 800-771-7627

SUNSHINE DISCOUNT CRAFTS
P.O. Box 301, Largo, FL 34649-0301; 800-729-2878

TEXAS ART SUPPLY
2001 Montrose Boulevard, Houston, TX 77006-1299; 800-888-9278

THAI SILKS
252 State Street, Los Altos, CA 94022; 800-722-7455

TINSEL TRADING
47 West 38th Street, New York, NY 10018; 212-730-1030

VIKING WOODCRAFTS, INC.
1317 8th Street S.E., Waseca, MN 56093; 800-328-0116

YANKEE CANDLE COMPANY
Catalog Sales, P.O. Box 110, South Deerfield, MA 01373-0110; 800-243-1776

ZIMMAN'S
76-88 Market Street, Lynn, MA 01901; 617-598-9432

CORRECTION
The "Fast and Easy Ottoman" in the Spring 1996 issue should have called for 6' x 1" x 3" dressed clear pine slats.
Compiled by Jennifer Putnam

Gilded Glitter Village

(*see* article, page 16)

NOTE: PHOTOCOPY ALL PIECES FOR THIS PROJECT AT 200%

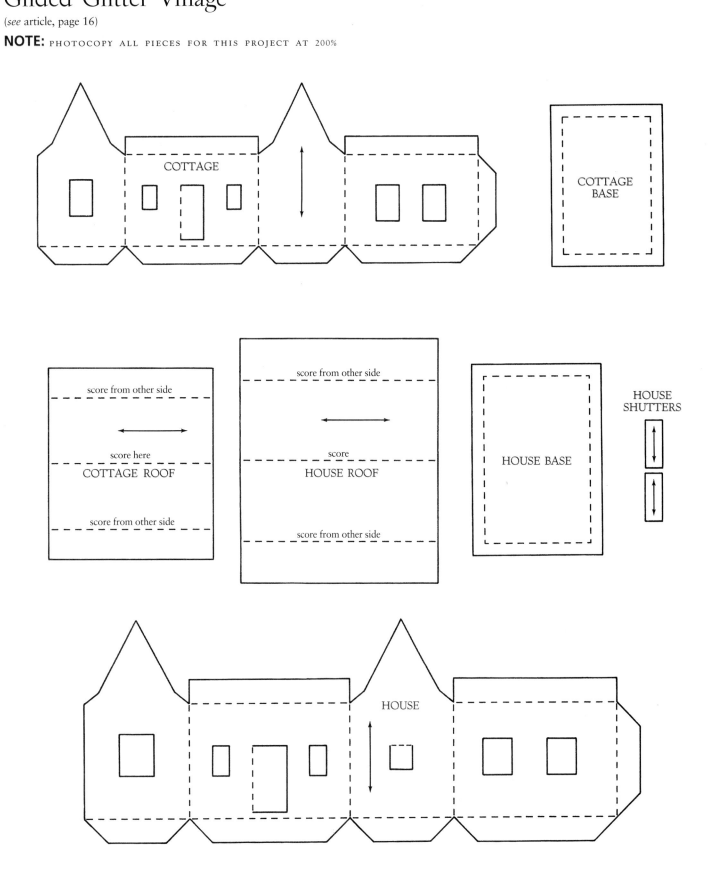

Quick Projects

For gifts or for your own table, "dressed" wine bottles lend a festive air.

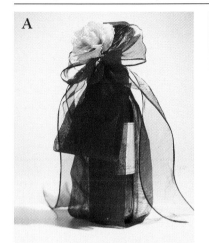

UNDER WRAPS

Looking for a different way to wrap your gift of wine or liquor? Consider novelty fabrics and trims, which combine to add festivity to any occasion. All of these wraps can be left on the bottle or can be easily removed before the bottle is opened.

A. Organdy with White Rose
Press a 15" x 42" piece of raspberry organdy into thirds for a 5"-wide band. Wrap the band once around the bottle vertically, fold the excess into a floppy loop, and secure the ends to the bottle neck with a rubber band. Tie a red organdy ribbon around the neck and slip a white silk rose into the knot.

B. Silver Mesh
Crush aluminum foil snugly around the bottle, then layer red cellophane giftwrap over it. For the final layer, wrap the bottle with silver metallic mesh fabric (if desired, use duct tape to secure overlap). Wind sculptor's aluminum armature wire around the bottle in an upward spiral, then twist the ends into tight curls.

C. Gold Voile Wrap
Wrap gold voile around the bottle tube-style, pleat and hand-tack the excess fabric at the lower end, and stand the bottle upright. Tie copper-glazed leather binding string around the base, then wind the string up around the bottle until you reach the neck. Wrap the cord snugly around the neck and tie it off. To shrink and crinkle the voile at the collar, hold it under hot running water for a few seconds, then blot it with a towel. Tie a wire-edged voile ribbon around the neck, then hot-glue artificial berries and leaves coated with silver glitter to the ribbon.

D. Organdy Slipcase
Machine-stitch two organdy place mats (one white and one gold) together on three sides, leaving one short edge open for the case top. Slip the bottle into the case. Crush the case around the bottle neck, then tie on a gold metallic cord. Wire a gold charm to the cord bow.

E. Cellophane and Jewels
Wrap the bottle in purple cellophane. Cinch the collar closed with a rubber band, then tie a wire-edged pink ribbon around it. Thread three different acrylic "crystal" drops onto a short length of thin, silver elastic cord and tie the cord in a loop around the bottle neck. ◆

COLOR PHOTOGRAPHY:
Carl Tremblay

Rose Petal Pomander

Sketch spiraling line around 4" teardrop or round Styrofoam ball from one end to the other. (The teardrop shape can be made by shaving and sanding a round ball using a knife.) Dent line with knife handle to make shallow groove. Brush Styrofoam with rubber cement, roll in loose crushed rose petals, and press gently with palms. Repeat until ball or teardrop is fully coated. Poke ¼" hole at each end of spiral groove. Hot-glue end of 1-yard length of twisted cord inside bottom hole. Then glue cord around ball, following grooved path, until you reach top hole. To create hanging loop, glue cord end in top hole, then loop and glue cord around itself once or twice. Pin wire-edged ribbon bow to top and glue a few dried roses and velvet leaves around it.

COLOR PHOTOGRAPHY: **Carl Tremblay**   STYLING: **Ritch Holben**